MY AFFAIR WITH ART HOUSE CINEMA

My Affair with Art House Cinema

ESSAYS AND REVIEWS

Phillip Lopate

Columbia University Press
New York

Columbia University Press
Publishers Since 1893
New York   Chichester, West Sussex
cup.columbia.edu

Library of Congress Cataloging-in-Publication Data
Names: Lopate, Phillip, 1943- author.
Title: My affair with art house cinema : essays and reviews / Phillip Lopate.
Description: New York : Columbia University Press, [2024] | Includes bibliographical references.
Identifiers: LCCN 2023059243 (print) | LCCN 2023059244 (ebook) |
ISBN 9780231216401 (hardback) | ISBN 9780231216395 (trade paperback) |
ISBN 9780231561266 (ebook)
Subjects: LCSH: Experimental films—History and criticism. | Independent films—
History and criticism. | Art in motion pictures. | Film criticism.
Classification: LCC PN1995.9.E96 L67 2024 (print) | LCC PN1995.9.E96 (ebook) |
DDC 791.43/611—dc23/eng/20240212
LC record available at https://lccn.loc.gov/2023059243
LC ebook record available at https://lccn.loc.gov/2023059244

Cover design: Julia Kushnirsky
Cover image: *Ugetsu Monogatari* (1954), Daiei/Kobal/Shutterstock

CONTENTS

CONTENTS

CONTENTS

Chapter Thirty-Two
Ernst Lubitsch 182

Chapter Thirty-Three
Sidney Lumet: *Long Day's Journey Into Night* 191

Chapter Thirty-Four
David Lynch: *Mulholland Drive* 196

Chapter Thirty-Five
Dušan Makavejev: The Wolf and the Teddy Bear 203

Chapter Thirty-Six
Kenji Mizoguchi: *Ugetsu* and *Utamaro and
His Five Women* 216

Chapter Thirty-Seven
Mikio Naruse: *When a Woman Ascends the Stairs* 224

Chapter Thirty-Eight
Yasujirō Ozu: *Late Spring* 228

Chapter Thirty-Nine
Christian Petzold: *Barbara* 231

Chapter Forty
Maurice Pialat: *Naked Childhood, Van Gogh,* and
Le Garçu 233

Chapter Forty-One
Alain Resnais: Middle and Late Resnais 242

Chapter Forty-Two
Dino Risi: *Il Sorpasso* 247

Chapter Forty-Three
Éric Rohmer: *La Collectionneuse, The Marquise of O,*
and *Le Rayon Vert* 253

CONTENTS

INTERMISSION: DOCUMENTARIES AND ESSAY FILMS

CONTENTS

INTRODUCTION

I am a lifelong movie lover—and a writer—so it was perhaps inevitable that I would write a ton about film culture.

I first fell in love with films when I was a little kid and my parents sent me and my siblings off to the local double-feature movie theater so that they could have more "private time." While they were engrossed in whatever that meant, I was drinking in the erotic magic of Veronica Lake and Ava Gardner doing their mischief onscreen. As a teenager I had the good fortune to be living through a cinematic highpoint (the French New Wave; the Italians Rossellini, Fellini, Visconti, Antonioni, and Bertolucci; Satyajit Ray; the last flourishing of classical American masters like Ford, Hawks, and Hitchcock; the American experimentalists Cassavetes, Mekas, Shirley Clarke . . .). I started a club in college called Filmmakers of Columbia and made a short film. But regrettably my working-class parents had little money to support my habit, so I put down my borrowed Bolex and turned to the typewriter instead.

Though I never held down a regular film critic post, I was often asked to write for various periodicals. In general, I wrote about films I liked, following the credo of W. H. Auden, who said it was pointless to waste time attacking mediocre work. My first collection of such pieces, *Totally Tenderly Tragically*, featured appreciations of Antonioni, Cassavetes, Fassbinder, Godard, Jerry Lewis, David Lynch, Mizoguchi, Naruse, Scorsese, Truffaut, Kiarastomi, and Visconti. Since then, I have written thousands more words about the movies. In gathering the best of those pieces for this collection, suddenly I was struck by an odd realization: the works I write about are all examples of what might be called art house cinema. The reason for this was simply that I had never been commissioned to review blockbusters; I was perceived by the periodicals that approached me (*Film Comment, Cineaste,* the *New York Times,* the Criterion Collection, the *Normal School, Moment, Oxford American, IndieWire,* the *New York Review of Books*) as a sort of specialist in the arcane field of the art film. Of course I, like everyone else, went to the big blockbuster movies from time to time and was entertained—or not—but even when I had the freedom to write about any motion picture releases I chose, I still gravitated toward analyzing new art movies with miniscule advertising budgets, which seemed to call more for my attention, or older classical films of substance that were being reissued.

I should explain that from my first infatuation with movies as an adolescent, I held fast to the notion that, at its best, film was an art form, on par with modern painting, music, literature, and dance. I vowed to seek out just those movies that were the most complex, the most artful, and. in a sense, the most challenging and intellectually demanding. It used to be customary for populist writers to sneer at the use of the word "cinema" or even "film" as pretentious, but I had no trouble embracing these terms. I was a truffle hunter, unashamedly seeking the highest form of cinematic art.

My grasp of the international art movie scene solidified when I was named to the selection committee of the New York Film Festival (NYFF). For eight years I went to Cannes, as well as periodic visits to film festivals in Berlin, Pusan (South Korea), Buenos Aires, and Vienna to scout films for the NYFF, and I participated in the selection committee's marathon summer screenings in New York to pick the final slate. That experience profoundly shaped my understanding of the filmic output of Teheran, Taiwan, St. Petersburg, Rio de Janeiro, Seoul, Paris, Berlin, Burkina Faso, Beijing, London, Los Angeles, and New York.

The result—this book—makes two claims. The first is that it represents a delineation, however scattershot, of my aesthetic. Not being an aesthetic philosopher or a critical theorist, I would be loath to articulate in so many words my critical principles. Still, anyone who reads the book can perceive what these mainly are: experiencing the integrity of each shot; relishing a flow of images that unfolds flexibly into its environmental space; endorsing a nuanced, humanistic psychology of character; and demonstrating some sort of wisdom. (Wisdom, a hard concept to pin down, but let's say it includes a stoical realism about human frailty and suffering and a compassionate sense of fairness over cheap, grindhouse thrills.) My aesthetic also inevitably draws from a set of partialities, prejudices, and preferences based in part on my class background, education, generation, and lived experiences, as is true for any critic.

The second claim I make in these pages is that they constitute a record of art house cinema in the last twenty-five years. Of course, this is not an encyclopedia; there are inevitable gaps. Not every significant art movie during this period could be discussed. I was restricted partly by assignment—so, for instance, I've never had the opportunity to write about Kelly Reichardt or Nicole Holofcener, two of my favorite American indie directors, or the uneven but sometimes brilliant Coen Brothers, nor did I get the chance to celebrate an Imamura, Oshima, or Wajda. And given the long piece I wrote about Visconti in my first book of film criticism, it made no sense to tackle him again. But on the whole, you will find registered here the art house field's tendencies and lineages—a map of that particular cinema landscape.

In my writing career, though I've written poetry and novels, I am known most as a personal essayist. In fact, when I edited my anthology *The American Movie Critics* for Library of America, I approached each seminal critic as if they were secretly writing personal essays in the guise of film criticism. So it is with this book. It is, in its way, intensely personal, even confessional. Perhaps that's why I am still loyal to approaching films from the standpoint of a director's individual expression—to auteurism, in a word. I realize, movies being such a collaborative medium, that there are sound objections to the auteur theory, but I still cling to it as a useful way of charting the personal arc of a filmmaker. At the same time, being a fan of movie acting, I will watch any film with, say, Edward G. Robinson, Claude Rains, Barbara Stanwyck, Burt Lancaster, or Bette Davis with a fascination that inadvertently assigns to them the picture's creative impulse, regardless of who directed it. I love the film noir *Criss Cross*, directed by the underappreciated Robert Siodmak, but in spite of its skillful mise-en-scène and intricate, flashback plot design, it is really Lancaster's performance that grips me—his combination of boastful macho and baffling insecurity in the face of Yvonne De Carlo's seductive allure. And the odd clothes he wears.

Most artists, I've long felt, have another art form they turn to for diversion and for comparison to an analogous set of aesthetic problems. With me, it has always been the movies. During the COVID pandemic, I was reduced to streaming movies rather than seeing them on a big screen. I missed that solipsistic and communal experience. But rereading these pieces has reawakened my enthusiasm for the art of cinema. I won't pretend the pages that follow represent an exact archival record: I've revised passages and even reversed a few judgments that now strike me as stupid. All in all, however, they convey my response to art movies as they came at me, willy-nilly. I hope they will set off your own thoughts, whether in agreement or dispute.

A few words about the structure of the book. It begins with two essays that are aimed at orienting the reader to my aesthetic leanings and taste preferences. They are followed by a lengthy section comprising reviews of feature films and appreciations of individual directors, organized in perhaps the most embarrassingly simplistic manner possible—alphabetically, by the surname of the filmmaker, because I could not think of any other way of dividing the material (nationalistic, genre, historical period) that would not come off as willfully arbitrary. At the very least, it should give readers the opportunity to hop around since there is no reason why this book need be read in strict order. The next section, given over to essay films and documentaries, speaks to a passionate interest of mine. I once thought of writing a whole book about essay films, but this selection will have to do. It is followed by a half dozen pieces about film critics. My love of movies and nonfiction writing could not help but lure me into a fascination with the craft of film criticism. The final section features a valentine to the art houses of the past and a few last thoughts on the future of cinema. I cannot contemplate current movies without thinking simultaneously of films of the past, their historic antecedents, on which their achievements or shortcomings rest. Murnau, Vigo, and Buster Keaton hover in the shadows as I write about the latest release. Moreover, regardless of whether a movie was put out in general commercial distribution or in a limited release, the classics of old Hollywood by directors such as Lubitsch and Ford can be seen only in revival or repertory theaters today, which is why I have included them in this collection devoted to art house cinema.

CURTAIN RAISERS

Chapter One

ON CHANGING ONE'S MIND ABOUT A MOVIE

For those who have ever tried to palm themselves off as film critics or even to assert confident judgments about movies in social gatherings, the nagging awareness of just how unstable and fluid these judgments can be is a secret embarrassment, a threat, possibly a stimulus. You feel sure you like or dislike a particular movie, and then, over the years, that certainty begins to waver.

I am not talking here about exhibiting a taste for the campy or the obviously awful. *Film Comment* would occasionally run a column called "Guilty Pleasures," inviting critics and filmmakers to confess the outré pictures they loved. The problem with that category is that, for the film buff, either everything is in a sense a guilty pleasure, or nothing. Once the film buff has accepted the guilt for wasting a good part of life chasing shadows and filling in gaps with encyclopedic pedantry, there are no "sinful" pleasures: cinephilia is a collecting avarice, drawn to marginal, half-good/half-bad finds as much if not more than to unarguable classics.

I had once thought of compiling a list of Guilty Displeasures, consisting of revered, paradigm-shifting movies I didn't much care for (such as *The Graduate* or *Bonnie and Clyde*), but this too seemed questionable, since, however much I personally found them overrated, I could still appreciate their contribution. A more valid category might be the movies about which I have changed my mind.

Pauline Kael asserted that she never went back to a movie twice because she wanted to trust her first, gut impression. Andrew Sarris took the opposite critical approach, re-viewing, mulling over, and altering his opinions about certain movies over a lifetime. He admitted, for instance, that he had been quite taken with *Sunset Boulevard* when it first opened but had shifted his view after some critics he respected sniffed at it, and he subsequently downgraded Billy Wilder, its director, for being too cynical, only to reopen the case years later and revise his estimation of Wilder upward. In that respect I am much more a Sarrisite than a Paulette, since my own tastes seem to fluctuate, whether or not I am paying attention.

To give an example: A few years ago, I was channel-surfing on a Sunday afternoon with my daughter Lily, then aged thirteen, when I discovered that the IFC channel would be showing Jacques Demy's *The Young Girls of Rochefort* in fifteen minutes. I got very excited. I hadn't seen it in since it had opened in 1967, and I had somehow missed the restoration print rerelease, though I recall thinking at the time about taking Lily (whose first exposure to a subtitled film, when she was ten or eleven, had been *The Umbrellas of Cherbourg*). "This is by the same director who made *Umbrellas of Cherbourg*. You liked that, remember?" She got that patient, forbearing, resistance-gathering look that appears whenever I try to foist an older, sometimes black-and-white, or even black-and-white silent movie on her. I told her it was very pretty—and in Technicolor! "What's it about?" she demanded, which I recognized as a sensible question for a normal viewer, if not a die-hard auteurist cinephile like myself, to ask.

"It's beautiful. The camerawork, the costumes . . ."

"Yes, but what's it about?"

"Love," I said, appealing to her taste for romantic comedies. "I don't remember. I saw it a long time ago."

Because she is essentially a kind daughter, she agreed to watch the beginning with me, and then, if it proved not to her taste, she would peel off into the other room and read her book.

I'd already decided that, even if she didn't like it, I would watch it from beginning to end. I felt sure I was about to be enthralled. What I didn't tell her was that the first time I'd seen *The Young Girls of Rochefort*, the movie had left me cold. It had seemed thin and insubstantial, precious yet overworked, the effort to retrieve the insouciant elegance of MGM musicals dooming it to taxidermy. The French New Wave's slumming adoration of Hollywood, the film's use of an over-the-hill, toupee-wearing Gene Kelly to give it American authenticity, had struck me (in my young man's severity) as misguided. How could I be so certain, then, that I would love it this time?

Before I can answer, let me backtrack. In my twenties, I counted myself a Jacques Demy partisan, having reveled in the bittersweet inventiveness of *Lola* and the mordant *Bay of Angels*. I had fallen for *The Umbrellas of Cherbourg*, which I found enormously moving, bucking the taste of my peers, who regarded it as retrograde corn. But *The Young Girls of Rochefort* seemed to foreground all of Demy's self-indulgences. I swore off him for a while. Later I was charmed by the fairy tale *Donkey Skin* and was puzzled by but able to find some peripheral merit in the misfire *Model Shop* and perhaps more in *Une Chambre en Ville*. In short, I climbed back on the Demy bandwagon.

The film began with a title in French, crediting Demy's widow Agnès Varda and various funding agents for the restoration. "This is boring!" Lily announced.

"Give it a chance."

"What's it about?" she demanded, and hit the TV guide remote button, to see if that might provide some plot information. Shocked, I grabbed it away from her, afraid I might have missed the first shot.

"Hey, calm down, Dad!"

We proceeded to watch the opening dance number.

"Is it a musical?"

"Yes, it's a musical. Lots of singing and dancing."

"Subtitles—eeoughh!"

But I had faith that the women's outfits would win her over, and soon she was watching it with engrossment. "See, it's like *Funny Face*," I murmured, bridging to a movie I knew she loved, meaning that it too had a stylized color scheme. I explained that the twins were played by sisters in real life, Catherine Deneuve and Francoise Dorleac, and that the red-headed one died shortly after making this movie.

"How?"

"In a car crash, I think." I was entranced watching every second of their duet. It struck me that Dorleac did look a little pale, like someone who foresaw she had not long to live. Part of what I appreciated this second time was seeing it all through the lens of death. Its very archness seemed tenderly endearing, alluding to a voluptuous, liberating, self-conscious "movie love" moment in cinema that was gone forever. Knowing as I now did that Jacques Demy was bisexual, that he had died of AIDS, I saw the telltale pink and mauve sweaters assigned to the male dancers as a defiant confession, and all those arias about finding the Ideal Woman came across as poignant, retrospectively. My emotional response was colored by the many gay friends and acquaintances I had lost to AIDS. Nevertheless, it would be wrong to think that I was giving the film only extra-cinematic credit. On the contrary, everything that had once seemed artistically weak to me had been turned on its head and appeared as a virtue. Artifice, serendipity, the fragile transience of happiness—I was seeing it the way Demy had intended, as a painful fairy tale about yearning and the improbable search for true love. This time I got the references to his earlier films and to those still to come. Demy was like a spider situated in the middle of his life, weaving a connecting web between his recollections and approaching fate that only now I could begin to understand.

If I attempt to isolate which factors contribute to changing my mind about a movie, they come down to: my particular stage of life, my overarching aesthetic, auteurist reconsiderations, public response, and peer pressure.

In adolescence I cherished, like many teenage boys, grotesquery: I delighted in seeing the gruesome wedding party scene of *Freaks*, with its dismemberment, or the beggars' violation of their benefactress in *Viridiana*. Now that I am middle-aged, the grotesque refuses to engage me as much; the siren song of the edgy sounds obvious and shrill; and extreme violence disgusts me. When my undergraduates loan me DVDs of their favorite Miike yakuza films, I have to turn them off at the first facial razor slice.

Big changes in one's life may also alter one's viewing tolerance. After I became a parent, I could no longer watch with equanimity any movie in which a child was kidnapped, endangered, or physically harmed.

I am more interested now in movies that reflect wisdom and compassion at their core, rather than mere sensation. This is not to say that I've become wiser with age. Youth has its own wisdom. I think I was right to react, as a young man, against what had seemed cloying in *The Young Girls of Rochefort*, but now I see that preciosity from a different perspective and cherish it. I was too young then to embrace the film's underlying romantic pessimism; I had plenty of yearning, but it was not yet infused with regret. The ultimate question may not be, "What is the correct critical judgment to make of a particular film?" but: "What are our different needs and understandings at various stages in life?"

In my teens and twenties I ate up everything Jean-Luc Godard did while disliking Ingmar Bergman's spiritual heaviness, his seemingly middle-aged, middlebrow gravitas. Though I still love much of Godard, a trifle like *A Woman Is a Woman* strikes me now as *only* playful, and even *Two or Three Things I Know About Her*, re-seen recently, seems underbaked. Conversely, Bergman's *Winter Light*, which looked to be so ridiculously strained and cosmically stodgy that I gave it a pass when it opened, I now regard as magnificent, approaching *King Lear* in its courage to contemplate harsh truths. I am no longer as threatened by unresolvable anguish.

Film magazines are infused with a bias toward youth culture. They are ever on the lookout for the cutting edge, which suits academic discourse to a T. The film that draws attention to itself *as* film is doted on because, we are told, it punctures the complacent illusions of realism. Do we really need to keep having pointed out the fact that film is an artificial construct? To my mind, self-reflexive cinematic gestures have become old hat; they've lost the daring they had for me in my youth.

When I was younger you could have me with a 180-degree camera movement. I've since seen many film school graduates circling their actors vertiginously to little point, but well-written dialogue has come to seem rarer. In my youth, I found Samuel Fuller the most refreshing filmmaker alive, exuding as he did a pulp gusto that upended prevailing pieties. But recently, when I watched *House of Bamboo* for the third time, the stilted dialogue and over-the-top performances made me wince. I hesitate to revisit all those beloved Fullers, given my lesser enthusiasm for shock edits and my enhanced regard for literate dialogue. I would probably now opt for Joseph Mankiewicz's talky *A Letter to Three Wives* over Fuller's hyperkinetic *Shock Corridor* (though I still prefer Fuller's *Pickup on South Street*: that much of a boy film buff I remain).

Then there is the matter of my overarching aesthetic. Regardless of further tweaks that may occur along the way, I have retained my loyalty to a formalist style that first won me over in adolescence: this Bazinian preference for long takes, flowing use of space, incorporation of the full body and the surrounding environment, implying a more detached sympathy toward human drama, and, on the other hand, a dislike of zooms, rapid-fire editing, tons of close-up reaction shots, or slow-motion has limited my taste options. There are certain films I can never change my mind about because I so embrace their worldview. I know, going into a Renoir, Mizoguchi,

Ophuls, Naruse, Minnelli, Ozu, Satyajit Ray, Nicholas Ray, Rossellini, Cukor, or Borzage for the first time that I will probably like it, and I almost always do; and if I see it a second or third time I still like it. To not like it would be to reject my own aesthetic DNA.

No, it is those filmmakers who run counter to this overarching aesthetic who cause me initial confusion and force me to reverse my judgments later. Robert Altman, for instance, whose technical gifts are unquestioned, has sometimes struck me as smart-ass: the first time I saw *Nashville* I found its satire of America too easy and patronizing. Having worked through my initial distaste, I was able in subsequent viewings to enjoy *Nashville*'s many terrific performances and fascinating digressions. Stanley Kubrick, a magisterial formalist, often puts me off with his superior scorn. To my shame, I walked out of *Barry Lyndon* for that very reason the first time I saw it; now I watch it with eager absorption and it seems to me a brilliant masterpiece, though I still cannot warm to *A Clockwork Orange* or the self-liberal-pleased *Dr. Strangelove*.

A nonformalist director like Sidney Lumet took me a long time to appreciate because his camera setups seemed muzzy and insufficiently rigorous. *Serpico*, the first time I saw it, looked ragged, slapped together; now I find it bursting with life, with an unrivaled feeling for 1970s New York City. Later Lumets, such as *Prince of the City*, helped me dig back into *Dog Day Afternoon* and *Serpico* and discover their considerable merits. Similarly, I was repelled, in my first exposures to Cassavetes's *Husbands* and *A Woman Under the Influence*, by what I took to be an overly operatic, boozy, hysterical approach to character, too many laughing jags and Method-indulgent performances. It was only when I saw *The Killing of a Chinese Bookie* that I revised my opinion about Cassavetes and detected the patient method underneath the seeming pandemonium. (But a part of me still wonders if I wasn't partly right the first time.)

I also find myself giving way to peer pressure. Much as one would like to believe oneself an independent-minded critic, one adapts to tribal consensus. I would be blind not to have noticed the reverential status accorded Cassavetes by my peers: he went from being scoffed at, a marginalized indie figure, to one of the key heroes in world cinema.

With each passing decade, the canon keeps readjusting itself. Hot newcomers who had seemed like sure bets run aground while once-mistrusted filmmakers stay the course, and their accrued quality begins to register as something unique and irreplaceable. The steady release of utterly worthless, forgettable product, year after year, cannot help but increase your benign tolerance toward anyone with a spark of originality. In death, their corpus complete, Altman, Kubrick, Cassavetes, and Lumet look like giants compared to the mediocre cinematic landscape that has come to surround them.

Some movies I resist, I'll admit, because they are simply so popular on release that I associate their appeal with pandering to the audience (*The Graduate, American Beauty, Titanic*, or *Avatar*). Though I enjoyed Woody Allen's early slapdash comedies, I had problems with his best-received films, such as *Annie Hall, Manhattan*, or *Hannah and Her Sisters*, because they struck me on first viewing as falsifying New York and the character played by Woody being smugly superior. Since then, now that he is less popular, I have come to regard Woody Allen as an American master, who goes his own way regardless of trends.

Peer pressure certainly plays a part in forcing critical revisions. However assuredly I may speak about a movie, I don't always completely trust my own opinion. Though I had liked Terrence Malick in the past, especially his *The Thin Red Line, The New World* struck me as a self-indulgent mess on first viewing, and I walked out before the last hour, telling myself that life was too short for such turgid neo-primitivism. Younger critic friends who adored the Malick film said I had missed the point, which resided in the final hour, and convinced me to give it a second chance. So I saw it again and virtually willed myself to admire it. I made a supreme effort to connect with Malick's mystical *The Tree of Life*, but nothing could make me take seriously his whirling dervish *To the Wonder*. In recent years I have sometimes parted ways with the enthusiasms of younger critics for art-crowd pleasers such as *Moulin Rouge, Lost in Translation*, and *2046*. I suspect this clash in tastes has something to do with a generation gap (gorgeous visual surface or hip, pop music soundtrack mattering less to me than to them), though I'm not sure. I may change my mind even about these films. It depends how much the internal quarrel between my critical selves and my own perverse openness might tip me toward the opposite pole and partly on the offerings of a slow afternoon's TV schedule. Just recently, while channel-surfing, I stumbled upon Fellini's *Juliet of the Spirits*, a movie I thought a confused, self-indulgent mélange when it first came out, but this time I relished its ambitious, over-the-top spectacle. "Not bad," I thought, compared to the offerings on other channels.

There are certain movies I can see over and over without worrying that I will lose my affection for them, precisely because they embody an enjoyable combination of shallow and deep, and the demands they make on me are minimal. Hitchcock's *North by Northwest* is such a movie; if I stumble upon it while channel-surfing, I can watch it happily from that point on when I have nothing better to do. But I need to steel myself for Bergman's *Persona* or Bresson's *Au Hasard Balthazar*; I do not always feel adequate to dipping into such great, exigent movies.

Some movies invoke in me a perpetually uncertain state of judgment. I've gone back and forth between thinking Charles Laughton's *Night of the Hunter* is an exciting one-off masterwork or a clumsy, semi-amateurish pastiche. With Max Ophuls's *Lola Montes*, at times I can embrace the weak central performance of Martine Carol's Lola as uncannily essential to its elegiac charm, and at other times I resist it as stultifying waxworks. Much as I revere Carl Dreyer, the first time I saw *Ordet*, at twenty, I found it interminably slow-going, a big letdown after *Day of Wrath*. Then I saw it again years later, in my forties, and had one of those transformative spiritual-cinematic experiences during the miraculous reviving of the dead woman; I was ready to believe in God, almost. The third time I watched *Ordet* I respected its craft but found the spiritual atmosphere a bit too morbid, even unhealthy, you might say. Maybe when Lily turns eighteen, I'll show her *Ordet* if she'll let me, and perhaps I'll discover what I finally feel about the film. One argument for having children is you get to revisit the cultural landmarks of your past, allowing their response to help change your mind.

You can wear out any film's magic if you see it too often. That is what happened to me about the eighth time I watched *The Third Man*—this seemingly irresistible, marvelous cuckoo clock suddenly struck me as tinny and calculating. I always recall what Chabrol said after he had seen *Vertigo* for something like the thirty-fifth time; he came to the conclusion that it was really a silly movie. To me, *Vertigo* is still sublime, but then, I sense where the cracks in my admiration may run, and so I am determined to ration my viewings of it in future.

FILM COMMENT (MAY/JUNE 2009)

Chapter Two

HOW I LOOK AT MOVIES

Not long ago, I was in Italy, where I took the opportunity to catch up with some Italian movies of the 1950s and early '60s. That was a glorious time for Italian cinema, when the instincts of postwar neorealism were still around to inflect and ennoble genres like comedy and melodrama, and almost every Italian studio product looked well composed and visually crisp. It could have been Visconti's *Bellissima* or De Santis's *Bitter Rice* I was watching, or something by the magnificently capable Pietro Germi, Alberto Lattuada, Dino Risi, Mario Monicelli, Valerio Zurlini, or even an early Antonioni; but no, it was *The Honorable Angelina*, a minor vehicle for the great actress Anna Magnani, and as it began, with a crane tracking shot of a Roman tenement and the surrounding slum at night, I was seized by such joy at the sensual intelligence with which this grimy milieu was being delivered to my eyes. A moment later, it occurred to me that in spite of having written hundreds of pages of film criticism over the years, I had never managed to convey the way I actually look at movies—what so enraptures me about a good movie, moment by moment, or so repels me when I think it's poorly made.

It is difficult to put these responses into words. For instance, take what I regard as a well-composed shot: do I mean it has a certain density of information, so there is enough detail throughout to please the eye, top to bottom, enough symmetry and balance? Yes, but too much symmetry can come across as stiff or merely "pictorial," like a trite postcard image. And sometimes it can be even more poetic to have an image not be saturated from back to front with concrete detail, but to let the viewer "feel" the background as a combination of suggested form and shadow. Certain thirties directors in Hollywood (John Ford, Frank Borzage), France (Marcel Carné, Jean Grémillion), and Japan (Mikio Naruse) were superb at that type of smudged, moody suggestion.

Call me arrogant, but I am convinced that I have a trained eye and can judge the difference between good and bad film technique. I can tell immediately whether a shot is well lit, illuminating expressively the salient details or catching them with natural lighting, and whether the cutting is appropriate or overdone. I am especially attentive to the unfolding of action in a space, knowing when to push against the borders of that frame and open it, through pans or tracking shots, or to cut neither too soon nor too late, and in such a way that there is logical continuity or stimulating dissonance between the two shots. I appreciate that moment when the director seems to seek out more of an overhead perspective, sensing that the viewer may want the larger picture or, conversely, that the viewer wants to get closer, see the protagonists' faces. But it would be too tedious to try to put into words that intuitive perception of cinematic fluency—which, by the way, many intelligent, cultivated moviegoers don't seem to have—so I end up writing about the psychological complexity or flatness of the characters and the questionable wisdom of the narrative arc. I write about all that too much, because otherwise I would end up like a film professor constantly freezing a shot for his class and saying "Look! Look!" then being dumbstruck.

I remember Renata Adler's mocking characterization of formalist film critics, whom she said would always begin with the solemn, self-evident assertion: "The screen is a rectangle." Like Adler, I am not that fond of the language of most formalist film criticism, which can feel like a chore to read. The problem is that when all is said and done, the screen *is* a rectangle, and my own appreciation of film is largely inflected by formalist considerations.

Then there is the matter of the way a film breathes. This is perhaps the most difficult aspect of movie watching to put into words—the necessary pauses, the tact by which climaxes may give way to reflective, in-gathering moments, so that one doesn't feel bludgeoned by wall-to-wall adrenaled intensities. On an intuitive level, when a film seems to breathe naturally, it can synchronize with one's own respiration, and surrendering to it becomes all the more pleasurable, easy to trust. This breathing pattern is something that occurs moment to moment, but in broader terms, think of the hoedown and chowdown sequences in a John Ford western like *My Darling Clementine* or *The Searchers*, which decelerate the tension from shootouts and chases.

Perhaps I am also reluctant to try to write criticism that more specifically captures the way I look at movies because I am aware that my own aesthetic was so conditioned by the historical period in which I developed it. Regardless of my conviction that I can tell good moviemaking from bad, I also know that film technique evolves, and what might look garish or arbitrary to an old-timer may seem perfectly acceptable to a younger viewer, who grew up watching music videos, playing video games, and streaming movies on iPhones.

I came of age as a film buff in the early sixties, when André Bazin's advocacy of deep focus and flowing mise-en-scène was taken up by the French New Wave and Antonioni, and I have been marked by that preference ever since. My eye was alerted to pick up the interplay among foreground, medium ground, and background. I saw that, long before *Citizen Kane* and Gregg Toland, D. W. Griffith used what the French *Cahiers* critics called "naïve deep focus." The silent filmmaker Maurice Tourneur used to carry around a tree branch, which he would prop in the front of a composition if there was nothing else to distinguish the foreground plane. A big part of what still pleases me is the way a film stitches its characters to their environments—how it allows us to see a larger sociological and geographical perspective, how it carves up the space and keeps a flow going, both within a shot and from shot to shot. The master of this fluidity was Jean Renoir. Then again, I am happy with some directors, like Robert Bresson or Yasujirō Ozu, who resist fluidity and call our attention to the isolation of each composed unit. What matters most is that the choices that make up a visual style (camera placement, camera movement, lighting, editing) be followed with consistency so that we can relax in the knowledge that the director knows what they are doing. Why this sudden zoom or 360-degree camera movement, that unnecessary close-up or reaction shot? As the great Carl Dreyer said about Danish film, it "has at its disposal clever and conscientious photographers and they just need the courage to choose a particular style for each individual film that must then be carried out with will and logic from first image to last."

Another historical development that conditioned my aesthetic was Cinemascope, which flourished in the fifties. As filmmaker Jacques Rivette observed, Cinemascope supplemented the Bazinian emphasis on spatial depth by emphasizing width and lateral movement. Suddenly there was more reason to connect the characters to their physical/sociological milieus because the image ratio let in more background and more incentive to build complex, long-duration two-shots though reframing, rather than cross-cutting all the time between actors or going to close-ups. To quote the film critic David Bordwell on Scope movies of the fifties: "Their images invite us to realms where people have bodies and move in real time." Cinemascope also privileged architecture in a new way, as the wide images could be partitioned in sections or modules.

I have a special liking for black-and-white movies in Cinemascope or, indeed, black-and-white in any widescreen format. Watching *The Hustler*, *Tarnished Angels*, *Bunny Lake Is Missing*, *Whatever Happened to Baby Jane*, *Forty Guns*, *Yojimbo*, *High and Low*, *Bitter Victory*, or *Bay of Angels* carries a special thrill: my eye is better able to pick out expressive accents in a black-and-white widescreen than in a color image. Is it just my imagination, or is there also something intrinsically suited to noir or pessimistic realism about black-and-white widescreen? Kurosawa was especially masterful in handling this technique: the bravura opening sequence of *High and Low*, which takes place in the industrialist's glassed-in modernist house, offers a magnificent example of the manipulation of horizontal planes through judicious reframings and cuts, while the awareness of a ceiling pressing down ominously on the protagonists sets up the grim, claustrophobic events of the ensuing kidnapping story.

I seem to be more receptive to the mysterious grace of an elegant camera movement in black and white than I am to a similar movement in a color image. Max Ophuls's black-and white, dolly-crazed movies, such as *The Earrings of Mme de . . .*, *The Reckless Moment*, *Letter from an Unknown Woman*, or *Le Plaisir*, will always affect me more deeply than his color masterpiece, *Lola Montes*. The elegant crane shot in *The Earrings of Mme de . . .* that follows Danielle Darrieux up the staircase to the jewelry dealer's office, or the whirling waltz between Darrieux and Vittorio de Sica, are some of my favorite cinematic moments, laying the groundwork for the tragic outcome, even reconciling us to it. The first ten minutes of Kenji Mizoguchi's *Sisters of the Gion*, with its tracking shot that takes us past the noisy auction of a bankrupt firm all the way to the back rooms, where the soon-to-be scattered remnants of the commercial family are huddled miserably, thrills me every time I see it, much more so than anything in his later color films, *Empress Yang Kwei Fei* or *The Taira Clan*. On the other hand, Hitchcock's color films, such as *Rear Window*, *Vertigo*, *North by Northwest*, *The Birds*, and *Marnie*, do much more for me than his British black-and-whites. One more reason to go easy on the formalist criticism: I am unable to put forward a consistent theory of my predilections or even account completely for them.

But I persist on thinking I can tell the good horses from the bad.

How I look at films affords me an ongoing source of pleasure and rapture, especially when what I regard as the proper artistic conditions are met. Still, one might ask, what chance is there for an aesthetic like mine, based as it is on the fluid carving-up of space, to survive at a time when celluloid itself is giving way to digital and people are watching movies on devices no bigger than their palms? I would argue that demandingly beautiful, exquisite films are still being made, often by filmmakers who are entranced by the power of full-sized projected images. Indeed, many filmmakers who have become darlings of the festival circuit in the last few decades champion a long-duration, long-shot aesthetic, with restrained cutting. I am thinking of such figures as Béla Tarr, Jia Zhangke, Hou Hsaio-hsien, Abbas Kiarostomi, Sergei Loznitsa, Chantal Akerman, Michael Haneke, Sofia Coppola, Lucrecia Martel, Olivier Assayas, Apichatpong Weerasethakul, and the Dardenne brothers. When I served on the New York Film Festival selection committee, there seemed to be a consensus among my fellow committee members, as well as the other festival heads, that good filmmaking technique proceeded from a respect for the integrity of the image and its rigorously choreographed moves. Those of us who see movies this way may be fighting a rearguard action, but if nothing else, we will be supplying a map to the cinema of the past, which will help explain why certain older pictures like William Wyler's *The Letter*, televised, say, on Turner Classic Movies, continue to be touched by magic, raising a shiver whenever we encounter their liquid shadows.

THE NORMAL SCHOOL (FALL 2013)

FEATURE FILMS

Chapter Three

MAREN ADE

The Forest for the Trees

The Forest for the Trees, by German filmmaker Maren Ade, is one of the deepest depictions of loneliness onscreen. After serving as a television producer and shooting two shorts, Ade made this first feature, based on her own screenplay, in 2003. A remarkable, unnerving work, it already exhibits some of Ade's trademark: complex psychology, a steadfast look at embarrassing situations, a mixture of melancholic and comic, and an utter refusal of sentimentality or, for that matter, redemption. What I find exhilarating is their willingness to treat as honestly as possible the conflicted, intransigent, squeamish parts of human nature.

My first encounter with this filmmaker came when I saw her second feature, *Everyone Else*, in 2009. I was astonished by its boldness about heterosexual couples and their emotional hang-ups, their inability to go that last extra mile of surrendering to love. Her third feature, *Toni Erdmann* (2016), was a more boisterous, deliciously comic romp, establishing Ade as a favorite on the international film festival circuit. I was curious to catch up with her maiden effort, which never received a theatrical release in the United States but was now streaming on the Criterion Channel. I didn't expect much, but sometimes these early features by auteurs, like Bertolucci's *The Grim Reaper* or Scorsese's *Boxcar Bertha*, display rough glimmers of genius that prefigure the sustained efforts to follow. In fact, *The Forest for the Trees* proved to be a fully accomplished artistic statement, no apologies necessary.

It focuses on Melanie (Eva Löbau), a twenty-seven-year-old woman who, when we first meet her, is leaving her boyfriend of eight years and moving to Karlsruhe to take up her first teaching job. Significantly, we are introduced to her in the process of jilting her longtime lover: since the rest of the film will show *her* being snubbed, we can't see her as a pure victim. Melanie is moderately attractive, but her ex is rather goony-looking, and she probably thinks she deserves better.

Eager to make friends in her new environment, she proffers homemade schnapps to her neighbors, calling them a "housewarming gift" and then catching herself with the realization that the term is usually reserved for residents welcoming a newcomer, not the other way around. We will come to recognize this as her pattern: she initiates the "nice" gesture as though modeling it, expecting others to return it and being disappointed. The aggressiveness beneath this conventional display of manners is subtly implied, if hidden from Melanie. She introduces herself to the other teachers at school with food treats but ruins it by saying she's been exposed to novel pedagogic methods and hopes they will welcome "a breath of fresh air." This does not go down well with these burnt-out veterans. who look at her with stony resentment.

Your heart goes out to Melanie as she sets about trying to employ these innovative pedagogic techniques, only to be met with rudeness, rowdiness, cruelty, and boredom. The children test the newcomer to the limit. One boy throws a carton of chocolate milk at her back, damaging the new jacket she'd bought in the hopes of looking more "professional." She calls in the boy's mother, a lynx-eyed blond who denies her son has done any such thing and blames Melanie for not being able to control the class.

True, Melanie doesn't seem able to summon the authority to keep the kids in order: she wants them to like her and have fun; she wants to be their pal. I saw this happening again and again during the open classroom era when I taught children: young teachers would strain to be nonauthoritarian, only to find kids preferred old authoritarians who set limits and forced them to do the work. There is a movie subgenre about idealistic teachers who encounter troublesome students and win them over (*Blackboard Jungle*, *Up the Down Staircase*, *Dangerous Minds*): this is not one of them. Melanie never does get the hang of controlling her classes; her plot arc lies in a different direction.

She becomes fascinated by a neighbor across the way, the beautiful Tina (Daniela Holtz), who works in a boutique. Tina has the looks and style that

Melanie covets: to the degree that her preoccupation with this neighbor is driven solely by admiration or has a homoerotic component, whatever "romance" exists in the film has to do with Melanie courting Tina. She insists on doing favors for Tina, keeps inviting herself to hang out with her, and pries into her love life. Melanie is both generously helpful *and* nosily intrusive. Tina, for her part, does not entirely rebuff her: she wants to get rid of her before her staff party at the store, so she gives her a dress as a present. She forgets to show up for a date with Melanie but then invites her to her birthday party. It's important to recognize that Tina is not intentionally cruel: she just doesn't need Melanie for a friend as much as Melanie needs her. Tina may have the upper hand, comparatively, but she would also like to act courteously to this needy neighbor. That is, until Melanie blows it by interfering in the complicated romance between Tina and her ex-boyfriend Tobias. When Tina discovers what Melanie has done, she shouts at her, "You're not all there, are you? You just don't get it, do you?"

Tina's right. Melanie does not get "the forest for the trees." She is so caught up in her version of herself as a kind, considerate person that she cannot see she was jealous of Tina's relationship with Tobias. With her one-dimensional take on human nature, she thinks she is always proceeding from good intentions and the others are "assholes," as she keeps muttering under her breath. She doesn't grasp how she is constructing self-fulfilling prophecies that will lead to her being rejected. Her lack of confidence extends even to a potted plant ("Maybe it doesn't like me") and to horses at a farm: she can't get some of them to eat from her hand. Such comic details show Ade having a little fun with her insecure, self-pitying character.

For much of the film, one's sympathies are entirely with Melanie as she gets battered around. I thought of Éric Rohmer's *Le Rayon Vert* (*Summer*), whose heroine is also somewhat of a pill though you root for her happiness. Rohmer is characteristically, gallantly sympathetic toward his female characters, whereas Ade seems less willing to give them a free pass. So we seesaw between our feeling sorry for Melanie in the face of her humiliations and impatient with her self-defeating behavior.

There is one character, a male teacher named Thorsten (Jan Neumann), who is drawn to Melanie. Obviously he would like to date her, but he also wants to reassure her that she's not the only one who had difficulties teaching their first year. Every time he tries to console her, she can't take it and runs to the bathroom to sob. Is it because Thorsten is another dorky-looking guy, below her attractiveness pay scale, or because it hurts her pride too much to be seen in trouble? She is quick to lie whenever she might be caught looking pathetically needy: these lies suggest a more pleasant alternate reality unspooling constantly in her brain, in contrast to the bleaker present.

Finally she loses her grip: the story morphs from a normal twenty-something undergoing difficult adjustments to one having a mental breakdown. The ambiguous, magic realism ending can be read two ways: either as suicidal or, by symbolically ceding control of the wheel, learning to be life's untortured spectator.

Ironically, while Melanie can't control her classroom, the film's technique is supremely controlled. A low-budget production, shot in handheld DV, the colors are somewhat muted, and there is little cinematic pizzazz; no beauty for its own sake, everything is strictly functional. But then again, why would you want visual poetry to distract from Melanie's drab circumstances? The framing is tight; no pictorial cutaway shots of the town or the surrounding landscape. Close-ups are given only to Melanie, underscoring her isolation. Eva Lobau's extraordinary performance registers stoicism, hurt, disappointment, suppressed rage, and fake bonhomie in quick succession. Periodically being photographed in shadows as she spies on her neighbor only underscores her clouded perspective. In Melanie, we have one of the most complexly shaded characters in contemporary cinema.

The theme of loneliness may be universal, but there is also something very Germanic about the plot of a decent, repressed, socially awkward individual broken by an icy, indifferent world. The prototype goes back to Georg Büchner's nineteenth-century play *Woyzeck*, through Berg's opera of the same name and Fassbinder's *Merchant of Four Seasons*. What is so unique in Ade's version is the degree to which the protagonist is shown complicit in her own suffering. The result is an uneasy sort of comedy, devastating in its capacity to keep its audience off-balance.

CRITERION COLLECTION WEBSITE, APRIL 22, 2020

Chapter Four

CHANTAL AKERMAN

No Home Movie

Chantal Akerman is gone. Hard to believe.

I was just explaining to a friend how much I liked her latest film, *No Home Movie*, which I saw last week at the New York Film Festival. Much of it is a documentary consisting of shots of her aged, infirm mother wandering around her very tidy Brussels apartment, as well as shots of these rooms and balcony emptied of people. There are also dialogues between Chantal and her mother, between the mother and her caregiver, and between the mother and Chantal's sister. Chantal descends on her mother from time to time, then goes off on her globe-trotting, filmmaking ventures, Skyping her mother to keep in touch. Signing off from these Skypes are multiple declarations of love and kissy-kissy, but when they are together in the same room the tension between mother and daughter is palpable. Chantal keeps trying to get her mother to tell her stories about her youth, including her years in a concentration camp, meanwhile slipping the noose of her mother's curiosity about her famous daughter's life. At one point the mother complains to her younger daughter, "Chantal never tells me anything." The sister replies wryly: "She never stops talking!" "But she never tells me anything important." We get the sense that Chantal is forever fleeing this comfortable, static, bourgeois mother's nest while at the same time desperately dependent on her mother for the maternal warmth she can find nowhere else.

The film is slow, annoying—and real. It has more truth in it than 98 percent of art cinema or commercial movies. Never mind the baffling cutaways to deserts and unidentified landscapes: are they metaphors or disorienting moves that the experimental filmmaker felt compelled to make? You keep watching these family members who love each other but are frustrated in their attempts to connect and think, "It is what it is." A slowed-down, plotless, Belgian version of *Long Day's Journey Into Night*.

The obituary in the *Times* noted that Akerman was depressed this past year over her mother's death, the implication being that that may have led to her suicide. Regardless, it's all there on the screen.

I thought back to a 1978 feature film of hers, *Les Rendez-vous d'Anna*. A woman filmmaker is on tour with her latest work: she takes trains around Europe, stays in hotels, picks up men when she's lonely, and returns to Paris, where she listens to her answering machine. It's a bleak picture of a sad, restless life, not especially satisfying as narrative, but touching: you feel Chantal is trying to make a personal statement about what it feels like to be in her skin. You couldn't get closer to her skin than in *Je Tu Il Elle*, where she rolls around the floor naked eating sugar then hitchhikes with a trucker who has sex with her. I haven't seen it in a while, but I remember being impressed with its raw honesty. I'm very partial to those early shorts she made in New York, such as *News from Home* (another mother-daughter dialogue, this time postal) and *Hotel Monterey*. Of course *Jeanne Dielman, 23, quai de commerce, 1080 Bruxelles* was her breakthrough film, her masterpiece, as good as everyone says—a cinematic game changer.

There was a time when I looked forward to her next movie more than any other filmmaker's. In *Golden Eighties*, a kooky musical, she tried to spread her wings, with amusing results. Rohmer-esque efforts like *A Couch in New York* were less successful, to my mind. *Histoires d'Amérique* was a clumsy if warm-hearted folkloric exploration of Jews in the Diaspora, with the sort of vignettes she was trying to get her mother to tell. She reached another pinnacle with the superb *From the East*, another documentary of unblinking looking, filled with long tracking shots of bundled-up bystanders. In her underrated adaptation of Proust, *La Captive*, she captured something of her favorite writer's moody obsessiveness while shrinking his social tapestry. And so it went: an uneven oeuvre, this one good, that one disappointing, but always making an effort to try something new, to reinvent herself.

Some words that spring to mind about Akerman's work are: *annoying, irritating, stubborn*—but in the best possible sense. She was not obliging, thank God. She was not afraid to try your patience. She would push past the stage when the alleged single "point" was made and get you to keep watching, a prisoner of reality as it unfolded. She was exceptional at showing process. The paradox was that so much alienation or depression could coexist with such wonderment and glee at being able to stare at the world as it is. As it was. It no longer *is* for Chantal. We are the poorer and will now have to look for her rigorous honesty and generosity elsewhere.

INDIEWIRE (OCTOBER 7, 2015)

POSTSCRIPT

Since I wrote that tribute, I came across a small book Akerman wrote, in tandem with her last movie: *My Mother Laughs*.[1] It is a beautifully written rumination on her last year taking care of her mother while itching to run away from her, and simultaneously her failed love affair with a much younger woman, C., with whom she shared an apartment in Harlem The fragments move backward and forward in time, always extraordinarily honest, vividly observant—but sad, so that one can't help regarding it in hindsight as a long suicide note. At one point she actually says: "One day I even tried to kill myself but was smiling, pointedly not forgetting to smile, as if it were a gesture without consequence. Luckily it was, since I survived. I have survived everything to date, and I've often wanted to kill myself. But I told myself I could not do this to my mother. Later, when she's not here anymore."

Chapter Five

ANTONIONI'S *LE AMICHE*
Another Look

I have always been partial to those four early, black-and-white features Michelangelo Antonioni directed in the fifties (*Cronaca di un Amore, La Signora senza Camelie, Le Amiche,* and *Il Grido*) before launching his great trilogy, *L'Avventura, La Notte,* and *L'Eclisse.* They have a relative modesty and freshness, a formal inventiveness that has not yet solidified into the grave, rigorous mise-en-scène of the trilogy, though you can see him trying out many of those ideas—the camera looking down, the poignant hitching of actions to architecture and landscape, the mobile long takes.

I was drawn to *Le Amiche* partly because it was based on a novella by one of my favorite authors, Cesare Pavese, *Tra donne sole* (*Among Women Only*). Though this was the first time Antonioni had adapted a literary work, it seems to me that during this entire period he was drenched in Pavesisimo—a feeling for the noble roots of Italian people as they collided with the more shallow, opportunistic, go-go materialism of the postwar years; the hope for a new, transformed society and that hope dashed; the individual's loneliness and alienation in modernity; the sympathetic treatment of women; the triad obsessions of love, sex, death—and the temptation to suicide. Antonioni featured suicides and suicide attempts as a key social problem in his section, "Tentato Suicido," of the anthology film *L'Amore in Città* (*Love in the City*) and in *La Signora senza Camelie, Le Amiche,* and *Il Grido.* Pavese himself committed suicide in 1950, despite having achieved great critical success, after suffering a failed love affair with a young American actress, but anyone who reads his diaries (*The Burning Brand*) can see the anguish building up. In any case, there has been a seam of pessimistic Italian literature from Leopardi down to Pavese and beyond, which features bitter disenchantment, as opposed to the *dolce fa niente*, *la vita e bella*, life-embracing stereotype many project onto Italians.

The novella is a rather cool portrayal of the smart set in Turin (Pavese's city), narrated by Clelia, a career businesswoman who has returned to her native city to run a regional salon for her boss's fashion boutique anchored in Rome. At the hotel where she is staying, a young woman in the next room has attempted suicide, and in being roped into that drama, Clelia finds herself in the midst of the young woman's friends. She herself says she has never had time to make friends and so hopes to latch onto this set, although they are all more moneyed and frivolous than she is.

The film shuttles through the entangled lives of this female group, their love affairs with irresponsible, emotionally stunted men (including Gabriele Ferzetti, wonderfully warming up for his Sandro role in *L'Avventura*), their betrayals of one another, their efforts to waste time with parties and drinking, all leading up to the successful suicide, this time, of the sad young woman, Rosetta, and the guilt-ridden fallout from that tragedy. The pace is brisk, moving right along with a light touch. We are a long way from those patient, lingering-in-the-moment set pieces that would come later in Antonioni, like the island sequence in *L'Avventura* and the party in *Il Notte*. Credit the great Italian screenwriter Suso Cecchi d'Amico, who cowrote the script with Antonioni, with dialogue that is sharp, light, bitchy, and tells us a lot about these characters' precise levels of awareness and unconsciousness.

In the Criterion DVD reissue of the film, Tony Pipolo, with his customary critical intelligence and diligence, does a fine job of detailing the differences and similarities between Pavese's novel and Antonioni's film. Nevertheless, I take issue with his conclusion, when he states: "Shocking as it is, Clelia grasps that neither Rosetta's so-called best friend Momina, nor the shallow, man-crazy Mariella exhibits more than passing concern. Similarly, later, Clelia perceives that Rosetta's despair in no small part reflects the cynicism and indifference of her friends." He is referring to a scene in which Clelia castigates Momina (Yvonne Furneaux) as a "murderer," blaming her and herself and the others for not taking better care of Rosetta. It is a dramatic scene, with Clelia unleashing her self-righteous grief and anger at the emptiness of their lives, and Pipolo appears to have bought it hook, line, and sinker. The question is: Should we?

(Incidentally, I don't agree that Momina exhibits no more than passing concern: she seems thoroughly involved in taking Rosetta to the hospital, and why else would we see her weeping in the corner while Clelia is raking her over the coals?)

As with Claudia in *L'Avventura*, Clelia is more upwardly mobile, rising from the tenements by dint of hard work to the middle class, compared to the well-born swells surrounding her, and therefore we may also be inclined to see her as an audience surrogate who shares our sense of values. On the other hand, she is thoroughly complicit in skimming the cream of the good life, just as Claudia would be complicit in shacking up with her best friend's guy so quickly after Anna's disappearance.

Part of the difference between the two heroines has to do with casting Eleonora Rossi Drago in the central role. When Antonioni moved on to making his four films with Monica Vitti, he found an actress whose facial expressions could always convey sincerity, vibrant openness, and amiability—she would later star in comedies—and therefore a note of hopefulness. True, Antonioni was also in love with her at the time, and that may have factored into the way he had her photographed. Rossi Drago, by contrast, has a more closed-off, toughened face, which suits the hardened career woman she is portraying—more Barbara Stanwyck, but without the ability to melt the mask at the end. This factor tilts the whole meaning of the film for me: Clelia may feel superior to the other women, may feel she has more of a conscience and better set of values, but does she? Isn't she toying with her handsome workman supervisor just as shallowly as the other women with their dalliances? When she is given the opportunity to return to her job in Rome, she barely gives it a moment's hesitation. Telling the workman how hard it is for her to leave him, after promising they would share a life together, she dashes off to the train station, but not before telling the waiter to put the tea on her tab. He says quickly, "I'll get it," but the insult has already occurred. She is the Great Lady making an exit, and he is the peon left behind. In that sense, I would like to believe that the director, in casting Rossi Drago, wanted to undermine the easy conclusion that Clelia occupies the moral high ground. She is just like the rest, and the film is the better for it, more consistent, if bleaker and more sardonic. (Pavese's novella makes it clearer that Clelia is enjoying herself insulting Momina "as if she were my sister" and later questioning whether anyone could have stopped Rosetta from killing herself).

Monica Vitti, as I've said, gave Antonioni a purchase on some trace of innocence, optimism, and hope, needed for contrast to the dour social satire, though by the time he got to making *Red Desert*, their private relationship in tatters, he was shaping her into more of a mental basket case, and the innocence had to be imported by way of a strained fable. He looked for a spark of youthful idealism and vitality to be delivered by Daria Halprin in *Zabriskie Point* and Maria Schneider in *The Passenger*, but increasingly, male vitiation and fatigue overshadowed their efforts. I don't fault him for that; he was pursuing his truth as it evolved. I'm simply drawing attention to a dynamic between pessimism and optimism that would affect his casting choices. Alida Valli, in the hinge film *Il Grido*, which he made between *Le Amiche* and *L'Avventura*, is a curious hybrid: her face always suggests a veteran who should know the score (*The Third Man*, *The Paradine Case*, *Senso*) but often still chooses men unwisely—in *Il Grido*, the inarticulate, suicidal lunk played by Steve Cochran.

Antonioni, in the wake of the critically successful *L'Aventurra*, began to make philosophical and political pronouncements about modern life ("Eroticism is the disease of our age")[1] and to project himself as a prophet. We young'uns looked to him for that very certitude. He was our God the Father, laying down the laws of cinema and modern life, just as Godard was our brilliant Older Brother, shaking them up. But the films he made abroad in the United States and the UK, *Blow-Up*, *Zabriskie Point*, *Passenger*, for all their rich images, suffered from, it seemed to me, a thinning, touristic grasp of the nuances of social texture. He missed the bedrock historical and social background of Italy that had supported him in the earlier works, thanks in part to Pavese and Cecchi d'Amico. In its place came a certain ponderousness.

Pauline Kael, in her devastating put-down of *La Notte*, nailed that fashionably sour, didactic side of Antonioni.[2] It's too bad she couldn't also appreciate the morose, purgatorial charms of the film (interestingly, she dropped that review from her selected, *For Keeps*), but she was onto something. It may have stemmed from the unresolved tension between Antonioni's left-wing, anticapitalist politics and his upper-middle-class social roots, along with his celebrity director deluxe status travelling in the haut-bourgeois, aesthetically elevated milieu he was critiquing. In that sense, he was like Clelia, wanting to hang out with the workers but deploring their poor taste in furnishings.

Not to take anything away from his artistry. Antonioni remains a colossus, not only of cinema but modern art in general, and all his works, early, middle, and late, remain for me an inexhaustible source of speculation and consideration.

CINEASTE 46, NO. 3 (SUMMER 2021)

Chapter Six

INGMAR BERGMAN

Scenes from a Marriage and *Saraband*

At the age of fifty-four, having already made some thirty-four features that established him as one of the world's undisputed cinematic masters, Ingmar Bergman embarked for the first time on a television miniseries, *Scenes from a Marriage*. It would be shot in Stockholm and the island of Faro for only $200,000, cheaper than his previous feature, *Cries and Whispers* ($450,000) and with none of that film's baroque color experimentation. Instead, it would focus closely on two characters, Marianne and Johan, played by Liv Ullmann and Erland Josephson, two of the most trusted members of his repertory company. Bergman's script would perforce draw heavily on autobiographical experience: the director already had several failed marriages behind him and his stormy live-in relationship with Ullmann had recently broken up. Premiering on Swedish television in six parts in 1973, it would subsequently be reedited and shortened for theatrical release. Thirty years later, in 2003 when Bergman was eighty-five and living on Faro, he made a sequel of sorts, *Saraband*, having these same two actors reprise their original roles. It is curious to observe the many continuities and discontinuities between these two works, both made initially for television, which constitute a sort of sandwich. Though *Scenes from a Marriage* is obviously more ambitious and novelistic compared to the more modest coda, they share a rueful warmth and muzzy affection for human frailty that is atypical of this often dour, severe director.

When *Scenes from a Marriage* was first released theatrically in the United States in 1975, it inspired the voyeuristic thrill of watching a live couple flailing themselves raw before our eyes. The three-hour film seemed to do for marriage what the spectacle of the Louds' disintegration in PBS's *An American Family* had done for the nuclear household. Indeed, in the long takes and ferreting camerawork, it bore resemblance not only to a cinema verité documentary but to passages in John Cassavetes's *Faces* or *A Woman Under the Influence*. To compare Cassavetes to Bergman may seem far-fetched, yet they both had an interest in scenes that went past the "normal" climax into a confusing, unpredictable zone of appeasement and retrenchment. Not that Bergman had ever shied away from lengthy dialogue scenes, but this time he seemed to be experimenting with a more improvisatory reactive camera, intent on keeping up with the actors as they straggled through interiors looking for some safe nook, as though for a boxing corner between rounds. The Swedish director's great cameraman, Sven Nykvist, relinquished the exquisitely balanced compositions of *Through a Glass Darkly* or *Persona* for a more decentered, darting, close-up visual look, which, however, had its own scruffy elegance.

By 1973 Bergman had worked through, or put aside, his anguished questioning about how to live in a world without God. Now he was probing another question: On what basis can men and women, natural antagonists, expect to sustain love?

Scenes from a Marriage is first and foremost a study of intimacy. Anybody who has been in a marriage or long relationship can recognize the alternations of tenderness and irritation, of mind-reading rapport and alienated conviction that one is being taken for granted or completely misunderstood. Such is the nature of true intimacy, not as some lofty ideal but as gritty reality. Bergman's method here is to attune the audience to the couple's segues of ambivalent mood reversals and flip-flops: they have only to reach an affectionate equilibrium for one of them (usually the husband, Johan) to force a breach. For instance, in the televised version's fourth, postbreakup episode, they are getting along famously, Marianne, the ex-wife, having put off David, her compensatory lover, on the phone in order to sleep with Johan, when her estranged husband asks her if she loves David. Is he just being obtuse, or is the exasperated anger this remark provokes in Marianne his intentional goal?

Johan, who is not above trying on the mask of misogynist, just to see if it fits, refers several times to the loathing that Marianne's body has provoked in him during their marriage, as she went about the business of daily living, going to the bathroom and so on. Since Marianne is so comely, we can only assume that this repulsion is something more basic, on the order of men's infantile fear of women, their maternal capacities, their mysterious secretions; he must run away from this scary intimacy, he must create a distance. If marital familiarity breeds contempt, then Johan, in order to rekindle romance and erotic feeling, feels obliged to rupture the comfort of their "ridiculously bourgeois" marriage and reestablish the couple on another, more playfully illicit level.

Part of the pleasure in *Scenes from a Marriage* is getting to watch two of the greatest modern screen actors, Ullmann and Josephson, tangle with each other. Josephson had been acting in Bergman films from the very beginning of the director's career, in 1946, and was an established star of the Swedish theater, as well as a writer and sometime director, while Ullmann, a celebrated Norwegian actress who had debuted with Bergman at twenty-seven as the nonspeaking heroine of *Persona*, would go on to make nearly a dozen films with him. The technical solidity, affective range, attractiveness, and chemistry of these two performers ensure that we are in secure hands, however bumpy a ride we may be in for. Bergman, following his master, Carl Dreyer, continues to reconstitute the cinematic art as a language of faces. Liv Ullmann has the ability to go from goddess to frump, from repressed to radiant, in a moment. Her face can look uncannily beautiful, flashing her luminous blue eyes, but she is never more moving than when they are distorted behind goofy glasses in the heartbreaking scene where she receives the news that her husband intends to leave her. A certain placid, rosy-cheeked, Heidi complacency often threatens Ullmann's movie star allure, but it is this very smugness, her goody-goody air, that Bergman maliciously undermines here, by using the bearded, existentially discontented Josephson as her sardonic goad. Marianne, accepting the gender role society has assigned her while working as a divorce lawyer, is the protector of daily life: the good mother and wife, the obedient daughter, the organizer of family holiday functions. She has bought into the dream of bourgeois domestic happiness, asking her husband: "Why can't we be fat and cheerful?" Yet always the perfectionist and self-improver, she obediently diets because she recognizes that her job description as an ambitious man's wife includes looking desirable and sexy. Together, Marianne and Johan constitute that terrifying contemporary behemoth, the professional couple. It is up to him to rock the boat.

Ullmann gives a powerhouse performance as Marianne; she seems the stronger, more assured of the two. Josephson may have the harder role as Johan, a man of signal potential of whom perhaps too much was expected—a scientist whose career has stalled and a failed poet—who must nourish himself on her strength while queasily rebelling against it, insisting that we are all isolated, true love is impossible. Even at her most disenchanted, Marianne expresses traces of tender pity for Johan, retaining an impulse to protect him. Much as he is horrified by the condescension implicit in her pity, he also feels sorry for himself—or is not above playing Little Boy Lost to buy a little time from his guilty conscience.

The supporting cast—a bickering married couple, a client of Marianne's, two of Johan's coworkers, her mother—cast fascinating sidelights on the central dyadic conflict. Interestingly, their two children are never shown on camera. Perhaps Bergman felt they would seize too much of our sympathetic attention, as children onscreen often do, from their parents. As it is, Johan's sanguine abandoning of his offspring will count heavily against him with some viewers—especially those who do not buy his explanation that he must act drastically to save himself from premature burial. We will see the consequences of his estrangement from his children play out more clearly in the sequel, *Saraband*.

The shorter film version of *Scenes from a Marriage* is more harrowing and theatrical: a string of high points. The five-hour, six-part TV version (which I prefer), at nearly twice the length, has more breathing room, which allows the characters to regroup. A TV miniseries, broadcast over several nights, has the ability to intersect with and form a quotidian relationship to viewers' lives: its characters become members of the family, and their resilience over time, however incessant the crises called for by the script may be, induces a more good-humored, forgiving atmosphere. Bergman's awareness of the buoyancy that repetition and length can bestow, and his stylized exploitation of it, show up in the TV version's drily witty, detached voiceovers, which summarize the story so far at the head of each chapter and invite the viewer to look at some footage from Faro during the end credits. The fact that these credits are read aloud conveys a jaunty, Wellesian self-reflectiveness, calling attention to the film's artifactual quality and implicitly mocking its protagonists' self-seriousness.

That the pair so palpably continue to care for each other in the face of much nasty provocation also suggests a bittersweet, comic, almost Mozartean undertone (Bergman's very next film project would be *The Magic Flute*) beneath the embattled goings-on. Nowhere is the filmmaker's puckish, *Smiles of a Summer Night* side more in evidence than in the last episode, where they are seen cheerfully planning to cheat on their current mates, faithless to their new marriage bonds if more deeply faithful to their own earlier one. Johan is seen reaching for the phone to make a secret assignation with his ex-wife and being continually interrupted. When they get together this last time in *Scenes from a Marriage*, Marianne is able to dispense her hard-won wisdom on how to live, and Johan is free to mock her by saying she sounds like a politician, without either taking deep offense. When she wakes from a nightmare and suddenly seems to subscribe to his pessimistic view of life, even doubting that she has ever loved anyone, he is there to comfort her with a reassuring pirouette, saying that indeed they have both loved each other in their selfish, partial, human ways. Whether such an ending comes across as transcendently moving or a trifle pat (maybe both) may depend on your own level of optimism at the moment. In any event, their détente seems earned: after twenty years, the two have reached an accommodation, a wry understanding. Only at the end do we grasp that *Scenes from a Marriage* is, on balance, one of Bergman's most life-affirming and hopeful constructions. But wait: we have not heard the last of these two.

Saraband (2003) would be the final motion picture directed by Ingmar Bergman—his parting gift to the medium. It was billed as a sequel to *Scenes from a Marriage*, and, up to a point, it is, since it returns to the now-older Johan and Marianne (again played by Josephson and Ullmann, the latter coming out of a decade-long acting retirement to participate in it). Bergman had already announced more than once that he had retired from filmmaking—not an unexpected decision, given that he was in his mideighties and had been turning over his screenplays in recent years to others (including Ullmann herself, for *Private Confessions* in 1996 and *Faithless* in 2000). Engrossing and respectfully filmed as these delegated assignments are, they lack the master's ferocious edge. The difference became obvious when he took over directorial reins one last time. *Saraband* is an astonishment: vital, powerful, and, in its own small way, magnificent. Granted, when an aged film master makes a late work that is sublime, it should not come as a complete surprise. We might place it alongside Dreyer's *Gertrud* as an uncanny last word on the capricious, destructive, and creative power of love.

In *Saraband*, Johan and Marianne have not seen each other for many years when she gets the sudden impulse to look in on her ex-husband, who has inherited millions from a rich old aunt and now lives in "the wilderness" by himself, in his grandparents' summerhouse. Marianne, competent, compassionate, and controlling as ever, still practices family law on occasion; Johan has long since retired from academia and has grown, if anything, more crotchety and intimacy-averse. (One senses an autobiographical note here since Bergman himself had become reclusive.) Though their old relationship wounds are touched upon, the film wisely spends little time revisiting them. By now each is supremely unillusioned, and they get by with a testy forbearance that is not without tenderness.

But they, as it turns out, are no longer the main story: rather, Bergman has shifted his focus to a new power struggle, this time between a father and daughter, who live in a cottage on Johan's property and whose contest of wills Johan and Marianne watch like speculating, meddling, Jamesian bystanders. The father is Henrik, Johan's son by his first marriage. Part of the collateral damage incurred by Johan's blithe neglect of his children, now middle-aged at sixty-one, chubby, needy, coming to the end of a disappointing career as a cellist, and despised by his father as a weakling, Henrik is full of confusion, rage, and self-pity. We are initially inclined to pity him, too, but eventually we realize this guy (phenomenally acted by Börje Ahlstedt) is a nasty piece of work. His beautiful nineteen-year-old daughter, Karin (Julia Dufvenius), is a talented cellist herself; the problem is that her widowed father, who has taken on the role of her music coach, won't let her go and is using her as a wife surrogate. It is alarming enough to see them sleeping in the same bed (though presumably without sex); when father kisses daughter hard on the mouth, we think, "Now wait a minute!" The plot is thus the reverse of Ozu's *Late Spring*: What happens when a father will *not* relinquish his grown daughter to the world? As with Moliere's classic comedies, the tension revolves around efforts to separate greedy old man from innocent young girl and restore the natural order of things.

The pivotal character in the story turns out to be one who makes no actual appearance: Anna, Henrik's wife, who died two years before from cancer. Anna, by all accounts, was a loving wife, and it was the "miracle" of her love, all the more saintly for being bestowed on such a seemingly unlovable character as Henrik, that sets all the others brooding. Johan, who seems to have been more than a little smitten with his daughter-in-law, keeps a framed photograph of Anna in his study. "It's incomprehensible that Henrik was given the privilege of loving Anna. And that she was so devoted to *him*!" he snarls jealously. Marianne remains agnostic when it comes to love. She, too, finds herself staring at the dead Anna's enigmatic photo smile and wondering what this woman could have been thinking and feeling—what gave her the power to love? Henrik is so obsessed with his late wife that her loss has left him feeling disabled and suicidal. Karin finds a letter from her mother addressed to her father, which prophetically warns him not to abuse

Karin's youthful affections by transferring his all-consuming conjugal love from mother to daughter. This letter, this deathbed effort to free her, "is what love is," young Karin asserts confidently.

The title, *Saraband*, refers not only to a cello piece played by father and daughter but to Bergman's intrinsic musicality as a filmmaker and to the specific character of this stately court dance form. The film is structured as a series of ten duets, with the dyadic personae shifting from scene to scene: first Johan and Marianne, then Marianne and Karin, then Karin and her father, then Johan and Henrik, then Henrik and Marianne, and so on. Each scene is introduced by its number and chapter title, reminding us, as was done with similar devices in *Scenes from a Marriage*, that we are watching a constructed narrative, with the theatricality of blackout skits. In addition, a prologue and an epilogue both show Marianne alone, addressing the camera with her thoughts. All these distancing formal devices, however, melt away in the face of the dramatic intensity and psychological plausibility of the unfolding dialogues.

In one memorable scene, Marianne enters a deserted church and hears Henrik playing Bach on the organ, they converse amiably, he, charmed by her, impulsively invites her to dinner and she accepts, only to realize she can't make it, at which point, disappointed, he starts spewing out poisonous venom toward her. In another remarkable duet, Henrik visits his father, sitting in his library surrounded by books, to ask to borrow some money; the two men spar angrily, and Johan says he prefers to see this "healthy hate" from his son rather than the usual mealy-mouthed response. Henrik demands, "Father, where did all this hostility comes from?" Johan reminds Henrik of how his son rejected him when he was eighteen or nineteen. Henrik draws close to his father and hisses, not unreasonably: "Words uttered fifty years ago are no excuse." Hate seems as much a mystery to Bergman as love. Once again, he shows an aptitude for going beyond the point of decorum to a more naked, violent expression of negative feelings—just as Josephson's brilliant acting is able to make his character both sympathetic and dislikable.

In a scene late in *Saraband*, Johan awakens with an anxiety attack (reversing Marianne's nightmare in *Scenes from a Marriage*). This time it is he who stands baffled in his nightshirt, saying "My anxiety is bigger than I am . . . I'm too small for my anxiety!" Could any line be more Bergmanesque? Marianne, who had been sleeping in a guest room, invites him consolingly into her bed. Josephson rips off his nightshirt and we see the old actor in all his splendid, foolish nakedness; then Ullmann takes off her dressing gown as well, and the sight of her nude body calms her ex-lover's disquiet—a wonderful moment, if gallantly under-lit. As often in the past, Bergman brings us to the edge of existential despondency then mocks it with a smile.

Saraband began as a made-for-television film shot on digital video. The framing and lighting are consistently intelligent, the camerawork unostentatiously fluid, the editing crisp, and the visuals as a whole entirely appropriate for their narrative purposes. I was on the New York Film Festival selection committee in 2004, and my colleagues and I were dying to include it in the festival. But Bergman was dissatisfied with the transfer from video to film and at first refused to allow it to be shown theatrically. The festival director, Richard Pena, asked Ullmann if she would intervene, and Ullmann agreed to phone the "stubborn old goat," as she called him, on his island retreat. She got him to relent and release the film, to our deep gratitude. Shortly afterward, three years later, Bergman died, alone, having seemingly outlived the need for intimacy. One cannot watch this final work now without sensing that impending end, and the calm equilibrium and vigor with which the filmmaker bequeathed this elegiac, sprightly late masterpiece to the screen. Then again, a similar maturity and wisdom were already fully in evidence in his earlier conjugal exploration, *Scenes from a Marriage*, in which Bergman demonstrated—whatever his shortcomings might have been in real life as husband or father—a sublime fair-handedness toward both marital partners, as befitted the great artist he was.

CRITERION COLLECTION, 2003;
FILM COMMENT (SEPTEMBER/OCTOBER 2004)

Chapter Seven

RAYMOND BERNARD

Wooden Crosses and *Les Misérables*

It is ever the dream of cinephiles to discover lost masterpieces, just as it is ever a nuisance to have to redraw the pantheon map and accept previously overlooked candidates for auteur status. But a great film usually implies the handiwork of a great filmmaker, so what to do? There is of course an expanding field of film scholarship that makes the case for regional masters unknown to the general film buff, such as this polished Finnish director of the 1940s or that Malaysian pioneer of the 1970s. The case of Raymond Bernard is more peculiar because he directed several movies that were hailed as extraordinary accomplishments in 1930s France, a territory hardly off the beaten path of film history, and then sank from sight. The Criterion Collection's new Eclipse line, which bills itself as "a selection of lost, forgotten, or overshadowed classics" (can something be a forgotten classic? Is this an oxymoron?) has now released Bernard's two best films, *Wooden Crosses* and *Les Misérables*, and together they make a compelling case for admission into the canon.

Bernard (1891–1977), the son of the playwright Tristan Bernard, acted in silent films and wrote screenplays, apprenticed with Jacques Feyder, and got his first big break taking over the troubled costume epic *The Miracle of the Wolves* (1923). He became known as a director who could handle crowds and epics. His 1932 antiwar film, *Wooden Crosses*, was a remarkable ensemble work using veteran actors who had served in World War I and a devastating, uncompromising portrait of a French regiment as it goes its episodic way from gung-ho enthusiasm to stoical disenchantment. The camaraderie of the men scarcely compensates for the fact that they are expendable cannon fodder, thrown into impossible situations by commanding officers safe at headquarters. The battle scenes were so realistically recreated that Hollywood bought the rights to the picture and cannibalized it for their own war movies. Made two years after the stiffer and more sentimental *All Quiet on the Western Front*, to which it is both a reproach and corrective, *Wooden Crosses* continues to sting. It is certainly one of the five finest films made about that war—a precursor to Stanley Kubrick's *Paths of Glory*, which explored some of the same material. Despite its pessimistic tone, the picture scored an impressive box office success when it opened.

Bernard was ready to take on the biggest assignment of his life, Victor Hugo's *Les Misérables*. The novel had been adapted previously, in the silent era, and would be adapted many times more, but Bernard's is by far the finest version. One cannot assess the quality of his 1934 film adaptation without considering the challenge of the source material. *Les Misérables* is a jaw-dropping book, 1,400 pages long, structured like a series of novellas, each building toward its own climax, and encompassing into the bargain vast digressions on history and philosophy (which encouraged Tolstoy to write his *War and Peace*). Hugo felt entitled to put in everything. The result is like a combination of *Moby-Dick*, Eugène Sue, Poe, *The Communist Manifesto*, and *Little Women*: monumental grandeur and kitsch wrapped in one package. A Christian fable and arguably France's national epic (its author believed France had a destiny to save the world), it contains more sentimental claptrap than any other great novel I know and, at the same time, more scenes of tremendous tension. Hugo was a man of the stage, and he delivers many *coups de théâtre*, hair-raising dramatic turns, and confrontations.

Bertrand and his co-screenwriter, André Lang, set about condensing. Of necessity, whole plot chunks disappeared or were elided, including some fairly gaudy events, such as Valjean's second imprisonment, the escape over the wall, Cosette's years in the nunnery school. But what is surprising is how much of the novel's sweep has been retained, and even more surprising, the intimate pace at which it unfolds. Each glance, each touch of an object, each moment is given its proper time to mature.

The fine acting of the leads sets the tone for the film's overall unhurried rhythm. Harry Baur plays Jean Valjean, modulating from animalistic hardened criminal to compassionate philanthropist. The difficulty with the character of Valjean—even more problematic in the novel than the movie—is that once he reforms, he turns into a plaster saint. Baur distracts you from this problem by the compelling, warm physicality of his performance—you just want to keep watching him, with his heavy-lidded narrow eyes, thick lips, and bulbous nose. Anything but an Adonis, he came from that era when movie audiences tolerated homely, forceful leading men such as Edward Arnold, Edward G. Robinson, and Michel Simon. A major star in France, Baur also played the lead in Abel Gance's sweet film about Beethoven and, ironically, was the judicial pursuer of Raskolnikov in Pierre Chenal's *Crime and Punishment*. This time Baur is the fugitive, and Charles Vanel, his bushy-browed, alert, relentless pursuer. The scenes between the two are staggering: you feel their hatred and grudging respect distilled into magnetic attraction.

All the shots are gorgeously composed yet never static. Jules Kruger, who was Gance's cinematographer on *Napoleon*, nudges each scene toward an active imbalance, either by tilting the camera, German expressionist fashion, or by hand-held lurching into fights and crowds. Close-ups, wipes, startling transitions up to the clouds and back to Valjean on horseback, long tracking shots, jittery little pans across the body—every technique of silent and early sound film is commandeered effectively. The country fair scene of little Cosette maneuvering her heavy water pail past carnival stands, dancing bears, monkeys, fire eaters, is a marvel. The long tragic episode of 1832 revolutionaries at the barricades is an intricately staged, convincing battle scene. The composer Arthur Honneger wrote a memorably haunting score. But what lingers most in my mind are the sets and the exquisite way they are lit to show just enough of their architecture. Bertrand's production designer, Jean Perrier, conjures a whole world of stark French villages and seedy Parisian tenements that are reminiscent of Seurat's smudged charcoal drawings, as graphically economical and ineffable.

Of course it is a highly stylized studio look, far from the casual *plein air* of Renoir's *Toni* and the neorealist films that were just around the corner. That may partly explain why Bernard's towering, monumental *Les Misérables*, which premiered as three separate films, ended up being butchered, trimmed to less than half, and eventually forgotten. When French studios, close to bankruptcy, turned away from competing with Hollywood via big productions and began supporting small-scale, psychological pictures by Carné, Renoir, and Grémillon—that alluring turn labeled "poetic realism"—Bernard got lost in the shuffle. Meanwhile, the official accounts of French cinema that ensued focused on only one thirties story, the development of poetic realism; the large-scale national epics that had preceded it began to seem embarrassingly rhetorical in comparison to the newer manner's lean, grimly fatalistic verisimilitude.

With the passage of time, Carné's fog-shrouded ports and Bernard's village squares have come to look equally fantastic, equally magical and fabricated. Now that *Les Misérables* has been restored to close to its original five-hour length and made to sparkle, we can see what a treasure it is and how much it shares, in its tenderness, lyricism, progressive political humanism, and melancholy spectacle, with the best of Feyder, Duvivier, Carné, Grémillon, and Renoir.

CINEASTE 28, NO. 2 (2008)

Chapter Eight

ROBERT BRESSON

Mouchette

One of the hardest things to pull off in a narrative is a convincing suicide. After all, people suffer so much in life without killing themselves, while those who do go through with it can often appear insufficiently motivated. If a character in a novel or film is rendered successfully, meaning *vividly*, the audience will likely be on the side of prolonging their life and apt to feel an element of the arbitrary or patly convenient in that character's sudden self-extinction. Suicide can seem both an over- and underdetermined action, in life and in art, finally inexplicable or mysterious (in short, the territory where Robert Bresson liked to hang out).

Among cinema's more memorable suicides, we might mention Louis Malle's *The Fire Within*, George Cukor's *A Star Is Born*, Michelangelo Antonioni's *Il Grido*, Jean-Luc Godard's *Pierrot le Fou*, Kenji Mizoguchi's *Miss Oyu* . . . the list could be prolonged indefinitely. The point is, adult suicides cannot help but take on an air of noble exhaustion and mature judgment, of Sydney Carton self-sacrifice. More germane to Bresson's *Mouchette*, comparatively speaking, would be the child suicides in Rossellini's *Germany Year Zero* and *Europa '51*. A child cannot hope to know enough about the twists of fortune ahead to make an enlightened assessment; therefore, the decision of minors to take their own lives is all the more horrifying and must indict the adult society surrounding them. Rossellini chose twice to dramatize the crisis of postwar doubt by showing children, the proverbial "hope of the future," refuse a future: in *Germany Year Zero*, at the end of accumulating harsh poverty and shame, the little boy jumps off a building in ruins; the other happens, more shockingly, near the beginning of *Europa '51*, off-camera and in a comfortable upper-middle-class home, driving the distraught mother (Ingrid Bergman) into a search for spiritual meaning. Rossellini and Bresson share a Catholic regard for child suicide as so monstrous an evil that it must awaken theological thoughts in the viewer. The difference is that Rossellini is more interested in the sociological and political context that would spawn such a despairing response, whereas Bresson fights shy of blaming historical conditions, being more intrigued with the possibilities of freedom and revolt as a desperate expression of the awakening soul.

In other words, much as we might want to see Mouchette simply as a victim, this is not Bresson's intention. Nor was it the aim of Georges Bernanos, who wrote the short, compelling novel, published in 1937 under the title *Nouvelle histoire de Mouchette*, which Bresson adapted for the screen thirty years later. This was the second time Bresson used a book by Bernanos as source material, the first being *Diary of a Country Priest*. Bernanos was fascinated with the perverse as a road to the sacred: he Gallicized and Catholicized Dostoevsky. For his part, Bresson, in addition to using *Crime and Punishment* as a template for *Pickpocket*, adapted the Russian novelist's *A Gentle Spirit* for another of his films, *Une Femme Douce*. The link from Dostoevsky to Bernanos to Bresson is thus very pronounced. "Suffering is consciousness," wrote Dostoevsky. In *Notes from Underground*, he famously gave validity to spite and spleen. And in *The Brothers Karamazov*, Ivan said the one thing he could not understand, nor forgive God for, was cruelty to children. This passage may well have been in the back of both Bernanos's and Bresson's minds when they undertook to exonerate God and tell the story of Mouchette, the barely teenaged girl who transforms cruelty against her into an inverted liberation through the perverse, spiteful action of suicide.

Mouchette is no angel: she throws dirt at her well-dressed classmates; she frustrates her teacher by refusing to sing in class; she curses her father; and she walks through life with a sullen pout. On the other hand, she helps her dying mother take care of the baby; she sees and understands what is happening around her with an animal cunning; and she exhibits powers of insight and sympathy (especially toward the poacher, Arsène). As is customary with Bresson, he has used a nonprofessional, Nadine Nortier, for the lead part and stifled any emoting, but within the confines of the Bressonian system of acting, Nortier expresses well the contradictory character traits of

Mouchette: stony, tender, resigned, rebellious. It should be pointed out that Bresson's screenplay takes many liberties with the novel, rearranging the order of sequences, building up certain parts, adding dialogues while radically compressing others, but temperamentally, it stays close to the book, especially in its handling of the main character.

Visually, the film has the graphic density of an Atget photograph and the material conviction and simplicity of a Victor Sjöström silent. Indeed, a good part of *Mouchette* plays like a silent movie: dialogues are minimal; characters respond mostly through glances; a judicious buildup of close-ups pulls the narrative along. (In other respects a hero of long-shot filmmakers, Bresson never signed on to the puritanical suppression of close-ups: *Pickpocket* is full of them.) His camera often stays low in *Mouchette*, picking out legs and skirts and shoes before granting us more of an orienting perspective. One of the ways Bresson structures the film is by setting up a bit of business, then repeating it: the motif of the boys who call out lewd proposals to Mouchette occurs twice, as does the image of her father and brother, standing side by side, belting down a glass of wine. This last gesture has the gravity of a solemn rite.

Alcoholism is the force, the puppeteer manipulating the automatism of the characters in the film. Bresson takes pains to show how deep its roots are in La France Profonde (deeper perhaps than Catholicism), how surely the disease is passed on from father to son, and how much harm it does to the women. *Mouchette* is, above all, a tragedy of alcoholism, from the viewpoint not of the imbibers but a recipient, the girl who is beaten by her father, raped by the poacher, and forced to watch her mother guzzle gin as she dies, her last words of advice to stay away from drunkards.

Mouchette wants to tell her mother about her violation the night before but is interrupted by the crying baby. Ironically, she had been raped by the one man who stirred her tenderness, and even while being forcibly penetrated, she could not help but stroke his hair consolingly. Now the baby's cry arouses in her another unexpected, maternal impulse. It is part of Bresson's point that the awakening of tenderness and love in Mouchette—of consciousness itself—proves dangerous to her survival. She discovers a realm beyond mute stoicism, is opened up and punished for that. A conventional contemporary reading of the film would argue that she commits suicide because she has been raped and is suffering grief from her mother's death, but there is no evidence given by the filmmaker that she was even close to her mother (Bernanos explicitly tells us she was not), nor does she seem overwrought by the loss of her virginity. Rather, her chain of humiliations seems part of the mortal package: just as the donkey Balthazar was a stand-in for Christ, so every creature on earth is doomed to reenact the Passion, in Bresson's vision.

After her mother's death, Mouchette wanders around the village, accosted by different older women, each of whom at first offers compassionate condolence then turns on the teenage girl with censorious venom. (Bresson's portrayal of French village life's poisoned malice is similar to Clouzot's in *The Raven*.) We feel society's mistrust toward the girl and her own estrangement building up inside her, even if we don't quite understand where all this vindictiveness against her is coming from. Here, Bernanos is much more forthcoming with psychological underpinnings, while Bresson refuses to advance us just that piece of information that would clarify the situation. What I never quite realized until I read the book was that the movie's cryptic, uncanny, elliptical manner comes partly from Bresson trying to render onscreen all the physical actions and gestures in the novel while suppressing all the mental processes, interior monologues, and commentaries that explain them.

Take this example from Bernanos's text, which adopts the momentary perspective of two old biddies: "The neck of Mouchette's blouse was open and the bruises on her chest were plainly visible. They had not yet turned purple. On her brown skin their dark red, with the lighter red of the scratches, stood out clearly. It was common knowledge that her father was free with his fists, but these marks had a deeper and more sinister significance. On her young girl's bosom they had written a story which the experienced glance of the two older women immediately apprehended."[1] In the movie, we see a close-up of Mouchette's neck, and her confused attempt to close her collar, but I doubt that one viewer in ten would be able to guess the two older women had gleaned from the sight of Mouchette's clavicle that she had slept with a man. So when one of them hisses "You slut!" at Mouchette, the hatred seems to issue from nowhere—precisely that lonely nowhere that is the vacuum Bresson keeps drawing from and pressing us to feel.

Where Bernanos and Bresson unite is in their insistence that her suicide has neither explanation nor justification. It comes out of nowhere, a negative miracle, like the reverse of the resurrection scene in Dreyer's *Ordet*. Instead of someone magically coming to life, someone magically dies. A short book (127 pages) and a short movie (80 minutes), both are kept intentionally brief so as to forestall the workings of that mesh-like causality that is the great promise of naturalist fiction. Listen to Bernanos: "People generally think that suicide is an act like any other, the last link in a chain of reflections, or at least of mental images, the conclusion of a supreme debate between the instinct to live and another, more mysterious instinct of renouncement and refusal. But it is not like that. Apart from certain abnormal exceptions, suicide is an inexplicable and frighteningly sudden event, rather like the kind of rapid chemical decompositions which currently fashionable science can only explain with absurd or contradictory hypotheses."

Those of us who are less hostile to psychological plausibility than Bernanos and Bresson, or more skeptical of the spiritual promise embedded in the inexplicable, might argue that a young girl like Mouchette, who had just been through such an eventful twenty-four hours (first being raped, then losing her mother) would probably not be inclined to kill herself right away. She would still be reeling too much to exercise this degree of volition. But it is the task of Bresson, as a religious artist in a secular age, to increase our sense of awe by the shaping power of art and to intensify our presentiment of destiny, just as it is our choice, as movie lovers, to go to Bresson and other great filmmakers to feel that there is some aesthetic design behind suffering—incomprehensible as it may be in our daily lives.

Mouchette lies down on the river bank, in the last scene of the film, and experimentally tests the angle of the grass, giving it an almost playful half try, like a kid enjoying the act of rolling downhill, before spiraling more purposefully and angrily into the lake. The camera stays on the reeds and the water as she tumbles out of the frame. Who can fathom it?

FILM COMMENT (MAY/JUNE 1999)

Chapter Nine

LINO BROCKA

Insiang

The haunting *Insiang* (1976) introduced its director, Lino Brocka, to the world stage when it showed at the 1978 Cannes Film Festival. Brocka had begun his career in 1970 making commercial genre films—domestic melodramas about marital infidelity, as well as action pictures and comedies. But wanting to create independent movies that addressed more problematic aspects of Filipino reality, he shifted directions in 1974. His first such venture, made that year, was *Manila in the Claws of Light*, a powerful, dark, sprawling film about country youth who come to the city, only to be ground down by urban poverty. (It was this movie that inspired Lav Diaz, today's most prominent Filipino director, to become a filmmaker). Brocka's next, equally provocative film was *Insiang*, which succeeded more than its predecessor by narrowing the focus and concentrating on one protagonist and one city neighborhood.

With these two films, Brocka joined a generation of filmmakers (including Ishmael Bernal, Mike de Leon, Kidlat Tahimik, and Mario O'Hara) whose aim was to wrench Philippine cinema from the slick commercial and soft porn product it had previously been known for and move it in a more personal, socially progressive, and artistically challenging direction. Of these New Wave–like innovators, who came to be known as the "Second Golden Age," Brocka was the most internationally visible. While also running an experimental theater troupe and directing for TV, he went on to make some sixty-odd features, many dealing with taboo subjects such as injustice and torture under martial law, governmental corruption, murderous militias, and prejudice against gays. Brocka became a cultural hero of the anti-Marcos protest movement. He died young, in a car accident which may or may not have been self-induced. It must be said that the artistic quality of his films varied widely, and that may explain why film preservers and festival curators keep coming back to *Insiang* as Lino Brocka's one unassailably compelling masterwork.

Insiang came from a novel by Mario O'Hara, who also wrote the screenplay with Lamberto E. Antonio. A small film in some respects, it is also an uncanny, resonant blend of neorealism and melodrama. It opens documentary fashion at a slaughterhouse with pigs being gutted, gushing blood into water tanks, then surveys the jerrybuilt shacks of a slum abutting a river, with children playing in the dirt. Eventually we pick out in the distance the heroine, Insiang, crossing a bridge. She (played by the Filipina screen goddess Hilda Koronel) is extraordinarily lovely, her beauty a counterweight to the shabbiness around her. She is also good and chaste; we see her vainly trying to keep peace in her squabbling household: her mother, Tonya, who sells fish in the market, is constantly haranguing the unemployed, parasitic relatives camped out in her house. These bickering ensemble scenes have a remarkable vitality, the camera framing shots of dense overlapping figures crossing and colliding. Tonya, played indelibly by the veteran actress Mona Lisa, is a shrewish, bitter woman whose husband, Insiang's father, deserted her for a mistress. In short order she kicks out her husband's relatives so that she can install a much younger male, the hunky, macho slaughterhouse worker Dado. She is relentlessly cruel to her daughter, Insiang, identifying the girl with her straying husband and jealous of the younger woman's beauty. As Insiang says in a matter-of-fact understatement, "I no longer feel any maternal bond from her." Dado, no surprise, is more drawn to Insiang than her aging mother. Thus a triangular situation is set up that can only lead to disaster.

The cinematic style is rough and ready: the film was shot in seven days and usually only one take sufficed. The talented cameraman, Conrado Baltazar, employed frequent zooms and pans to keep up with the jittery action. You come to know well the interior of that shack: the kitchen, the dining table, the toilet, everything out in the open. (In one shot, Insiang is cooking on the stove while her mother squats nearby, taking a piss.) Keeping in mind that Brocka had developed his own theatrical troupe and commandeered them to act in his films, one senses he was more concerned with staging the action as a theater director might, and getting the best possible performances out of the cast, than devising an elaborate mise-en-scène for the camera. Indeed, Peter Rissient, the extraordinary scout who first brought *Insiang* to Cannes and helped produce several of the filmmaker's later films, confirmed to me that Brocka knew nothing about lenses, leaving those decisions to the cameraman. In certain respects Brocka resembled Rainer Werner Fassbinder: both had theater troupes; both worked quickly and were inordinately prolific; both were gay and put forward a harsh vision of the strong preying on the weak.

In *Insiang*, the laws of physical attraction trump any ethical considerations. The two men who take sexual advantage of Insiang conveniently excuse their rapacity by saying that they are only men—in effect, animals—and can't help themselves. Insiang's muscular, feckless, mechanic boyfriend Bebot (Rez Cortez) is shown shirtless throughout, while Dado (Ruel Vernal) recalls Marlon Brando's Stanley Kowalski, pouncing on every female in the household. It does not take much to imagine a gay storyteller like Brocka projecting his own fascination with the handsome, cruelly exploitative Dado. Tall, mustachioed, with a tattoo on his chest, Dado dominates the smaller Bebot, taunting the other man by fingering his earring and questioning his masculinity. Dado may be a lout, but by the end it does seem that he genuinely loves or cares for Insiang. It is Insiang, initially pure and virtuous, who turns out to be the monster, bent as she is on deadly revenge.

Much of the film's fascination derives from the way the main character keeps revealing unexpected aspects. Insiang surprises us initially when she declares her hope of getting married to the boyish, immature Bebot (she deserves so much better!), and then she startles us with the boldness of her declaration that she hates her mother. If in the first half she seems an innocent, wanting only to be rescued from a sordid situation, in the second half she becomes more calculating, having learned to use her sensual power over men. This change corresponds to an alteration in the film's pace and tone, slowing down to savor the moment. There is the prolonged, awkward scene when Bebot starts to pay for the room in the hot-sheet hotel and then turns to Insiang for the money when he comes up short. There are slow night scenes where we glimpse Insiang behind a mosquito net, dimly lit: they suggest the awakening of her sexuality, side by side with her repugnance and disgust. These scenes plunge us into a dreamlike, surreal mood, reminiscent of the way Buñuel incorporated dreams into his portrait of slum dwellers in *Los Olvidados*. There is also an undercutting of realism in the many scenes that end with a zoom onto Insiang's expressive but inscrutable face, like the close-ups in a cheesy television soap opera, while the same limited musical refrain churns in the background and then gets abruptly chopped. It is hard to say what part of this is crude filmmaking and what part a conscious stylistic device, meant to draw us further into an oneiric, meditative space. Both, perhaps.

In the background is a third suitor for Insiang's hand, a serious, studious-minded boy, and of course she barely notices him. He is the one who keeps telling her she must "leave this place," as he has every expectation of doing. This idea of escaping the shantytown is articulated repeatedly by different speakers, but the film casts a claustrophobic net over the barrio and will not permit them or us to exit the premises. The ending (without giving it away) is very strong and forces us to reinterpret all that has gone before: now we are invited to see it as a thwarted mother-daughter love story. Each is encaged separately in her own pride and anger.

The film's psychology is intricate and subtle. Still, it is the tactility of desire and matter that leaves the deepest impression. The press of flesh on flesh, the tropical heat and sweat, the water dripping in the faucet to drown out the sounds of sex, the smell of fish that Tonya tries to get rid of before her pig-butcher lover comes home. . . . Most of all, there is the physicality of the barrio in all its gritty concreteness. *Insiang* may not have been as explicitly political as many of Brocka's later movies would be, but it insinuated a clear politics about the urban poor, merely by depicting their living conditions. This Filipino reality was one the dictator Marcos would have definitely not wanted the world to see. At the same time these slum dwellers are never presented as mere victims; they possess agency and enormous, if spiteful, vitality and a willingness to engage with one another, inflicting pain or tenderness as the situation arises. "Just endure it," Insiang advises the recipient of her mother's tongue-lashing early on, but stoicism is finally not an option. Rarely has Fate been more convincingly orchestrated.

"SLUM GODDESS," CRITERION COLLECTION/
MARTIN SCORSESE'S WORLD CINEMA PROJECT, 2017

Chapter Ten

JOHN CASSAVETES

The Killing of a Chinese Bookie

In John Cassavetes's personal cinema, the director was always trying to break away from the formulae of Hollywood narrative in order to uncover some fugitive truth about the way people behave. At the same time, he took seriously his responsibilities as a form-giving artist, starting with a careful script (however improvised it may have appeared). Nowhere was the tension between Cassavetes's linear and digressive, driven and entropic tendencies more sharply fought out than in *The Killing of a Chinese Bookie* (1976), one of his most fascinating achievements.

Following up his success with *A Woman Under the Influence*, the director thought it might be interesting to try a gangster picture to stretch himself, in effect, by exchanging the domestic suburbia of quarreling married couples for a more raffish milieu and meeting the audience halfway with some traditional Hollywood entertainment values associated with the mob genre: suspense, murder, double-cross, topless dancers. An amiable, courtly nightclub owner, Cosmo Vittelli (Ben Gazzara), already in debt to loan sharks, indulges his unfortunate weakness for drinking and gambling and ends up owing $23,000 to gangsters, who demand that he pay off the debt by executing a competitor of theirs, a mob boss whom they inaccurately describe as a Chinese bookie. The story obeys the step-by-step, film noir fatalism of an unfolding nightmare, whereby small mistakes and temptations lead to deeper consequences. Looked at purely as narrative, there is surprisingly little waste in the script: each scene advances and intensifies the central dramatic situation. Cassavetes even fulfills the genre contract with action sequences (rare for him) that involve shootings, chases, sinister underlit garages, perhaps drawing on his own past experience as an actor in crime movies and television series. On the other hand, the film's enduring power comes across most in subtle details of setting and character that play against or in inertial counterpoint to these obligatory propulsive scenes.

Cosmo's strip club, the Crazy Horse West, functions as a viscous flypaper to which the film keeps attaching itself, where time dawdles and dilates in a constant night. (Cassavetes insisted these nightclub scenes be shot through gels, the effect of which created stylized pools of isolating red or blue light for the owner-impresario to walk through.) Cosmo has gilded his tawdry peep show with a series of fantasy backdrops, all introduced by the dumpy, epicene master of ceremonies, Teddy, known as Mr. Sophistication, who "takes" the audience to exotic locales. Unforgettably portrayed by screenwriter Meade Roberts, Mr. Sophistication belongs to that tribe Dostoevsky called "the insulted and the injured." He oozes affronted, buffoonish humiliation. But he also epitomizes the needy, oversensitive artist, a self-parody of Cassavetes, who is hungry for the spotlight but believes himself fundamentally homely and unloved. Teddy's theme song, "Imagination Is Funny," becomes the film's bleak anthem.

At bottom, *The Killing of a Chinese Bookie* is a character study of its grinning, self-estranged protagonist, Cosmo, a small-time, rough-around-the-edges businessman trying to maintain an invented persona of Mr. Lucky suavity and charm. The corsages he brings each of his "lovely ladies"—rounding them up as escorts to the gambling joint, Ship Ahoy, where they will be forced to witness his defeat—are the perfect expression of his self-conscious, formal punctilio and hunger for class. Ben Gazzara turns in a brilliant performance as the unhappy Cosmo. (That Gazzara was unhappy himself through much of the shooting, finding it hard to sympathize with or admire his character, only reinforces our sense of Cosmo as discomfited with his chump role in life.) Cosmo seems always to be sniffing himself for something rancid or fraudulent. Trying to live up to an elegant standard of sophistication, he mutes his Sicilian street temper with a false veneer of politeness and seductive blather. In a long, revealing speech near the end, he admits that he is always betraying his real nature: "Look at me—I'm only happy when I'm angry, when I'm sad, when I'm playing the fool, when I can be what people want me to be, rather than be myself." Ironically, he utters this false-self confession as a way to motivate the troupe to get back on stage and give the customers what they want—saying, "Choose a personality," or in other words, *Fake it for me.* Even at his most sincere, he's calculating, and even at his most calculating, he is lost, unable to decide what he is undergoing or who he is. One moment he says, "I've never felt better in my life," the next moment it's "I don't feel so good." (No surprise, since he has a bullet lodged in his gut.)

Cassavetes clearly believed the self to be a constant bluff, a desperate improvisation launched in heavy fog. He told an interviewer: "People don't know what they are doing, myself included. They don't know what they want or feel. It's only in the movies that they know what their problems are and have game plans for dealing with them." The closest thing Cosmo has to a game plan is *The show must go on.* In one hilarious scene, en route to his prospective hit job, he stops in a phone booth to check up on the evening's performance: what number are the girls and Teddy doing? He berates his help for not knowing the acts better after all these years. At bottom he is a man of the theater, at its most flea-bitten. He understands two things: "I own this joint" and "Everything takes work; we'll straighten it out." You do your job the best you can, even if it's just shaking your tits onstage, in the no-win situation life hands you. It is this sort of philosophy that informs what nobility there is in Cassavetes's grubby universe.

The plot's biggest gamble was to make Cosmo, this likable if screwed-up schnook, actually go through with the killing. Is it plausible that someone seemingly so decent would do such a thing? We don't know—any more than we know enough about his past to say with certainly whether it's even the first time he's killed someone. But if we accept Cassavetes's model of the self as constantly in flux, provisional, unknowable, yet susceptible to the immediate claims of duty, then we may be better able to make the leap and accept the possibility.

Cosmo's counterpart in the gangster world is Morty, shrewdly played by that superb Cassavetes regular, Seymour Cassel. Morty is another character with a false self, a smiling company man hiding behind an oddly decorous manner: "Will you excuse me please, I have to freshen up," he says to his dinner companions before ordering another rubout. Not everyone surrounding Cosmo is as empty and amoral, however. Rachel (Azizi Johari), the beautiful Black showgirl who is Cosmo's lover, and her mother, Betty (Virginia Carrington), offer him an alternative of tender care. So it is all the more startling when, in a powerful scene toward the end, Betty interrupts his monologue of childhood reminiscence and sweet talk to tell him she doesn't give a shit.

"Cosmo, I think what happened was wrong," she says, rising to full moral stature, and adds that if he won't see a doctor to have the bullet removed, then he can't stay in their house. Without wanting to know how he came by that bullet, she indicates to him that he represents a danger to her and her daughter and she has an obligation to protect her family. Thus his fantasy that this black mother and daughter are his true "family" crumbles, and he retreats to the club, his only haven. So might Tony Soprano lick his wounds in the Bada Bing! club.

Thirty years ago, when *The Killing of a Chinese Bookie* was first released, it bombed at the box office, much to Cassavetes's disappointment. Critics found it disorganized, self-indulgent, and unfathomable; audiences took their word for it and stayed away. Today, the film seems a model of narrative lucidity: we have caught up to Cassavetes, the reigning aesthetic has evolved steadily in the direction of his personal cinematic style. Now we are more accustomed to hanging out and listening in on the comic banality of low-life small talk; to a semidocumentary, hand-held camera, ambient-sound approach; to morally divided, not entirely sympathetic characters, dollops of "dead time," and subversions of traditional genre expectations.

The film, seen today, generates considerable suspense, part of which comes from classic man-against-the-mob conventions: seeing how the noose of fate is tightened. Part of it, however, comes from Cassavetes's perverse reluctance to play the game of simple entertainment, offering more complex rewards instead. An example is the scene where Cosmo stops off at a hamburger restaurant to pick up some meat with which to placate the guard dogs before murdering their owner. The waitress, a well-intentioned, matronly blonde, tries to convince her customer to take the burgers individually wrapped, so they won't make a greasy mess. Cosmo obviously cannot share with her the real reason why he refuses this amenity, and is reduced to repeating his request with mounting frustration, while the bartender acts as a bridge between the two. Classic gangster movies or film noirs often feature sharply etched cameos of garage attendants, hotel clerks, or hash slingers, but generally they perform a strict narrative function and then disappear. In this scene, however, the waitress goes beyond that point, threatening to pull you out of the hit-man narrative by insisting on her reality. Cosmo, looking tired and aggrieved, is being forced to acknowledge that every human being has a distinct point of view—something he will again have to take into consideration soon enough, when he faces the old Chinese bookie, naked in the bathtub, before deciding whether to blow him away.

In Cassavetes's cinema, these delays, these eruptions of the messy, frustrating, time-consuming, and inconvenient ways that everyone, bit player to star, asserts their right to be taken seriously, are not impediments to the plot, but are the plot. This point is made clearer in the original, more leisurely (and, to my mind, better) version of the film, which lasted 134 minutes, as opposed to the second, tightened version of 109 minutes. In the longer version, we learn more odd details about the De Lovelies (the one who doesn't like champagne, for instance) and get an introduction to the Seymour Cassel character at his most unctuously ingratiating. We are allowed to sink into each moment voluptuously, to see more stage routines in the nightclub, which reinforces Teddy's/Mr. Sophistication's role as Cosmo's grotesque doppelganger, as well as making for a better balance between crime and show biz film. The shorter version is in some ways tougher, colder, more abstract, like a French *policier*; in the longer, more exploratory version, Cosmo takes a while to seem completely lost, alienated. Both versions, however, end the same ironic way, with Teddy mistaking his "padrone's" philosophical spiel as proof that Cosmo "practices the best thing there is to be in the world—to be comfortable." Cosmo goes off we not know where, bleeding, possibly to death, and we never him see again. The focus shifts back for the final time to the nightclub, where Teddy sings a despicably hostile rendition of "I Can't Give You Anything But Love" to the audience (and, by extension, us), and the last line heard in the film is one of the chorus girls reassuring Mr. Sophistication that they really do love him, even if he thinks they don't. We could say the same to the now-departed Mr. Cassavetes.

"JOHN CASSAVETES: FIVE FILMS," CRITERION COLLECTION, 2004

Chapter Eleven

CLAUDE CHABROL

The Swindle

The Swindle (1998), a.k.a. *Rien Ne Va Plus*, is the fiftieth feature film made by Claude Chabrol. A decidedly and almost obstinately minor work, falling into the category Chabrol himself calls "light entertainment," it gives us, if nothing else, a chance to take a step back and contemplate this director's strange career.

I began with an active enthusiasm for this director, who seemed the early sixties peer of his other Nouvelle Vague confreres, Godard, Truffaut, Rohmer, Malle, etc. I was particularly drawn to the raw-edged, semidocumentary freshness of *Le Beau Serge*, the saucy cynicism of *Les Cousins*, and, best of all, his resolutely unsentimental ensemble masterpiece, *Les Bonnes Femmes*. He continued to dazzle me with the unreliable narrator of *The Third Lover* and the capricious camerawork in *Leda*. All in all, Chabrol seemed a provocateur, like Buñuel, trafficking in perversities and shocks to the bourgeois nervous system. His *Bluebeard* (*Landru*) fit thematically into this pattern of subversion, though I could not help wondering at the eerie evenness that was starting to infiltrate his visual style.

There ensued a period alternating slight, campy "entertainments" (*The Tiger Likes Fresh Blood, Marie-Chantal Contre le Docteur Kha*) with art films of almost glacial smoothness, somber plotting (infidelity, murder), and silky sensuality (*Les Biches, La Femme Infidèle, Le Boucher*), usually featuring his lovely wife, the actress Stéphane Audrin. The anarchist rebel had turned into an arch-purveyor of high-bourgeois taste. All of these middle-period, chic films had their moments, but none of them moved me especially, except for *Just Before Nightfall*, the one masterwork in the batch.

By the time *Violette* (1978), his film about a murderess, came out, I was starting to get bored with Chabrol's programmed frissons. Either I no longer cared as much about shivers of perversity as I had in adolescence, or he'd lost his inner fire and was merely going through the motions. I wondered if Chabrol had nothing more to say but was too much the old pro to retire. Still, you had to give him credit as a survivor. Truffaut, Demy, Malle had all died, and Godard was permanently self-marginalized. But Chabrol kept churning them out. There is something admirable about an aging director who keeps doing skillfully made, modest little genre films that may not amount to much, that may even be empty inside, but that have a classical sense of composition and flow.

Then I started to see a return of visual ambition, to tense, conscientious mise-en-scène in *Betty, L'Enfer, La Cérémonie*. Each seemed to project a feeling of ritual, mystery, and curiosity about obsession. (It must be said that obsession can be as much a narrative trap as a hook, leaving nowhere to go except some sort of implausible explosive violence). Though these films indeed tended to collapse into mechanical catastrophe, as is Chabrol's wont, they at least drew me in for the first two-thirds. Having dismissed him as a hack, I was changing my mind again. Now he seemed among the most underrated directors, and I looked forward to his next efforts.

Which brings us to *The Swindle*. It stars those two warhorses of French cinema, Isabelle Huppert and Michel Serrault, as a couple of scam artists, Betty and Victor: Betty picks up conventioneers in bars, takes them back to their hotel rooms, already drugged, and she and Victor rob the men while they sleep. In between jobs, the two lead a quiet, nicely observed domestic life while bantering back and forth. He is much older than she and her mentor in crime and assumes he is the brains of the operation. She bristles at this condescension and dreams of reeling in a big score. Their relationship has the easy charm of Nick and Nora Charles or the Lubitsch comedy *Trouble in Paradise* about sophisticated jewel thieves.

So delightful and relaxed is the first-half setup that it seems a shame when the film takes a plot turn. Chabrol starts planning mischief: a valise filled with millions of Swiss francs turns the partners into adversaries, and there are double-crosses galore, masquerades, a killing, a gangster who loves *Tosca*. None of it matters, really, or else Chabrol can't get us to feel it matters to him. Since he wrote the screenplay, there is no one else to blame. He keeps inserting lines like "You're the most perverse creature I know!" but this devil-may-care perversity is asserted rather than ever realized. Similarly, she says, "Where's your sense of fun?" but this larky aspect is proposed instead of achieved. It's as if Chabrol had written in the margins "fun TK." By the end, I am not having fun because I no longer believe in or care about these characters, and no number of plot twists will compensate.

Part of the problem is a muffling of emotion. Huppert's reserve carries, as ever, its own useful suspense: you wonder if she'll ever drop her "cold nonchalance" (as one of her marks, played by the superb François Cluzet, describes it) and become more open. She does for maybe a few seconds, but this is a film in praise of character armor, not vulnerability. Serrault, given precious little inner conflict to work with, does what he can with shticks and tics, but we are a long way from the depth he showed in Claude Sautet's *Nelly et Monsieur Arnaud*. Wondering what Chabrol might have had in mind with such an ultimately bland narrative, I turned as a last resort to the publicity booklet. There I learned that Chabrol considered *The Swindle* to be his "first autobiographical film. . . . Of all the characters in all of my films, Victor is the one that most closely resembles me. The nature of his relationship with Betty is unclear because it is a blend of my relationships with my wife and my daughter, both of whom work with me." So this lack of clarity is meant to be a plus? Betty, a vengeful Elektra? And Victor, a Prospero figure? The filmmaker as scam artist, just playing around?

Future dissertation writers can sort it out, but I suspect Chabrol had more on his mind than ever got on the screen. If this is meant as an autobiography, then he simply did not put enough of himself, particularly his dark side, into it. Unless he is telling us that he has become no more than a Victor in real life, given to momentary irritations but sunnily complacent about his prudent professionalism. It happens to the best of us.

FILM COMMENT (JANUARY/FEBRUARY 1999)

Chapter Twelve

GEORGE CLOONEY

Good Night, and Good Luck

Good Night, and Good Luck, George Clooney's dramatic reconstruction of newscaster Edward R. Murrow's confrontation with Senator Joseph McCarthy during the 1950s, is about the responsibility of American network news to speak truth to power. This theme is so relevant to our present political nightmare over the wars in Iraq and Afghanistan that its timeliness—obviously intentional—nevertheless risks overshadowing any discussion of the movie's artistic quality. For this reason, I would like to hold off on these comparisons until later and analyze why I think it is such a singular, austere piece of work for an American commercial film.

The strength of the movie issues as much from its avoidance of pitfalls (the average docudrama's melodramatic triumphalism, the biopic's episodic attenuations, the art director fetishization of vintage props) as from its achievements. This air of restraint is all the more remarkable in that actor Clooney's first directing effort, *Confessions of a Dangerous Mind*, seemed crude, sophomoric, and slapdash in its satiric approach to the recent past and the television medium.

His new film is in black and white: the decision to suppress color, however commercially risky, solves a multitude of problems. It permits the use of old kinescopes and news footage of hearings, and, more important, it allows us to see and hear the real Senator Joseph McCarthy. It is one thing to get an actor (David Strathairn) to play the buttoned-down newscaster Edward R. Murrow, quite another to come up with a credible impersonation of the flamboyantly larger-than-life McCarthy, who almost seemed to relish an oily, demonic self-mockery, with his inimitably rasping, insinuating radio orator's voice and forelock bobbing from a balding dome. The fact that the two men fought each other through the media and never squared off in the same room, is accentuated by the many shots of Murrow watching his adversary holding forth on a TV monitor. Even more frequent are shots of the tele-journalist in profile, counterpointed against monitors showing his face from a different angle: just as Douglas Sirk employed mirrors to suggest how fractured and self-alienated his characters were, so Clooney uses monitors to multiply his protagonist's images as an indication of self-unease.

Robert Elswit's sure cinematography eschews high contrast, giving us instead a spectrum of gray tonalities that matches the grainy texture of the kinescopes and picks up the smudged, smoky swirls of that unapologetically nicotine-addicted era. The fifties have often been characterized as a gray period, morally a "scoundrel time" and sartorially (gray flannel suits) conformist: the film's decision is to emphasize that limited palette, letting glints of courage or integrity shine forth the more splendidly from a neutral corporate milieu. Often the ostensible light source, such as a desk lamp, is placed within the frame, casting half of Murrow's face in shadows. At other times, characters' features are flattened under fluorescents. No interior is warmed by sunlight.

Artificial light underscores the fact that there is not a single exterior in the film. The filmmakers have made a conscious decision to restrict the locations. I counted only seven: 1) the CBS Studios, a warren of bullpens, smaller offices, hallways, and broadcast studios through which the camera often darts and flitters in mobile shots; 2) the boss's office upstairs, done in impeccable fifties-modernist taste, teak woods and nonobjective paintings, as befit the man, William S. Paley, who served on the Museum of Modern Art's board of trustees for years; 3) a bar nearby, where the *See It Now* staff goes to unwind; 4) a hotel ballroom where Murrow receives an award in 1958 and gives a speech warning of the increasing vapidity of television (the film's framing device); 5) the apartment of Joe and Shirley, two staffers who live there in clandestine conjugality (no CBS news employees were allowed to be married to each other in those days); 6) a public government building lobby, where Joe meets an underling of Senator McCarthy; and 7) the apartment of newscaster and Murrow protégé Don Hollenbeck, shown for ten seconds as he turns on the gas and sits calmly awaiting suicide, watching television.

The restriction of locations dovetails with the film's structure, a limited set of dramatic scenes that keep recurring with variations: the group meetings preparing for a program, the tense on-the-air process, the tête-à-têtes between Murrow and his bosses or underlings, the after-hours unwinding. . . . Again, it's no accident that only two locations feature private, residential space. *Good Night, and Good Luck* is a film about work. Unlike most American movies, which gravitate toward after-hours romance and weekend leisure, it keeps a tight focus on the workplace struggle between Murrow's staff and McCarthyism. Since Americans bring so much of their energies to their jobs, though you would never know it from the movies, this particular film's single-minded emphasis on the workplace offers a salutary redress. Murrow's wife and son are mentioned but never shown onscreen—nor, wisely, I think, is any attempt made to get behind the man's professional persona, which is compelling enough. We learn in passing that Murrow's producer, Fred W. Friendly, is Jewish, loves Christmas, and lives in Riverdale but beyond that discover nothing that is not contained in *his* work demeanor. (Clooney himself plays Friendly and has himself photographed in a resolutely non-movie-star manner as Murrow's cohort and sounding board). The two have moments of splendid rapport, as when Friendly, hiding under the table, taps Murrow's leg the moment he is supposed to speak on-camera or Murrow says, "I can always tell when you're lying to me, Fred: you light my cigarette." They function as a kind of couple.

The film has two subplots, the sketchier of which features Robert Downey Jr. and Patricia Clarkson as clandestinely married staffers, the only characters afforded a private life. Since Downey and Clarkson are such attractive and able performers, their scenes together are never less than winning. Yet their period-specific dilemma, clearly intended to echo or complement the tensions at the heart of the narrative, seems superfluous, not unlike those glimpses of the outside world meant to "open up" cinematic adaptations of plays. Their story remains something of a red herring since we never do learn the extent of their past involvement in left-wing causes.

Much more compelling is the subplot involving Don Hollenbeck, brilliantly played by Ray Wise as a weak, self-pitying character in awe of Murrow, whose big-brother protection he craves. When Hollenbeck finds himself under attack from the right-wing columnist Jack O'Brien because of past left-wing activities, he pleads with Murrow to go after O'Brien. Murrow sensibly tells him that he cannot take on both the U.S. Senate and the Hearst papers simultaneously. We see Strathairn, as Murrow, repressing an instinctive dislike of the cringing Hollenbeck while gently attempting to instill the man with courage—his own courage, which the underling will never have. And when Hollenbeck kills himself, we see Strathairn's complicated face reflecting the guilt and despair that haunts him for not having done more.

Certainly, Strathairn's performance as Edward R. Murrow is the film's anchor, and he does pull off a tour de force of nuance and controlled tension. Since I remember the real Murrow coming into our homes, I can testify that Strathairn is close enough, though not a ringer, physically or emotionally, for the man he portrays. Strathairn's Murrow seems more on the edge, about to blow any moment; the Murrow I remember was a little more poker-faced, basset-hound deadpan. For instance, there is a hilarious scene in which Strathairn's Murrow, forced to wear his other hat as congenial interviewer for his show *Person to Person*, asks the pianist Liberace, who is living with his mother: "Have you given much thought, Lee, to getting married and settling down?" The real Liberace, in kinescope, responds with wonderfully airy nonsense about not having met the right woman though Princess Margaret interests him; then a close-up of Strathairn, cheek twitching in telegraphed recognition that he knows he is being lied to by his gay interviewee. The real Murrow would never have made it so obvious that he felt soiled lending his talents to celebrity blather; he could play that game calmly when he needed to.

But perhaps in a feature film we don't have enough time for such double masquerades. We need to read the protagonist clearly, and Strathairn's Murrow is lucid and internally consistent from the start. He always acts morally, with dignity and enough humor not to be a prig. Still, the film takes a chance by not making him more of a "mixed" character. He's a hero in the agony of a noble action, and if the film gets away with such a white-hat protagonist, it is partly because Strathairn gives a very Henry Fonda–like performance (virtue absorbed in a wary, self-mistrustful, standoffish vigilance that doesn't invite audience merger) and partly because the story is finally less about Murrow than about the historic challenge to a network. The staff's frequent overlapping dialogue, à la Welles's *Citizen Kane* (another newsroom drama and clearly an influence) helps convey that sense of collective effort.

Murrow is also given a remarkable foil in the character of William S. Paley. As played to perfection by Frank Langella, this worldly, elegant employer, clearly no fool, would also like to do the right thing, morally, but does not want to see the network he has so lovingly created injured in the process.

Their confrontations (filmed in stern shot–counter shot, for the most part) are classic standoffs of equal intelligent force, a competing impatience between two shrewd professionals. The last confrontation, the best-written scene in the movie, has you sympathizing with each man's point of view— until Paley finally pulls the plug on Murrow and says he is moving his news program from Tuesday night to Sunday afternoon and cutting it down to five shows a year. The result feels eerily inevitable; this time Strathairn's Murrow responds with well-tempered pragmatism rather than anger about to blow.

A mournful tone holds sway throughout the film, which is surprising given the narrative's potential for *Norma Rae*–ish exulting. After all, Murrow gets the better of McCarthy; Joe Welch has his big moment; McCarthyism is defeated. Yet all of that political esprit, as represented by the youthful *See It Now* staff whooping up their victories, seems hollow in the end, like college kids who still don't know the score, and their joy is undercut by the many shots of Murrow or Paley alone in the studio at night—the two equated by their solitary burdens—as well as by a bluesy, downbeat jazz score that overrides the soundtrack during those scenes of triumph. The Black singer Dianne Reeves, standing in as a kind of fifties amalgam of Billie-Dinah-Ella-Sarah, has no fewer than five numbers punctuating the movie, and these songs ("TV Is the Thing This Year," "I've Got My Eyes on You," "You're Driving Me Crazy," "How High the Moon," and "Straighten Up and Fly Right") comment sardonically on the unfolding drama, rather like Brecht-Weill musical interludes. They also articulate a more straightforward sadness than these uptight white men can bring themselves to utter on their own. And that too is very fifties, when modern jazz captured the temper of the times as much as did the burgeoning Madison Avenue culture (lightly satirized here by an Alcoa ad and a Kent cigarette commercial).

The film's lingering melancholy is perhaps meant as a commentary on our own situation, as if to say all those battles were fought and dragons slain, and now we're back where we started, with the National Patriots Act, Muslim Americans held in jail without evidence, Jim Lehrer called a traitor for showing dead American soldiers in Iraq. And indeed, my first response on seeing this film was to feel acutely ashamed that our media had not challenged more outspokenly the "weapons of mass destruction" charade by the Bush White House or confronted more strenuously his bad economic and environmental policies—and to long for an Edward R. Murrow superhero to take on these iniquities.

But I wonder. After all, those stories *have* been aired in the media, without changing the mind of the electorate or altering governmental policy. We are not being censored, precisely. Murrow's 1958 warning speech (reproduced in the film) that we have become "fat, comfortable and complacent" and that TV has degenerated into escapist entertainment, when it could illuminate or enlighten, is not entirely accurate. Television carries mature dramas, comedies, news shows along with the usual inanity. One thing that has changed is that there is simply more of everything, hundreds of channels, so that a single newsman may never enjoy the same impact Murrow had.

In that 1958 speech, Strathairn/Murrow quaintly calls for an Ed Sullivan show to be turned over one Sunday to a clinical discussion on American education and for one Steve Allen show to be dedicated to an analysis of American policy in the Middle East. I started to think, maybe Paley was right for pulling the plug on Murrow; the guy just didn't get it. And what about Clooney: does he get it? The way he films the scene gives no indication whether he thinks Murrow's schoolmasterish recommendation is right on or dunderheaded. It's at moments like these that I fear the film is settling into a smug, sentimental nostalgia for a time when there were giants of rectitude walking the earth

One area where I can share in this nostalgia is the diction of newscasts. Murrow is shown typing away at night on a manual typewriter. Unlike many news personalities today, he wrote his own material and took pride in his prose style. Indeed, part of my fascination with Murrow's on-air rhetoric is that it sounds so literary, with diction such as "insofar as" or "rather precisely." It is a formal language meant first to be written down then read aloud for an audience that could still delight in witty turns of phrase. The screenplay is adept at transmitting traces of this Latinate starch in Murrow's offhand dialogue, as when he counterattacks Paley with: "I would submit that we have done very well by one another." Strathairn beautifully conveys Murrow's own ironic awareness of the anachronistic game embedded in such Senecan locutions.

Hard to imagine a newscaster today getting away with this lofty, self-consciously educated tone. How did even Murrow get away with it? I wonder. The film lets us see that his authority derived in part from the "This Is London" dispatches he filed via radio during the Battle of Britain. The American public would listen to him because they knew he had been under fire. But they would also listen to him because he "stood behind his words," as in the Chinese calligraphic character for honesty. If there is a lost world invoked by this movie, it is one in which written language still had a significant role to play in the oral/visual culture of its day. Clooney, who cowrote the screenplay with Grant Heslov, has attached himself here to that ideal of literate seriousness.

But he is also making a pertinent political point about language. Avoiding ideological constructions of the Right or the Left, Murrow appears able to commandeer the rhetorical middle ground of *decency* (Welch's famous cry, "Have you no sense of decency, sir, at long last?" is shown in a video clip). When Murrow says to his staff, "If none of us had ever read a dangerous book, or had a friend who was different—well, we'd be just the kind of person Senator McCarthy wants us to be," he is speaking decency's language. When he warns on the air not to confuse "dissent with disloyalty," he is invoking American democratic ideals and recalling his audience to that civic path. When he says that though he is not a socialist he believes in "the clash of ideas," in dramatic terms he is positing a high-minded, Athenian speech against McCarthy's sniping, religious-martyr oratory about left-wing traitors and "jackals" who go for America's throat. (There is an interesting moment in the elevator when Paley says that McCarthy had wanted to use William S. Buckley instead of himself to rebut Murrow's show on the air but Paley turned down the request. All who remember Buckley's sneering syntactical convolutions will appreciate what a Thucydidean duel that would have been).

In appropriating the middle ground of American decency, Murrow drew on an advantage we no longer have: he could respond against McCarthyism with the supporting ballast of a Left movement that had been vibrant as recently as the thirties and forties and that, while chased into hiding by the Cold War, nevertheless bequeathed a moral pressure that continued to reverberate.

Clooney's recasting of Cold War issues as a simple matter of decency versus intimidation fudges any hope of clarity regarding the film's politics. We never do learn whether Murrow was a member of a communist front organization involving international education in the 1930s, as McCarthyites charge in the film, though we hear him deny in high dudgeon that he was an IWW member. To what degree was Murrow's "taking sides" dictated by his own personal politics? What, for that matter, are Clooney's politics? What does he make of the influence of Stalinist Russia on the American Left at that time and whether it held any possible danger for the republic or was entirely illusory? By treating the so-called communist threat as a merely an irrational, nutty fear on the part of some fanatic right-wing patriots, the film pays no compliment to the potential power of the Left to affect radical change, nor does it take into account the anti-Stalinist Left at the time, which was as frightened and suspicious of Soviet Russia as was Senator McCarthy. We must be content with a moody, rueful elegy for a passing titan and no clear sense of how to get out of our current mess, except to stand tough and be prepared to follow similar heroes of sober integrity. Maybe the unintended message of this very decent film is a more realistic intuition about the limits of decency.

FILM COMMENT (SEPTEMBER/OCTOBER 2005)

Chapter Thirteen

DAVID CRONENBERG

eXistenZ

David Cronenberg is one director who knows his themes. Perhaps too well. The body's extrusions and betrayals, the fluidity of self and its bizarre transformations through technology, the unpredictable portal between life and death, dream and reality, are what we expect to encounter The most intellectual of American directors (although perhaps he should be seen as Canadian), Cronenberg has a self-consciousness that rarely translates into a sufficient payoff onscreen. I didn't always think this way: a huge fan of his early low-budget, stylishly grungy pictures from the seventies (*Shivers, Rabid, Scanners, Videodrome,* and my favorite, *The Brood,* the only horror film I know of that places psychotherapy and emotional expression at its scary center), I found his subsequent A-movies, literary adaptations, and remakes such as *The Fly, Dead Ringers, Naked Lunch, M. Butterfly* less to my taste. It seemed to me that the more lofty his intentions and production values grew, the more half-baked the results.

eXistenZ is a return to his low-budget Toronto environs and has a likable hit-and-run, cheesy-elegant style. Written by Cronenbeg (an increasing rarity), it's a conceptual B horror movie that keeps moving. The futuristic premise has to do with a new electronic game, eXistenZ, which you download directly into your body via a "bioport" punctured into your spine. The program thus becomes part of your nervous system, picking up on your anxieties, desires, and preoccupations and changing the direction of the game accordingly. It's "interactive," in short.

The plot has to do with eXistenZ's inventor, Allegra Geller (Jennifer Jason Leigh), who is being hunted down by evil competitive forces who want to kill her. After being wounded, she is entrusted to a nerdy trainee, Ted Pikul (Jude Law), and the two become an odd couple on the run. Allegra is the techie goddess who, like an addict, sinks into inanition when not plugged in; Ted is a game virgin who has never played and even lacks a bioport. In spite of his fears of penetration (read: latent homoerotic panic), she talks him into being fitted with a bioport so that they can play the game together. Cronenberg is fascinated with the game's paraphernalia: he gives special attention to the game pod, which is organic, flesh-colored, hillocky, and activated by plucking a nipple-like protruberance. The prong of the "UmbyCord" that plugs into the player's back is bulbous at the tip, and Leigh wets it suggestively in her mouth before insertion. Once the game starts, Allegra and Ted enter a dreamscape where the physical scene can change at any moment. Their characters change as well, in line with the evolving game plot: the reclusive, shy inventor becomes more boldly sexual while the uptight Ted starts swaggering like a tough guy and giving in to his inner impulses. Their hairdos and outfits alter as well (she turns tartish; he, greaser); they mutate into their ids' cartoonishly cool projections. But always they are at the mercy of the game/dream narrative: just as Allegra and Ted are starting to get it on, the scene shifts.

There is the cinema of character (Rohmer) and the cinema of visual dream (Lynch). The first is generally what is taught in film schools; the second is what the young often flock to on their own. At its best, Cronenberg's work has inhabited both camps. What makes *eXistenZ* so intriguing is that we are invited to follow a core of self in the two leads, a continuity of personality that we can still see, in and around the transformations brought on by the game. So even at the new Ted's most thuggishly violent, blowing away a Chinese waiter, he still seems a trifle nerdy, not toughened up at all. Allegra, for her part, retains a schoolmarmish pique at her partner's slowness to adapt to the game, however raunchy her costume.

The film is shot mostly at night: lots of bruised blues and greens, edge-of-town exteriors, gas stations, factory interiors. The city has been banished; horror is a small-town product. Partly the child of the mating of science fiction and film noir, as in *Blade Runner*, *eXistenZ* is also a road movie: the exasperated runaway pair recalls Hitchcock's reluctant fugitive couples in his British films. "I need to play with someone friendly," Allegra keeps saying. "Are you friendly?" It is a reasonable question since all the characters around them keep shifting from friend to foe. Toward the end, *eXistenZ* become more a road movie in the manner of Godard's *Weekend* as chaos breaks out everywhere, fires are set, and guerrilla armies battle each other.

One of the factions, lightly satirized, is called the "Realist Underground" (Cronenberg's critics?). They are dead set against games. Are we to see the film itself as a warning about the spread of gaming or a brief for invention? Allegra is particularly split in her self-reflexive meta-annoyance at the cliché turns the game plot takes. Even as she finds herself rubbing her body sexily against Ted, she mutters something like "This is obviously a cheap attempt to generate plot tension." At such moments, the film wittily reflects the culture of screenwriting courses and rewrite meetings. The audience is invited along as insiders in the sophisticated game of keeping a screenplay "fresh." The problem is: How are we supposed to care about the outcome if actions have no real consequences or if the ostensible situation on hand keeps opening into a set of Chinese boxes, a game within a game? Cronenberg succumbs to the seduction of one narrative twist too many. The question of who is in whose dream may make for a nice haiku, but it becomes tiresome as a storytelling premise for a feature film. Ultimately, *eXistenZ* is not a movie that asks to be taken seriously. Fair enough. Cronenberg, the philosopher-filmmaker, raises clever questions about characters in search of their proper milieus, but he lacks the tragic depth of Pirandello. He keeps getting sidetracked by a sort of adolescent sensationalism. We are left with the afterimage of Jennifer Jason Leigh fellating a bungee cord . . . to what end? Yet one has to admire his *Naked Lunch*–like loyalty to the radical destabilizing of the quotidian and his ability to create a sustained dark mood within a self-enclosed universe.

FILM COMMENT (MAY/JUNE 1999)

Chapter Fourteen

JEAN-PIERRE AND LUC DARDENNE

In three intensely naturalistic, psychologically powerful features—*La Promesse* (1996), *Rosetta* (1999), and *The Son* (2002)—Jean-Pierre and Luc Dardenne, a Belgian brother directing team, have developed their own signature cinematic style (characters shot close up, often from the back), carved out their regional universe (working-class Liège), captured numerous awards (including the Palme d'Or for *Rosetta* at Cannes), and catapulted to near the top of the international film festival circuit. Which does not mean the cultivated American public has the foggiest idea who they are. But before we lambaste our countrymen for their imperial incuriosity, let us frankly admit that these Dardenne brothers' films are not exactly date movies ripe for crossover success: they are rigorous, wrenching, and grim workouts, however original.

The Dardenne brothers, now in their fifties, learned their trade as documentarians (Belgium has a strong, gritty documentary film tradition). Traces of industrial documentary manner persist in their use of direct sound (harsh clanking noises, no music scores), a loving respect for fact and real-time work processes, now joined to a brisk narrative style of jump cuts and economical storytelling. The contradiction between these two senses of duration forms a complex tension of its own.

Typically, a Dardennes film follows one industrious character on his or her work rounds while trying to resolve a crisis of conscience. In their first feature, *La Promesse*, a fifteen-year-old boy, Igor, helps his father run an illegal immigrant labor network. No slacker, Igor also works in a garage and does a dozen other odd jobs, mostly illicit. Never has criminality seemed such hard work: the film is really about labor and keeps up a breakneck, handheld-camera pace as it follows Igor and his father on their exhausting, shady rounds. The laborers, from the Eastern bloc, Africa, and the Middle East, are put up in Igor's father's fleabag hotel. If our first glimpse of Igor is filching an old lady's wallet, by midstory his conscience undergoes a reluctant awakening when he is pushed too far by his father's brutal pragmatism. (An African laborer falls from a scaffold and is allowed to die rather than be taken to the hospital, which would alert the authorities. Igor's father buries him then lies to the man's wife, saying her husband has run away.)

The father—unshaven, with thick glasses, not so much evil as doing what he feels he has to—is uncannily played by Olivier Gourmet. Particularly powerful are those scenes where the father, used to dominating his son, tries to win him over again. He tickles Igor in bed (a disturbing scene, this); he tries to get him laid for the first time by setting him up with a tarty young woman. It is a measure of the film's subtle economy that we never find out if the boy had sex or not; we just see him the next day grimly doing his chores, more determined than ever to resist his seductive father's manipulations and to protect the widow of the African laborer. In this film, becoming a man means something more than losing one's virginity.

Their second film, *Rosetta* (my favorite), is another hymn to work. As we know from their earlier *La Promesse*, there are no slackers in the Dardennes' chore-laden universe; a job is the summa of one's existence. The camera-person must be as indefatigable, running pantingly after in long, handheld shots that keep reframing the protagonists. Newcomer Émilie Dequenne is terrific as the fiercely determined eighteen-year-old Rosetta, who does not want to become like her alcoholic, sluttish mother any more than she feels free to abandon her. Rosetta cannot help but remind us of Bresson's Mouchette, being just as sullen-faced and alienated, rushing between forest and town, but with a more powerful survival instinct. We see her always engaging in physical processes, catching fish when there's nothing to eat, making Belgian waffles at work, trying to go it alone—though the film is intent on teaching her that she can't, quite. Its ending (exhaustion, dependence, stasis) flows inexorably out of the relentless driven motion that preceded it.

The Son reverses the generational pattern, focusing not on an adolescent resisting the influence of a corrupt parent but on a middle-aged man who must forgive a teenager's horrific destructiveness.

Specifically, Olivier is a carpentry shop teacher at a vocational center for troubled youth, divorced and living a spare existence except for his work, where he feels "useful." He seems stoical but burdened with an inconsolable sadness, which, we come to learn, issued from the death of his son, killed by an eleven-year-old thief in a botched petty robbery. (Presumably, his marriage was also a casualty of that tragedy.) Now the killer, having served five years in a juvenile lockup, Fraiport, is paroled to Olivier's center. Olivier must decide whether to take him on as an apprentice.

The instructor is played by Olivier Gourmet, in an exceptionally physical (and cerebral) performance that won him the best actor award at Cannes. Gourmet has been a consistent Dardenne brothers' standout, playing the slimy father in *La Promesse* and the girl's boss in *Rosetta*. Here he goes further, inhabits the role until there seems no boundary line between character and actor (they share the same first name). The Dardenne brothers acknowledge this ambiguity in their diary notes: "The storyline is the character, opaque, enigmatic. Maybe not the character, but the actor himself: Olivier Gourmet. His body, the nape of his neck, his face, his eyes lost behind his glasses. We could not imagine the film based on another body, another actor."

Gourmet is not your average matinee idol: a stocky man with thinning hair and thick glasses, slightly cross-eyed, with a mole above his lip (how well we come to know his face!), he yet has a magnetic presence onscreen, with a sort of handsomeness that derives from his alert intelligence. And he moves like a whirling top, an acrobat graceful on his feet, forever in motion. In Donald Phelps's essay entitled "The Runners" (a title applicable to the Dardenne brothers' films), he perfectly describes what Gourmet does: "The actor, onscreen, manufacturing the film from his body, silk-worm-like." Significantly, the carpentry teacher has a bad back and must wear a wide leather belt around his midsection. We see him periodically doing therapeutic sit-ups and tightening or loosening the notches of his harness (a systole, diastole that mimics the film's breathing; rhythm is a Dardenne brothers' forte). In the outfit he wears in every scene—denim overalls atop a wool maroon shirt—the orange belt bisects his body into two uneven halves, twisted by pain. "The body of Olivier in permanent disequilibrium," the Dardenne brothers' notes refer to this torsion.

Off-centered himself, he provides his trainees a model of balanced, accurate feedback: "Your mortise is not ready. Put it back in the vise. No. Push the lever," he tells a youth, demonstrating. He has made himself into a tool. His trainees mostly have foreign names like Filippo, Omar, Fouad—the maladjusted outsiders of Belgian society. Francis, the boy who killed his son, is Belgian working-class stock but orphaned by his misdeed: his mother wants nothing to do with him; his father has disappeared. At first Olivier, too, rejects the chance to work with Francis. It is only when, later on that day, he receives a visit from his ex-wife, Magali, who tells him she is pregnant and getting remarried, that he reverses his decision (to spite her?) and takes the boy on.

Much is made about his motives for training his son's killer. Magali accuses him of being crazy when she hears he is even thinking of it. Later she faints after seeing them together. "Nobody would do this," she says, coming to. "I know," he says. "So why you?" she demands. "I don't know," he replies. Is he trying to be a saint, exchanging good for evil? Or to intensify his torment, in the hope of release? I have to say that his decision did not seem so perverse or mysterious to me: first of all, he sees his purpose in life as training troubled youth; this is what he does. Second, he has been at a standstill; he needs a jolt to get him feeling alive again. Third, it is not unreasonable for him to want closer contact with the agent of the most important event in his life, if only to understand it more deeply. Curiosity alone plays its natural part. He does not know why, he admits. His scientific side is experimenting.

The spectator must tease out all these motivations since Olivier offers no spoken rationale. The filmmakers give us only a subjective side entry into Olivier's mind by employing a handheld camera technique that trains in on the actor's head plus a bit of his shoulder and, past that, scraps of bumpy plastered walls, heavy metal doors with spy windows, the street. A shot will begin in close-up from behind Olivier, race alongside him, let him by, and end in a long shot as he continues off-screen. In this way we get pieces of Liège and the surrounding landscape: not a scintilla of Old World tourist Europe, though, only factories, lumber yards, roads, fast food diners, filling stations. The Dardennes' determined refusal of elegance extends to the screen's compositions as well, which eschew formal beauty. The camera moves jitterily, sweeping up Olivier's arm, catching his trusting relation to objects (he is wedded to *things*): the thermos from which he pours coffee, the carpentry tools, his locker, his cigarettes, his harness. It is not that we actually enter Olivier's mind through this claustrophobic camera style as that we come to like him from what we see on the outside and so go along with his choices.

We want to find the boy sympathetic as well, but he makes it difficult because he seems so washed out, unsure. In his first film role, young Morgan Marinne does a terrific job of conveying Francis's shyness as a black hole:

his eyes are hooded, give back little (just as our view of Olivier's eyes is restricted by his glasses). He has that torpor of many adolescent boys, increased by sleeping medicine, probably antidepressants. The first time Olivier comes upon Francis in the locker room, the slight-figured boy is cat-napping, curled fetally on a bench. This gives the older man a chance to spy unimpeded on the younger man, who is blond, full-lipped, sulky, and rather pretty in a bereft way. So the camera watches Olivier, the filmmakers' sur-rogate, watching Francis.

Here begins an almost Chabrol-like section, with Olivier "stalking" the sixteen-year-old through town while trying to stay out of sight. At one point he goes so far as to slip into the boy's room when he is away and lie down on his bed—a secret sharer gesture, inflected with obsession. Meanwhile, the affection-starved boy—eager to please, a pathetically poor inspiration for Olivier's hatred—tries to prolong every exchange with his reluctant teacher. A grudging current of tender feeling begins to flow both ways between them. The boy must become a man, and the man must help him to do so by teaching him how to balance a beam on his shoulders, for instance. Olivier cannot help projecting fatherly feelings onto his son's killer as a surrogate son (the film's title points to this irony), all the more because the boy has much in common with him: a quick aptitude for carpentry work, a mathematical fascination with measurement, and a comparable loneliness. Each provides the other with the only opportunity for intimacy. (In all three Dardenne films, the main characters deflect sex or romance as an option, preferring work and friendship).

The boy's requests for closeness, beginning with "May I lean on your car?" graduate eventually to "Can I call you Olivier?" and "Would you consider being my sponsor?"—"Why do you want me for a sponsor?" demands the older man, gruffly. "Because it's you who's teaching me my trade" (i.e., teach-ing me to become a man). Olivier knows he must come clean. Each of the three films is structured by suspense. In *La Promesse*: will Igor "snitch" and tell the African woman her husband was left to die in a covered-up accident at his father's construction site? In *Rosetta*: how will this poor girl keep her head above water, and will she allow her suitor to drown so that she can take his job? In *The Son*: when will the man tell his apprentice who he is?

The opportunity arises on a trip Olivier and Francis take to the lumber-yard. The car functions as a confessional box. Olivier, casting sideways glances at the boy, who only wants to nap, starts interrogating him about why he was locked up. Francis's response is evasive: he stole, and "some other stuff." Olivier lets it slide; later, they stop at a roadside café. Francis challenges him to a pinball machine game of table soccer, and Olivier resumes the questioning: "What was the other stuff you did besides theft?" "There was a death," the youth says, his use of the passive tense abjuring responsibility. He changes the subject: "In Fraiport I was the champion at this." Back in the car, Olivier probes further: "Why did you kill? You want me to be your guardian, so I should know, right?" The boy mutters that there was a radio in the car. "You killed for a radio?" Francis replies that he tried to steal it but a boy "wouldn't let go." Olivier, frustrated at every turn in extracting remorse, or at least consciousness, wants to wake up the robot, to shake the future laborer free of his automatism, get him to admit his complicity: "You strangled him!" he says. "But he wouldn't let go!" "No 'buts.' Did you or didn't you?" No reply. Angrily, Olivier slams on the brakes: "I went too far." (Meaning both "I overshot the lumberyard" and "I let my emotions out too much, I was unprofessional.") It is a beautifully written scene, and it underscores the Dardennes' insight that violent criminals often feel sorry for themselves rather than gleefully vicious.

The film has built, gyre-like, to a full confrontation between the two principals. At the lumberyard, a scene staged with exquisitely tactful mise-en-scène, we see the teacher quizzing his student about types of wood, handing down planks from above, and finally telling him, "The boy you killed was my son." Which causes the trainee to bolt and run. "Don't be afraid," Olivier calls, giving him chase. "Come back. I won't hurt you!" Francis yells, understandably: "I don't believe you!" In fact, when Olivier finally catches up with him and they wrestle on the leaves (like cop and killer at the climax of Kurosawa's *Stray Dog*, merging into one via their tussle), he puts his hands around the boy's throat and starts to squeeze. So much for St. Olivier! From the start he had embodied power held in restraint; now we see his rage, repressed all along. But the moment passes: having experimentally measured Francis's throat for a strangling, he realizes he is no avenging killer. He gets up and walks off into the woods, and the film ends with Olivier and Francis loading lumber into the truck, communicating best in the way they always had, through working together.

Each of the three films closes in the recognition of human connection. Igor, by telling the truth to the African woman, is freed from his father's domination but handed over to the larger social system with its stern laws. Rosetta realizes she can't go it alone; she must turn for help to the young man she had earlier betrayed. Oliver and Francis reach a tentative respect for each other's right to exist, out of exhaustion if nothing else. No man is an island: all are interdependent. This is the Dardenne brothers' cautiously optimistic, redemptive social message. Seen this way, they follow a neorealist cinematic lineage. But they also belong, it seems to me, to a more stringently Bressonian tendency.

How can I claim the Dardennes as Bresson's children when their films are so crammed with movement and Bresson's transcendental cinema aspires to stasis? I see Rosetta as a Mouchette who gets pushed in the pond and crawls out. *The Son* reprises *Pickpocket*'s restricting of information, refusing easy empathy, shutting doors to end scenes. Then there are certain Catholic overtones: the necessity to forgive the sinner, the ritual of confession, and the narrative strategy of testing the limits of God's grace by challenging it with a monstrous crime. Finally, the film asks: Is a human being's totality to be defined by one action, however heinous?

Earlier I said that *Rosetta* is my favorite Dardenne film; permit me to explain why. *La Promesse* had a riveting father-son dynamic but is bogged down in its surrender to exoticism (African spirit religions) and its pat division between evil Belgians and noble Blacks. *Rosetta* was like one long whoosh, the obstinate drive of the young girl exhilaratingly in sync with the marathon-run cinematic style. In *The Son*, the camera continues in manic pursuit, but the soul of the movie is graver, heavier. Man and boy are both depressed, and their depression, though observed honestly, casts a pall, seems mismatched with the film's energetic rhythm. Also, *Rosetta* was driven by necessity every moment; that girl had no time to stalk, even if she'd wanted to. In *The Son*, there is something more arbitrary about the man's tailing the boy.

Actually, *The Son* hinges on several coincidences and far-fetched premises: first, the boy-murderer ends up being assigned to the same vocational center where his victim's father works (fair enough, they both come from the same locale, with ostensibly limited parole resources). Second: the boy never recognizes that the name of his teacher and the boy he murdered are the same. Didn't the parents ever attend the trial of their son's slayer? Wouldn't he have seen their faces somehow? Harder to swallow is that Olivier's ex-wife, Magali, also "spies" on Olivier to find out if he is helping the boy after she had expressed a definitive request to put the tragedy behind them.

Such points raise a larger doubt, that maybe there is something tricky about the Dardenne brothers' filmmaking in general: their plot crises seem melodramatically forced at times; their camera style, expressive and useful as it is, may be on its way to becoming a mannerism; and their politics can programmatically intrude. Perhaps they do not yet deserve to be placed on that pinnacle with other recent masters of film poetry, such as Maurice Pialat, Abbas Kiarostami, or Hou Hsiao-hsien. Still, *The Son* delivers very satisfyingly on its narrative promise: if not quite a masterpiece, it is mitered together with the skill of a master carpenter, and it demonstrates anew the Dardenne brothers' genius for creating complex, vivid characters, tested to the limit.

FILM COMMENT (2003)

Chapter Fifteen

ARNAUD DESPLECHIN

A Christmas Tale

In the eight films he has made since 1991, Arnaud Desplechin has been developing his own visionary world, his own unique personal style, and it is one that goes against the grain of standard cinematic practice today. A master of ensemble mise-en-scène and a brilliant director of actors, his interest tends to fan out over many characters, whose mixed strengths and flaws jolt the viewer out of easy identification with any of them and instead compel a more complex, delayed type of sympathetic judgment. This environmental, "novelistic" approach, with its digressive and converging plot lines, is admirably suited to the family romance as well as the collegial circle, which becomes a second, substitute family.

Desplechin was born in 1960, the same year the French New Wave crested internationally. Fifty years have passed since that famous movement's inception, and it is worth considering how the important French filmmakers who grew up in its shadow both took from and departed from it. The New Wave auteurs, at least at first, disdained Freudian psychology and rarely embedded their protagonists in familial contexts: think of Godard's characters, who spring to life in an existential present, with no hint of having had parents, much less grandparents. Since then, we have seen Philippe Garrel use his own father and son in his movies, Olivier Assayas trace the fortunes of a family at the point of dispersal in his lovely *Summer Hours*, and Desplechin focus again and again on family or affinity group dynamics, starting with his first film, *La Vie des Morts*, up through *The Sentinel*, *My Sex Life . . . or How I*

Got Into an Argument, *Esther Kahn*, *Kings and Queen*, and, most recently, *A Christmas Tale*. This impulse to tackle intergenerational narratives may say something about the state of French politics or a conserving impulse (even on the part of left-wing filmmakers) toward traditional culture at a moment when globalization is eroding any sense of national identity. We do know that the families in Desplechin's films are deeply messed up— "dysfunctional," if you prefer—riven as they are by jealousies, enmities, and unsettled scores. There is never quite enough love to go around. Yet the center somehow holds: the family unit is inescapable.

In *A Christmas Tale*, the members of the cultivated Vuillard family, all of whom play instruments and spout aphorisms, seem to have divided up between them the possible responses to life's trials. The paterfamilias, Abel (capably played by the veteran actor Jean-Paul Roussillon), is a kindly stoic who counsels forgiveness and tolerance and is more often than not shot down for his pains. His wife, Junot (Catherine Deneuve, in a performance beyond praise), is a cool-hearted realist who knows the limits of her capacity to love and the power of her survival instinct. Their dour, unhappy daughter, Elizabeth (Anne Consigny), has taken the path of self-righteous anger, condemning her scapegrace scapegoat younger brother, Henri. And Henri (Mathieu Amalric) stirs the pot with buffoonish stunts that do little to allay the others' mistrust of him. Then there is youngest brother Ivan, who tries to be peacemaker; his wife, Sylvia, cousin Simon; troubled grandchild Paul; and several relatives and hangers-on. All are brought together at Christmas time to engage an immediate crisis: mother Junot is suffering from a rare form of cancer and needs a bone marrow transplant from one of her children or grandchildren.

By collecting a large group of characters in one big house over several days, Desplechin pays homage to that great French classic *Rules of the Game*. We can, if we wish, see it as well as a tougher version of an American holiday staple, such as *The Family Stone*, which also featured a mother with cancer. There is also some resemblance to *The Royal Tenenbaums*, another film about an argumentative family with an immensely complicated past. (*A Christmas Tale* has so much back story it takes almost the entire film to be sorted out.) Finally, Desplechin has declared his admiration for Ingmar Bergman, and there are echoes here of the Christmas preparations in *Fanny and Alexander*, as well as many Bergman films where a quite breathtaking animosity breaks out between couples or parent and child.

Desplechin has always been an immensely competent, vigorous visual stylist who stops short of making a fetish of the pictorial. Here, the film employs a catch-all of self-conscious devices that draw our attention to its fabrication: chapter headings, actors directly addressing the camera, iris shots, split-screens, a montage of nightspots, shadow puppets representing the characters, multiple first-person voice-overs, and a third-person omniscient narrator. Oddly enough, none of these devices has the Brechtian alienation effect of taking us out of the action in order to induce critical reflection. Rather, they propel us further into the naturalistic narrative through shortcuts. They are all warming, amusing modes of storytelling, very Nouvelle Vague in a sense (think of Truffaut's high-speed openings in *Shoot the Piano Player* and *Jules and Jim*). Their ultimate effect is to keep us off balance. The same could be said for the director's approach here to individual shots, a stutter-step technique that includes short pans, tracks, multiple takes of actions that last only a few seconds, and a good deal of cutting. The aesthetic of deep-focus, long-duration takes that Desplechin had employed in earlier films has been jettisoned, replaced by the visual equivalent of turntable rubbing and scratching (as we see Ivan doing when he deejays the town dance).

It is fair to ask: Why this set of techniques for this particular film? For one thing, the shot instability reinforces our doubt that any of the protagonists' testimony should be trusted entirely. Each of their perspectives is distorted by rationalization, and the image onscreen often suggests a subjective camera viewpoint. For instance, when Elizabeth narrates her flashback about why she hates her brother Henri, taking us back to the courthouse scene, Amalric's Henri is shown skulking in a weasel-like, malevolent manner. (But are we to take this as how he actually responded or as Elizabeth's prejudiced memory? Desplechin leaves it to our judgment.) Another instance: Patrick, Elizabeth's disturbed son, is shown looking at a mirror with a black dog in the background. Actually, as we later learn from his own spoken testimony, he is having a hallucination. All we can do when we first see the scene is store it in our memory, not really sure what it means, but the unsteady way it is shot casts uncertainty about its reliability.

A second reason the director keeps us off balance, I think, is to dilute the melodramatic overtones of the story—the cancer of the mother; the death of her first child, Joseph; the despair of her daughter, Elizabeth; the emotional breakdown of the teenage Patrick; the sad, soul-destroying pining of Simon for his cousin's wife, Sylvia. All of this potentially "heavy" plot material is undercut not just by a virtuoso array of self-conscious cinematic technique but by a taste for comedy. Elizabeth's husband, Claude, pummeling Henri, a scene that could have shocked us as violent, comes across as ridiculous farce, partly through intercut reaction shots of Henri's girlfriend, Fauna (the wonderful Emmanuele Devos), laughing with embarrassment and partly through the victim's seeming indifference to the blows. As he showed in *Four Kings and a Queen*, Desplechin tends to turn obstinately playful in the presence of the grim story lines he has set in motion, such as serious mental illness, familial antipathy, and the looming death of a parent. For this reason, the director's most often used actor, Mathieu Amalric, with his clown's self-mocking, sardonic grimace, is the perfect interpreter of Despleichin's refusal to be crushed by mourning or to surrender to sentimentality.

For all its dark notes, there is considerable lightness and joy in the film. When Fauna hugs Henri from behind, saying merely "My friend," you could not ask for a more eloquent testimony of affection between man and woman. Even the expressions of hostility have a cauterizing, engaging honesty. One of my favorite scenes is between Deneuve and Amalric on the outdoor swing in the snow. "Still don't love me?" he asks. "I never did," she says. "Me neither," he retorts. "I wasn't a good mother?" she asks with detached curiosity. The two of them seem to understand each other so well, in their ability to look calmly at their lifelong mutual dislike, that you wonder if their antipathy is in earnest or a form of role-playing both have settled into with gusto.

Another highpoint is when Sylvia (played by the irresistible Chiara Mastroianni) gives herself to her long-suffering adorer, Simon. Without attempting to read too much religious symbolism into this Christmas tale, I can only say that her adulterous disrobing is made to look like an angel's appearance in an annunciation. (The lighting in this scene, as at other key moments, is both expressionistic and epiphanic). When the time comes for Sylvia to send Simon on his way, returning to her children and her husband, Ivan, she says: "I invented Ivan by living with him. I'll invent you by not."

Desplechin and his cowriter, Emmanuel Bourdieu, offer us the wittiest French dialogue this side of Sacha Guitry. They dare push the envelope of how much syntactical and semantic complexity the ear can absorb, and the film succeeds in being as literate as it is visually vibrant. References to Kafka, Emerson, and the duc de Saint-Simon abound; poems are quoted and long prose passages read aloud. These literary texts are just one of many cultural layers in the movie: we hear snippets of music ranging from Vivaldi to Indian raga to Cecil Taylor and glimpse film clips from *A Midsummer Night's Dream, Funny Face, The Ten Commandments*. . . . The Vuillards surround themselves with cultural artifacts that might teach them how to live, but their ability to cope finally comes down to a roll of the dice. Will Junot's body accept or reject the bone marrow transplant?

That still leaves the crisis of Elizabeth's melancholia. "Why am I always so sad?" this successful playwright asks her father. He offers a number of answers, including that she expects people to be perfect and that she has taken on the grieving function for her whole family, still mourning the loss of her little brother Joseph. Another reason might be that she has no sense of humor, making her an anomaly among the director's personae. But it is a chicken-and-egg riddle: Which came first, her sadness, her humorlessness, or her self-righteousness? Somehow, by the end even Elizabeth gets her bearings.

Desplechin makes longer than normal films because he wants to explore a set of crises and then move beyond them to arrive at some greater wisdom of acceptance. Yes, one goes crazy, he says, or becomes melancholy because life suddenly seems unbearable, but then one gets over it and comes out the other end. That there is another end ranks him finally with the optimists.

CRITERION COLLECTION (2009)

Chapter Sixteen

CARL DREYER

Gertrud

There is no other movie like *Gertrud*. It exists in its own bright, one-entry category, idiosyncratic, serenely stubborn, and sublime.

When it premiered in 1964, Carl Theodor Dreyer's last film, one of his greatest, generated a scandal from which it has never completely divested itself. New York Film Festival audiences, attuned to the sixties jump cuts of the French New Wave and Richard Lester yet prepared to honor the legendary filmmaker of *Vampyr, The Passion of Joan of Arc, Day of Wrath*, and *Ordet*, were baffled by its provokingly patient procession of scenes in which the main physical action seemed to be moving from one divan to another. Husband and wife sat on a couch for minutes at a time, talking about the past and the end of their love. Audiences hissed, critics accused it of being uncinematic. But as the filmmaker André Téchiné admiringly put it, "an attentive eye on two figures talking even in a prolonged and static shot will never cease to astonish us." In fact, for all that it disdained to disguise its roots in a play, *Gertrud* is pure cinema: every frame is composed and lit exquisitely, balancing pools of light and shadow; its small, gliding camera movements encircle the characters; it is anything but static, to those who can enter its rhythm (and Dreyer is a master of the atmospheric uses of rhythm).

Set at the turn of the century, the film and its discontented heroine cannot avoid echoes of Nora in *A Doll's House*, Hedda Gabler, and Miss Julie. But there is a difference, as the filmmaker tells us: "I had chosen the work of Hjalmar Soderberg because his conception of tragedy is more modern; he was overshadowed for too long by the other giants, Ibsen and Strindberg. Why did I say he was more modern? Well, instead of suicide and other grand gestures in the tradition of pathetic tragedy, Soderberg preferred the bitter tragedy of having to go on living even though ideals and happiness have been destroyed . . . [and he made] conflicts materialize out of apparently trivial conversations." It is precisely the eschewal of melodrama and the counterpoint between suffering and triviality that point the way toward a reading of this sly, cunning film as a comedy of sorts. We do not often think of Dreyer as a humorist, but there is certainly satiric mockery in the ceremonial pompous speeches honoring the returning poet, and there is a deliciously playful balance between the claims of transcendent passion and the grubby realities of daily life.

"*Gertrud* is the kind of masterpiece that deepens with time because it has already aged in the heart of a great artist," wrote Andrew Sarris. Dreyer was seventy-five when he shot it (he would die four years later), and the film belongs to that confidently autumnal canon of Old Man's Cinema, along with John Ford's *Seven Women*, Mizoguchi's *Street of Shame*, Billy Wilder's *Fedora*, and Luis Buñuel's *That Obscure Object of Desire*, all analyses of passion made from the detached perspective of one already half-situated beyond the grave.

For years Dreyer had unsuccessfully sought funds to make his Jesus film; instead his last testament would be an ironic study of another kind of martyrdom—a martyr to the exigent requirements of romantic love.

Dreyer thought the camera should register the soul, and in Nina Pens Rode he got a brilliant lead performance from an actress who knew how to take a close-up and project uncannily her character's inner states, from migrained lassitude to ecstatic surrender. She is wonderfully supported by Bendt Rothe as Gertrud's stodgy husband, Kanning, a politician about to be named to the cabinet, and Ebbe Rode as her ex-lover, Gabriel Lidman, now a famous poet returning from abroad. Both these middle-aged men seem weighed down by self-importance, expecting the love of a beautiful woman as their due and, not getting it from Gertrud, retreating to self-pity. She accuses them of lack of feeling, caring more about their work than any sincere investment in love. We can agree with her assessment of these men while questioning her own capacity to love. She bolts as soon as the man she is with betrays his self-absorbed limitations. Gertrud herself is a zealot: she wants to take men to the emotional place she inhabits—to make them feel her need for love not just as a fleshly diversion or a hedge against loneliness but as the highest calling.

In *Day of Wrath*, Dreyer showed the persecuting spirit of a sanctimonious puritanical community in the face of marital infidelity. By contrast, in *Gertrud* the men are more forgiving of the woman's carnal straying; it is she who acts as the prosecutor. Feeding her resentment are the power relations between men and women, here scrupulously dissected: Gertrud, having been forced to give up her singing career to be Kanning's wife, rejects these eminent males while choosing a third man, an upstart composer who will reject her. She dotes on the younger man, Erland (memorably played by the fox-faced Baard Owe), and enjoys his sarcastic digs at her husband's generation, but she takes instant offense when the composer, after meeting her husband, reports with wonderment that he's a pretty nice guy. At that point she knows their affair is doomed. Even then, she might have held onto the composer had she been willing to compromise and accept his dalliances, but instead she takes herself off to Paris to study psychoanalysis, like a fictional version of Lou Andreas-Salomé.

The coda, decades later, is filled with ambiguous poignancy. A white-haired Gertrud, now living in seclusion, welcomes the visit of her old friend, Axel, who had originally invited her to study psychology with him in Paris. Axel seems polite and gallant, bringing her a copy of his new book, but lest we jump to the conclusion that friends are better than lovers, she intuits that he has another motive for his visit. He wants his old letters back, and he destroys them in front of her by throwing them into the fire. Then he leaves, with a sweet wave of his hand, and we are left looking at the door of her cottage: a liminal divider that could stand for her imminent entrance to eternity, a journey she will soon be taking, or, on the contrary, the rigid separation between one human being and another. Has Gertrud, through all her thrashing about, transcended ego and achieved autonomy and enlightenment? We would like to think so, yet there is the rather harsh way she tells her manservant to mop the kitchen floor. It appears she is still positioned between the angelic and the human-all-too-human.

As with everything in this supremely uncoercive film, Dreyer doesn't tell us what to think or whom to judge: he challenges the audience to draw its own assessment, treating us like adults. That invitation, even more than its unhurried pace, may undoubtedly frustrate some viewers, but those who surrender to it will never tire of its subtle beauty.

CRITERION COLLECTION (2001)

Chapter Seventeen

LENA DUNHAM

Tiny Furniture

Comedy evolves. We've long ago bid adieu to the physical acrobatics of Buster Keaton, the wisecracks of Bob Hope, the witty repartee of Cary Grant and Irene Dunne. The now-reigning comedy of embarrassment, seen in Judd Apatow, the Farrelly brothers, and loss-of-virginity farces, seems particularly appealing to younger viewers, who can relate to the awkward silence of fart jokes, crushes, being stuck with someone who is clearly physically undesirable, or being oneself the nerdy companion of some repulsed hottie, that power imbalance being the kernel of the jest—though by final credits, the nerd usually ends up with said hottie. The work of Lena Dunham is distantly related to that mainstream comedy of embarrassment but is subtler and more intellectually sophisticated. It bears a slight resemblance to mumblecore but has none of that subgenre's inarticulate tentativeness. Lena Dunham takes the comedy of embarrassment one bold step further, into the comedy of chagrin, and there is no happy ending, only, for the moment, an illuminating realism.

When *Tiny Furniture*, which won the South by Southwest festival award for best narrative feature, premiered in 2009, it was hailed as a remarkably assured debut. Actually, the twenty-two-year-old filmmaker, Lena Dunham, had already been honing that sensibility via a dozen inventive shorts made in college and a first feature, *Creative Nonfiction*, which was both poignantly hilarious and excruciatingly painful. Using herself as the actress/protagonist in narratives that dwell on humiliation, sexual rejection, immaturity, and general floundering, Dunham has put herself out there, defiantly and without the usual safeguards that male comics employ. Her only protection is her self-aware artistry.

Dunham's films have so far focused on the dilemma of being young, in that transitional stage before becoming a full-fledged adult. Our culture flatters the young, holding them up as the standard of beauty and insouciance. But Dunham shows the other side: what it's like to be powerless, at sea, lonely, forced into low-paying, soul-destroying jobs that have nothing to do with one's intended life work, and not nearly as sexually liberated as envious elders would like to believe. (In the words of a Philip Larkin poem, "everyone young going down the long slide / To happiness, endlessly.") At the same time, in *Tiny Furniture*, she exposes with wry detachment the maddening self-pity and entitlement of Aura, her protagonist. It is both privilege and curse to be able to drift and mooch off one's parents and to feel sorry for oneself in the bargain. In the film, the mother asks Charlotte, Aura's friend: "Do you have as much sense of entitlement as my daughter?" Charlotte answers: "Oh, believe me, mine is much worse."

Both Aura and Charlotte are the children of artists. Lena Dunham's parents, as she makes clear in her films, are both artists: her father, Carroll Dunham, is famous for his shock-value paintings with barnyard animals and exposed genitalia; her mother, Laurie Simmons, is known for her uneasy-making photographs and sculptural miniatures, including a photographic series on a day in the life of a Japanese love doll. These kids of downtown New York artists are in certain respects quite jaded, at home with talk of transgender, blow jobs, and film theory, in other respects naïve, with the provincial narrowness that comes of being raised in a permissively protective liberal environment. Growing up underfoot at art openings and poetry readings, watching their parents being fawned over, what is left for the children of avant-garde rebels but to be more torpid, more cautious, more skeptical, more uncertain? James Mangold, the filmmaker son of two eminent painters, went Hollywood; Azazel Jacobs made a movie, *Momma's Man*, about retreating to the womblike loft of his avant-garde filmmaker parents. Lena Dunham, whose own films chart her flight to a midwestern liberal arts college and return after graduation, dramatizes how difficult it is to leave the Manhattan bohemian nest.

Tiny Furniture begins with the prodigal daughter coming home from college to find a less-than-warm welcome. Her mother is distracted with art making; her younger sister is studying for the SAT and in any case is disdainfully competitive with Aura. (Both parts are played well by Lena Dunham's actual mother and sister). The white-walled, book-lined duplex loft, clinically dissected by the camera, appears elegant but chilly—anything but homey. Charlotte's judgment is witheringly dismissive: "Art people are assholes." Aura is more loyal to that upbringing, though her artist mother comes across as self-absorbed (the way creative people often are), distracted, coolly reserved, or maybe just tired.

While the film at first seems to be about the protagonist's testing the romantic and vocational waters in her new postcollege life, I view it at heart as a mother-daughter story. Aura keeps trying to show her mother that she doesn't know how to be self-sufficient: she still needs her guidance. Jealous of the access her younger sister and her mother's assistant have to the older woman, Aura reads the diaries her mother kept when she was her age as a way to bond secretly with her and reassure herself that her own lack of direction is normal. The only way she can think to get a maternal response is by breaking the rules of the household and making her mother angry at her. Meantime, she rejects her college friend who was planning to be her roommate, saying she can't move in with her because she has to stay at home, her mother "needs" her too much. This is the opposite of the truth but very much an expression of her fantasy. All through the movie, Aura has been asking for permission to sleep in her mother's bed, and in the last sequence this privilege is granted. They have a quiet, communicating catch-up talk. "I just want to be as successful as you are," she admits. Her mother reassures her that she will. She gives her mother a massage. She has finally managed to return to the comfort of her mother's body. But her mother is still wiry, tense, wracked by back pain and annoyed by some clock ticking nearby. Aura is at last able to feel that her mother needs her, if only for a brief moment.

In one of Dunham's very funny conceptual shorts, Lena's parents buzz the intercom to be let in, having forgotten their keys. Lena "directs" them with lines they must say before she will buzz them in, meanwhile filming their bewildered, increasingly annoyed faces in the building's TV intercom hookup. It is a fairy tale reversal: the child now has control over the family domain; the parents must beg to be let in. In *Tiny Furniture*, the child, no longer a child, seems desperate to return home, but permission is granted provisionally, obligatorily, and reluctantly.

Who controls the domestic realm, and what sleeping privileges accrue thereby? In each of Dunham's feature films, the protagonist takes in a young man who needs a place to sleep, with the tacit hope on her part that he will make love to her. And he, being a narcissistic jerk, not attracted to her, doesn't. Both films follow this pattern: the boy who won't make love to her, though he abuses her hospitality, and the boy who will, though the sex is crude, without a shred of tenderness, and it changes nothing,

The Dunham character is consistent, in that she is always thrusting herself on people and situations, courting rejection, and, though basically shy, demanding that she be seen. She parades her somewhat overweight tattooed body on-camera like an exhibitionist's dare: look at me. One of the most cringe-worthy scenes in *Tiny Furniture* has Aura walking pants-less through the high school party of her younger sister. Her sister accuses her of being willing to do anything to get attention; there is some truth to that. In her short *The Fountain*, her ex-boyfriend draws a distinction between her disrobing and a stripper's, asking her why she wants to show her body to others who may not want to see it. (*The Fountain*, by the way, is the very same short that we see Aura agreeing to exhibit at a group art show in *Tiny Furniture*). Is her exposure of her zaftig flesh intended as a feminist statement? Or is she simply saying: This is what ordinary people look like, not movie stars?

Dunham keeps growing as a filmmaker: formally and compositionally, she has come a long way from the cheerfully low-tech, low-resolution images of her early work. Those shorts belong to a YouTube aesthetic that proclaims *anyone can be a filmmaker.* Dunham parodies that do-it-yourself élan and distances herself from it in *Tiny Furniture* via the character of the narcissistic jerk, who calls himself the Nietzschean Cowboy, "kind of a big deal on YouTube." The narcissistic jerk makes himself at home, interestingly, by reading her mother's paperback copy of Woody Allen's *Without Feathers* in bed. Woody would seem to be both a major influence on Dunham and a cautionary contrast, the embodiment of the guarded male auteur. She has adopted his strategy of being the performer of one's self-mocking material; she uses the streets of New York City in a similarly emptied-out way; and the loft scenes, with their wide angles bisected by wall verticals, seem to quote Gordon Willis's interior cinematography in *Manhattan*. However, the difference is that Woody Allen's early films were built around much more exaggerated situations, and in all his starring roles, he contrived to give the wittiest lines to his own character—there was something smug about his enactment of self. In Dunham's case, we have a comedic filmmaker who bravely admits, no, insists in interviews that the humbling situations onscreen more or less happened to her. What we are witnessing is the Awful Truth.

The title of her first feature, *Creative Nonfiction*, draws deliberate attention to the narrative's personal sources. Dunham, a nonfiction creative writing major in college, is a highly literate filmmaker: she writes stunning dialogues, like the all-too-real argument between mother and daughter where Aura tries to evade the blame for her misdeeds by casting a wide net of past recriminations. She scatters literary references about (the sous-chef reads Sebald and Cormac McCarthy). For all her candor, it is important to remember that Dunham has sifted and shaped this material to achieve its compelling dramatic form and psychological richness. Like all autobiographical artists, this filmmaker has decocted a persona that is drawn from her but is not her. (One suspects that in contrast to the inertial fetal-seeking Aura, Lena Dunham herself is a much more dynamic, driven personality, managing to direct her own features while barely over twenty.) She is also, though rarely given the credit, a gifted actress, able to register every shade of perplexity, pride, and pain. If she is "only" acting a convincing replica of herself, that alone is no mean feat. In *Tiny Furniture*, she proves herself a deft director of other actors, both nonprofessional and professional. The cloak of the amateur no longer fits her, however much it may have helped her achieve this particular level of freedom and accomplishment. Of late, she has been preparing a television series for HBO, writing scripts, and acting in other people's productions. Lena Dunham is shaping up to be a force to be reckoned with and is already an extremely engaging talent.

CRITERION COLLECTION (2012)

POSTSCRIPT

The above was written before *Girls* took the country by storm, becoming the emblematic portrayal of and for millennials. Its success made manifest the advantages and limitations of turning an artistic direction into a brand.

Chapter Eighteen

PAUL FEJOS

Lonesome

Paul Fejos's *Lonesome* is one of those no-longer-forgotten treasures that knowledgeable cinephiles cherish. A frequent retrospective highlight at film festivals, lovingly restored, it has a fresh, dashing charm and brio that repay numerous visits. The visual virtuosity of this film alone might argue for Fejos's placement in the auteurist firmament. Much of the rest of his oeuvre has unfortunately not survived, although the few features and fragments that remain all attest to his consistently inventive cinematic flair. Still, it is this one picture, *Lonesome*, that has secured his reputation in the annals of film culture.

The Hungarian-born Fejos (1897–1963) studied medicine and served as a medical orderly in World War I then made his living as a set painter before embarking on a peripatetic moviemaking career that, over about fifteen years, took him from Hungary to Hollywood, France, Austria, and Denmark. In the mid-1930s, however, his frustrations with the studio system's commercial constraints led him to venture on a series of ethnological documentaries in Madagascar, Indonesia, New Guinea, and Thailand before settling down at his last, successful career as an anthropologist and head of a foundation for anthropological research. Indeed, he is probably more widely known today in anthropological than cinematic circles. This ethnological curiosity should be borne in mind in the stunning, evocative, documentary-like passages of *Lonesome*, capturing New York in all its feverish vitality. What also needs to be stressed is that Fejos from the beginning saw film as primarily a medium of moving images, of visual poetry concerned with light and shadow, of stunning effects for the eye's delight—in short, more allied to painting than literature. His style combined the flowing camerawork of Murnau and the German school with the rapid-cutting montage sequences of the Russians.

His first feature in the United States, a silent, unfortunately now lost, called *The Last Moment* (1927), about a drowning man reliving his past in flashbacks, was reportedly astonishing, highly experimental, relying on pure visual storytelling, without any intertitles. Impressed with the success of his low-budget film, Universal signed up the director for a studio feature. Their plan was to have him direct something action-oriented and sexy, maybe an aviation picture, but Fejos, already showing his prickly independence and determination to make something new and artistically worthy, insisted on being shown all the properties in their story department. He found an idea for a documentary short subject about life in the big city and saw that its very sketchiness would give him the freedom to build a more personal narrative feature around this slender premise.

The film was shot and premiered in 1928. Sound had already come in but was used sparingly, and *Lonesome* constitutes one of those peculiar hybrids made on the cusp between silent and sound cinema. Some few exchanges are spoken while others are mimed, with intertitles used to carry the dialogue. It is hard to tell whether the sound sequences are intentionally awkward, to convey the shyness of the romantic principals, or whether this clumsiness issues from the abrupt transitions between silent and sound technique. Clearly, the film's heart is still rooted in silent cinema, and *Lonesome* can be considered a late blossoming and recapitulation of that medium's potential to dazzle.

Fejos had lived a hand-to-mouth existence earlier in New York, taking jobs in a funeral parlor and a piano factory and as a laboratory technician. He was determined to draw on his mixed feelings about that city. He loved the extroverted humanity of New York, while aware that it came at a cost, As he later explained: "I wanted to put in a picture New York with its terrible pulse-beat, that everybody rushes, that even when you have time, you run down to the subway, get the express and then change over to the local . . . this terrible pressure which is on people, the multitude in which you are always moving but in which you are still alone, you don't even know who is your next door neighbor."

The film begins in the manner of European city symphonies of the twenties, such as *Berlin: Symphony of a Metropolis* and *Man with a Movie*

Camera, with a montage of the metropolis waking up. We see the sun peeping through the clouds, ships crossing the harbor through the Brooklyn Bridge's harp-strings, legs stampeding the pavements, elevated trains careening aboveground and cars careering below, as policemen haplessly blow whistles trying to control the traffic's pace. A title tells us: "New York wakes up—the machinery of life begins to move." The key word here is "machinery": not only is the city to be interpreted as a vast machine, à la Fritz Lang's *Metropolis*, but the people in it will be seen as robotic cogs rushing to their work stations. The editing of these street scenes is both exuberant and ominous. How is a lone individual to hold onto any unique sense of purpose, dream, or desire in the face of this million-headed crowd? The ordinary Joe, the "common man" (as they used to be called) crushed by the anonymity of the great city, was much on the minds of social critics of that period. It could be seen in other Hollywood films of the day, such as King Vidor's classic *The Crowd*, also made in 1928, or in the opening of Allan Dwan's 1924 *Manhandled*, with its rushing feet. From those heedless masses, one or two individuals, a Boy, a Girl, will be picked out and introduced to the audience. So it is with *Lonesome*, only this time the specific emotional problem of loneliness is emphasized. "In the whirlpool of modern life—the most difficult thing is to live alone," a second title announces.

In the following sequence, we meet Mary (Barbara Kent) and Jim (Glenn Tryon), each bestirring in a modest hotel room, performing their toilettes, getting dressed (she primping, he scrambling), and going off to work. The tone in these sequences is wryly amusing, and Glenn Tryon, with his rubber face and limber body, seems cut from the mold of silent comics, a cross between Keaton and Lloyd. He stuffs a doughnut in his mouth and squeezes into a subway car, under a sea of panama hats: we get some comic vignettes of the other passengers, beleaguered, squashed, or indifferent. Then the principals settle into their work stations: she as a smiling switchboard operator, he grim-faced at a punch press—both highly repetitive, mechanical jobs. In this remarkable sequence, the camera keeps panning laterally from her workplace to his, as though they were coterminous in space as well as time. Meanwhile, both are framed in the roman numerals of a clock-face, for it is the clock and the calendar alone that control this otherwise chaotic urban universe.

A factory whistle blows at one, fortunately: a holiday has been declared, and all are free to amuse themselves for the rest of the day. The women workers dash off to the locker room to adjust themselves in the mirror while the men splash water on themselves in their washroom. This sexual segregation loosens a bit outside the workplace, where each of the protagonists witnesses coworkers pairing off. Now they are faced head-on with their loneliness. They retreat to their separate hotel rooms, where loneliness is compounded by boredom. But even here, their efforts to distract themselves have been choreographed with charm and brio.

The film has a good deal to say about mass culture. Our protagonists' inner lives seem to have been formed largely by the magazines they read (he, *Popular Mechanics* and *Police Gazette*; she, *Saturday Evening Post* and fashion periodicals) or the phonograph records they play, and these media have taught them to aspire to the lives of millionaires and princesses. The protagonists are working-class—it was still possible in the 1920s and 1930s for Everyman to be represented by the proletariat, unlike today—but they have virtually no working-class pride; when they finally meet, each tries to attract the other by pretending to have a yacht and membership in the social set. (The movies themselves, as Fejos well knew, were one of the chief purveyors of such upwardly mobile dreams, and without ever mentioning the medium, he seems to be staking out a subversively progressive position regarding the value of the worker.) At last the young man confesses apologetically; "I'm only an ordinary working stiff. And I'm so sick of being alone that I can't stand my own company." (Somehow, his lower social status and the shame of being isolated are conflated in this character's mind, as though lonesomeness were merely a problem for those with too little money.) Mary, flashing her dimpled smile, says with relief, she's glad he's a worker like her: "I bet we've been both reading the same serial in the *Saturday Evening Post*." But it turns out that serial is about a guy who ends up a millionaire. Later, Jim reiterates his uncertainty that he has any right to romantic bliss when he says: "Can you imagine me, a simple working stiff, talking about love?"

It is only by going to the beach and enjoying the amusements at Coney Island that they are able to shed their social insecurities. Coney Island is the People's Riviera. Here they ride the roller coaster, laugh at themselves in the funhouse mirror, toss balls for a prize, have her dress blown up by a wind tunnel, and spin around vertiginously. These scenes are packed with giddy spectacle: Fejos may well have been influenced by the great city sequence in Murnau's *Sunrise* (made in 1927, the year before), but he ramps up the carnivalesque visuals of these images. The density of confetti, streamers, and balloons surrounding the two is really quite mad. When their romance starts to take hold, at nightfall, the director pulls out all the stops, superimposing colored, hand-painted lights in the background sky as though their love is manifesting in an explosion of neon. Fejos celebrates the value and innate potential of these seemingly plain, ordinary lives with every sort of visual dazzlement.

In fact, for a film that is sometimes spoken of as a precursor to neorealism, there is considerable stylization employed throughout. We see it from the very beginning, with the art deco, Scheeler-like drawing of skyscrapers behind the title card. Then there are the multiple superimpositions and the aforementioned camera pans between workplaces and the framed clock face. The Coney Island sequences approach surrealism as they toggle between subjective shots portraying the lovers alone on a stage set swirling with dry ice and others of crowds rudely jostling them. The two are never able to be free from the mass, and ultimately they lose each other in this very crowd. The heavens open up, the storm arrives, and the atmospheric camerawork goes to town, as each lover plunges around in the soaking rain looking in vain for the other.

Maxim Gorky, the Russian socialist writer, penned a description of Coney Island pointedly titled "Boredom," in which he excoriated the amusement park as a cynical way to distract the working classes from their lives of drudgery: "From the very moment of arrival at this city of fire, the eye is blinded. It is assailed by thousands of cold, white sparks, and for a long time can distinguish nothing in the scintillating dust round about. Everything whirls and dazzles, and blends into a tempestuous ferment of fiery foam. The visitor is stunned; his consciousness is withered by the intense gleam; his thoughts are routed from his mind; he becomes a particle in the crowd. . . . A man must make a great effort not to lose himself in the crowd, not to be overwhelmed by his amazement—an amazement in which there is neither transport nor joy." Gorky is here arguing that there is something ultimately deadening in this giddy spectacle and that mass culture is the other side of the coin from wage slavery.

Fejos's own attitude toward Coney Island is a good deal more positive and lighthearted: his bizarre steeplechase world offers diversion and even many moments of pleasure and joy, if two strangers can just stay focused on each other while experiencing the recreational environment. But it also poses the continuous threat of separation by the crowd—and with it, a return to loneliness. In the end, in classic Hollywood fashion, the script pulls happiness out of a hat, when the two bereft souls discover they live next door to each other. But this reconciliation is barely sweet enough to counter the bitter foretaste of romantic loss that had preceded it. We can almost see the streamer-filled panicky search in *Lonesome* as a precursor to the finale of Carné's *Children of Paradise*, when the lovers are separated by a parade of merrymakers and never do manage to reconnect.

CRITERION COLLECTION (2012)

Chapter Nineteen

EMMANUEL FINKIEL

Voyages

With one and a half films—the forty-minute short, *Madame Jacques sur la Croisette* and the feature *Voyages*—Emmanuel Finkiel has staked out his own corner of the cinematic universe. His Yoknapatawpha County is populated with European Ashkenazi Jews over seventy years old, mostly nonprofessionals who speak a combination of Yiddish, French, Russian, and Hebrew. Many are concentration camp survivors, forever exiled from what would have been their normal destiny by the tragic disruptions of history; they constantly search for lost relatives, more appreciative children, and a feeling of home, equally out of place whether Diaspora displaced or resettled in Israel, the so-called Promised Land. Perhaps the deepest sense of exile is from youth and productive adulthood: you wonder whether these works by Finkiel are finally about the fate of the Jews as much as they are about the loneliness and resiliency of old age.

Voyages is a three-part film, composed of interlocking stories. The first depicts a busload of elderly Jews going from Warsaw to Auschwitz, on a grim pilgrimage to the monuments, cemeteries, and concentration camps. Our shock is that—in startling contrast to so many movies revisiting these grounds, with programmatic solemnity and triumph-of-the-human-spirit messages—here the pilgrims are portrayed in a sardonic, irreverent way as Holocaust tourists: arguing pettily, grousing about medical ailments, one-upping each other with war stories and prejudiced remarks about the Poles. An elderly man tartly tells the other passengers, "I'm here mainly for my son;

I want him to understand," and the longhaired son, equally unsympathetic, says the Polish people never did anything to harm him. Meanwhile, the isolating shield of a bus window frames and distances the world it passes.

At the heart of this first episode is Rivka, a sixty-five-year-old Frenchwoman now living in Israel, who has joined the tour to pay her respects to the dead. Played by Shulamit Adar, an attractive, curly-haired, twinkle-eyed actress who seems to be Finkiel's muse, Rivka radiates a warmth toward everyone but her husband, whom she regards with icy disgust. He, having let the bus leave without her the day before, grumbles, "How long do I have to be punished?" and insists "Everyone forgets." In a movie that is all about what is and is not remembered, the crime of forgetting lingers, unforgiven. The bus breaks down; the couple quarrels; he tries to badger her into peace ("Stop this endless brooding"); she retorts, "Shut up. I don't feel well"; he answers sarcastically, "When do you feel well?" and she says with queenly dignity, "Respect me, please." Just as we are all set to sympathize with her as a condescended-to, oppressed woman, she tells him that he disgusts her and she will never go back to him. A look of fear comes over the old man's face, and our sympathies momentarily shift to him. As their conjugal bile flows, we seem to be in Ingmar Bergman territory—or is it Rossellini's *Voyage to Italy*, with George Sanders and Ingrid Bergman bickering between the statues?

The episode ends with the wife, who had closed her eyes to block out her husband, sleeping when the bus arrives at Auschwitz. Through the window we see the husband, who had never wanted to come along on this trip in the first place, pacing, uncertain whether to wake his wife, then going into the camp without her.

It would seem that the episode's power derives from the ferocity of her rejection of him. Later, however, during the last episode, when we seen Rivka settled in Tel Aviv, Finkiel waits until the last minute to show us that the couple has remained together. The husband returns from his walk, newspaper in hand, casually asking, "Everything okay?" The redemptive moment, the Rossellinian miracle of the couple embracing on the street, never occurs onscreen. But Finkiel tweaks us for having thought that anger and not forbearance must have the final word.

Something similar happens in the second episode. Regine, a Parisian, is contacted by a man who bears her last name, Graneck, and claims to be her long-lost father. Regine had thought that her father, mother and sister had all perished in concentration camps, but this Graneck insists he survived and they are blood relatives. What follows is a dance of jubilation and doubt: the miracle of reunited family begins to crack after she takes the old man into her home and questions him. Clearly, he is a nice old man looking for a comfortable place to rest his head in his final years, and she is a virtuous middle-aged woman with a warm protective streak, but does that necessarily entail any obligation to each other?

Her suspicions mount after comparing his wallet pictures with her family photos. She spits out: "You're wrong! Wrong all along!" Later, finding him packing, she softens and says that he can stay for a while; she will help him continue the search. She invites her children and grandchildren over, and he is desperate to please. He lets one of her grandchildren ride him ("Was I a good horse?"), then holds the newest arrival in his arms, singing a Yiddish lullaby to the infant. He is "home," but does that mean he will stay with the woman? We don't find out. As his singing continues in the voiceover, the visuals show us the beginning of part three.

Many feature films have about thirty minutes of intriguing narrative, whose possibilities then get run into the ground. What gives *Voyages* its richness and its light touch is that the director cuts away to another story at precisely the point of maximum quandary. The third episode of the film follows an old Russian Jewish woman, just immigrated to Israel, an outsider comically plunged into a baffling new world. Vera, white-thatched and round-faced, crisscrosses Tel Aviv, looking for her cousin's address, begging for instructions in Yiddish, which none of the locals can understand. "It seems there are no more Jews in Israel, only Israelis!" she laments. Finally, she finds her cousin, who is complacently set up in an old people's residence. Vera has no option but to say, "You look very happy," and leave. Taking the wrong bus, where she feels faint from the heat and passes out, she is rescued by Rivka, the same Rivka who looked so pinched in snowy Poland but who now has a sundress on, and the serenity to match. She invites Vera back to her home to rest. The encounter between Vera and Rivka is one of pure acceptance and tenderness, no needy men to mess things up, just a middle-aged woman admiring and administering care to a still older, braver one. But ultimately Rivka watches Vera disappear into her bus in a shot that mirrors the one of her husband watching Rivka, at the end of episode one. The phone rings, and it is the man from part two, looking for his daughter: it seems Rivka also has the same last name as his. We are left with the Borgesian sense that many people could substitute for one another and exchange identities in a pinch.

If we go back and look at *Madame Jacques sur la Croisette*, we see both a dry run for *Voyages* and a satisfying film in its own right. The pace is more leisurely, less condensed, perhaps because it has only one story to tell. Set in Cannes among a group of elderly Jewish retirees, it centers on a widower, Maurice (Nathan Cogan, who was also in *Voyages*), an ex-tailor, nattily dressed, narcissistic, acting superior, who becomes attracted to a widow, Madame Jacques (Shulamit Adar again). The treatment of this pair, with their slow courtship dance in a vacation spot, has echoes of Chekhov's "Lady with the Dog," but this time the woman rebuffs the man. "What do you want from me?" she demands. When he says he wants to share his remaining years with her, she responds: "If you're lonely, that's old age. Nothing to do with me." She seems repelled that he may expect sex with her, at their age, and that he doesn't seem to understand she can never give herself to another man after her husband. So she retreats. Once again, the narrative has been structured around a rejection, but then it continues, and in the end Madame Jacques decides she does not want the courtship of her to end quite so quickly. She secretly rips off a button on her blouse, giving him the opportunity to sew it back on for her, which he does, coming close to burying his head in her breast as he bites off the thread. It's one of the most erotic moments I've seen onscreen in a while.

There is a telling scene before this reconciliation, when Maurice is still at loose ends, feeling rejected, that characterizes Finkiel's even-handed, sympathetic approach. The tailor's middle-aged son comes down to Cannes for a surprise visit to his father. He seems troubled, and Maurice has to extract from him that his marriage is going badly. Maurice says, "Well, at least your children are grown up," and a moment later, confesses his own distress: "I'm bored stiff." The son takes offense, saying, "You were always selfish, but this . . . !" Unpacking the moment, you realize that the son is probably right about that, and we're glad to have it out in the open but, on the other hand, maybe the father was trying to make contact with his son by telling him his own troubles, after having listened to the younger man and drawing him out.

Everyone has his reasons, as Jean Renoir famously stated, and Finkiel understands how everyone's self-absorption constructs self-serving scenarios to justify their pain. *Madame Jacques sur la Croisette* took a César for best short and helped the director raise the money for *Voyages*. Finkiel is clearly no beginner: between 1979 and 1996 he was assistant director to Godard, Kieslowski, and Tavernier, and sometimes you can detect their influence (the camera moving slowly across a seascape between two conversants in *Madame*

Jacques, like the lamp-tracking scene in *Contempt*). Mostly, though, what you sense is his visual tact. In an interview, he cited Ozu and Kieslowski's *Decalogue* as key influences: both exhibit trust in the camera's ability to bring out the depths of a human situation and a willingness to be digressive.

Characters who seem on the point of confronting a crisis will suddenly stop to watch a sunset or listen to a singer. Yiddish songs and dances, the archipelago of a lost continent, surface from time to time and everyone stops to take them in. There are a fair amount of cutaways or "pillow shots," as they are called in Ozu movies, to remind us that a world exists beyond the egos of the protagonists. Finkiel also shows a penchant for shooting backs, which capture the eloquent sag of body weight or the force of rejection. We retain most, of course, the lined faces of his characters, hunting each other's eyes for some sign that they are understood. And we are left to ask ourselves what we owe one another as human beings, Jews and non-Jews alike. It is noteworthy how much conventional storytelling is left out and how many meditative, breathing moments are inserted. Finkiel has, so far, had the courage to remain a miniaturist, a teller of ironic short stories in a field that rewards more amplified narratives. I hope to see his civilized intelligence continue its development onscreen.

FILM COMMENT (JANUARY/FEBRUARY 2001)

Chapter Twenty

JOHN FORD

The Sun Shines Bright

In 1953, John Ford directed *The Sun Shines Bright*, his paean to the traditional South. Throughout his career Ford utilized the South frequently as a trope for authentic folk America. It should be noted, however, that Ford was born and grew up in Maine, which is as far north as you can get in these United States. When he arrived in Hollywood with his brother, the actor Francis Ford, one of his first jobs on the set was as an extra, a hooded Ku Klux Klan rider in Griffith's *The Birth of a Nation*. I don't want to make too much of this curious fact, only to say that there is a direct link between Griffith's whitewashing, ennobling treatment of the South around the period of the Civil War and Ford's sympathy for the defeated region. Many of John Wayne's performances in Ford movies, most famously *The Searchers*, feature him playing a disillusioned, embittered Confederate soldier returning to the post-war South. Ford was not unique in this regard: from the silent era until the desegregation battle of the sixties, Hollywood had lopsidedly condoled the loser of the Civil War, giving the South a free pass for its support of slavery and equating its plantation culture with gallantry and romance. We might charitably surmise that stories of defeat and underdog rebound tend to generate more dramatic sympathy than those of winners. Certainly, Ford's deepest lyrical genius came into play when he evoked loss and mortality, so it is not entirely surprising that he should have found in the defeated South a perfect setting for his preoccupations.

The Sun Shines Bright was the third in a trilogy of genially melancholy films Ford made about Judge Priest, drawn from the stories of Irvin S. Cobb. The first two, *Judge Priest* (1934) and *Steamboat Round the Bend* (1935) starred Will Rogers as the wily justice, but the popular entertainer had died by the time Ford returned to this material, twenty years later, and so the veteran stage actor Charles Winninger (Cap'n Andy in *Show Boat*) was cast in the leading role. Winninger, with his white curls and paunch, brings a much older, more avuncular, and deceptively soft, jolly look to the part. The judge, coming up for reelection against a confidently energetic, forward-looking candidate who disparages any sentimental ties to the Confederacy, is surrounded by a claque of old geezers, all of whom pessimistically expect him to be defeated. A young hero, Ashby Corwin (John Russell), comes off looking absurdly stiff, as square-jawed as a Superman cartoon. His lack of impact onscreen only underscores the fact that *The Sun Shines Bright* takes place in the country of old men.

The whole film is poetically wrapped in an elegiac decrepitude. This is Ford without the cavalry charges or "Indian raids." What is left but the rituals, so cherished by this director: a chorus of "Dixie" that stops court proceedings, an election parade, a town dance, a funeral, and patently silly meetings of ancient CSA veterans, where the trumpet is played and the flags (both Old Glory and the Stars and Bars) saluted. There are many comic bits around the alcoholic frailty of old men. The film's pace is obstinately leisurely: it proceeds by fits and starts, stubbornly taking its time, the better to savor its valedictory, valetudinarian self-regard. As it turns out, the old judge and his seemingly washed-up generation of elders are able to save the day after all, by recourse to simple humanity: Priest faces down a lynch mob while protecting an innocent Black man; he dignifies a prostitute's death by giving the sermon at her funeral; and he defends a young schoolmistress whose questionable paternity had ostracized her. Each time he does the tolerant, compassionate thing, in opposition to the rigid morality of the town's proper citizens. In the end, of course, they reward him by voting him back into office.

As I watched the film, I found myself deeply satisfied. Part of my pleasure came from Ford's exquisite visual artistry, the beautifully lit and composed night scenes, the spatial elaboration of the town, its wooden sidewalks and storefronts and columned mansions. But I also accepted the fantasy on its own terms, in spite of—or because of—the fact that it was unrolling like a fairy tale, without the slightest connection to social reality or psychological complexity. The judge was a good man, through and through, and you wanted him to triumph, and he did. There were none of those dark shadings of character to be found in later Ford, like *The Searchers* or *The Man Who Shot Liberty Valence*. It embraced its stately sentimentalities without the least resistance, like a noble dream, and its internal consistency won me over.

I saw the movie with my friend Jim Harvey, a knowledgeable film critic, who hated it. He thought every scene emotionally false and cliché. We argued on our walk home. I claimed that it was not emotionally false but true to its dominant feeling, self-pity. Ford was obviously feeling old when he made it, at fifty-nine, the civilization around him was changing beyond recognition, and if you can accept self-pity as a valid emotion in art, then you can be stirred by it.

"But it's so reactionary!" demanded Jim. "It says you should obey the old order, just conform to what they tell you to. The military is the most important social institution, and the hierarchical arrangement from the army on down should dictate over society. Blacks should know their place, and the South dealt better with Blacks because it knew how to treat them, paternalistically."

"Yes, I agree that the presentation of Blacks is appalling. They're portrayed as childish and obscenely grateful for Judge Priest's tolerance. And Ford never squares his hero's veneration of 'Dixie' with his defense against the racist mob. That contradiction is never addressed."

So does one negotiate with a friend by meeting him halfway while holding onto one's initial judgment. I had loved the film; I couldn't help it. I was both fascinated and troubled by Stepin Fetchit's performance as Jeff, the judge's grinning Black servant. He seemed grotesquely clownish, yet his character kept making astute remarks from behind a mask of obsequiousness. Here is how the film critic Gilberto Perez deconstructs the discomfit, in his thoughtful analysis of *Judge Priest*:

Stepin Fetchit is an actor who has been maligned for his portrayal of a type that some find demeaning to his race. Some find all types demeaning and think that people should be portrayed as individuals. But types are a representation of people in society, of individuals as part of a group. Comedy especially calls for types in its rendering of the human accommodation to society, an accommodation not without its troubles, but the troubles allow for laughter when seen as something shared. To be against types is to be against comedy. Still, it cannot be denied that some types are objectionable. What about Stepin Fetchit? He is alleged to portray black people as dumb and lazy. But his character is neither dumb nor exactly lazy. In the white supremacist society in which he lives, he must play dumb—or else he would be seen as surly or insolent—in order to get away as much as he does with doing what he wants. His dumbness is a mask that Fetchit subtly lets us see through so we can glimpse the intelligence beneath. And as for his being lazy, in that regard Jeff Poindexter is at one with Judge Priest. They're both easygoing Southern types. Their relaxed quality, which matches Ford's own directorial style, is construed positively.

I would be happy to let Perez's analysis speak for me and leave it at that, but there is also the matter of certain sequences that treat the Black population not as comic types but as a picturesque frieze, a sort of solemn folk chorus. Some of the same choral set pieces, with grateful Black characters revering their white masters, pop up in another of Ford's film, *The Prisoner of Shark Island* (1936). That intriguing picture is about Doctor Mudd, the man who helped patch up Lincoln's assassin, and there are jaw-dropping sequences in it that feature Blacks massed together, willing to die for their former Confederate masters—magnificent in their way, possessing an undeniable graphic power, though I doubt I would find them so if I were African American. Moreover, even if you buy the argument that these films must be judged in their historical contexts, not by present moral standards, Ford made *The Sun Shines Bright* in the mid-1950s, which was rather late to be toying with such racial caricatures. You watch it and gasp at the tenacity with which Ford holds fast to his conservative dreams of the past. By building the film around an elderly southern protagonist for whom racial tensions are simply not a problem, the director finesses away the problem of white supremacy.

John Ford is on record as having said *The Sun Shines Bright* was his favorite of all the films he ever made. This pronouncement has provoked much head-scratching on the part of Ford scholars. Some have willed their way into seeing it as his greatest masterpiece. (I think it good but not great.) Others have dismissed the remark as mischievous slyness on the part of an old fox. Clearly, Ford liked the film in part because he was able to indulge himself mightily, ignoring the usual requirements of a Hollywood feature for attractive young leads and a snappy pace. He even coproduced it, though it was hacked up a bit by the studio on its initial release. But his personal preference for *The Sun Shines Bright* must also have been because it was the last time he would be able to recreate a southern idyll just exactly as he wanted it: a sweet, static place where chivalry and decency continued to hold their own. The year before, he had directed (and coproduced) *The Quiet Man*, so it was as if he was taking one last victory lap around his two idyllic mythical kingdoms, Ireland and the Southland.

The Old South, for him, embodied emotion, blood loyalty, tradition, instinct, simple enjoyments (including corn liquor), the darkies singing spirituals; it stood in opposition to mercantile civilization, hustle and bustle, and cold, calculating intellectuality. Ford's South was a place that would have had no use for me, yet, such is the power of movies, I found myself enchanted spending ninety relaxed, cloistered minutes there. I did wonder, however, if such a film could have ever been made by a native southerner. My gut instinct tells me no. The real South may still have its echoes of chivalry, decency, or folly, but to one born and raised there, the setting could not be so idealized; its complexities would've had to be registered, if not honored.

OXFORD AMERICAN (JUNE 2007)

Chapter Twenty-One

JEAN-LUC GODARD

Breathless and *Band of Outsiders*

BREATHLESS: HOW DOES IT PLAY TODAY?

An amiably cocky Frenchman in sunglasses steals a car, mugs people for petty cash to romance a cute American coed, tries to collect funds from shady characters so he can run away with the American girl to Rome, but she, Patricia, seems more interested in flirting with contacts to secure a writing job, besides which she is pregnant by the Frenchman and he seems indifferent to this fact while a police manhunt closes in on them both . . . No wonder they called it *Breathless*! Actually the original French title, *À Bout de Souffle*, might be better translated as *Out of Breath*, with darker connotations. Forty years after it shook up the movie world, Jean-Luc Godard's brilliant provocation has been revived nationwide in a new print. For his debut feature, Godard wanted to make a film where "anything goes," and there is still a strong whiff of the anarchic and dangerous in his concoction.

Susan Sontag once compared Godard's impact on his medium to Arnold Schoenberg's introduction of atonal music and the cubists' challenge to traditional painting. Having been a young, impressionistic film buff when *Breathless* first exploded on the scene, I can't help but experience some nostalgic memory of its freshness. Granted, *Breathless* had plenty of company: The early sixties was a time when such masterworks as *L'Avventura*, *La Dolce Vita*, *Psycho*, and the Apu trilogy were thrilling audiences worldwide while Godard's confreres in the *Cahiers du Cinema* French New Wave—Francois

Truffaut, Claude Chabrol, Eric Rohmer, Jacques Rivette, Louis Malle—were astonishing us with everything from *The Four Hundred Blows* to *Zazie dans le Métro*. Yet only *Breathless* struck us as a revolutionary break with earlier cinema. It seemed a new kind of storytelling, with its saucy jump cuts, digressions, quotes, in-jokes, and addresses to the viewer. Yet underneath these brash interventions was a Mozartean melancholy that strongly suggested classical measure. (We actually get a little of Mozart's clarinet concerto when Patricia puts on the LP and tells us her father used to play it.) "Classical = modern," that Godardian paradox announced later in *Bande à Part*, was already operating in *Breathless*.

What seemed miraculous when it first opened remains its greatest coup: Godard's ability to infuse an improvisatory manner with an underlying mood of grave inevitability. The spontaneity came from working with a five-page outline by Truffaut rather than a finished script; from the director's writing the day's dialogues at the last moment, often in the car on the way to the set, and speaking it to the actors just before they were to deliver their lines; and from the employment of a hand-held camera and a wheelchair to save the time of laying tracks. The gravity came from somewhere deep inside Godard, a defeatist quality symbolized by those overhead shots he said he was borrowing from Fritz Lang.

Godard remains the darling of film studies, if only for the way his self-reflective moves highlight cinematic fabrication. But will seventeen-year-olds be as stunned by this breaking of the fourth wall or still respond to Godard as revolutionary now that his technical innovations have been so universally assimilated? Some might, if only because its attitude of rebellious impudence still speaks to the young. In a curious way, it could even be seen as a progenitor of the youth-cult film.

"If you don't like the sea, and don't care for the mountains, and don't like the big city either, then go hang yourself," the film's protagonist, Michel (Jean-Paul Belmondo) soliloquizes to the camera while driving. So he rattles on with his views on France, hitchhiking, women drivers; a few moments later, he shoots a traffic policeman to death. (This combination of yakking and violence would later lead a Godard-smitten Quentin Tarantino to attempt the same in *Pulp Fiction*.) Whether meant as a Gidean "gratuitous act" or one of survival, the shooting certainly complicates our attitude toward Michel. Is he a sociopath or just a likable none-too-bright guy in a jam? Perhaps both. He makes himself up as he goes along. Michel/Belmondo is forever adjusting his performance, doing faces in the mirror, imitating his hero,

Humphrey Bogart, and aspiring to a tough-guy role he insecurely tries to occupy.

Life is a bluff; we are none of us authentic, the film seems to say (just as Godard is bluffing at genre, pretending sometimes to make a Monograph B-gangster movie.) Meanwhile, death awaits. "We are dead men on leave," the film quotes Lenin. *Breathless's* existential pessimism and air of self-invention fit right into the mood of the young exiting with relief from the conventional fifties. Godard also struck an antiauthoritarian note by mocking the police, who are portrayed as bumbling Keystone Kops (in what looks like a cheap shot today).

The son of a family of Swiss Protestant physicians and bankers, the film-maker came to his antibourgeois sentiments early. As David Sterritt percep-tively observed in his book *The Films of Jean-Luc Godard*, "Michel's character—including its more menacing side—draws some of its dark power from the filmmaker's own brushes with this territory. . . . Godard as late as 1952 was known as a chronic thief (relatives and the *Cahiers* office were among his targets), a failed homosexual prostitute, and enough of a social misfit to be committed by his father to a psychiatric hospital for what one biographical sketch describes as 'a considerable period.'"[1] These antisocial impulses were not the whole story, however: Godard was also an ethnology student; a sober, thoughtful film critic; and of course a conscientious artist of severe integrity.

It's odd that this particular director, who in his later career so disdained the public's appetite for pleasure, should have struck such a popular chord with his first feature. Much of the film's appeal derives from its inspired pair-ing of Belmondo (a bit player before this role launched him as an interna-tional star) with Jean Seberg, as his American girlfriend. The complexity of their psychological duet goes a long way toward restoring a sense of realism that Godard's alienation-effect tactics elsewhere strip away. Belmondo, with his boxer's physique, is animalistic energy, impulsive in crime, masochistic in love; Seberg, with her short, boyish hairdo and striped polo, seems more cultivated and self-reflective. Their relationship is a reversal of the pattern in Henry James novels: this time the Frenchman is the romantic naif and the American woman the cool skeptic. She defines herself by ambivalent Carte-sian epigrams, like "I don't know if I am unhappy because I am not free, or if I am not free because I am unhappy."

The director, obviously charmed by Seberg's gamine air of mysterious reserve, shot her profile in close-up like a silent movie star—Louise Brooks, say. She had been discovered by Otto Preminger, who launched her, miscast, in *Saint Joan* and subsequently and more suitably in *Bonjour Tristesse*. Godard, that most filially respectful, ancestor-worshiping of iconoclasts, cast her in what he viewed as a continuation of her role in *Bonjour Tristesse*. Most critics have assumed that Belmondo was Godard's autobiographical stand-in, but there is at least as much of him in the analytical outsider, Patricia, as the pantherlike Michel. In an interview, Godard said that he found the theme of *Breathless* during the shooting when he "became interested in Belmondo. I saw him as a sort of block to be filmed to discover what lay inside." When Patricia says to Michel, "I've been staring at you for the past ten minutes, and I can't see anything but a mask," her words might as well have been Godard's.

Their long scene indoors, when Michel keeps coaxing Patricia to make love, is famous for its jump cuts, which eschew traditional film continuity. The conversation jumps all over the place, from fornication to Faulkner, from Renoir to remorse, and when the long-awaited sex scene finally arrives, Godard tweaks our prurient interest by filming it as undistinguishable shapes under bed sheets. What to show, what to leave out, which dialogue to render audible, what to drown out with car horns—all this is part of the cat-and-mouse game the filmmaker plays with us, to our off-balanced enjoyment.

The story goes that Godard, faced with an overlong three-hour film, decided that instead of losing the subplots (as his mentor, the director Jean-Pierre Melville, had advised him), he would cut within the sequences. The jump-cutting gives the film a jittery rhythm, which paradoxically plunges us into a prolonged sense of dawdling, since we can't judge real time anymore. The resulting effect is that of "hanging out" with these characters rather than being pushed through a plot. As it happens, hanging out is something young people are obliged to understand; indeed, the attempt of Godard's imitators to capture the mystique of that (non)activity may be one of *Breathless*'s enduring legacies, for better or worse.

Godard discovered in filming *Breathless* that storytelling was not his strong suit, so he compensated by privileging lyricism over narrative. Lyrical rushes break out in *Breathless* in many sensual directions: Seberg's sunniness as she twirls in a new frock, the joy of motion in long walking or driving sequences, the quoted allure of poetry and Hollywood movies, and always Paris. As soon as the film moves outside, Paris swirls around and threatens to seduce the camera. Godard, who broke into filmmaking with nonfiction shorts, said that "fiction is interesting only if it is validated by a documentary context," and certainly there is half-buried in *Breathless* a jaunty documentary about Parisian streets, bistros, travel agencies, monuments. Some of the documentary look comes from the use of newsreel stock, and some from the head-on style of the film's great cameraman, Raoul Coutard.

What stands out forty years later is how elegant the city looks. Godard makes no attempt to startle us with grunge; surprisingly, this is tourist Paris, the Arc de Triomphe, the Champs Elysée. Michel points out with pride how beautiful Place de la Concorde looks at night. The cunning score by Martial Soleil, with its cool xylophone jazz or lush violin passages, counterpoints with ironic premonition the grubby end of a petty thug.

Godard took the atmospheric pessimism of the French gangster film— the poetic realism of Marcel Carné and Jacques Feyder, down through Jacques Becker's wonderful *Touchez Pas au Grisbi*, in which Jean Gabin in pajamas drinks a glass of milk before going to bed—and hot-spliced it with the plot-driven fatalism of American film noir (Bogart, *Criss-Cross*, the double-crossing dame). *Breathless* still plays beautifully as a charming ode to Franco-American relations. Godard had not yet hardened into his foolishly doctrinaire anti-Americanism (for instance, making the preposterous claim that Americans had no history so they had to buy up the Europeans'); there was a fluidity in his feelings about the United States, both pro and con. What does date is the film's lack of resistance to such sexist notions as the betraying female and its willingness to discuss women in terms of their body parts. Another weakness of *Breathless* is simply that it is a young man's film: full of spectacular effects, vitality, but without the consequential depth that would mark Godard's later efforts, such as *Vivre Sa Vie* or *Contempt*. It runs on nerve until it stops, out of breath. "A shallow masterpiece," we might conclude, as Pauline Kael said, with less justification, about *Citizen Kane*. Its beguiling lightness seems both its strength and limitation. Still, that brio captivated and influenced filmmakers everywhere: in the United States (Robert Altman, Martin Scorsese, Hal Hartley), Japan (Nagisa Ōshima, Shōhei Imamura), Brazil (Glauber Rocha), Yugoslavia (Dušan Makavejev), Cuba (Tomás Gutiérrez Alea), Germany (Wim Wenders), Iran (Abbas Kiarostami), Georgia (Otar Iosseliani), Hong Kong (Wong Kar-wai), to name just a few. *Breathless* lit the fuse for the whole independent movement in cinema. If some of today's young directors may not even know how indebted they are to his work, and if Godard himself has become something of a curmudgeon, unsupportive of the latest cinematic trends, the fact nevertheless remains that *Breathless* is where it/they all began.

NEW YORK TIMES, JANUARY 16, 2000

BAND OF OUTSIDERS

We do not often think of Jean-Luc Godard as a charmer. But in 1965 he shot his seventh feature, *Band of Outsiders* (*Bande à Part*), which, while never a box office success, cast a spell over susceptible audiences and critics ("Godard's most delicately charming film," wrote Pauline Kael) and has since influenced a generation of vanguard filmmakers. Quentin Tarantino went so far as to name his production company "A Band Apart," and he, Hal Hartley, and countless others have paid tribute to (or ripped off) the line dance that sends the middle section soaring. The rerelease of this film by Rialto Pictures gives us a chance to speculate on the nature of its peculiar appeal and why (unlike some other Godard films) it holds up so remarkably well.

"All you need to make a movie is a girl and a gun," Godard famously asserted, and *Band of Outsiders* is his demonstration of how to concoct a film out of the materials at hand. Since it's a feature, a sort of story is required, and characters. It doesn't hurt to start with three strong actors, who compensate for the emblematic sketchiness of their roles. Two young idlers, Franz (played by Sami Frey) and Arthur (Claude Brasseur), are drawn to a "romantic girl" (Anna Karina), who lives like a Griffith heroine in a villa by the river with her aunt and a wealthy lodger. They decide to use the girl to rob the house, meanwhile vying for her favors. Franz, with his mournful long face, inevitably suggests Kafka while Arthur's last name is "Rimbaud," to link him with the poet-adventurer.

Franz, in love with Odile, becomes tongue-tied around her; so naturally, she gives herself to the smoother, more cynical Arthur, who seduces her to help in the burglary. It is hard to imagine a trio less cut out for crime: Arthur, supposedly tough, wears a hat with goony earflaps; Franz pauses in the midst of the robbery to swipe a book; and Odile, in her ingénue plaid skirt, seems too sweet to harm anyone but goes along with the scheme, ostensibly to hold onto the two men's interest. It's as though they have been playing at robbers, like children in a schoolyard, and suddenly the game turns serious. In Kael's perfect description, *Band of Outsiders* is "a reverie of a gangster movie."

Part of Godard's playfulness here is to draw you into caring about the characters while denying their naturalism when it suits him. The film is constructed like a series of cheeky set-pieces that call attention to its narrative technique: Odile's English teacher dictates a long passage from *Romeo and Juliet* while providing the film's aesthetic credo with a T. S. Eliot quote ("Everything that is new is therefore automatically traditional"); the trio race through the Louvre in fast-motion to break the record for doing that museum; a minute of silence is called for and the sound track goes blank (only for forty seconds, however); the action stops while the trio perform a dance called the Madison; in the park, Franz and Arthur read newspaper accounts to each other of grisly murders. Meanwhile, the narrator (Godard himself) comments on the action in a lofty, literary manner that is sometimes comically at odds with the humdrum events onscreen. ("They descend to the center of the universe," he says sonorously, when Arthur and Odile take the metro.) The audience, thrust out of its mimetic dream by these self-reflexive meta-devices, is also flattered into becoming collaborators in the filmmaking process.

What Godard seems to have been most after was capturing the sensation of life in flux. He referred to "my *Bande à Part* mood . . . characters who live off the cuff and whose speech is recorded directly. . . . The interesting thing is this sort of fluidity, being able to feel existence like physical matter: it is not the people who are important, but the atmosphere between them."

The film, shot in black and white, takes place in a wintry Paris and its outskirts. At one point the narrator compares the cityscape of Parisian bridges onscreen to a Corot, and indeed, Raoul Coutard's inspired cinematography uses the cloudy, drizzly ambience of a Paris winter to bestow a consolatory mist, reminiscent of that painter, on what could have been harsh tragicomedy. At other times, there are shots of brute materiality, like a car going around and around a snow-filled lot with large cable spools on end. Transition scenes in the plot are skipped; cutaways to the streets provided in abundance. A documentary urge vies with a fate-tinged fairy tale, each enriching the other.

Still, what prevents this lark from becoming coy, in the manner of shallow, postmodernist gamesmanship? First of all, there is Godard's inventiveness, what the film critic Robin Wood called "that sheer delight in creating that continually balances and colors our awareness of the near-despair that the film expresses and that makes us feel it, not as a litter of fragments, but as the expression of a single and strong creative impulse." The emotional tone—Godard's grave romanticism, if you will—draws every stray filing to its magnet. Michel Legrand's melancholy, calliope-like score, with its unresolved circularity, dignifies the restless, aimless transit of these protagonists.

Then there is the tenderness and grace of Anna Karina's performance. Modulating from naïve schoolgirl to cool, alluring chic, she is the one who puts the verve in the famous dance sequence, the Madison. All three line up, never touching, each in their dream of Bob Fosse perfection. Their physical nonimpingement foreshadows Franz's later comment, that "people never form a whole, they remain separate." Yet despite their different thoughts as they dance (which are told to us by the narrator in voiceover), Karina functions as a bonding agent. In the metro, she recites a poem by Louis Aragon, the French communist poet, declaring her unity—"I am the same as you"—with the worn subway riders (Of course, she only identifies with the masses, never the bourgeois victims whom she and her friends will rob. Godard would eventually embrace Marxism, but for the moment it was his sympathy for alienated youth rather than any evolved politics that dictated the film's moral sense.)

In *Band of Outsiders*, Godard treats Karina as his very own screen goddess, with Garbo-like close-ups accentuating her mystery. He had already turned her waiflike face into a sixties icon by having her star in five out of his first seven movies. She'd been a spy's mistress, a prostitute, an unfaithful wife, and now he was restoring her innocence by making her a schoolgirl with pigtails. Odile declares that she hates the cinema and the theater; she prefers nature. Woman as Nature, Love, Mystery, the Eternal Feminine—all those categories that we now find so dubious, Godard was insisting upon, without irony, through the layered images of Karina. She remained a screen on which he projected his movie love. (Odile may have hated the movies, but Godard cared for little else.)

Here is how he spoke about Karina's role in the film:

For a minute, Odile is Leslie Caron in *Orvet* or *Lili*; then suddenly she's Cathy O'Donnell in *They Live By Night*. For three seconds she follows the winding river like Jennifer Jones in *Cluny Brown*, and suddenly fate brings her to the point of tears like Sylvia Sidney in Lang's immortal film (*You Only Live Once*). It needed a young and beautiful girl like Anna Karina to play this part. . . . Brought up in the great and rigorous tradition of artists like Asta Nielsen, Garbo (Stiller's), Pola Negri, Anna (she's my wife and I love her, but that really changes nothing) knows how to let a little fresh air into this exalted but suffocating framework, so that one can breathe a very modern perfume, that of the improvisation dear to Italian comedy, the neo-realism of an earlier age.

In their movies together, Godard both celebrated his love for this beautiful woman who happened to be "my wife" and reached back through her to summon the ghosts of other film immortals (as when he "merged" Falconetti's Joan of Arc and Karina in *Vivre Sa Vie*). It's a lot to put on a young performer, even one as talented as Anna Karina. The result is that she comes across at times more as muse than actress. She never quite attained, after their breakup, an independent screen presence. Though she appeared in many films for other directors, they were usually small, unmemorable roles; Karina was only able to be a star with Godard.

There is also a nasty, sadistic side to this filmmaker that emerges in the sometimes brutal treatment of heroines played by Karina. Odile gets slapped around by Arthur when the robbery starts to go wrong. Franz rushes chivalrously to her defense, and Arthur is "recompensed" later for his meanness by taking a bullet. Played by an actor, Claude Brasseur, who bears a certain resemblance to Godard, Arthur is another of the filmmaker's surrogate male protagonists who is killed or commits suicide—the masochistic, self-destructive obverse to his sadistic impulse.

Ultimately, regardless of Karina's waiflike allure, *Band of Outsiders* is a kind of buddy movie. The triangle of two friends in love with the same girl echoes an earlier New Wave landmark, *Jules and Jim*. Arthur may resemble Godard, but Franz brings to mind another French filmmaker, through the character's name and Frey's alert, beaklike profile: Francois Truffaut. (If that premise is granted, then Godard is being uncharacteristically gallant in having the character based on Truffaut come off as more noble and letting him get the girl in the end.) It is possible to see *Band of Outsiders* as an elegy to their frayed friendship, conjuring up a time, before their filmmaking debuts, when Godard and Truffaut both engaged in petty thefts, ran afoul of the law, experienced humiliating powerlessness, and had big auteur dreams. The original "band of outsiders," were they not the young cinephiles of the New Wave, who hung out together and did odd jobs (press agent, film critic) while scheming to make movies? The loss of that camaraderie is partly, to me, what accounts for the nostalgic ache underlying Godard's 1965 bagatelle.

NEW YORK TIMES, APRIL 12, 2001

Chapter Twenty-Two

HONG SANG-SOO

The 2017 New York Film Festival featured two new films by the South Korean director Hong Sang-soo, *On the Beach at Night Alone* and *The Day After*. Such a double honor has been reserved in the past for only the most important directors, such as Jean-Luc Godard and Rainer Werner Fassbinder. Hong actually directed a third film in 2017, *Claire's Camera*, which the festival's organizers also liked but reluctantly turned down, I was told, only because one filmmaker taking three slots would be unseemly.

Such prolific output is noteworthy in its own right, but the consistently high level of Hong's films makes it even more remarkable. Since 1996, he has made twenty-two features, at least half of which have premiered at the New York Film Festival, and he is routinely included in the Cannes and Berlin Film Festivals. If one were to ask international critics and festival programmers who they consider the best filmmakers working today, Hong would undoubtedly rank high. He is, however, virtually unknown to American audiences because so few of his films have received commercial distribution here and also because of Americans' resistance in general to subtitled movies and even to learning the names of non-European auteurs.

For all his appearances at Cannes, Hong has also never won a Palme d'Or. The reason, I think, is that despite their pleasurable, engrossing nature, each of his films gives the impression of being slight—intentionally so. Hong eschews the self-important and ostentatiously ambitious, preferring instead to build delicate cinematic structures out of seemingly offhand, casually

playful, sardonic observations. This modesty is partly a function of his production methods, low budgets being a tradeoff for maximum freedom.

Hong, born in Seoul in 1961, studied at the California College of Arts and
Crafts and then got a master's degree at the Chicago Art Institute. A professor at a Seoul university, he gets free rent there for his company (two employees) and relies on students as interns; he shoots on location without building
sets and is able to hold the costs of a feature film down to about $100,000.
Some of his films, like the delightful *Oki's Movie* (2010), which moves back
and forth in time—relating a love triangle between two film students and
their professor in a series of four quick sketches—are all the more charming
and fresh for their unassuming nature. *Yourself and Yours* is about a man
who is still in love with his ex-girlfriend and refuses to believe the rumors of
her promiscuity, preferring to think there are two women in town who look
exactly alike—and he may be right. As Martin Scorsese put it, in Hong's films
"everything kind of starts unassumingly—but then things unpeel like an
orange." The pleasures are additive: if you see one of his movies, you are apt
to be amused but may think "Is that all?"; see five, six, or ten of them and
you are likely to be hooked, a happy captive of Hong's world.

What are its common elements? A good deal of drinking, passive-
aggressive miscommunicating, romantic misalliances, and male competitiveness. The men tend to be loners, doggy-lustful yet timid seducers,
commitment-averse but given to needy clinging. Often they are film directors
teaching in the academy and hitting on attractive female students. The
women, ambitious to become actresses or filmmakers themselves, are typically looking for a mentor, a letter of recommendation, or a way to gain entry
into the industry. So the power game begins.

On the Occasion of Remembering the Turning Gate follows a handsome,
spoiled, but likable out-of-work actor as he is pursued by and pursues two
women. The film is set up in chapters and well-composed tableaux, during
which a sly comic feeling starts bubbling up in the embarrassing zone between
sex and love. The three sex scenes are especially amazing, deftly revealing
character through bedroom intimacies. The protagonist is clearly an unfin-
ished man, an actor waiting to be filled by other people's lines, accommodating and yet averse to being trapped. Banging up against his self-limitations,
he begins to change, moving from ambivalence to desire, but is the world
ready for him? Having it both ways, the film cleverly offers a fortune-teller's
preview of the hero's fate near the end, even as it leaves him in narrative
limbo, standing in the rain. The freshness of his movie is that you never know

where it's going from scene to scene. Hong Sang-soo is perpetuating a surprising cinema of understatement and psychological richness, based on the colliding needs of contemporary men and women.

All of Hong's films are drawn from his original screenplays, which feature pointed and penetrating dialogues. But he does not prepare scripts in advance. In fact he limits preparation time (normally an elaborate process) to a minimum, usually just scouting locations a few weeks before filming. When he's ready to shoot, he calls together the crew and cast a day or two before. He writes the dialogues for each day's shoot in the morning, starting at four AM. By nine or ten he is usually done writing and gives the actors their lines to memorize, allowing forty minutes or at most an hour for them to do so. (The dialogues may appear improvised, but as with John Cassavetes's films, the lines all have been scripted by the director).

It is worth remembering that Godard often worked in a similar fashion, composing the day's script in a car on the way to the set; borrowing lines from a newspaper, the radio, or a book at hand; and even whispering lines into the earpieces of his actors. Hong is not a collagist like Godard, being much more invested in the realistic situation and psychological complexity of his characters, but his reasons for working this way are perhaps analogous: to trick himself into coming up with something spontaneous and unconventional, putting pressure on his unconscious to come through at the last moment while relying on his observational antennae to tune opportunistically into the immediate surroundings and his cast's off-camera behaviors. Keeping the actors in the dark is also a way to draw more natural performances from them: they have no time for their lines to grow stale through overpreparation. Nor can they overthink their characters' motivations since Hong refuses to provide them with background about their characters' past. They are obliged to be in the moment. The moment, indeed, as it passes second by second is what you are most aware of in watching a Hong film. Time is distended, and the experience of presentness is allowed to bloom.

The paradox is that Hong is so keen on slipping the noose of intention, inviting chance and impromptu impulse, while on the other hand imposing certain restrictions that limit the amount of variation from film to film. For instance, there is his habit of working with similar character types from the same milieu, which he explains as follows: "It's convenient. It's not that important that they are directors of films, I just know more about them. I don't have this need to go to different professions, different types of characters. . . . My temperament is to work with the things I know already, and then find new things. . . . I don't want to make films about a plane pilot; if I try to describe him maybe I will be very stereotypical."

Surely no one else has made as many pictures set in film schools or focused so relentlessly on the power dynamics between teacher and student, the envy and competitiveness between one promising male student and another, or the chagrin that can arise between a director and his flunky. Lest we leap to the assumption that Hong is simply channeling his own autobiography, consider his statement that he simply knows more about film directors, not that he is the only one on which he bases his scripts.

Nevertheless, all this has rendered Hong susceptible to the charge that he is making the same film over and over. It's an intriguing if faulty accusation, especially since the same was said at times about Yasujirō Ozu, Éric Rohmer, and Woody Allen. Hong has been called "the Korean Woody Allen," as much to associate him with a familiar brand—comedies about rationalizing males who receive their comeuppance—as because the two are really that similar. There are funny touches in every Hong film, but I would not necessarily classify them as comedies. They seem more to be psychological investigations about the difficulty of sustaining romantic relationships or friendships, closer to the Rohmer prototype.

Hong says he appreciates the compliment of this comparison and admires Rohmer but does not see much similarity between them, beyond the fact that both use extensive dialogues and have developed low-budget strategies. I do see more of a kinship, especially considering how many of his films start with a protagonist on vacation at loose ends, recalling the vexed heroine in *Summer* or the narrator-antihero of *Claire's Knee*. Hong would probably also concur with Rohmer's disclaimer: "You should never think of me as an apologist for my male character, even (or especially) when he is being his own apologist. On the contrary, the men in my films are not meant to be particularly sympathetic characters." Both filmmakers are tireless analysts of male self-ignorance, immaturity, and cowardice.

Hong is pretty much alone working this vein in South Korean cinema, which specializes in technically polished genre pictures featuring crime, violence, sci-fi, fantasy, sex, or politics. He stays away from politics and violence, neither of which seems to interest him, and though his earlier movies sometimes had steamy sex scenes, he hasn't included one in many years.

Visually, his films are simply if well photographed with a functional priority placed on the actors' words. There may be cutaways to images of natural beauty, but there are no elaborately choreographed crane or dolly shots.

In dialogue scenes between a man and a woman meeting for the first time or with a group at a bar, he will often hold the camera on the speakers for long periods without changing the framing. Sometimes he will pan from one speaker to the other, just to vary the shot. From his sixth film on, he began using a zoom lens, which raised some cinephiles' ire (zooms were thought by purists to be vulgar technological shortcuts, performing an act that the human eye could not). Explaining his preference for the zoom, Hong told an interviewer: "I just felt one day that I would like to get closer to the actors without cutting the shot. By doing it I discovered that I could create a special rhythm in continuity. And it's so easy. I just kept doing it ever since. I didn't want to make it my trademark."

The area where Hong most experiments cinematically is in his handling of narrative structure. He will frequently break the film into two or three parts, each section set in a different time frame or doubling back on itself. Thus, though his filmic style may be naturalistic, you are often suddenly made aware, through chapter headings or self-reflexive shifts in points of view, that you are watching a construct, a movie whose realism Hong feels free to undercut at any moment. *Tale of Cinema* (2005) has a tricky Möbius strip structure that follows an Underground Man–like filmmaker envious of the short film of a former classmate and includes scenes from that film. Rarely has the male psyche, in all its dogginess, competitive resentment, and self-pity, been so unsentimentally probed. This time, the less successful of two film school graduates is hung up on the notion that the other man stole elements of his life to make a first movie. The film employs a figure-eight construction that shows how life and art mutually influence each other. But the real achievement is in creating shaded characters (even a strong woman) who keep you in suspended judgment: one moment acting impetuously generous, the next obnoxiously self-defeating. The voice-over narration adds a literary, Nouvelle Vague ambiance to the enterprise, with Seoul standing in for Paris. *Nobody's Daughter Haewon* is a forlorn, heartbreaking narrative told in diary entries, flashbacks, and dreams. The exquisite *Hill of Freedom* follows a Japanese tourist trying to reconnect with a former girlfriend who has disappeared by hanging out in a coffee shop hoping to spot her.

An even purer example might be his 2015 *Right Now, Wrong Then*, a wry comedy about a nerdy filmmaker, at loose ends in the provinces before a showing of his film, who hits on a pretty young aspiring painter. This time Hong covers the same narrative ground twice, showing the protagonist making mistakes and then correcting them, like a Korean *Groundhog Day*. The first half is taken up by the filmmaker seeking to impress the artist, though he keeps putting his foot in his mouth, offending her by his false praise of her artwork and unconscious sexism. In the second part, we see the same action played out but with subtle differences: this time the man adjusts his level of honesty, with better results. (Subtle, too, are the slight variations in camera placement, which reinforce the shift from the man's subjective viewpoint to the woman's.) In neither part do the two end up in bed, but the result is a demonstration of the choices we make every second to be merely presentational or more authentic—one of Hong's main themes.

The woman painter in *Right Now, Wrong Then* is played by Kim Min-hee, a prominent South Korean actress (*The Handmaiden*) who has frequently been cast by Hong in his recent films. She has also had an affair with Hong, who is married, which provided much scandalous fodder for the South Korean tabloids. Hong's (defiant? self-mocking?) response was to make *A Woman on the Beach Alone*, starring Kim as an actress named Younghee who has had an affair with a married film director and who, for the duration of the picture, is shown trying to console herself and waiting for the lover to resurface. In doing so, Hong was essentially inviting his national audience to read the film as an autobiographical confession and to judge him severely while being fully aware of the ways in which it is a work of fictional imagination— not least because it enters so deeply and sympathetically into the woman's point of view.

The film begins in Hamburg, Germany, where Younghee is taking some time off and distracting herself from heartbreak, wondering if she should move permanently to Germany. She has just met another Korean woman, and they are hanging out together, comparing notes on life and love. The other woman, who is rather plain-looking, states that she is not given to passionate romance because she lacks "desire." Obviously she also envies Younghee her beauty and healthy libido, but neither mentions that. Younghee, admitting that she has played around a lot, insists that she doesn't care anymore whether her lover will join her in Hamburg as he has promised or not; what will be will be. She seems to be fooling herself.

The second part moves to South Korea, where Younghee runs into some acquaintances from her past while visiting a small city. (Getting away from Seoul, the capital of ambition, and trying to find contentment in a less hurried corner of Korea is a frequently expressed if disabused hope by Hong's characters.) These acquaintances, deferential to her as a successful actress, are mostly curious about the rumors of her relationship with the film director and invite her to dine with them. She regards them as losers who are stuck in a provincial rut. Over the course of a meal she becomes more and more aggressively rude, telling one man that he is incapable of loving and moreover they all lack the "qualifications to love."

In Hong's films, awkward conversational standstills are suddenly broken when the characters start drinking. Alcohol is necessary to advance the plot, releasing these otherwise polite, repressed middle-class South Koreans to express their desires, resentments, wild guesses, or acute insights about one another. We see a less likable side of Younghee as she turns on her friends with haughty superiority. Bragging about having slept with several German men abroad, asserting that they are bigger down below than Korean men, she impatiently declares, "Men are idiots!" and starts making out with the woman closest to her.

In the last part of the film, she repairs with a few of these same companions to a beach town. As they debate in their fancy hotel suite what to eat, a window washer is manically scrubbing away on the other side of the glass, a characteristically zany, surrealist touch on Hong's part. Surreal, too, is the dream sequence (which we initially assume is real) where she fantasizes about a reconciliation with her director lover, who keeps sloppily telling her how pretty she is, then reads a passage from a Chekhov story about love. But ultimately, to the grave accompaniment of a Schubert passage that keeps recurring, she is left "on the beach alone at night." (The title comes from a Walt Whitman poem). Meanwhile we have spent time in the company of a singularly vivacious, strong-willed female character. Kim's performance—fierce, quicksilver, and riveting—won her a Silver Bear at the Berlin International Film Festival.

Kim appears again in *The Day After*, this time playing a decorous, proper young woman interested in writing who goes to work for a book publisher and respected critic, played by Kwon Hae-hyo. He is torn between his ex-mistress and his wife, who flies into a jealous rage when she discovers a love letter. *The Day After* begins in a somewhat mystifying manner, as Hong intercuts between his protagonist's guilty-husband present tense and his past adulterous affair. Soon, the new office worker (Kim) appears on the scene, and he can't keep from flirting with her. The three women converge on the increasingly hapless, bemused publisher, who finds himself less and less in control of his destiny. The wife, mistaking the new worker for her husband's mistress, slaps her around and refuses to acknowledge her error.

Eventually the confusion sorts itself out, and the film builds to an explosive confrontation. Hong pushes the dramatic tension in ways that could seem melodramatic but instead play as sly, ironic farce. Unhappiness being a guarantee, the hysteria of the characters trying to flee that conclusion seems a waste of time. As though aware of that futility, they take a break from anguish to order Chinese takeout. The last shot in the movie shows the Chinese takeout food man's arrival, a sort of consoling presence.

The superb cinematography in both films is the work of Kim Hyung-koo. Whereas the color photography in *On the Beach at Night Alone* looks sun-kissed and open-air, *The Day After* is shot elegantly in black and white, in grimly grey, snowy conditions that underscore the trapped, bleak situation of the publisher. In the last scene, the office worker (Kim), who had lasted only one day at the job before quitting, returns some months later to congratulate the publisher on winning a prize for his criticism, and the publisher gives her a parting gift, a new translation of a Sōseki book, *And Then*. Hong likes to drop literary references casually, as we can gather from his quotations of Whitman and Chekhov in *On the Beach at Night Alone*. In *The Day After*, the choice of a novel by the great Japanese author is particularly significant, since Sōseki also was accused of writing the same book over and over and specialized in dissecting his male protagonists' isolating egotism.

Solipsism would seem to be the ultimate source of Hong's characters' unhappiness. As he stated onstage at the New York Film Festival, each of us operates on a different plane of reality, and these planes rarely align so as to bring about a knowledge of what the other is feeling. One is reminded of Emerson's statement in his notebook: "Man is insular, and cannot be touched. Every man is an infinitely repellent orb."

A depressing notion. Yet underneath the misbegotten behavior in Hong's films, the doomed attempts to free oneself through alcohol and sexual affairs, I sense another quest, which might be called spiritual. It enters in the silences and gaps that filter into moments when his characters are at a loss. The protagonist in *On the Beach at Night Alone* startles her friend by bowing and kissing the ground before crossing a bridge in Hamburg. The office worker in *The Day After* demands of her boss, "Why are you living?" She scoffs at his inability to answer and confesses that she herself believes in God, which she knows will cause her to lose credit in the eyes of the sophisticated literary crowd that she aspires to join.

Kim Minhee may be Hong's muse, as Anna Karina was for Godard or Monica Vitti for Antonioni, but in addition he seems to be exploring through her roles his own transcendental yearning. Hong titled an early film of his *On the Occasion of Remembering the Turning Gate*, about a man at a cross-roads, eerily recalling another Sōseki novel, *The Gate*, which was about some-one who goes off to a Buddhist retreat only to realize at the end of his visit that the hoped-for release didn't work for him. Perhaps, Hong is saying, one's spiritual hungers cannot be appeased, any more than one's carnal appetites, but that does not prevent one from trying. Finally, what is one to make of the odd admission of Hong's that the movie that made him want to become a filmmaker was Bresson's *Diary of a Country Priest*? There is little of Bresson's Jansenist severity in Hong's droll, melancholy rondos, but perhaps there is something of the same faith that in confronting unyielding reality head-on, we can begin to surmise a larger, more hidden truth or possibility of grace.

NEW YORK REVIEW OF BOOKS, DECEMBER 7, 2017

POSTSCRIPT

Recently I saw a new Hong film, *In Front of Your Face*, which struck me as one of his best (and most poignant). In it, a middle-aged woman who used to be an actress and who has resettled in Canada returns to her hometown in Korea to visit her sister. She has also received an invitation from a younger director to discuss the possibility of working with him. At one of those long eating and drinking scenes for which Hong is noted, the married director keeps telling the woman what a fan he is of her older films and how much he would like to make a movie about her, any film, even a documentary with no script. Suddenly she says, in one of those dawning realizations that cuts through the blather, "Oh, you want to sleep with me." He confesses embarrassedly, "Yes." She explains that she cannot shoot a film with him because she is dying of cancer. He seems utterly taken aback (as are we) but still insists that they start shooting the next day. As they leave the restaurant, she pats his head in a tender gesture, as if to return the compliment of his erotic interest in her. The next morning, she plays a message on her answering machine from the director, awkwardly apologizing that he cannot possibly make the film with her. She laughs and laughs. Of course, now that he knows she is dying, he has lost his interest. (Men are idiots.)

Chapter Twenty-Three

HOU HSIAO-HSIEN

Could it be that one of today's most important film artists—the critic J. Hoberman calls him "the world's greatest active narrative filmmaker"—is a Taiwanese director virtually unknown here? American audiences, accustomed to gauging a movie's importance by its advertising budget and buzz, may understandably scoff at such a claim. Regardless, the director in question, Hou Hsiao-hsien, is a star of the international festival circuit. Six of Hou's last seven pictures have been shown at the New York Film Festival, yet none has been released theatrically. His movies are considered difficult—and they are, compared to the latest action picture. Yet it says something about how incurious American audiences are that they must be "protected" from great, demanding cinema from abroad.

Part of Hou's significance is that he is both a compassionate humanist storyteller and a great formalist. Imagine a cross between Satyajit Ray or Vittorio De Sica and the rigorously framed, meditative works of Bresson and Ozu, with gritty urban echoes of Scorsese thrown in. His films constitute a running commentary on Taiwanese history and identity while drawing deeply on classical Chinese art. If Hou's style bridges the old traditions and the jagged, modernist edges of a rootless global culture, it is partly because he himself embodies these contradictions.

This maker of contemplative masterworks is, at fifty-two, youthful-looking, roguish, and a hard-drinking karaoke habitué, as we see in *H.H.H.: Portrait of Hou Hsiao-hsien*, a documentary by his fellow filmmaker and admirer Olivier Assayas. We learn that Hou had a wild youth; many of his gang members met violent ends. After military service, which settled him down, he was unsure whether to aim for pop singing, acting, or filmmaking. He joined a movement of cinematic progressives (including Edward Yang, whose *Taipei Story* featured Hou as the acting lead). The New Taiwanese Cinema identified with the French New Wave, rebelling against the previous Taiwanese studio comedies and melodramas and favoring real locations and socially conscious materials. Their first effort was an omnibus film, *The Sandwich Man* (1983). Hou directed the title section, and already one can see his patient observation of everyday people caught in a trap. Other early Hou films, *The Boys from Fengkuei* and *A Summer at Grandpa's*, displayed an open storytelling approach that captured the irregular rhythms of growing up. But it was not until the more autobiographical *A Time to Live and a Time to Die* (1985) that Hou made his first genuine masterpiece.

He chose the story of a schoolteacher, much like his father, who transplanted his family from mainland China to Taiwan in 1948 for work reasons then was unable to go back after the Maoist revolution. The first generation's tragedy was that they died in Taiwan deluding themselves that they would one day return to China. Their children, Hou's generation, accepted that they belonged in Taiwan, though that meant subscribing to an uneasy, fractured identity, buffeted politically between the Nationalists and the Chinese Communists. These larger tensions are reflected in the story of an exiled family, in which the death of both parents leads to the adolescent children's delinquency. Hou's camera recorded, with anthropological interest, life's task-laden dailiness, which continues through dramatic disruptions. The mournfully consoling noises and rituals of everyday life go on in the surround (you can't even say "background," because the key dramatic action is not always in the foreground). The performances also seem nonprofessional, making you forget you are watching acting, so absorbed is the camera with real-time behavior. For instance, there's a stunning, almost throwaway moment when the mother, who has throat cancer, is being clumsily strapped into a rickshaw by its driver, to be taken back to the hospital. You watch the rain falling, the driver buckling the straps around the mother, her own stolid, indrawn expression, and her grown children more or less assisting. The director's restraint lets you feel, and swallow, the full effect of severe illness.

One might generalize in broader terms about a Taiwanese cultural sensibility, which is melancholy and fragilely quotidian, reflecting the apprehensive circumstances of the island's modern history: occupied for fifty years by the Japanese then placed under martial law for forty years by the émigré Nationalists, initially under Chiang Kai-shek. Hong Kong films tend toward the brashly kinetic; Chinese mainland films, toward the panoramically epic; Taiwanese films, toward the quietly moody. Hou's trademark heartbreaking stoicism has been supported immeasurably by his two screenwriters, the novelists Chu T'ien-wen and Wu Nien-jen.

His next work, *Dust in the Wind*, based on Wu's authobiographical script, focused on the problems of country youth moving to the big city and getting lost in the big shuffle. A small, wrenching film, it features some astonishingly beautiful long shots, which, like classical Chinese painting, assign the place of humanity within a larger picture.

From this point on, Hou steadily perfected his technique, moving from that "attractive plainness" to a much higher level of refinement, justifying the director Peter Sellar's claim that he is "one of the last great craftsmen in cinema." Visual elegance permeated his next film, the haunting *Daughter of the Nile*, which portrayed disaffected Taipei teenagers trapped in the aqua fluorescent glare of Burger Kings, and came to an apotheosis in his ambitious, three-hour *A City of Sadness*, which won the grand prize at Venice in 1990.

A City of Sadness was a breakthrough for Hou in many respects: by telling the taboo story about the February 28 incident, a massacre of native Taiwanese in 1947 by the Nationalist Chinese, he struck a national chord (the film set box office records in Taiwan). By layering so many characters and themes with a minimum of orientation, he created an epic both richly textured and austere. The film traces the fortunes of a family, led by Older Brother, a brusque, gravel-voiced, endearing gangster, who tries to honor the codes of family, clan, and professional confederates while keeping wife and mistress happy. Meanwhile, we learn about the Japanese occupation, competition from Shanghai gangsters, and left-wing political movements.

The film's narrative reach and fatalistic undertone owes something to that other gangster epic, *The Godfather*, which Hou says inspired him. In *A City of Sadness*, violence often erupts from seeming tranquility and then spends itself, the site returning to calm. A man slowly walks up a mountain road; a rickshaw appears in the middle distance; the man turns and strolls toward the rickshaw occupants, then pulls a samurai sword and starts thwacking at them. This spasmodic aggression gets swallowed up by the mountain landscape. (There is also a hint of Godard—another influence of Hou's—and his shootouts between gangsters in long distance.) "I always tell my cameraman,

'Pull back! More detached!'" says Hou. By striving toward a detached point of view, without leading us ideologically by the elbow, he compels a more active spectatorship. With Hou, you feel your way into a scene, sorting as you go the characters' relationships and objectives. The film critic Kent Jones has written: "There is truly nothing but in medias res in Hou." After a while you abandon your quest for the key action and surrender to the perplexing, multifarious life unfolding before you. In a sense, Hou's work is not difficult at all: you need only slow down your metabolism and submit to the pace, the images, the information onscreen. What he offers is a plenitude of life as it accumulates in the moment: the screen fills with being like water in a fish tank. He forces you to attend to the unfolding present—a quality he shares with other "ontological filmmakers" like Andrei Tarkovsky, John Cassavetes, Godard, Hong Sang-soo, and Frederick Wiseman, all of whom allow the moment to flower rather than coercing it into the one-point-per-scene formula of most Hollywood movies.

"He probably understands framing better than any director in the world," observed New York Film Festival director Richard Pena. Hou often subdivides the frame, with lattice or door frames, letting several actions go on at once. Increasingly, each scene is presented as a self-contained shot, without interior cutting, which places more pressure on camera movement and choreographed action within the shot. Yet if you're not always sure why you're watching a scene, given his abjuring of transition shots, a second viewing of the film reveals that it has been tightly constructed, with no narrative flab.

A City of Sadness was the first in a historical trilogy, which also included *The Puppetmaster* and *Good Men, Good Women*. All three paid their respects to the sacrifices and resilience of an older generation as a way of trying to come to terms with Taiwanese history and to contrast it with the pessimism and malaise of young Taiwanese today.

Having performed this filial duty, he next made *Goodbye South, Goodbye*, in which he cut loose with Taiwanese punks talking on cell phones, riding motorcycles through the mountains, hanging out, and trying to pull off harebrained cons. Hou paints Taiwan as a society so corrupt and lawless— "pure" capitalism—that only a frayed system of familial and clan loyalties is left to adjudicate disputes. *Goodbye South, Goodbye* has a vivid nightclub scene late in the film, which begins with an elderly man crooning a karaoke number about love and betrayal, then drifts leisurely over to a row of banquet tables where a senator and a cop discuss with a gangster how best to mediate a row that has resulted in the gangster's relatives being kidnapped by the police. In the background sit various relatives and retainers of the warring sides, eating with deadpan politesse.

Hou has—wrongly, I think—been compared to Ozu because of his contemplative style of long takes. A formal purist he may be, but he is also something of a wild man. *Goodbye South, Goodbye*, with its depictions of wannabe hoods and molls, of scams gone sour, may be closer to Scorsese territory than to Ozu. One particularly lame scheme involves trying to pass off ordinary pigs as prize studs, with government subsidies to sweeten the deal.

Hou has always had a magnificent compositional sense, creating dynamic background-foreground relationships. In one scene, a young woman nicknamed Pretzel who has just attempted suicide is stretched out on a mattress in the background with a bandaged wrist while Kao, the head of their gang, demands to know how this could have happened. Kao's body mostly blocks off our view of Pretzel's boyfriend, Flathead, except for Flathead's legs, between which the teenager bounces a basketball while his boss berates him for allowing the suicide attempt to occur. Flathead's shame at being upbraided is bought home by this odd framing and the distracting thud-thud-thud of the basketball. I cannot get that bouncing basketball out of my head.

In his subsequent film, *Flowers of Shanghai*, Hou abandoned Taiwan for the first time and focused on a period drama. *Flowers of Shanghai* is a visually ravishing masterpiece, one that induces the calm fatalism of an opium high. The film is shot entirely in interiors: at various brothels in fin-de-siècle Shanghai, rotating between five elegant "flower girls." Often we will start by seeing a dimly gaslit parlor, inhabited by one or two characters; our eyes will slowly make out the muted background colors, the plums, the golds, which open to reveal their richness; the camera will begin its patient oscillations from side to side, sometimes revealing other characters (servants, trainees, go-betweens) who we had not known were in the room. In this society, no one is ever left alone for long, though their inner isolation remains untouched. It takes awhile for courtesan and client to shed their retinue; we never see them having sex, but we spend time watching other rituals (gambling, eating, drinking, the preparing of opium pipes) that take place unhurriedly in "real time." Even the dramatic eruptions—a jealous argument between a courtesan and her patron, a suicide pact gone awry—arise ritually, sputter, and fall back onto the bedrock of everyday routine, rooted in a granitic economic system.

Hou builds on the geisha melodramas of Mizoguchi and Naruse—the cruelty of sexual commerce; the women's debts; the madam's bossiness; the self-protective, two-faced nature of a courtesan's attachments—and strips down this narrative genre to its essence, by way of formal blackouts, frontal compositions, and gyroscopically rigorous camera movements. Hou's scriptwriter, Chu T'ien-wen, deconstructed an 1894 novel by Han Ziyun into a set of pungent dialogues, purged of any sentimental condescension toward the "flower girls." The main story involves Crimson, a lovely courtesan whose patron, Master Wang (played by the sad-eyed movie star Tony Leung) is beginning to drift away. The film's one voiceover has Master Wang wondering what Crimson is feeling. Throughout, you keep anticipating she will commit suicide or smash up, but it never happens. Nor is Crimson entirely innocent. We are left with the enormous gulf between male and female as Master Wang, about to be transferred, gazes at Crimson in the end, still wondering what is going on inside her, while she prepares his pipe. I regard *Flowers of Shanghai* as perfect and one of the most beautiful film ever made.

NEW YORK TIMES, OCTOBER 10, 1999;
FILM COMMENT (NOVEMBER/DECEMBER 1998)

Chapter Twenty-Four

OTAR IOSSELIANI

Otar Iosseliani is one of the missing links in our Anglo-American map of world cinema. In France, where the Georgian-born filmmaker has settled, he is treated as a master, with his own lavish DVD box of collected works; in Italy, dense critical books are devoted to him. His movies have played the international film festival circuit for decades and won awards at Venice, Cannes, and Berlin. He is a first-rate, resolutely minor artist—a noble category that in literature encompasses superior stylists such as Max Beerbohm and A. J. Liebling. From his first student short onward, Iosseliani seems to have possessed his own personal, ironic film style. Fluent but not prolific, he has made a small, carefully deliberated body of work: only nine features since 1966, plus a few documentaries.

Iosseliani's are, for the most part, what the French call "composite" films. Rather than focusing on a single character's conflict, they track groups of people who interact in inadvertent or volitional contexts: family members, neighbors, fellow vagabonds on the road of life. It takes awhile to figure out the specific relationships that tie the different protagonists to one another, though each one's role becomes apparent in time. Often the characters are introduced through an everyday, seemingly static pattern at a stable location, a country estate or village or city block, and move off from there in all directions. Though no central conflict may unite these episodes, plenty of plot happens: terrorists blow up trains; fathers desert their families; prisoners are tortured; people lose their homes or end in very different straits from where they started; sometimes a whole way of life is turned upside down—but all these developments occur with the same imperturbable deadpan, the same lack of melodramatic emphasis, as occurs in the inertial passages. Fate is dealt out with sangfroid. Human desire may come to naught or occasionally even be satisfied; whichever, the beauty of the physical world remains.

Other Iosseliani leitmotifs include: alcoholic consumption and communal drinking songs, the ramshackle tatters of an aristocratic life, large Borzois that wander underfoot, children practicing the piano, a tall De Gaulle-looking guy, and a bearded Rasputin-resembling Slav. Iosseliani favors nonprofessional actors (or actors, used in cameos, who are his personal friends), and there is very little playing to the camera.

His film style favors the long shot. Few close-ups occur in Iosseliani's mature oeuvre, and these are invariably of objects or people's torsos, never their faces. A shot is held with patience until the gag or ironic point is made. The result is an accumulation of wryly telling moments: gestures or grimaces that betray secrets of character, frustrating encounters with obdurate objects such as carpet runners. Almost no musical score, and what little there is (usually early twentieth-century piano pieces) won't tell us what to feel. Dialogue is spare, and that little is more ornamental than crucial to the narrative. One can watch a Iosseliani film without subtitles and still get most of it. In that respect, his work seems rooted in the universalist aspirations of silent cinema.

Some comparison to Jacques Tati (née Jacques Tatischeff) is unavoidable, given the same structure of droll comic moments, the tactful spying on private struggles with intractable objects, the aversion to dialogue, the master-shot aesthetic, the rebuilding on silent cinema, even the small, carefully evolved corpus. Iosseliani, understandably irritated by being compared too frequently to an older filmmaker he knew and admired, is quick to cite in interviews the differences: that Tati comes out of the "clown" tradition, whereas he works more in fables; that Tati used an alter ego or guide, M. Hulot, to weave together films, whereas he never does, relying more on a musical structure . . . and so on. Frankly, these distinctions sound picayune. Iosseliani might do better to embrace the association and admit he is working in a Tatiesque vein. The real difference between them, it seems to me, is temperamental: Iosseliani's films come across as mordant, not so benign as Tati's; his world is crueler, more sexually explicit, more treacherous. Where Tati tended toward inquisitive bemusement at modernity's gadgetry and modular design, Iosseliani is angrily at odds with the globalized postmodern world and attached to the myth of a lost Eden. Sometimes that Eden may be a geographically specific place, such as the African village in *And There Was Light*; at other times it may be childhood or the half-buried traditions of a slower, lazier, peasant/aristocratic way of life or an ancient viniculture or even the lost kingdom of silent cinema.

Otar Iosseliani was born in 1934 in Tbilisi, Georgia, a handsome old city whose crooked streets he often captured on film to charming effect. His first love was classical music; he received his diploma in piano, composition, and conducting. He then studied mathematics and engineering before switching to film school at VGIF, the famous Moscow institute that also graduated Tarkovsky and Parajanov. His main teacher at VGIF was the great Alexander Dovzhenko—a wonderful old man, according to Iosseliani, but unfortunately still duped by Soviet communism, "because he was a peasant," who was flattered to be accepted into the inner circle of state-approved artists. Iosseliani makes no bones about coming from a more illustrious family background, a French-speaking, cultivated Georgian upper class. There is absolutely no love lost between the Georgians of Iosseliani's background and the Soviet Russians. In any case, Iosseliani was skeptical of the communist dream from early on and firmly convinced, in his words, "that all on this earth was vanity and everything ended badly."

One of his first student shorts, *April* (1962), tells of a young couple in love, living in a poor but lively tenement, who are given sterile new housing; so much furniture keeps arriving from the tenant council, like Ionesco's *The Chairs*, that they end up quarreling, almost breaking up, and finally throwing the furniture out the window to rekindle their love. The Soviet censors banned it, deeming its stance against new household goods antiprogressive—which it was.

Iosseliani subsequently made three Russian features, *Fallen Leaves* (1967), *There Was Once a Songbird* (1971), and *Pastorale* (1976)—all gems of black-and-white filmmaking, whose inventiveness, youthful sadness, and legerity have a kinship with the first features of Dušan Makavejev, Ermanno Olmi, Jerzy Skolimowski, Raúl Ruiz, and other regional internationalists responding in fresh ways to the French New Wave and the sixties' liberating promise.

In *Fallen Leaves* (its episodic manner and vivid background characters upstaging the doleful young protagonist have much in common with Olmi's *Il Posto*), a young man is apprenticed in a wine-selling business. Like Jean-Pierre Léaud in *Masculin Féminin* he is attracted to a pretty brunette above his physical station. A popular friend keeps giving him advice about how to act cool. Timid and pushed around by everyone—a woman at the bus stop tells him to pick up the butt he dropped, another orders him to give up his seat to the elderly—he finds himself miraculously promoted at the factory and starts officiously issuing orders. But in the end his reluctant integrity—he happens to know a lot about wine—surfaces, and he rebels, spoiling the company's awful mass-produced wine product by pouring in gelatin, which costs him his job. (It should be noted that Georgians take pride in their wine, which is one of their main exports).

Iosseliani's delightful second feature, *Once Upon a Time There Was a Singing Blackbird*, tells the story of an appealing, distracted young scamp who is always on the verge of losing his job as an orchestra tympanist; he shows up at the last possible moment to play the final drum rolls, keeps various girlfriends dangling, and roves around a Parisian-looking Tbilisi of chestnut trees, boulevards, and cafes, making promises and breaking them, wondering why "everyone finds fault with me." Suspecting there may be something physically wrong with himself, he is told by his doctor that no, he's just lazy. Iosseliani treads delicately between sympathy and detached objectivity in his psychologically astute portrait of this Georgian Alfie, who keeps disappointing everyone. The one instance by this filmmaker of a sustained conventional narrative about a single protagonist, it shows what Iosseliani could have achieved along these lines had he pursued realistic storytelling strategies with professional actors.

By his next film, *Pastorale*, he had already begun experimenting with ensembles and the barest minimum of plot. Four young musicians who constitute a string quartet repair to a collective farm in the country to find the simple life, only to discover the villagers are infected by petty vendettas while they themselves keep getting on each other's nerves. This simple narrative spine functions as a pretext for many delicious throwaway moments observing daily rural life, some of which are documentary in spirit (an old man carrying a mound of straw on his back, metaphorized into an Everyman Sisyphus) and others enacted; the effect of both is to pull the viewer into a timeless, casual realm. With this film, Iosseliani starts to perfect the dispersed narrative, using figure-8 camera movements that follow one character, then drop him to pursue another who has crossed his path. The musicians attempt to tape-record the old folk songs that are fast disappearing, but they end up "corrupting" the locals by taking them out of their work rhythm through the novelty of picnics. In the end, entropy and idleness, the ultimate threats to the Soviet system, take over.

It seems remarkable that Iosseliani got away with making these three features. He explained to me in an interview that it was partly because the head of the studio in Georgia encouraged young filmmakers to do creative work and partly because Georgia was on the periphery. "Then the Soviet censors started tightening the screws. Making good films suddenly became a heroic act." Iosseliani's own films were banned, and when he was offered the option by the Soviet authorities to leave the country (at about the same time that his friend Andrei Tarkovsky was shown the door), he took it and went to France. "Tarkovsky made the mistake of leaving permanently. And that's what killed him," Iosseliani told me. "The sadness of all émigrés is the impossibility of ever going home. With me, I never emigrated. I made a film, I went back home, I made another film, I went back home. Always to Georgia—I never returned to Moscow. No one understood why I kept coming back. You have to know Georgia, the beauty of the place, its antiquity, its suffering. I returned to Georgia, to my friends, to my songs, to each corner of the mountains that I knew by heart."

Iosseliani comes across in person as testy—a man who has fought so hard for his artistic integrity and independence that he cannot quite lower his dukes, even in the presence of a fan. (I made the mistake of turning down a shot of brandy he offered me, which may have set off his wariness. I am not much of a drinker, I'm afraid). When I asked him how he got started professionally, he launched into a disquisition about Georgian and Russian cinema that went back to 1904. He took pains to insist that Georgia was *not* Russia; the latter had merely dominated the former politically. Georgian cinema began in 1904 and was tragic, dramatic, romantic, and popular. Soviet cinema, he said disdainfully, followed the same line as Hollywood. He expressed particular dislike for Eisenstein, whom he regarded as a cold-blooded, cynical intellectual and a liar ("The truth is that the Russian navy was the best nourished of any, and the *Potemkin* revolt was a rebellion of officers, not sailors."). Nevertheless, he granted Eisenstein his brilliance: "There is an old Chinese saying: 'Even if you hate a fox, don't say that he doesn't know how to run.'"

It was characteristic of Iosseliani that his answer to my mundane personal question should immediately revert to the silent era, before he was born: his interest in film history and his antagonism to dialectical montage could not be contained. Iosseliani's own model from early Soviet cinema was Boris Barnet, a fun-loving renegade who directed with panache movies such as *The Girl with a Hatbox*, *Okraina*, and *By the Bluest of Seas*. In an article

Iosseliani wrote celebrating Barnet, he said: "Above all, he must show imag-ination and a sense of fantasy by refusing, for example, to adapt famous lit-erary works or film the biographies of famous people." This dubious idea that there is something corrupt about adapting literary works for the screen was popular with the French New Wave directors when they were writing for *Cahiers du Cinema*, but most of them abandoned it in the course of their careers. Not Iosseliani.

When I asked Iosseliani to name, besides Barnet, the directors he thought had inspired him, he listed René Clair and Jean Vigo. France was the logical country for him to move to. "I am no competition with anyone in France because I don't eat the grass from their lawn. I'm nibbling on the grass of René Clair. But since he left without mowing it, there's still something to nib-ble on." I find it interesting that he identifies so strongly with the whimsical, unfettered, anarchistic lyricism of Clair, Barnet, and Vigo since his own style seems tighter and darker.

His first feature in France was *Les Favoris de la Lune* (*Favorites of The Moon*), made in 1984 in color—from this point on, all of his films would be in color. It revolves around an apartment building in Paris and the interlock-ing lives of its occupants. Its cast includes, among others, the filmmaker Pascal Aubier, the film critic Bernard Eisenschitz, the actors Mathieu Amal-ric and László Szabó; Iosseliani himself puts in a cameo appearance as an elderly gent who frequents the prostitutes stationed outside the building. One absurdist moment out of many may suffice to show the way the filmmaker both satisfies and frustrates the viewer's desire for action: a maker of remote-control bombs keeps warning his turbaned client not to push the red but-ton, and of course the client does, and the arms-maker's assistant gets blown sky high, pulverized into dust, a Méliès magic trick that yields no further con-sequences; the indifferent onlookers give a collective shrug.

He next directed *Un Petit Monastère en Toscane* (1988), an hour-long documentary about five French monks who inhabit an Italian monastery, making wine, of course, and the daily life of the villagers—peasants, bour-geoisie, loner types—who surround them. The film exhibits Iosseliani's anthropological engrossment with traditional ways of life that face extinc-tion and his eye for the throwaway five-second anecdote. This documentary seems to have been good preparation for his next effort, *Et la Lumière Fut* (*And There Was Light*, 1989). A film of dazzling cinematographic beauty and clarity set in a small village in the south of Senegal, at first it seems a radical departure from his previous work, given its African setting. We watch the everyday, ancient practices of this rather matriarchal, mostly happy tribe, their mating rituals, prayers for rain, hunting expeditions, couple squabbles, and every bit is fascinating, even if we are unsure whether these events are being captured documentary-fashion or staged for the camera—perhaps both, in the manner of Jean Rouch's ethnographic fictions. The village seems a paradise: another of Iosseliani's lost Edens. But a timber company has been moving in on the area, and before long the forest which had been the tribe's habitat and protective covering is stripped, and the villagers are forced to disperse—some to nearby towns, where they get enmeshed in social welfare bureaucracies, others abroad, becoming world travelers, still others adapting to the market economy by turning out commercial copies of their sacred statues. No longer is any place safe from globalization and modernity, a point Iosseliani neither belabors nor sentimentalizes. If anything, he imposes an even tone—call it comically deadpan observation—on the before-and-after sections, which reinforces the underlying strand of human endurance.

His next work, *La Chasse aux Papillons* (*Chasing Butterflies*, 1992), continues this theme of the inexorability of displacement and globalization, albeit in a more Chekhovian, *Cherry Orchard* vein. Two elderly Russian sisters peaceably share a chateau in a French town, surrounded by local villagers, Hare Krishnas, and others; one dies. The chateau is inherited by a third sister, who lives in Moscow, and she sells it quickly to some Japanese speculators, who transform the place into a chic hotel, the old iron gate replaced by plate glass. In Iosseliani's vision of flux, property keeps being usurped, and the powerless if rightful owners evicted by parvenus; it scarcely matters whether the usurper is the communist state or international capital. One of his best and most delicately lepidopterous of films, *Chasing Butterflies* also marks the first time he would collaborate with the exceptional cinematographer, William Lubtchansky, who has shot all of Iosseliani's movies since. Though Iosseliani insists that he designs all his own camera movements and tells the cinematographer exactly what to do, what Lubtchanksy brings to the image is a classic compositional balance and a luminous sensitivity to lighting changes, particularly outdoors.

In his next film, made in 1996, *Brigands #7* (a title that suggests incessant narrativizing, like a Feuillade serial, which is the other face of "plotlessness"), three time periods are juggled: a medieval narrative involving a cuckolded king; a story set in the early Bolshevik era, in which a dandyish robber ends up some high mucky-muck in the communist bureaucracy; and the contemporary moment, wherein a sculptor threads his way through a Serbian landscape torn by civil war in order to stay drunk with his buddies. The same actor, Amiran Amiranashvili, plays the gallant king, the swinishly opportunistic people's commissar, and the wine-befuddled clochard; there is some suggestion that the various episodes are all dreams in the drunkard's mind. There is also a Parisian episode that climaxes in the massacre of arms merchants and a frame story involving an alcoholic movie projectionist, since everything we see is part of a movie shown to some Russian studio hacks. All this invention may be too wacky for its own good, yet the film—as always with Iosseliani—has many deeply engrossing, plausibly human passages, particularly in the Bolshevik episode, that transcend the farcical or narrowly fabulist thrust of the material.

Iosseliani's two most recent features are both satisfying, accomplished works in the manner of *Chasing Butterflies*. *Adieu, Plancher des Vaches!* (*Farewell, Home Sweet Home*, 1999) concentrates on an aristocratic family coming apart at the seams: the father (played by Iosseliani himself) is too lazy to do anything except drink and envy the clochards their freedom; the mother is a go-getter who sells real estate and takes lovers, flying in helicopters from one deal to the next; their downwardly mobile teenage son goes into town every day and transforms himself into a street beggar. In the end, the father runs away to the sea ("The boat is a sort of romantic dream, like death," Iosseliani told me.)

In *Lundi Matin* (*Monday Morning*, 2002), a ripely beautiful work by an old master (Iosseliani was sixty-eight when he made it), a welder, whose only pleasure in life is Sunday painting, fruitlessly tries to evade the no-smoking rule at his factory. When he gets home, his wife bosses him around to make house repairs, and his children ignore him. In the first half, the film also spies on a neighbor who owns a farm, his shapely wife, a peeping-tom priest, some gypsies, a child who refuses to brush his teeth, a Black immigrant farmhand who writes love letters to a high-school girl, and several old people slowly moving through the day—daily rituals are one of Iosseliani's chief subjects. Then the welder takes off without preliminaries and wanders to Venice, where he falls in with a drinking crowd, gets his pocket picked, and ends up working on a crew not dissimilar from the one he fled. Meanwhile, back home, life goes on: the oldest son makes a hang glider with his girlfriend; the Black farmhand marries his heart's desire; and eventually the welder returns and is gratefully accepted back into the family's routines. Dwelling on the struggle between freedom and repression in bourgeois society, Iosseliani would seem to be arguing for an anarchistic, *in vino veritas*, clochard position, but he is too much the realist to claim it will work out. If it makes no sense to obey unthinkingly the Monday-morning factory whistle, neither is flight and the avoidance of all responsibilities a viable solution. Either way, wage slave or vagabond, you are screwed. The penultimate shot is of the son's hang glider, suggesting freedom, transcendence; the final shot is the factory's smokestacks, invoking all the world's constraints.

Life on earth, as depicted by Iosseliani, is a tight little place with few variables and many limits. Indeed, despite occasional attempts to break out of his mold, through departures to Africa or the Middle Ages, there is a sense in which he keeps making the same film over and over. Which is not necessarily a bad thing—think of Ozu—and just as with Ozu, the enjoyment of Iosseliani's films is moment by moment. The pieces of his mosaic blur together. Perhaps an alcoholic's impassivity informs his movies' contemplative air of floating resignation, though I would not want to give the bottle too much credit: many drunkards do not have a scintilla of Iosseliani's artistry or intelligence.

I asked Iosseliani to explain the role of alcohol in his films. He said: "I am singing the praises of everything that is not permitted. Of the ancient vices of humanity, I chose the one that is most traditional—to drink. It demands a lot of work, a lot of savoir faire. It's a culture and there are consumers, thankfully. Otherwise, the culture would die. I think people who don't drink are dangerous," he said, looking (or did I imagine this?) straight at me. "Because they imagine they are good and they understand everything. That's pride. Because none of us understands anything in this world, and I prefer people who understand that we don't understand anything. In addition it's sociable, it creates connections between people, and everyone becomes equal, as idiots."

FILM COMMENT (JANUARY/FEBRUARY 2005)

POSTSCRIPT

I spoke to Julie Bertuccelli, the director of the lovely Georgian film *Since Otar Left*, about Otar Iosseliani. She had worked with him as an assistant director on two films, *Chasing Butterflies* and *Brigands #7*, and is currently preparing to make a documentary about Iosseliani shooting his next feature. She also played a waitress in *Chasing Butterflies*.

"He never works with actors. He prefers to cast friends or people he sees in the street who have interesting faces and ways of moving. He wants his characters just to move, and he choreographs their gestures, giving them very little dialogue. It's the body that counts. No psychology. He always shows the cast how to do it, mimicking the action like a clown. He has a very funny face. He talks to the cast during the takes, tells them what to do, as though he were directing in a silent movie, which drives the soundman crazy. He says, 'So we'll fix it in the post-synchronization, don't worry.' After he shoots he adds sound and dialogue, sometimes clumsily, but that doesn't bother him.

"He's like a poet; he has his own world. We recognize in his films always the same family—rich people who want to mix with poor—and the notion that life goes on or that friendship is more important than love.

"He is a perfectionist who will fuss over every detail until he gets it right. He may take the same shot over and over, although sometimes one or two takes is sufficient. He's an aristocrat; his glance is always a little above everyone else's head. At first I was very nervous about saying something that he would think ridiculous and excite his scorn. Sometimes he gets very angry and makes us all nervous. Then five minutes later he says, 'Have a little vodka,' and everything's fine. Usually he wants you to drink with him. I'm a girl so it was okay not to drink. When we were shooting in Georgia, it was terrible because his old friends kept coming around and asking for jobs and getting him to drink with them. They were old; they were drunk; they weren't competent like the French crew. But whenever anything went wrong, Iosseliani would blame the French crewmembers for messing up.

"He has a big book where he paints very precise storyboards. At the last minute he may change the shot on the set, but he begins with these shots carefully mapped out. He's the one who choreographs them, not the DP [director of photography]. In the morning when he's had too much to drink he can take comfort knowing he has something on paper already, a complicated *plan sequence*, say. Although sometimes he'll dawdle too long getting every prop just right, and the light will be gone. Usually Lubtchansky is very flexible and adjusts; he doesn't insist on imposing his vision on Iosseliani's film. He's philosophical; he's not a prima donna, unlike some directors of photography. But sometimes the two of them start arguing and they're like bears growling at each other.

"Iosseliani takes a lot of pleasure in making the mise-en-scène. It's always a long shot and little gestures inside it. The frame or the edge of the picture is not so important as the action and the humor, the gesture, which dictates the mise-en-scène.. He uses big camera movements with a zoom. It's very fluid. To me he's like a magician. He finds ideas suddenly, puts a tree in the middle of a closed set. He's always searching for sets or locations that will symbolically support the action.

"He believes in the director being uncompromising and insisting on his vision. When I was having doubts about my first feature, he was very encouraging. He told me: 'Don't compromise; push forward on your ideas no matter what.'"

Chapter Twenty-Five

ELIA KAZAN

Any biographer of Elia Kazan faces daunting challenges. There is first the fact that Kazan himself wrote one of the most candid, compelling, and exhaustively self-aware autobiographies, *A Life*, which would seem to have said everything necessary on the personal aspects of its subject. Second, Kazan's achievement was not just in movies but in the theater, the record of which mostly doesn't exist. Third, there is the difficulty of threading one's way through the political labyrinth which led to Kazan's testimony before the House Un-American Activities Committee (HUAC) and delivering a credible judgment on his being an informer. Fourth is the rather anomalous position Kazan holds in the rankings of American cinema and how to assess it.

Fortunately Richard Schickel, the veteran film critic for *Time* and biographer of D. W. Griffith, Marlon Brando, Clint Eastwood, and Woody Allen, is more than up to the task. He has a written a fine biography, deeply knowledgeable of all aspects of show business, abounding in wonderful throwaway aperçus (like this one about Dana Andrews's performance in *Boomerang*: "Bad actors are often good in courtroom scenes, since the emotions of lawyers, in the adversary system, are generally false—full of fraudulent outrage and fake moralizing"), thoroughly researched, analyzed, satisfying. Schickel also saw all of Kazan's theatrical productions from the 1950s onward, an advantage younger biographers would not have had. The fact that he was friendly with Kazan during his lifetime adds sympathetic warmth to the text without compromising its objectivity.

Schickel's way of avoiding duplicating Kazan's autobiography is to claim at the outset: "This book is a *critical* biography. Inevitably it contains a certain amount of information about Elia Kazan's personal life because it often intersected, to palpable effect, with his public life. But the emphasis in my research and in my thinking was always on his professional activities." In doing so, he has studied the director's voluminous production notes, deposited at Wesleyan University, which Kazan himself failed to consult while fashioning his memories into a self-lacerating, Rousseauesque confession. We come much closer here to the day-to-day mental processes of directing, and we get a more rounded picture of Kazan from the many interviews the biographer conducted with his artistic collaborators. Schickel also differs frequently with Kazan's own judgments about his work. (For instance, he rates, as I do, Kazan's first film, *A Tree Grows in Brooklyn*, much higher than the director did while refusing to be as moved by the ponderously Oedipal *East of Eden*, by which Kazan set great store.)

He gives us with quick strokes the needy, insecure immigrant who sought to seduce and manipulate everyone with his "Anatolian smile," the Group Theater hanger-on who earned the nickname "Gadget" by his knack for fixing production problems, the intense actor whom a critic labeled "the proletarian thunderbolt" for his electrifying performance in *Waiting for Left*, the quintessential actor's director who gave performers room and saw no need to tear down their egos, the uxorious husband and chronic womanizer. We are led through those heady years of Kazan's stage direction of Arthur Miller's *Death of a Salesman* and Tennessee Williams's *A Streetcar Named Desire*, his unleashing the force that was Marlon Brando, his filmmaking apotheosis with *On the Waterfront*. Kazan is portrayed as a dynamo drawing on an endless supply of exuberant energy and—however muddled his personal life—happy in his work.

There was, of course, that painful business in 1952 of his HUAC testimony, which frames and centers the biography. Schickel tackles it from every angle, including the studio politics, the non-benign activities of the CPUSA, and, not least, Kazan's expression of regret and remorse in *A Life*. He concludes, with a balanced statement: "To testify, as Kazan was obliged to do in 1952, is not a pleasant matter; it sticks in one's craw. But it should not have been, as it has become, the defining (and in the eyes of many, the indefensible) event of his life."

Some of Schickel's assertions about Kazan's significance I find more arguable. He considers Kazan's ability to command an important place in both movies and the theater unprecedented, which scants Welles, Visconti, and Bergman. He also tends to give Kazan sole credit for developing the prevalent style of modern movie acting (emotional struggle springing from an interior life), which seems to me a wave that broke on many fronts during the fifties: consider Ray's *The Lusty Men*, Zinnemann's *From Here to Eternity*, Preminger's *Man with the Golden Arm*, Cukor's *The Marrying Kind*, not to mention Cassavetes's films, which were just around the corner.

My main criticism of the book is that it fails to embed Kazan sufficiently in the context of postwar Hollywood movies, so that the reader might better understand how Kazan's punchy, aggressive filmmaking coexisted with the more formally composed styles of Nicholas Ray, Otto Preminger, Vincente Minnelli, George Cukor, Robert Aldrich, Orson Welles, as well as the older masters still practicing, Ford, Hawks, Walsh, Hitchcock, and Lang. Schickel does tell us how Kazan was initially influenced by the montage style of the Russians: the movies "offered him a visual language—close-ups, editing, insert shots—that more efficiently and powerfully permitted the poeticizing of reality than the stage ever could." He details Kazan's struggles to learn from studying John Ford a filmmaking approach that emphasized pictures and action over dialogue and delineates Kazan's shift to gritty locations, but it is still difficult to assess how conscious was Kazan's visual technique. The awkward scenes in his films lead one to wonder how much the choreographer Agnes de Mille's observation about his stage direction ("He had no visual sense. Kazan had no eyes at all.") may have carried over to his filmmaking.

In Schickel's view, Kazan was the victim of technological forces. "Kazan did not seem to notice that the kind of pictures he had been making—intense, relatively small-scale realistic dramas, shot in black and white—were becoming outmoded."

The larger question is: Where exactly does Kazan belong in the canon? I sense that he is not taught much in university film studies courses because he does not fit naturally into the familiar parade of American auteurists, Ford, Hawks, Hitchcock, Sirk, Welles. . . . Andrew Sarris placed him in that hellish category, "Less Than Meets the Eye," in *The American Cinema*, noting with some justice, "There is an edge of hysteria even to his pauses and silences. . . . Unfortunately, his career as a whole reflects an unending struggle between a stable camera and a jittery one."

My own assessment of Kazan is that he is presently underrated among cinephiles. I still resist the coercive shrillness of his big films, most notably his alleged masterpiece, *On the Waterfront* (I know I am in the minority here but dislike its sham religiosity and self-satisfied redemption), and am drawn more to his calmer works, such as *A Tree Grows in Brooklyn* and the lovely *Wild River*. I admire the magician who rendered *A Streetcar Named Desire* so beautifully onscreen and who could keep me engrossed watching the sweaty, neorealistic *Panic in the Streets*, the silly tease that is *Baby Doll*, the satiric pyrotechnics of *A Face in the Crowd*, and even the glamorously trashy *The Arrangement*. There was a smooth professional showman inside that rebel outlaw, and it is a paradox of Kazan, and of auteur criticism in general, that he was not always at his best when he was being most personal. Schickel's book, reasonably enough for a biographer, tends to argue the opposite, finding Kazan most exciting when he is closest to his primal themes: the hatred of the overbearing father, the question of loyalty, the unfulfilled promise of America, the damaged man who craves redemption. His biography does a good job of redeeming Kazan and hastening a time when film scholars can regard him neither as "less than meets the eye" nor more, but simply approaching eye level.

Chapter Twenty-Six

ABBAS KIAROSTAMI

Through the Olive Trees and *Taste of Cherry*

THROUGH THE OLIVE TREES

Abbas Kiarostami was both a neorealist filmmaker, in the tradition of De Sica, Rossellini's *India*, the Apu trilogy, and a playful formalist, with a penchant for complexly choreographed shots and meta-reflexive gestures. His method was to start with a skeletal script, which he embellishes on location with documentary footage and serendipity, giving the films an unpredictable, real-life texture. In *Through the Olive Trees*, as in the earlier two films of his trilogy, he has mostly used nonprofessionals as actors. Playing the role of the Filmmaker is a bearlike man who looks nothing like Kiarostami. Ostensibly a film about shooting a movie in an earthquake-riven area, it evolves into a romantic comedy about a genial but illiterate poor ex-bricklayer, Hossein, who keeps asking for the hand of a girl from a better family. Hossein expounds the theory that social classes *should* intermarry so that there will be more opportunity for upward mobility and cooperation: "Since I can't read, she could help our child with homework." As it happens, the girl ends up playing his mate in the film they are shooting. This leads to an enchanting scene in which Hossein, between takes, courts his taciturn beloved by telling her he would never act toward her as the Husband in their scene behaves toward the Wife.

As with the ending of *And Life Goes On*, the film's last shot is a stunning tour de force, merging landscape, title, and plot in one braided whole. The camera, high above the olive grove, watches as Hossein chases the girl and finally catches up with her in the distance. We hear not a word of their dialogue, but the sprightly music and the alacrity of his gait as he runs off suggests that maybe she has finally said yes.

TASTE OF CHERRY

Taste of Cherry solidifies Abbas Kiarostami's position as the most important filmmaker working today. In terms of international art cinema (though Americans don't know it yet), we are living in the Age of Kiarostami. Godard and Kurosawa have publicly "anointed" Kiarostami, even as the Cannes jury awarded him the Palme d'Or. This praise cannot be politically motivated solely by anti-American sympathy for an Iranian filmmaker. No, I think it is because Kiarostami offers thoughtful, concrete solutions for the cul-de-sac of the art film with his *cinema povera*, which combines modest means with large themes and emotional power; which reinvents neorealism (amateur actors, slice-of-life stories), with self-reflexive, structuralist gestures; and which employs a polished visual style that fights free of prettiness.

The New York Film Festival's program note succinctly sums up *Taste of Cherry*'s plot: "A solitary man contemplating suicide drives through the hilly outskirts of Teheran in search of someone who will bury him if he succeeds, save him if he fails." The protagonist, played by Homayon Ershadi, who has the dourly handsome looks of an Iranian Bruno Ganz, accosts in his search a laborer collecting plastic bags, a soldier, a security guard, a seminarian, and finally an assistant taxidermist who alone is willing to accept the proposition. In a sense, it's the same pattern as Kiarostami's script for *The White Balloon*—someone elicits help from a wide range of ordinary citizens—only this time, the cause is less benign. Kiarostami seems fascinated with the theme of the individual turning to the People, throwing himself on the mercy of the community. What's so piquant here is that the more they respond by wanting to help him survive, the more frustrated he gets. They can't really hear or take seriously his wish to die, nor does he bother to give them the personal details accounting for his anguish, which in any case would trivialize it. Kiarostami has enough respect for suicide as a valid option that he understands one can get to that point without having to demonstrate a lethal burden. He also knows that the suicidal prospect can have a willful, petulant side. When the seminarian starts saying that suicide is a sin against Islamic law, the driver cuts him off by retorting that if he had wanted a religious lecture he would have asked someone who had already earned his degree!

The genius of the movie is that it keeps in perfect balance the arguments for life and death. Optimism and pessimism are both seen as right—each side locked in its isolation—and so the tension builds. Strange for a film about suicide, but typical of Kiarostami, there are many comic moments and fascinating topical digressions, such as one about the Afghanistan and Iran-Iraq wars. The camera keeps pace with the protagonist, sad and restless, backgrounded by construction sites and army maneuvers. Then night falls, and we watch in a harrowingly beautiful long shot as the man sets out in a taxi through the hills to go lie in his ditch. This part is excruciating. I wanted the movie to end; I couldn't take it any more; and then Kiarostami, as if appreciating my panic, offers his controversial postscript: rough video footage of making the film, with the man who played the suicide up and about, showing that "it's only a movie"—showing that (the title of another Kiarostami film) "And life goes on." Would it have been better if the picture had ended in uncompromising bleakness, like Bresson's *Mouchette*? But then, Kiarostami apparently could not bear to let his audience leave the theater, he explained at his press conference, in such a despondent mood.

FILM COMMENT (NOVEMBER/DECEMBER 1994);

FILM COMMENT (NOVEMBER/DECEMBER 1997)

Chapter Twenty-Seven

HIROKAZU KORE-EDA

This year's Cannes Film Festival jury, chaired by Cate Blanchett, awarded its top prize, the Palme d'Or, to Hirokazu Kore-eda's *Shoplifters*. It was an uncontroversial choice, as Kore-eda's features have been appearing in the international festival circuit since the midnineties, and this latest film was applauded by critics as tightly controlled, beautifully acted, humanistic (often a requirement for Palme d'Or winners), moving, and clearly one of his best. There was, however, a lingering resistance on the part of some high-art cinephiles to Kore-eda's coronation, perhaps because in the past he has shown crowd-pleasing tendencies or because he lacks a signature art house visual style, along the lines of recent global masters like Abbas Kiarostami, Hou Hsiao-hsien, the Dardenne brothers, Wong Kar-wai. That he is considered by many the leading Japanese director of his generation may say more about the decline of that country's film industry, once on a par with the United States and France, than about his own merit, considerable as that is. Nevertheless, he consistently explores a set of personal themes, writes as well as edits his films, and is entitled to be regarded as a genuine auteur.

The movie revolves around a group of poor, non-blood-related individuals who have reconstituted themselves as a "family." If their primary reason is economic survival, they have also developed affection for one another. There is Grandma, on whose pension checks they partially subsist; a middle-aged, marginally employed couple who may or may not be married but who (we learn in time) have bonded over their long-ago murder of the woman's husband; "Sister," who earns her living at a peep show; a twelve-year-old boy who was abandoned at a pachinko parlor and adopted informally into the family; and finally, a five-year-old girl whom they come across, seemingly abandoned in the street, and whom they also take in. When the little girl is eventually reported missing by her negligent parents, the couple rationalizes that they can't be prosecuted as kidnappers because they haven't demanded a ransom.

They live and sleep together in one big room, Grandma's place, whose dense comings-and-goings are deftly captured by cinematographer Ryuto Kondo's restless, panning camera. Osamu, who occupies the father role in this unofficial family, is a construction worker who is incapacitated by a job accident. His partner, Nobuyo, is seen working in a laundry, but when the boss decides she or her work-share partner must choose who is to step aside, the other woman threatens to turn her into the police for housing the little girl, so Nobuyo is forced to relinquish her job. Neither of these employment losses registers as catastrophic; they are shrugged off as part of the expected hard-luck pattern for those at the bottom of the social scale. Nor does supplementing their slender incomes by shoplifting make them anything like hardened criminals; they are simply trying to get by. Osamu has taught the twelve-year-old boy, Shota, how to steal items in supermarkets, and Shota is now trying to pass on his knowledge to the (willing) five-year-old girl.

The pack has adapted to their constrained circumstances, and for the first two-thirds of the film we watch them operating more or less harmoniously within a daily round. Though the clan mother, Noboru, says that people like her who grew up raised by indifferent parents usually end up being cruel and indifferent to others, the opposite appears true here. Casual kindness and inclusiveness are the rule. Examining scars on the little girl's body, she says she was similarly treated: "If they say they hit you because they love you, that's a lie. If they love you, this is what they do," she tells the girl, wrapping her in a hug and beginning to tear up.

The clan goes off to the beach, where they seem at their happiest, but it is here that Grandma dies, at which point the whole scheme starts to unravel. Unable to pay for a funeral, they bury her secretly. The authorities catch on and the family is dismantled, thanks to the inflexible bureaucratic machinery of the legal system and social welfare. Key to this turnabout is the growing conscience of the twelve-year-old boy, Shota, who had begun to have doubts about shoplifting. He betrays the family by allowing himself to be

caught, injuring himself in the process, and they in turn betray him by trying to run away while he is recovering in the hospital.

Earlier, he had had trouble acceding to Osamu's request that he call him
"Dad." Toward the end, there is a scene briefly reuniting Osamu and Shota,
where the two confess their mutual betrayals. Osamu apologizes for abandoning the boy, and says, "From now on, I'm not your dad." But in Kore-eda's
universe, what makes someone entitled to be considered a parent is not so
easily determined. Shota whispers "Dad" to himself for the first time as his
bus pulls away, leaving Osamu waving on the sidewalk.

Hirokazu Kore-eda, born in 1962 in Tokyo, began his film career making television documentaries. The subject matter he chose for them would reverberate in his features. *August Without Him* (1994) initiated his studies of marginalized individuals: it focused on the first Japanese gay man who had
openly declared himself HIV-positive through sexual contact. We see him
cleverly developing and orchestrating a community of volunteers who assist
and nurse him, including the filmmaker himself. We follow the subject's
plucky activist efforts and his slow dying of AIDS, along with a coda, wherein
his community of helpers begin their grief work.

Without Memory (1996) was a documentary about a man who, because of
an illness worsened by medical malpractice, has been left with short-term
amnesia. He cannot remember anything longer than a few moments. Distressed by being unable to distinguish between dream and reality, he has to
outsource his memory to his wife and children. The fact that he had been a
paramedic to the disabled before he became ill makes his helplessness all the
more tragic. Outrageously, his condition had been brought on by hospital
budget cutbacks, which deprived him of the necessary post-op vitamins that
would have prevented the amnesia. (Kore-eda's films typically touch on some
aspect of social injustice, sometimes quietly in the background.)

An earlier documentary, *However . . .* (1991), about two suicides and the
people they left behind, fed directly into *Maborosi* (1995), his first dramatic
feature. *Maborosi* is a critically acclaimed film about a young widow whose
seemingly happy husband kills himself and who becomes obsessed with trying to figure out why. It pursues a slow, dirge-like pace, with many static
location shots emptied of people. Kore-eda admits he was smitten at the time
by his great Taiwanese contemporary, Hou Hsiao-hsien, whose long-shot,
melancholy, semiautobiographical films such as *A Time to Live and a Time*

to Die and *Dust in the Wind* set an influential standard for Asian cinema. *Maborosi* was Kore-eda's most Hou-like, self-consciously composed effort: the result was visually ravishing if a bit too arty and lugubrious. In any case, he would quickly abandon this fly-in-amber manner for more dynamic, fast-paced editing and a darting, catch-as-catch-can camera, both techniques more in keeping with his documentary background.

His next feature, *After Life* (1998), an international hit, braided together the filmmaker's preoccupations with memory, bereavement, and resilience. Its imaginative premise had the dead being sent to a processing center where each must conjure up a single memory that will allow for transition into eternal afterlife. What brought freshness to this sorting-the-dead premise was its setting, a perfectly mundane, grubby structure, most likely an old schoolhouse—in which the interviewing team try to pry open the precise memories of the recently deceased. Part interrogator, part therapist, these angelic bureaucrats view their task as getting the interviewees to face the truth while prodding even the most crabby, morose, disenchanted among the dead to admit there may have been shining moments when they were loved or were contented. The whole first hour of the movie is brisk and original while the latter part drags, as the interviewing team turns into a film crew recreating choice recollections for the benefit of the deceased.

If it's my sense that many of Kore-eda's films go on too long, I would guess it's because he labors to extract a solacing conclusion from a conflict-laden situation. Some of these redemptive moments come across as squishy, as does the frequently corny tinkling music he places in the background or the borderline-kitsch montages he assembles of characters having fun. It is part of what makes him so difficult to characterize: part commercial filmmaker, part art house auteur.

A quirky little film, *Distance* (2001), came next: this time, a group of people united by the tragic circumstance that some of their relatives were members of a suicidal sabotage cult, like the Aum Shinrikyo group that released sarin gas in the Tokyo subway, gather together in the woods to honor the deceased and to contemplate the meaning of that loss. It was followed by *Nobody Knows* (2004), also inspired by news stories, which many consider Kore-eda's masterpiece. *Nobody Knows* is about four children whose party-girl mother (played by the rock star Who) abandons them for weeks at a time, leaving them in the care of the oldest child, an ultra-responsible twelve-year-old boy. He could be the twin of Shota in *Shoplifters*. This is a repeating figure in Kore-eda: an eleven- or twelve-year-old boy, coming of age, stolid and precociously mature, who watches the indiscretions of adults and shoulders the burden of conscience. The mother is less monstrous than self-absorbed. In fact, when with her children she seems felinely charming, like their big sister: the problem is that she keeps going off with different men and forgetting to come back. The calm air of "normalcy" in the first hour, with its Ozuesque interiors, subtly plays against the audience's expectations of a horror story about child abuse. The children keep adjusting to increasingly intolerable circumstances until they are left penniless on their own, to roam the clean, suburban-looking streets of Tokyo. The film generates an uneasy suspense and is very moving, especially since the children give marvelous performances. The fourteen-year-old boy, Akira (played by Yuya Yagira, who won best actor award at Cannes) is especially poignant: I will not soon forget the withering look he gives his mother when he accuses her of being selfish and she whines, "Don't I have the right to be happy?" Unfortunately, Kore-eda doesn't know how to conclude the film and stretches it out to two hours and twenty-one minutes, its multiple endings searching for the right balance between despair and hope, with a sappy music score employed to mitigate the harshness. A powerful film it remains, albeit locked inside a bloated one.

Kore-eda has been justly celebrated for his handling of child actors. Whether professional or amateur, they have none of that coyness and insufferable preening often seen in movie children. Rather, they tend to be reserved, dignified, wary, holding secrets inside, playful among other children but never flirting with the camera. In *Nobody Knows* and *Shoplifters*, when the children converse with one another, they are far less secretive than with adults. Kore-eda's cinema-vérité background allows him to eavesdrop, to watch them covertly as though he were filming a documentary.

His stories about children under duress fit squarely in the neorealist tradition, from de Sica's *Shoeshine* and Rossellini's *Germany Year Zero* through Satyajit Ray's *Pather Panchali*, Mira Nair's *Salaam Bombay!*, and Héctor Babenco's *Pixote*. That so many hallmarks of neorealism and its descendants have focused on children must derive from the opportunity of dramatizing their vulnerability and relative innocence against a harsher social backdrop. In Kore-eda's films there is also the recurring theme of "throwaway children" who live on their own by their wits and who grow up too quickly, relinquishing the protections of childhood.

In *Still Walking* (2008), one of his most personal films, Kore-eda switched to a middle-class milieu: the stern, withdrawn patriarch who keeps his grown children at a distance; his wife, who at first seems grandmotherly but comes to reveal a much more carping, unforgiving side and whose grieving for a long-dead son prevents her from fully acknowledging her living one. "That kind of relationship, where the parent and the child are very out of sync emotionally, it's very reflective of my personal experience," Kore-eda told a *New York Times* interviewer, Dennis Lim. The surviving son has, in the face of his mother's disapproval, married a widow with a young boy, who also can't bring himself to call his stepfather "dad." Sibling rivalry and competition for scarce parental approval produce a tense, resentful atmosphere that inevitably leads to confrontation. Whatever familial reconciliations ensue feel more like a smoothing-over than a true entente. The grandmother is momentarily placated by a butterfly that follows her and that she is convinced is the spirit of her dead son. (The dead don't ever really go away in Kore-eda's films: the young widow reassures her son that his father is still inside him.)

In *After the Storm* (2016), one of Kore-eda's most delightful and consistently sustained works, a shaggy, likable novelist with writer's block and a gambling problem supports himself as a private detective, meanwhile tailing his ex-wife and trying to get back together with her. The writing is comic and the characters sharply drawn, including a marvelously pragmatic grandmother and another of Kore-eda's thoughtful eleven-year-old boys, who confesses, "Sometimes I'm a child, sometimes I'm a grownup." In the end, after the protagonist's attempt to stage a rapprochement with his ex-wife aborts and she tells him, "It's over," he says, with resignation, "I understand. I've always understood."

Between *Still Walking* and *After the Storm*, the prolific Kore-eda made several other features and television series and even tried his hand at genre pictures. *Air Doll* (2009), a mildly erotic fantasy about a life-size inflatable sex toy who comes alive and goes to work in a video store, was seen by some critics as an embarrassment, though I found it steadily watchable and finally touching. It is, in any case, another study of a marginalized figure trying to fit into an increasingly technology-crazed, dehumanized world. As she perishes in a heap of garbage, to be recycled, some floating milkweed fuzz becomes a symbol for her escaping soul. Recycling itself is a kind of reincarnation, though it remains unclear whether Kore-eda believes in an afterlife or is merely showing how his grieving characters cling to superstitious consolations.

Further branching out into genre pictures, he made *The Third Murder* (2017), a competent if by-the-numbers legal thriller that doubles as a polemic against capital punishment. But his specialty has always been the family film. His 2013 feature, *Like Father, Like Son* was well received, even winning the Cannes Jury Prize that year for best film: the plot revolves around an effort to correct an error by which two boys, now around eleven, were switched at birth, raising the characteristic Kore-eda quandary of who is the legitimate parent, the biological one or the one who can best love the child. In a follow-up feature, *Our Little Sister* (2015), three siblings discover their father has had another daughter and try to take her into the familial fold. I must admit I found *Like Father, Like Son* and *Our Little Sister* too studiously heart-warming and their visual technique too close to a conventional made-for-TV product.

They did, however, reinforce this director's exploration of his favorite theme, which I take to be the attempt, in the face of illness, emotional damage, loss, divorce, abandonment, or death, to rebuild the family unit. We see it in *August Without Him*, where the HIV patient enlists a cadre of volunteers to care for him; in *Without Memory*, where the loss of identity via amnesia is compensated for by farming out memory to the protagonist's wife and children, in *Maborosi*, where the widow remarries and tries to root herself in a second family; in *After Life*, where the processors of the dead form a supportive community; in *After the Storm*, with the effort in vain to heal the couple's separation; in *Like Father, Like Son*, via the reassignment of the two boys, for better or worse; in *Our Little Sister*, with the attempt to incorporate the newly discovered sibling; and of course in *Shoplifters*, which is explicitly about an artificially reconfigured family. That point is made explicit when Noboru, in *Shoplifters*, tells the grandmother, "Sometimes it's better to choose your own family." The grandmother replies: "If only to have no expectations."

This theme has special meaning in Japanese culture, as the traditional extended family, with its reverence for the elderly and its stay-at-home moms, began to break down. In postwar films such as Ozu's *Tokyo Story*, Kurosawa's *Ikiru*, Naruse's *Mother*, Kinoshita's *A Japanese Tragedy*, and Mizoguchi's *Ugetsu*, Japanese directors took up narratives about the fractured family unit. The theme particularly colored a type of film known as *shomin-geki*, which Joseph L. Anderson and Donald Richie defined in their classic *The Japanese Film* as "the drama about the common people.... Essentially a film about proletarian or lower-middle-class life, about the sometimes humorous, sometimes bitter relations within the family, about the struggle for existence, it is the kind of film many Japanese think of as being about 'you and me.'"

Kore-eda's warm sympathy for ordinary people may explain why his characters so often seem normal, un-quirky, relatable like "you and me," and also why a film like *Shoplifters* is popular at the Japanese box office. He refuses to pathologize his characters' misdeeds, to turn them into grotesques, as might his more edgily perverse predecessors Ōshima and Imamura. Compare, for instance, his rather tolerant handling of the parents' exploitation of their son's light fingers with the creepy couple in Ōshima's *Boy*, who collect on insurance by having their son "accidentally" hit by vehicles. Even the shocking revelation that the couple in *Shoplifters* once killed the woman's husband is casually finessed by their self-defense rationale: he'd have killed them if they hadn't gotten to him first. The tenderness with which Osamu treats his adopted son, Shota, while waiting patiently for the boy to call him "dad," makes it impossible for us to view him as anything but a good man. Noticing the boy eyeing a woman's cleavage on the beach, he assures him a man's interest in female breasts is normal, as is the boy waking up "big" with an erection in the morning. He is helping to steer the boy through puberty by quelling his fears of being weird. As a father figure he has good instincts, and even his bad ones extend from plausible premises. When the authorities demand to know whether Osamu feels guilty for making his children shoplift, he says, perplexed, "I didn't know what else to teach them."

Their lower depths humanity is underscored in a lovely scene involving sex. Earlier, Osamu had been asked when he and Nobuya "do it," given the lack of privacy in their one-room flat, and he answered solemnly that there's no need any more for that sort of physical activity, their love is on a different plane, it comes from a heart connection. Shortly after Nobuya has lost her job at the laundry, we see them alone in the flat; it's raining outside, it's very hot and the couple, stripped down, are eating noodles. Noboru is wearing a new nightgown, which she explains she treated herself to after getting fired, along with some toiletries. They discuss the possibility of opening another bar, as in the old days, but the idea goes nowhere. She whispers in his ear coquettishly. He seems alarmed, falling backward as she mounts him, he stalling for time, not ready. We cut to later: he is humming, obviously pleased with himself. "I did it. Hey, I did it, right?" She is smoking a cigarette, amused by his pride, and says, "I didn't break a sweat." She then proposes "another round?" He says, "Hey, how old do you think I am?" Just then the children enter, soaked from the rain; Osamu is spared having to do it again.

The scene works beautifully in part because of the chemistry between these two fine performers: Osamu is played by the well-known Japanese actor

Lily Franky, whom Kore-eda has used in the past and who brings a comic touch to his role as an aging, near-derelict paterfamilias. Sakura Ando's Nobuya goes from being gruff to revealing unsuspected layers of sexiness and mischief. The scene is also shrewdly written and shot in an unfussy way, with the camera remaining still the entire time, making full use of the shabby room's crowded décor. When the plot takes a darker turn soon after and the couple's way of life collapses, the memory of that warm exchange continues to resonate.

It is clear, even without his having confirmed it in interviews, that the filmmaker regards this poor family's crimes as petty. "Of course," said Kore-eda, "these criminals should be criticized but I am wondering why people get so angry over such minor infractions even though there are many lawbreakers out there committing far more serious crimes without condemnation." Yet having abstained from harshly judging the group's law breaking, he nevertheless steers them in the last part toward a climactic atonement. In a scene near the end when Osamu and Shota visit Noboru in prison (she had taken the rap for the family's illegalities since Osamu already had a criminal record), we see her uncharacteristically in a luminous close-up. No longer trying to justify her appropriation of semi-lost children, she tells her mate, "We're not good enough for him," indicating Shota, and tells the boy, "If you really want to, you can find your mother and father." I can't help thinking the shot's auratic quality is a tribute to Bresson's transcendent final scene in *Pickpocket* (referenced earlier by the shoplifting hand techniques), and maybe even a reaching for similar spiritual depth. The destruction of this atypical family's arrangement has forced them all into a more self-critical awareness of the unthinking way they had been operating. That positive conclusion is offset by a bitter last shot of the little girl, returned to her abusive mother who never wanted her, staring off in the distance and trying to make sense of it all.

NEW YORK REVIEW OF BOOKS, JANUARY 17, 2019

Chapter Twenty-Eight

AKIRA KUROSAWA

Rashomon

Review of *Kurosawa's* Rashomon: *A Vanished City, a Lost Brother, and the Voice Inside His Most Iconic Films*, by Paul Anderer

In September 1951, the Venice Film Festival awarded its top prize, the Golden Lion, to *Rashomon*, by a little-known Japanese director, Akira Kurosawa. Immediately, the film and its maker became international sensations. It is easy to see why, given its dynamic, virtuoso cinematic technique, sensationalist story involving a bandit raping a samurai's wife, Bolero-like musical score, and tantalizing if schematic structure of flashbacks contradicting one another. The title quickly entered the English language and became shorthand for the relativity of truth: "the *Rashomon* effect," invoked to indicate how witnesses to the same event may see it differently.

Paul Anderer, a professor of Japanese literature and film at Columbia University, has written a well-researched study that is part biography of Kurosawa, part cultural history of modern Japan, and part film monograph. Previously the author of two scholarly works, his prose here is energetic, straightforward, and free of academic jargon—if rhetorically overheated at times, seeming to mirror his subject's excitable style. He has chosen to focus on *Rashomon* as the fulcrum of Kurosawa's career, emphasizing what he regards as the early influences in the filmmaker's life that fed his thematic vision—specifically, its mixture of the appalling and the redemptive, the apocalyptic and the humanistic.

Among these influences was a pair of catastrophes that left his city devastated: the earthquake of 1923 and the firebombing of Tokyo in 1945. "Kurosawa's was an imagination of disaster, lined by fear and an often overwhelming darkness. His most daring work, though, moves beyond the shadows, perseveres to locate some slivers of light," writes Anderer. Kurosawa was only thirteen when the earthquake occurred, but his older brother Heigo insisted they walk through the ruins and view the corpses, ostensibly to overcome fear by staring reality in the face. That older brother exerted a major influence on Kurosawa: a movie buff, he took Akira along to silent film classics, mostly foreign, and even became a *benshi*, "The benshi were there to explain the plot but also to impersonate the characters. Such a narrator, standing at the podium to the left of the stage, made faintly visible by the lectern light, would declaim from the start to the finish of a feature film." Heigo was a celebrated *benshi*, but when sound came in, his profession evaporated. Depressed, he committed double suicide with a waitress.

Anderer views the newspapers' contradictory accounts of that tragedy as a template for *Rashomon*. More importantly, he sees the older brother looming over Kurosawa throughout his career, imbuing him with a love of 1920s silent, experimental cinema and a passion for Russian literature, especially Dostoevsky. So taken is the author with this brother motif that he locates Kurosawa's "core" narrative as "variations on a story about one brother's rise and fall, and another brother's efforts to recall their life together in its vitality, complexity, and memory-shaping force." This seems a bit farfetched, but Anderer presses on, squeezing the brother into the tail of sentence after sentence: "Kurosawa knew, of course, that a shadow character was more than just a filmic cliché, that such a character could be someone you knew intimately, someone you feared or relied on, as you would a brother." He also hits the shadow/light metaphor pretty hard.

The book's strength lies in its grasp of Japan's cultural history: the dominant literary figures; the political currents that drew the young Kurosawa into the proletarian art movement; the country's rightward shift in a militaristic direction; and the war years, when Kurosawa began directing under heavy censorship, keeping his head down; followed by the American occupation and a chance to make more expressive films. Throughout, Anderer engages in animated dialogue with Kurosawa's own written account, *Something Like an Autobiography*, at least as much as with the films themselves.

Curiously, given the book's title, there is not that much formal analysis of *Rashomon*. There is scant discussion of the acting: the seductive star, Michiko

Kyō, is mentioned only once in passing, and the superb Masayuki Mori, who plays the samurai, is singled out not for his performance but for his writer father, who committed double suicide. The great cinematographer Kazuo Miyagawa, so crucial to the film's appeal, is complimented without exploring how his work for Kurosawa contrasted with that done elsewhere. More crucially, there is no attempt to place *Rashomon* in the larger context of Japanese cinematic practice. Part of what made Kurosawa's technique stand out—and be accused by Japanese critics as too "Western" in spirit—were his extreme close-ups and the way he moved the camera. Kenji Mizoguchi and Yasujirō Ozu both disdained close-ups, and Mizoguchi used elaborate, choreographed camera movements but in long shot, affording a more detached perspective. Kurosawa has the bandit rush through the forest, keeping the mobile camera close, for a blurred, visceral effect. "Visceral" was Kurosawa's word for what he was going after. No wonder the New Hollywood princes— Martin Scorsese, Francis Ford Coppola, George Lucas, and Steven Spielberg— embraced Kurosawa as their master: he was employing a propulsive rhythm and impulse to entertain more in keeping with Hollywood films and far removed from the contemplative, transcendental style that had been the hallmark of Japanese cinema.

Anderer argues that Kurosawa required "a more melodramatically charged, allegorical framework for his postwar film project, which was to shock what had become a cultural dead zone back to life." And he quotes Kurosawa's rather self-serving 1945 statement that Japanese "'films have lost their youth, vigor, and high aspiration' [and] look like the work of tired, old men, 'who make petty judgments, have dried-up feelings, and whose hearts are clogged.' He adds, 'if we say films made by such people are mature, we should throw such "maturity" to the dogs.'" So much for the sublime postwar efforts of Ozu, Mizoguchi, Naruse, and Kinoshita.

Anderer sees Kurosawa as retrieving Japan's honor after its shameful war defeat by winning the Golden Lion for *Rashomon* and going on to make *Seven Samurai* and *Ikiru*. Those two later films are great, but in my opinion he overrates *Rashomon*. The fact that it is "iconic" does not necessarily make it a masterpiece. Visually dazzling, yes, but the hammy and naive aspects remain irksome. Toshiro Mifune's monkey-scratching bandit, charming at first, becomes one-note; the drifter's cynical laughter is excessive; and the woodcutter's rescue of the baby at the end is a crudely sentimental device. Kurosawa's Big Thoughts, like "What is truth?" and "Is humanity inherently evil?" seem trite. The problem is not that these questions are undeserving consideration but that Kurosawa poses them in a didactic, simplistic manner.

The novelist Yukio Mishima said that "Kurosawa's ideas were those a middle schooler might have." Anderer quotes this judgment but isn't fazed by it: he shrugs off the charge of sentimentality and continues to treat the director's films as philosophically profound. He is, in short, a Kurosawa enthusiast, and his book should be warmly welcomed by all who share his passion. Myself, I am a Kurosawa enthusiast more for his other films, like *Seven Samurai, Ikiru, The Idiot, Yojombo, Stray Dog,* and *High and Low*; less for the flashy *Rashomon*.

NEW YORK TIMES, DECEMBER 2, 2016

Chapter Twenty-Nine

ALBERTO LATTUADA

Mafioso

The 1960s were a heady time for Italian cinema. On the one hand, the post-war art-film demigods (Visconti, Fellini, Antonioni, Rossellini, and DeSica) were all still at the top of their form, with a younger crop, Pasolini, Berto-lucci, Zurlini, Olmi, Rosi, and Scola, bringing up the rear. On the other hand, you had an imitable strand of popular, cynical Italian comedy, by such polished directors as Alberto Lattuada, Pietro Germi, Mario Monicelli, and Dino Risi. The auteurs versus the craftsmen, you might oversimplify the situation by saying. With the passage of time, commercial comedies such as Germi's *Divorce Italian Style*, Lattuada's *Mafioso*, Monicelli's *Big Deal on Madonna Street*, and Risi's *The Easy Life* have come to be regarded as masterworks in their own right, equal in psychological complexity, visual élan, and social observation to those by the art house auteurs.

Lattuada is an especially interesting case. Brought up by his father, the composer Felice Lattuada, in an opera-drenched atmosphere, he trained as an architect but was movie-mad and helped start Italy's first film archive. He began his directorial career by making literary adaptations in the "cal-ligraphist" manner, the Italian equivalent of what the French New Wave disdainfully called "the cinema of quality," partly to evade the fascist cen-sors. After Italy was liberated by the Allies, Lattuada called for a neorealist cinema: "We are in rags? Then let us show everybody our rags," he wrote. He directed neorealist melodramas, visually exciting, such as *The Bandit*,

Without Pity, and *The Mill on the Po* (1949), before turning to the masterful comedy *Variety Lights* (1950). This bittersweet ensemble film about a troupe of traveling players—which he cowrote and codirected with his friend Fellini—was a full-fledged demonstration of Lattuada's flair for exposing the weakness of masculine vanity and the strength of female opportunism. It also demonstrated what Lattuada himself called his main theme: the isolation of each person, trying to pursue a glimmer of individual happiness in the face of society's opposing pressures to conform.

Lattuada's hard-nosed comedy *Mafioso*, which won the Grand Prize at San Sebastian in 1963, further elaborated on this theme of the individual versus the group. The plot centers of Nino, a go-getter foreman in a Milanese car factory. Though he grew up in Sicily, Nino has, for all intents and purposes, become a northerner, pacing the factory floor with stopwatch in hand, hawk-eyed against malingerers, thinking himself shrewd, nobody's fool. Now he is taking his wife and two daughters on vacation back to his native Sicily. It is the first time his slim, sophisticated, blonde wife will be meeting her husband's family, and Nino, who has been away from his homeland for years, tries to counter her trepidation by singing the praises of Sicily as a joyous place filled with scented oranges. What they encounter is instead a dour, suspicious populace, wily, cretinous, upholding a bloody code of honor. Nino's wife (Norma Bengell brings an endearing air of baffled estrangement to the role) offends the traditionalists by lighting up a cigarette and bringing gloves to her father-in-law who, unbeknownst to her, has lost a hand through gunplay. Half the townsmen are unemployed lechers; the other half work for the Mafia.

The film can be seen as a parable of regional/class tensions between the go-getter, optimistic modern northern Italy of the economic "miracle" and the poor, backward, pessimistic south, still ruled by bandits and gangsters, embodying a corrupt past that has never gone away. Nino tries to bridge these two worlds with an increasingly desperate bonhomie and gregarious flattery, but no one is fooled, especially not the old Mafia chieftain, Don Vincenzo, who calls in a favor and reenlists Nino as a hit man. Nino thus enters a world where even glib words (he had promised to do anything the old man requested) have consequences. In its pre-*Godfather*, antinostalgic, unromantic treatment of the Mafia, *Mafioso* uses the criminal-society plot to impose implacability on an otherwise random, frivolous world. Without this engine of fate we would have had merely a stock if amusing comedy about culture clash; with it, the stakes are raised. Like *Divorce Italian Style*, this grim comedy does not flinch at murder.

No one could better embody the "average Italian" in all his swagger, cowardice, hypocritical geniality and reluctant decency than Alberto Sordi, and Nino is undoubtedly one of his greatest performances. Known to his fans and critics as the Emperor, Sordi was almost handsome enough to be a matinee idol, had not a certain pudginess of cheek and largesse of nose gotten in the way. Sordi's character here is essentially that of a conceited boy who has never grown up; his vanity prevents him from understanding the iron forces arrayed against him. Yet we can't help liking him, partly because, as Sordi put it in an interview, conflating his character and himself, "Impulsiveness and vitality are part of my character," and partly because Nino takes such touching pride in his little family. He is certainly not a macho, even correcting one of the Sicilian toughs: "It's not a sign of weakness to go along with what your wife wants." Yet even here, Nino's city-dude smugness undermines his enlightened feminist message, so you're not sure whether to applaud him or laugh at him.

One peculiarity of this golden age of Italian screen comedy was that while it grew out of neorealism and never abandoned grubby locations or social facts, it nevertheless drew the opposite emotional conclusions by substituting mockery for pity. To my mind, the best Italian comedies of this period draw on a deeper sympathy than say, the manipulated bathos of a *La Strada*, by showing their protagonists' craven flaws yet still regarding them with affection.

Mafioso is filled with delicious touches, such as the discussion about alienation by several Sicilian beach bums, the alarmingly abundant welcome-home feast, or the dilemma surrounding Nino's unmarried sister's mustache. Comedy is perhaps more reliant on good screenwriters than any other genre. The bedrock of Italian film comedies was its magnificent corps of veteran dialogue writers, and *Mafioso*'s screenwriting team boasted not only the great duo Age and Scarpelli but also Marco Ferreri (who later directed his own comedies) and Rafael Azcona. Together, they imparted a ferocious satiric edge to Lattuada's smooth, agile penchant for the comedy of vanity.

When we have subtracted the contributions of superb comic acting, brilliant scriptwriting, and a splendid music score by Piero Piccioni and Nino Rota, what is left to characterize Lattuada's direction? Vivacity, in a word. He keeps the action moving by any means necessary: sometimes tracking, sometimes employing enormous close-ups or cutaways to the landscape or zooms or stylized lighting. In short, he doesn't bother to assert an austere signature style but draws pragmatically on every technique available and melds them into a vibrant, well-proportioned whole. As Edgardo Cozarinsky, the South American film director, wrote admiringly, Lattuada's "eclecticism has obstructed an evaluation of his unusual achievement. . . . The capacity to work with given materials and achieve something else, in quality and tone, has been one of Lattuada's elusive talents . . . [and his films] often prove more biting, more complex than the flashy concoctions of most 'new' Italian directors."

The alluringly realist aesthetic of sixties widescreen black-and-white has never looked better. (Granted, "realism" itself may be an artificial construct, but what makes black-and-white Cinemascope films from the fifties and sixties so convincing a signifier of the real is the amount of extra detail that spills over from the center's symmetrical emphasis, thanks to the screen's greater width relative to its height and the convention that color photography prettifies whereas black-and-white gives us a more nitty-gritty feeling of life—a carryover itself, perhaps from Italian neo-realism.) Lattuada uses the widescreen format both for a fluid mise-en-scène that embeds his characters in detailed social environments and for expressionistic effect, as when he floods the screen with noirish shadows in the night sequence before Nino's departure.

The most startling stylistic tour de force occurs when the film suddenly shifts location to New York City. We move from the horizontal parched landscape of Sicily to New York's vertical cityscape (Nino plays tourist, craning his neck at the skyscrapers, to distract himself from the murderous task ahead) and from the operatic intensity of Verdian *verismo* to the sunlit, semi-documentary manner of Don Siegel's *The Killers* or Irving Lerner's *Murder by Contract*. The Queens barbershop killing is both climactic and strangely matter-of-fact, illustrating the notion that we could all be murderers, given the appropriate circumstances.

Mafioso, this ostensibly diverting entertainment, takes us to a horror-film conclusion where Nino is left quivering with terror—at himself and the way the world operates. Yet by shuttling Nino between the dehumanizing, regimented factory and the more small-town, bestial Mafia, Lattuada suggests a rough equivalency between the two systems. They are part of the same dog-eat-dog continuum. The film has not dated in the slightest: Recent statistics show organized crime still occupies the largest sector of the Italian economy.

If anything, in its portrayal of the Mafia's long international arm, *Mafioso* looks prescient today about the globalization of crime. Faced with such fecund and enduring corruption, you can only sigh or laugh, and Lattuada's ingenious comedy inspires us to do both.

FILM COMMENT (SEPTEMBER/OCTOBER 2006)

Chapter Thirty

RICHARD LINKLATER

Before Midnight

Before Midnight, like its two predecessors, is about the flowering of a mood over a period of less than a day between two characters, an American man, Jesse, and a French woman, Céline. But where the first two films built toward erotic release, this third keeps veering off into irritable argument, which curiously seems the proof of the couple having finally achieved a true intimacy.

For those who have seen the first two movies, the shock, which comes early in the film through back-story dialogue, is that Jesse and Céline have apparently been together ever since he missed his plane to prolong his stay with her at the end of *Before Sunset*. So forget any *Same Time Next Year* schema. There will be no more chance encounters ending in sex. The spousal future they had fantasized about and dreaded in the two previous movies has arrived. For better or worse, they are a functioning couple. Toting around twin daughters—children change everything—they can no longer con each other, he with his hangdog aw-shucks Texas guile, she with her sexy Nina Simone imitations. They are stuck with each other—or not. In any case, knowledge has replaced seduction and its idealizing projections. If in their first romantic encounter they asked what might piss each other off about the other, then fudged the question, now they are prepared to enumerate.

It is hard to think of anything quite like the Before triptych in the history of American movies. We might range farther afield and consider the British 7-Up series for analogous longitudinal insight into the aging process or Bergman's *Scenes from a Marriage* for similar dissection of a couple's divergent dynamics or the exquisitely talky, modest-budgeted films of Eric Rohmer or late Alain Resnais, but these comparisons won't account for this trilogy's uniqueness. What began as a light-melancholy romance about appealing, ambitious twenty-somethings having a one-night stand in *Before Sunrise* (1995) and took on chastened but still hopeful shadings (he unhappily married, she still single) for the thirty-somethings in *Before Sunset* (2004) has now deepened immeasurably. The onset of middle age has brought the series, with timeliness, to a harsher, tougher, more implacable redoubt. The infinite possibilities of youth having permanently narrowed, the persistence of a boyishly immature or ingénue self into one's forties has lost its allure.

Ethan Hawkes's Jesse looks somewhat the worse for wear, scruffy, sloppily dressed, and no longer dewy-cute. This actor has always had something ratlike about him, with his scraggly half-beard and shifty eyes: conveying an air of apology in advance for disappointing, he's not the star you want to see in an action movie saving the planet. He's in effect the ideal representative of a self-mistrustful, vain Generation X, paralyzed by multiple options. Hawkes, brilliant here, has no qualms about making Jesse look glib and not entirely dependable: you can't blame Céline for suspecting him of trying to weasel out of his familial responsibilities. She is utterly onto his entitled sense of himself as the Writer, going on book tours and leaving her to take care of the kids, given to daily pensive strolls while she is running the household and trying to maintain a career, accepting the sexual favors of groupies and the flattery of fellow writers. At the same time Delpy's Céline has herself become rather a pill: a mother superior all too quick to get on his case. This actress, vivacious as she may be, has always conveyed an annoyingly coy, gamine self-righteousness. Together, the two principals show a nuanced understanding of their characters' vulnerabilities and contradictions, having honed them through a participatory filmmaking experience spanning three decades.

The "auteur" of the Before series must thus be considered a triumvirate. Linklater has given us a slew of fine, intelligent films about the arrested-development male, from *Slacker* to *School of Rock* to *Bernie* to the Before trilogy, his masterpiece: Hawkes and Delpy again share two-thirds of the screenwriting credit with their director. It is likely that a fair amount of the dialogue was improvised between them. No surprise that the two actors collaborated on the script, since Hawkes has himself written books of fiction while Delpy has directed and written several films of her own.

Although *Before Midnight* works as a stand-alone piece, one of the delights of seeing the three films together is realizing how much they echo one another. For instance, the "time machine" motif keeps recurring as a device for cheating fate. Jesse's seduction of Céline in *Before Sunrise* hinges partly on the premise that she should get off the train and spend time with him because she would regret it later on if she didn't. She would think of him romantically as a mysterious stranger to whom she could have gotten closer but didn't, whereas this way she has a chance to learn that he's nothing special. At the end of *Before Midnight*, Jesse again invokes the time machine, saying he has been to the future and learned that the sex they will have this night will be fantastic, so she had better stick with him. More importantly, the fault lines in their relationship (his condescension and passivity, her humorless political moralism) are to some extent anticipated in the first two films so that when the tension erupts in the third, we are not surprised.

The central conflict resolves around Jesse's belated remorse and sense of responsibility toward Hank, his thirteen-year-old son by his previous marriage. Whatever romantic ache hovers over the movie has more to do with Jesse's feelings toward his absent son than with his present partner.

While *Before Midnight* is not as locked into real-time as *Before Sunset*, it is more radically constructed around a series of five scenic blocks or units. (Linklater, who has flirted with unity of time in the past, here goes further in the experimental direction of long-duration takes, aided by the stunning cinematography of Christos Voudouris, which snares the beautiful Mediterranean light without softening it.) The first scene shows us Jesse parting from his son in the airport of a Greek island where they are vacationing. The second scene is a long drive to their vacation house, the twins sleeping in the back of the car and Jesse and Céline conversing in front. It is here that Jesse tentatively half-raises the possibility of uprooting Céline, the girls, and himself from Europe and relocating the family to Chicago, where he could at least see his son every other weekend. What is remarkable is how quickly Céline sees through this still-inchoate maneuver and how fiercely she puts her dukes up against it. She rightly judges his sense of paternal duty toward Hank as too little too late and if anything a potential fleeing of his responsibility toward her and the girls. She is also furious at him for not appreciating the important government job offer she is considering, which would keep her in Paris. The argument is side-tracked, thanks partly to Jesse's confrontation-avoiding diplomacy, and Céline asserts herself as "the general," issuing orders to the girls, now awake, and consigning her husband to the role of private.

The third scenic block is a long outdoor luncheon with friends and neighbors, in which the discussion roams from futurist technology to the creative process but inevitably keeps circling around the differences between men and women and what it might take to keep love alive between them. (This al fresco Symposium has the air of something indigenous to European art cinema, say a scene from Rohmer's *Claire's Knee*, or Sautet's *A Heart in Winter*). Shards of feminist resentment crop up in Céline's gender distinctions, but in a sense this is nothing new: from their first meeting in *Before Sunrise*, she and Jesse have always needled each other by attributing stereotyped polarities to one another: I Man, You Woman; I French, You American. She does a hilarious send-up of a bimbo gushing over Jesse upon learning he is a Writer. In turn, Jesse affects a Latin lover growl, alternately Spanish or Greek, as a come-on. Underneath the parodies they seem to be fumbling to find some way back to their original romantic spark. No longer able to wow the other with their everyday natures, they try on different personae. This role-playing is indicative of a larger problem: the unstable, provisional self. They are stuck acting the part of grown-ups while trying to remain forever young, true to their adolescent dreams, their limitless desire to get the most out of life. In any case, we know from *Before Sunrise* that they are generational imposters: Céline often thinks of herself as an old woman pretending to be young, and Jesse often feels like a thirteen-year-old boy.

Their friends, volunteering to babysit the twins, have given them the present of a night alone together in a luxurious hotel. So begins the fourth act, a long rambling Steadicam walk through the Greek island, in which the couple alternately make nice and spar. They know they are supposed to be having a romantic, sexy evening, but the conversation keeps revolving around kids and mutual mistrust. They stop in at a chapel with candles and icons. Eventually they reach the hotel suite, where the longest and most climactic block, scene 5, occurs.

The room is rather impersonal: Céline hates it while Jesse, connoisseur of anonymous luxury hotels from his book tours, approves. They start getting down to business, when a phone call from Hank interrupts the foreplay. Céline takes it, speaks sweetly to her stepson—but this time it is Jesse who ruins the mood by disapproving of a comment she makes to Hank about his mother. Sex gets tabled in favor of a no-holds-barred fight, and one realizes that quarreling has taken precedence over fornication as the means this couple has evolved for kick-starting emotional connection. Céline criticizes Jesse for his monotonous love-making and for abandoning her when the twins were first born while Jesse insists she is insane, a madwoman who revels in anger. They thus square off as jousting knights, Anger and Depression. Accusations of past infidelities ensue; Céline keeps storming out of the hotel room then coming back to fight anew, and finally she reaches a revelation, declaring that the real problem is that she no longer loves him. She leaves, this time not returning.

This could have been the Nora-slamming-the-door moment that brings the trilogy to a halt. But it is now up to Jesse to remedy things, and he does so with some resourceful fast-talking (he is, after all, a writer), deconstructing her statement and pointing toward a less romantic definition of love. In this coda, roused from his customary coasting, he has managed to spring into action, activate his old charm and bring about a temporary truce, and so the film ends, on a satisfactory note of irresolution. Of course there is nothing to say that a fourth or fifth chapter may not someday appear, but I rather think it has been taken as far as it can go. In any case, *Before Midnight* is the triumphant capstone of Richard Linklater's extended project and a remarkably sage achievement. With Terence Malick floating off into the wonder and Stephen Soderbergh retiring from the field (at least for the moment) and Quentin Tarantino clinging to the movie-mad grindhouse of his youth, Linklater seems the only one of his generation willing to address the disenchantments and readjustments of mature adults.

FILM COMMENT (MAY/JUNE 2013)

Chapter Thirty-One

HAROLD LLOYD

Speedy

In his memoir, *An American Comedy* (cowritten with Wesley W. Stout), Harold Lloyd asserted that in growing up "I was average and typical of the time and place." He continued: "Supposing Atlantic City had been holding Average American boy contests, with beauty waived, I might have been Mister America most any year between 1893 and 1910."[1] This insistence was not random; it suited someone who doggedly set out to create a type onscreen as close as he could make it to an average specimen—a mirror image of the American audience. The fact that the man who said this was anything but average, a brilliantly gifted physical performer with a genius for constructing comic gags, who moreover understood the film medium with greater sophistication than all but a handful of his peers, speaks to both his modesty and vanity. It also approaches the mystery of why audiences today may find it harder to connect with Harold Lloyd than they do with, say, Chaplin or Keaton. He embodied the spirit of the American dream that any average individual with gumption could attain success, an ideal which still seemed within reach in the twenties, pre-Depression, Vietnam, and national disenchantment.

Chaplin flirted perennially with pathos, Keaton with melancholy, while Lloyd went his merry way, positive thinking and triumphant. "It's the optimism," wrote his defender Richard Griffith, "which chiefly sticks in the highbrow craw and accounts for the continued fundamental lack of interest in him and the continued rating of him below Chaplin, Keaton and even

Langdon. *Weltschmerz* is hard to find in him." Not just world-sorrow, but alienation of any sort. David Thomson gets it right, as usual: "Early clowns are all outsiders, men incapable of, or uninterested in society's scale of merit. Chaplin admits the scale but criticizes it. Langdon never notices it. Keaton is bewildered by it, the Marx Brothers know it is a lie, Laurel and Hardy believe it will never come their way. But Lloyd became the least deviant of comedians, a man who never dreamed of being out of the ordinary." Still, this judgment needs to be complicated because only a profoundly and uniquely imaginative artist—by definition, an outsider—can take on his shoulders the burden of synthesizing the entire society around him and fashioning an archetype from it that will play in Peoria. A lack of deviancy, moreover, does not account for the sheer inventiveness and pleasure that can still be found in abundance in Lloyd's films, particularly his four best features, *Grandma's Boy*, *Safety Last*, *The Freshman*, and *Speedy*.

As good a place to start as any is *Speedy* (1928). The title alone tips off Lloyd's comic approach, which is to keep up a pace so rapid that no lingering sentimentality or sadness can attach. Fittingly, the film is set in New York City, where, the opening titles tell us, everyone is in such a rush. Whether or not the expression "a New York minute" was yet current, the idea that the city represented the forefront of hectic modernity already held sway, We see establishing shots of trains, tugboats, crowds hurtling by. Eventually we are brought to a slower neighborhood, where the most gradual, archaic of conveyances is introduced: a horse-drawn carriage, driven by Pop Dillon, the grandfather of Lloyd's love interest, Jane (played winningly by Ann Christy).

At a very basic level the film is about modes of transport, and its rhythm is largely dictated by many shots of people rushing via taxi, subway, streetcar, and motorcycle. It is also about an older way of being, a more traditionally communal, unhurried morality, in conflict with the new, headlong capitalism that sprang up in the Gilded Age with the railroad barons and now seemed well-nigh unstoppable. The plot hinges, in fact, on a villainous railroad company that seeks to drive the old horse-carriage line out of business and take over its tracks.

The protagonist, also named Harold and nicknamed Speedy, would appear to be in harmony with this burgeoning capitalist ethos: he is ambitious and in a hurry to succeed, the very prototype of "the aggressive bourgeois ego which George Santayana saw emerge in the industrializing U.S.—the go-getting American with no higher aim than diligent imitation of the rich" (Pankaj Mishra). But because he is in love with Jane and she with him, he ends up allying with Pop Dillon and his elderly neighbor-friends against the big shots. Lloyd's character may be a go-getter, but he is also fundamentally decent and in sympathy with the little guys, his coworkers at the soda fountain and the small shopkeepers who support him and Pop Dillon when the railroad company tries to seize the horse carriage. A full-scale donnybrook occurs between the neighborhood geezers and the railroad thugs, and the point of it is that our hero needs all the help he can get from the People. A veteran uses a peg leg to his advantage. A Chinese laundryman applies his hot iron to the seat of the bad guys. (There is also a loyal dog that keeps coming to Speedy's aid). A sort of popular-front politics can be read into these scenes, which if nothing else celebrate the enduring values of neighborhood diversity and local community against the impersonal corporation.

Speedy is an urban variant of the "boy with the glasses character" that Lloyd had been painstakingly refining for years. Lloyd had stumbled on the idea of giving his character a pair of horn-rimmed spectacles (lens-less, since glass would becloud the eyes' expression). The glasses were meant to signify a nerdy milquetoast type, from whom one would not expect much derring-do and who would therefore pleasantly surprise the audience when he rose to heroic challenges. Speedy is given a few other characteristics, such as being unable to hold down a job because he is so obsessed with Yankees baseball (the cameo featuring a game Babe Ruth who gets bounced around in Speedy's cab is a funny eye-opener). But in general, we are asked to accept that Speedy is simply Youth in its most healthy, energetic and accident-prone form.

Lloyd divided his movies into "character pictures" and "gag pictures": the former, like *Grandma's Boy*, took longer to set up the plot and had more psychological shadings. *Speedy* is decidedly a "gag" picture: the pace alone, with its wealth of sight jokes, dictated that there would not be enough time for much character development. In various sections, such as the long taxi-driving sequence, the gags flow outrageously yet organically into one another. "Lloyd was outstanding even among the master craftsmen at setting up a gag clearly, culminating and getting out of it deftly, and linking it smoothly to the next," wrote James Agee.[2] One extended sequence, Speedy's date with Jane in Coney Island, may suffice as example.

It begins in the subway, with much pushing and shoving. In his memoir, Lloyd quipped: "the Subway is a comedy all by itself, except to those who have to ride in it." We are treated to an ethnically and physiognomy-diverse batch of New York humanity. Speedy contrives to get seats for his girl and himself by a trick involving a dollar bill on a string, which he dangles before the seated passenger to entice him to stand, then pulls it away. A bit shady, unfair, not entirely what you'd expect from the supposedly proper Speedy, but—entrepreneurial, shall we say. At Luna Park, Speedy is the height of fatuous self-content, with his loving girl beside him and a week's wages in his pocket and a new white suit that makes him feel dressed for success. It does not take long for the suit to be marred, first by an over-friendly dog whose paws deface his trousers, then by his leaning against a freshly painted fence. Passersby laugh at the black bars on his jacket, and he has no idea why until he turns around and sees the pattern in a funhouse mirror. Next he passes a fish stand, and a crab lands in his pocket, leading to a set of mishaps in which the crab pinches ladies' behinds and steals their nightgowns. The women slap Speedy, thinking him a masher, and he reacts with astonishment and self-righteousness. The humor here flows from the Lloyd character's thinking he is an utterly normal, upstanding citizen while those in his vicinity view him as a pervert. Here I am making the case that Lloyd's comedy derives precisely from challenging his character's assumptions of being the quintessence of average and normal.

Lloyd was a veteran on one- and two-reel comedies made for producer Hal Roach (Max Sennett's rival). It was a school that taught him to brainstorm ideas with story and gag writers but never to work from finished scripts, instead trusting to improvisation and inspiration on location for building elaborations on a gag onto a comic bit. "Our lack of method is deplorable, but somehow it works," he testified. While he often directed parts of his pictures, he omitted taking directorial credit, preferring to help out the ex–gag writer designated for that job and perhaps feeling it was sufficient that the public knew the film reflected his own comic vision. Ted Wilde is listed as the director of *Speedy*, but the whole notion of directorial auteurism seems a little spurious when it comes to silent comedy. By whatever collaborations the film came about, the result hangs together as a kinetic, fast-moving affair. The Coney Island sequence, for instance, has some beautiful cutaways to the fairway at night, some surreal dream-swirls when Speedy and Jane are trying out every punishing ride, and a hysterical fantasy shot of twin babies with Harold-like spectacles in the moving van driving the couple home, which they pretend is their future abode.

By the film's conclusion, Speedy gets his girl by saving Pop Dillon's horse-carriage business, and all ends happily. In an interview with Lloyd long after he retired (he did not self-destruct, like many silent film stars, but was a business-shrewd steward of his heritage), he was asked to compare Chaplin's tramp to his boy with glasses. "Well, Charlie generally had to play the losing lover because his character was the little tramp—who was a little grotesque. If he won the girl, she generally had to be off-beat, a little screwy. . . . But with this boy with the glasses character—that was one of his virtues, he wore ordinary clothes the same as the boy next door. He was somebody you'd pass on the street—and therefore his romances were believable. And I would say that I got the girl most every time. Generally, in many of Charlie's pictures, he walked down the road at the end, which had *its* own virtue."

We see in this passage Lloyd's even-handed sense of perspective. Each—Chaplin's final saddening aloneness and his own cheerful romantic triumph—has its place. Lloyd had a purer sense than most of what it means to keep audiences laughing. He was a profound student of the art of comedy, as well as one of its most ebullient practitioners.

CRITERION COLLECTION, 2015

Chapter Thirty-Two

ERNST LUBITSCH

Review of *How Did Lubitsch Do It?*, by Joseph McBride, Columbia University Press

Jean Renoir said of Ernst Lubitsch, "He invented the modern Hollywood." Orson Welles thought him "a giant. . . . Lubitsch's talent and originality are stupefying." John Ford remarked: "None of us thought we were making anything but entertainment for the moment. Only Ernst Lubitsch knew we were making art." François Truffaut had his children watch Lubitsch movies so often they knew the lines by heart. A number of his pictures—*Trouble in Paradise, Design for Living, Ninotchka, The Shop Around the Corner, To Be or Not to Be*—are firmly enshrined in the canon of classical American cinema. Yet despite the veneration for Lubitsch by fellow directors and cinephiles, Joseph McBride feels that "Lubitsch's name has largely been forgotten" and his reputation sadly in need of recuperation. McBride, one of our foremost film historians, the author of solid, well-informed books on Capra, Welles, Ford, and Spielberg, has taken up the cudgels for his favorite master of sophisticated comedy.

Not that there doesn't already exist a body of strong writing about the filmmaker, including James Harvey's *Romantic Comedy in Hollywood: From Lubitsch to Sturges* (1987); Scott Eyman's biography, *Laughter in Paradise* (1993); and William Paul's *Ernst Lubitsch's American Comedy* (1983). But these books are all over twenty-five years old. McBride has set out, he states, to write not a biography (no need for that, since Eyman's is so satisfying) but an in-depth "essayistic investigation" of the entire oeuvre: "What has been lacking until this critical study has been a sustained, systematic, fully integrated overview of both Lubitsch's German and American work. Without seeing his career as a single, unified whole, it cannot be fully understood or appreciated." His commentary on the recently restored silent German films, many of which are now available on YouTube and DVD, is especially pertinent.

Lubitsch was born in 1892 and grew up in Berlin. His father, a Russian Jewish émigré, ran a tailoring establishment, specializing in coats for large women. He was something of a dandy and ladies' man (a prototype, perhaps, of the filmmaker's many philandering characters) and left most of the day-to-day operation to Lubitsch's practical mother. Young Ernst, an indifferent student, was enthralled by acting and managed to join the troupe of the great theatrical director Max Reinhardt, who cast him in minor roles—a source of frustration, though he picked up technique and aesthetics by observing Reinhardt.

He also began acting in his own short comic films, such as *Meyer from Berlin* (1919) and *Shoe Palace Pinkus* (1916), often playing a clumsy go-getter shop boy named "Sally," which drew on his family background in retail. While Lubitsch's parents were only secular, assimilated Jews, his onscreen persona read as blatantly Jewish. It was ethnic comedy, a staple at the time, though McBride worries at length whether Lubitsch's screen persona might have inadvertently fed antisemitic sentiment. I doubt it—any more than Jerry Lewis, Mel Brooks, or Woody Allen did. If you can overcome Lubitsch's outrageous facial mugging in the broadest silent film manner, these comedies centering on a lusty schlemiel are actually quite fun.

Having become a popular screen presence in Germany if not quite a star, Lubitsch was at the same time directing movies with other actors. There was the risqué cross-dressing comedy, *I Don't Want to be a Man* (1918); a deliriously zany *The Wildcat* (1921), with its frame adjustments in every geometric configuration; *The Doll* (1919), in which a young girl pretends to be one to offset the fears of a leery bachelor; *Kohlhiesel's Daughters* (1920), a delightful tale in the snow about two sisters, a plain, hard-working one and the other pretty and frivolous (both played by the same actress); and most accomplished of all, *The Oyster Princess* (1919), revolving around the marriage-intent daughter of an American millionaire.

You can see Lubitsch trying out in these films every stylistic camera flourish (getting them out of his system, as it were), as well as employing motifs and plot devices he would incorporate later. *The Doll*, for instance, opens with the director himself putting together, like a magician assembling his props, a cardboard set that will dissolve into a life-size replica—a forerunner of his meta-gestures conversant with the audience (like Maurice Chevalier addressing the camera in the 1929 film *The Love Parade*). The full-out wacky dance sequence in *The Oyster Princess*, "the Foxtrot Epidemic," prefigures choreographed numbers in his and everyone else's musicals. These silent German comedies are a minor revelation: they may not be masterpieces, but they are exuberantly entertaining and inventive.

Lubitsch next tried his hand at a series of historical spectacles, the most satisfying of which was *Madame DuBarry* (1919), starring the seductively sensual Pola Negri as a factory girl who sleeps her way to the top (Louis XIV, played by Emil Jannings). Its international box office success was followed by *Anne Boleyn* (1920) and *The Loves of the Pharaoh* (1922), huge, laboring machines with "casts of thousands," as they used to say, which earned him the nickname "the European Griffith."

Though left-wing critics disapproved of Lubitsch's neglect of socioeconomic historical factors, opting as he did to focus on the personal conflicts and passions of his regal protagonists, McBride tries to make the case that he was smuggling in liberal progressive ideas. Essentially, Lubitsch was apolitical and oblivious to Germany's upheavals, preferring to build dream worlds out of his imagination and to hone his craft. By the early 1920s he had acquired a mastery of every aspect of film production and could handle big and small budgets and even the most difficult actors—and so he was summoned to Hollywood in 1922 by Mary Pickford to direct her in a departure for America's sweetheart, *Rosita* (1923), in which she played a street singer in Seville who is propositioned by the king.

It is sometimes incorrectly assumed that Lubitsch was part of the wave of German émigré talent fleeing Hitler. In fact he was already ensconced in the American motion picture industry a decade before their arrival. Facing initial hostility from American patriots bristling at employment of "the Hun," Lubitsch made a quick adjustment to his new country, loving as he did the American spirit of casual optimism and the technical superiority of American film crews, though he never lost his thick German accent.

Of the dozen silent films he made in Hollywood during the 1920s, two stand out as masterpieces: *The Marriage Circle* (1924) and *Lady Windermere's Fan* (1925). In these narratives of conjugal misunderstandings, adulterous temptations, love triangles, self-deceptions, and stoic readjustments to spousal flaws, he refined his visual approach, tamping down the theatrical German expressionist mannerisms and replacing them with more American, "invisible" storytelling conventions. There were subtle tensions arising from engaged and averted glances, movements toward and away from suitors, in high-ceiling settings that dwarfed the occupants and emphasized their emotional solitude. Intertitles were cut down to a minimum so as not to interrupt the camera's telling.

Most important, perhaps, was the sophisticated, adult treatment of male-female relationships. In *The Marriage Circle*—the film Renoir regarded as commencing the modern Hollywood film—a contented wife's best friend tries to steal her husband away. The woman's sexual hunger is stunningly overt yet also understandable, an occasion for sympathy, with none of the judgmental Puritanical attitude found in other Hollywood films of the period. Lubitsch would always evince a tolerance and even affection for human frailty.

So arose what came to be known as "the Lubitsch touch." I wish it were possible to write about this great filmmaker without invoking that hoary, reductive cliché, but at the very least it tells us that long before the auteur theory, critics and the public alike appreciated that this director had a personal style that persisted from film to film. Usually the term referred to something naughty: his ellipses when it came to couples having sex, the closed door from which one could infer what was happening. As Truffaut said about these ellipses: "In the Lubitsch Swiss cheese, each hole winks."

Certainly Lubitsch was celebrated for getting around the censors, partly by innuendo, partly by setting most of his films in Europe, where morals were assumed looser (those continentals, what can you expect). But the Lubitsch touch also had to do with respecting the audience's intelligence, not spelling everything out. I like what film critic Andrew Sarris said: "A poignant sadness infiltrates the director's gayest moments, and it is this counterpoint between sadness and gaiety that represents the Lubitsch touch, and not the leering humor of closed doors."

For someone who had perfected silent movie grammar, taking it to a point of "pure cinema" (as Hitchcock, a Lubitsch fan, approvingly termed it), one would think the introduction of sound might have posed problems, but Lubitsch again adjusted. If anything, the addition of sound helped him develop his most urbane comedy by allowing him to emphasize the disparity between the stated and the unexpressed. Though his films were critical successes and highly influential within the industry, they rarely scored big at the box office. He was able to keep making them because, even when they lost money, they brought the studio prestige. Still, Harry Warner feared they might be *too* intelligent and worldly, going over audiences' heads, and finally Lubitsch departed Warner Brothers for Paramount Studios, where he found a more congenial home for his European reconstructions. As he famously quipped, "I've been to Paris, France, and I've been to Paris, Paramount. I think I prefer Paris, Paramount."

At Paramount he launched a series of five musical comedies, starting with *The Love Parade* (1929) and concluding with *The Merry Widow* (1934), which usually featured Maurice Chevalier and Jeannette MacDonald. He is often credited with initiating the musical genre; his biggest contribution may have been liberating it from a revue structure and integrating musical numbers as parts of the story. The best of the series was the last, *The Merry Widow*, but by that time, in the midst of the Depression, audiences were tired of films about queens and millionaires in Lubitsch's mythical kingdoms. McBride speculates on what this middle-class Jewish boy was doing making so many pictures about English aristocrats and Mittel-European royals: was this a form of social climbing? "Lubitsch's continual return to the closed world of nobility that he, as a doubly exiled Jew, could not enter can be seen as the sign of a blocked attempt to keep repeating an act of fealty in the vain hope that the kings and princes, the uniformed nobles, and their grandly gowned women would eventually allow him entrance, that they would welcome this brash upstart as an equal."

Perhaps, but I see it differently. Lubitsch was no royalist. His sympathetic interest was in showing how these crowned heads were human and fallible, prisoners of their unfulfilled desires like everyone else, at the same time providing entertaining fantasies (with pinches of gritty humor) set in dreamy architectural environments. As Samson Raphaelson, the preternaturally gifted screenwriter who collaborated on nine Lubitsch films, said, "We just laughed our heads off at kings. . . . We were just having fun."

Trouble in Paradise (1932) marked the apotheosis of Lubitsch's and Raphaelson's subtle, indirect style. This comedy about a pair of romantically involved jewelry thieves (Herbert Marshall and Miriam Hopkins) who try to bilk a wealthy widow (Kay Francis) gets complicated when the man finds himself falling in love with his prey. Since both women are so desirable and appealing, the audience finds itself wondering how this "insoluble conflict," in McBride's words, can ever be resolved. Lubitsch may not have been moralistic, but his intent was "to explore the kind of moral issue he finds most compelling: how men and women should treat each other." In this case, as in *The Love Parade*, he is showing how "men who are toying with women's passions are forced to face the consequences of their deceptions and recognize their own deeper emotional natures."

When he first saw *Trouble in Paradise* in college, McBride was convinced that "I've just seen this guy's masterpiece," and he has apparently held tight to that opinion, devoting roughly three times more space to it than to any other Lubitsch film. I find the film brilliant but a trifle glacial. My favorite would be *The Shop Around the Corner*, with its warm, squabbling ensemble of Matushek & Company employees. Raphaelson himself felt similarly: "I cared more about those people than I did about the people in *Trouble in Paradise*. I thought the people in *Trouble in Paradise* were just puppets." Lubitsch adjudicated the matter thus: "As for pure style I think I have done nothing better or as good as *Trouble in Paradise*," while "As for human comedy, I think I was never as good as in *Shop around the Corner*." I guess I prefer human comedy to pure style.

Puppets or no, Lubitsch managed to extract magnificent acting out of his three leads: Miriam Hopkins was her usual bouncy self, but Kay Francis, elsewhere often decorously becalmed, was never so sparkling and vivacious, and the sometimes wooden Herbert Marshall conveyed a pained sense of ambivalence beneath his suave exterior. There is a beautiful moment near the end of *Trouble in Paradise* when these two, Francis and Marshall, the latter's con exposed, stare at each other for long seconds with supreme awareness, a look filled with disenchantment, affection, and regret, shame on his part and forgiveness on hers.

Lubitsch was famous for getting actresses to deliver their best performances. Greta Garbo, as the Soviet zealot who bends under the charm of Paris in *Ninotchka* (1939), was at her most luminous and quicksilver, and Irene Rich was great as the maternal blackmailer in *Lady Windermere's Fan*. Margaret Sullavan's tightly wound, melancholy charm and tremulous voice adroitly suited the idealistic, disputatious Klara in *The Shop Around the Corner*. Jeannette MacDonald was never as vulnerable or touching as in the Lubitsch musicals. Molly Haskell singled out the way "he created women characters of depth and complexity whose originality was glossed over in the general designation of 'Continental sophistication.' But Lubitsch's worldliness was as deceptive as his touch. If anything, it was in going against the grain of the polished surface, in the hints of awkwardness with which he invested his men and women, that they—particularly the women—acquired complexity."

A female reporter, interviewing Lubitsch on the set, came away thinking that no man understood women better. Here we see the difference between filmmaking and daily life: both his wives divorced him, claiming neglect. The first said that her husband was "99 percent in love with his work and had no time for home." She cheated on him with his first screenwriter, Hans Kraly. Raphaelson thought the problem was that "he liked women who treated him badly." But Lubitsch himself cheerfully admitted he was a workaholic. "I think I am possessed only of a fascination for the work I have chosen to do. I am so engrossed by the production of a film that I literally think of nothing else."

His involvement was total: he produced; directed; cowrote the screenplay; oversaw every detail of the set designs, costumes, and music; and even edited the films. It explains how Frank Capra would say: "Ernst Lubitsch was the complete architect of motion pictures. His stamp was on every frame of film—from conception to delivery."

Conception began with the script. Lubitsch and his screenwriters would talk through every line and gesture, looking for ways to avoid cliché and do it differently while a stenographer took it all down. Billy Wilder, who was the director's chief acolyte and who later kept a sign in his office, "How would Lubitsch do it?" (hence the title of McBride's book), said that Lubitsch was at bottom a writer, and in fact the best film writer he ever knew. When they worked together on *Ninotchka*, some of the best dialogue bits came from Lubitsch, such as "the last mass trials were a great success. There are going to be fewer but better Russians."

Once the script had been nailed down, Lubitsch rarely deviated from it. Improvisation was for the scriptwriting phase, not the actual shooting. Lubitsch, the ex-actor, would act out each role—a practice that some professionals might ordinarily take offense at, but it "was his way," notes McBride, "of ensuring that they would follow his preferred rhythms, which are integral to the humor and emotion of his work." It was also his way of keeping the actors entertained, which he regarded as his directorial duty. He would play the piano between takes: his love of music was a constant.

Toward the end of his short life—he died in 1947 at the age of fifty-five—he expressed some reluctance at having become so entranced with the spoken word that he'd neglected telling the story purely via the camera. The purity of his cinematic technique, however, was if anything enhanced by its rigorous economy: if you look at the scenes between James Stewart and Margaret Sullavan in *The Shop Around the Corner*, the blocking and compositions are perfectly appropriate, the camera movements slight yet pleasingly adjusted to the mood. Truffaut said of Lubitsch: "There's not a single shot just for decoration; nothing is included just because it looks good. From beginning to end, we are involved only in what's essential."

At the same time, he was able to stage the bravura theatrical scenes of *To Be or Not to Be* (1942) with panache. In that outrageously audacious film, Lubitsch is exhibiting his affection for the communal theater milieu while reviving memories of his apprenticeship with Reinhardt's troupe. Jack Benny, previously wasted in movies, gives an unforgettable performance as the vain, hammy actor Joseph Tura, who is trying to protect his sorely cuckolded ego while jousting with the Nazi commandant, known as "Concentration Camp Ehrhardt." By the way, with this picture Lubitsch returned to the Jewish themes he had begun as a young man—though perhaps his comic sense all along can be seen as an expression of typically Jewish humor. Enno Patalas, the German scholar who restored many of Lubitsch's silents, wrote: "Lubitsch was not ashamed of being Jewish—quite the contrary. In a 1916 interview—the earliest that survives—he says that 'Wherever Jewish humor is seen, it is likable and well-crafted, and it plays such a major role everywhere that it would be absurd to dispense with it in the cinema.' Jewish culture is the only culture with a feeling for comedy at its very heart. Jewish humor cuts the ground from beneath the earnestness of life—a way of asserting oneself in a hostile world." That could certainly serve as a rationale for *To Be or Not to Be*, a movie that riled feathers when it opened by refusing to be earnest about Nazis.

In "removing some of the barriers to appreciating Lubitsch," McBride brings up ways that the director might be seen as out of touch with contemporary audiences, only to defend or excuse him. He queries that wonderfully elegiac late Lubitsch work, *Heaven Can Wait*, about an unexceptional man (Don Ameche) who loves his wife (Gene Tierney) but cannot stop chasing women. In her patient acceptance of her husband's straying eye, is not Lubitsch condoning the double standard? My own reading of the film is that he is neither condoning nor condemning it, only saying it exists. It is the wife who emerges as the film's hero, stubbornly determined to wait out her "little boy" of a husband. And the casting of the soft, amiable Ameche as the skirt chaser instead of a more virile type, like Clark Gable or Robert Mitchum, lends an air of pathos to the story. In general, Lubitsch seems to ridicule the Don Juan figure by exaggerating his magnetism to the point of absurdity— like the multitudes of women camp followers who crowd the streets in *The Wildcat* or the dozens of women at Maxim's who congregate around Maurice Chevalier in *The Merry Widow*. Chevalier is such a preening, self-satisfied caricature of a fop in these musicals that one cannot take him seriously as a lady-killer.

Was Lubitsch a sexist or a feminist? To me the question seems pointless. When we watch a Lubitsch film, we reenter not only the past mores of an old movie but also a past that he conjured from his imagination, that was fast disappearing or had already vanished in the eyes of his contemporaries. His penchant for adapting old Hungarian plays and Viennese operettas ensured a certain off-kilter relationship to the American present. Even in his heyday he was always one step ahead of being dated, or two steps behind. There was always something delicate and fragile about his graceful constructions that invited special consideration.

Maybe we have to examine the whole notion of being dated. I'm sure there are young people who feel that any black-and-white movie is dated, not to mention any silent, but that's their loss. As I see it, when enough years after the introduction of a truly fine artwork have passed, it has outlived the threat of datedness. Think of Lubitsch's miraculously tender last film, *Cluny Brown* (1946). Can such tenderness date?

McBride concludes his excellent, authoritative book, which offers all the necessary points to be made about Lubitsch, is chockful of cultivated insights and astute quotes, and is even forthright about his subject's clinkers (*The Man I Killed, That Uncertain Feeling, Bluebeard's Eighth Wife*) with a lament. Having decried the gross-out comedies of today and the action movies showing "giant robots smashing into each other," he wonders what became of the Lubitsch sophistication, maturity, and wit. Is there some way to get it back into films? (We need to remember how rare it was, even in its day.) "Whether or not Lubitsch's cultural influence can be revived, those of us who love him need to keep insisting on its importance," writes McBride. Insisting? How un-Lubitschean. Those of us who love, I mean *love*, Lubitsch know that such clamorous advocacy is unnecessary. His lovely pictures await those who are meant to find them.

NEW YORK REVIEW OF BOOKS, JUNE 28, 2018

Chapter Thirty-Three

SIDNEY LUMET

Long Day's Journey Into Night

Where does Sidney Lumet belong in the cinematic firmament? In his forty-year, forty-film career, this man gave us a surprising number of satisfying movies—or let us say satisfying *parts* of movies—exceeding almost any other American director of his time. Whether we are talking about his peaks (*Long Day's Journey Into Night*, *Dog Day Afternoon*, *Prince of the City*, *The Verdict*), his partial successes (*Serpico*, *Twelve Angry Men*, *Running on Empty*, *Bye Bye Braverman*, *Just Tell Me What You Want*, *The Hill*), or even an overripe hit like *Network*, which initially seemed preposterous and meretricious but that now looks compelling thanks to the dissonant but curiously meshing acting styles of William Holden, Faye Dunaway, and Peter Finch, all have an absorbing, warm vitality. In his long career he careened cheerfully all over the map, working in a variety of genres, and nourished as independent a producer-director identity as Otto Preminger, without ever sinking to studio hackery. Even his debacles, like *The Wiz* and *A Stranger Among Us*, seem to have been freely chosen, embraced with as much gusto as Preminger's awful swan songs, *Rosebud* and *Skidoo*. Unlike Preminger, however, Lumet ended his career with a fiercely well-made movie, *Before the Devil Know You're Dead*, featuring beautiful performances by Philip Seymour Hoffman and Ethan Hawke. Perhaps because he lacked a signature visual style, Andrew Sarris, Pauline Kael, and David Thomson all expressed doubts about his auteurist credentials, though European cineastes valued him more. Even I, a dedicated Lumetian, would not place him in the pantheon, albeit in a more elevated category than the "Strained Seriousness" accorded him by Sarris. I would rather grant him a corner in "Lightly Likable," along with such veterans as Michael Curtiz and Delmore Daves. But Lumet *is* maddening because his virtues (humanity, strong direction of actors, vigorous storytelling, novelistic background detail, an amazing feel for New York locations) are inextricably knotted up with his vices (visual sloppiness, improbable plotting, a penchant for moralizing). Just when you want to venerate him, he disappoints, and just when you want to discount him, he entertains.

Even his most exigent critics admit that Lumet's 1962 adaptation of Eugene O'Neill's *Long Day's Journey Into Night* was superb, and any evaluation of the director must hinge partially on what one thinks of this acclaimed, imperfect, but magnificent film.

Lumet, who grew up in the Yiddish theater, was never one to shy away from filming a play, as his adaptations of Chekhov, O'Neill, and Tennessee Williams attest. So it was only natural for him (prodded by producer Ely Landau, a tireless proponent of filmed drama) to take on O'Neill's masterwork, arguably America's greatest play. Though written in 1941, *Long Day's Journey* did not see publication until 1956, when it also premiered on Broadway, in a legendary production directed by Jose Quintero that included Fredric March, Florence Eldridge, Jason Robards Jr., and Bradford Dillman. Of the original Broadway cast, only Robards, as Jamie, the older son, transitioned to the film version. Ralph Richardson as the miserly, ex-matinee-idol head of the Tyrone family, was a significant upgrade, being a much more resourceful actor than March, and Katharine Hepburn, likewise a cut above Eldridge, turned in one of her most indelible, eerily incandescent performances. Dean Stockwell replaced Bradford Dillman, an even trade, looking very James Dean–ish as the younger brother, Edmund.

Lumet made no attempt to "open up" the stage play cinematically, instead restricting the action almost entirely to the living room of the Tyrone's Connecticut cottage, with a few scenes on the grounds outside. This strategy reinforced the claustrophobic intensity of an Irish American family getting on each other's nerves. Interesting to consider that the play was written in the forties, the same decade that the Irish playwright Beckett wrote *Waiting for Godot*, and though the two works are generally viewed as representatives of opposite realist/absurdist aesthetic tendencies, from today's vantage point they would appear to have much in common. The Tyrones are as trapped in their existential wasteland, their endlessly recycling conversational dead ends, as Vladimir and Estragon. Indeed, O'Neill's dialogue pattern here is for one Tyrone to begin rehashing some boast or resentment, only to be interrupted by another, "Not that old story again!" or pointedly told to shut up. Harsh reproaches are followed by smoothing over and forgiveness, only to give way to more emotional scab picking; self-deceptions are caught in midair and converted into bursts of self-awareness, only to be succeeded by more lies, denials, self-defenses. Some revelations do make appearances along the way, moving the action forward, though they are soon covered over by the same wounding retorts and passive-aggressive maneuvers. The pleasure is in watching this skilled verbal clan go at it, stymied as much by their love for each other as by their willingness to blame one another for their misery.

The elder Tyrone receives the brunt of this blame, and Ralph Richardson, as the vain, testy, stubborn, baffled patriarch who seeks to ward off the scapegoat crown, both admitting and refuting the charges, is a wonderment of behavioral shadings. Katharine Hepburn, as the drug-addicted mother who is losing her mind, gives a quicksilver performance full of sudden transitions. The Parkinson's disease that had made this actress's later performances sometimes painful to watch is here suitably matched to the character, whose hands, according to O'Neill's instructions, are meant to be seen trembling. Of course, the rail-thin Hepburn cannot fulfill the play's description of Mary as having put on weight; her statements to that effect sound like the delusions of an anorexic. But her real achievement is in not coming across as gallant: she doesn't try to win the audience's sympathies over to her character's self-pity. What can be said of Robards's riveting, bravura performance as the drunken failure who seeks to protect his younger brother at the same time as ruining him, other than that it is pitched at the exact borderline between stage and film acting, sometimes bravely or heedlessly crossing to the former. Dean Stockwell seems the only one functioning within the more restrained conventions of screen acting, but there is good reason for that: the two older Tyrone characters are, after all, professional actors given to posturing, Mary Tyrone is a hysteric actress manqué, and Edmund is, by contrast, an introverted would-be writer, an autobiographical surrogate for O'Neill himself. His is the most weakly developed character, the family's spectator, and there is only so much Stockwell can do with this underwritten part.

If Lumet refuses to disguise the theatricality of the source material, he brings an impressive array of cinematic technique to its moment-by-moment realization: tracking shots following Mary around the room, severe close-ups of Edmund, camera placements extremely high and low, framings through banisters, frenetic pans of tussles, and long sequences when the camera just stays put, watching these phenomenal actors interact. There are the occasional gauche, unnecessary cuts, but overall, the impression is one of a director in vibrant sync with the material, trying to extract the most dynamic visual response to the characters as they form into duets, trios, and quartets. Lumet was aided by the great cinematographer Boris Kaufman (*L'Atalante*, *On the Waterfront*), whose masterful black-and-white photography played cunningly with shadows, in line with the characters who keep turning lamps on and off—the father to save on electricity, his sons to thwart their miserly dad. Richard Sylbert's production design was quintessentially genteel-shabby, the editing by Ralph Rosenblum crisp and on point.

Lumet, extremely proud of this film, defended it from critics like John Simon, who accused him of making "canned theater." He said: "They didn't know cinematic technique from a hole in the wall. There was more sheer physical technique in that movie, in its editing and camerawork, than anything you are likely to see for twenty years." I agree. Lumet's forte was the persistence with which he was able to look at weakness and failure in his characters without flinching or proposing premature redemption, and *Long Day's Journey Into Night*, in retrospect, seems the perfect vehicle for this director's bleakly humane vision. Moreover, the film is one more refutation of that old, false idea that the two media, theater and movies, are bad for each other and must be kept apart. At 170 minutes, this adaptation is not quite the full play (some dialogue has been trimmed), but it's still staggeringly monumental and will wring you out.

Lumet himself compared filmmaking, in an interview with Peter Bogdanovich, to "making a mosaic. You take each little tile and polish and color it, and you just do the best you can on each individual tile and it's not until you've literally glued them all together that you know whether or not you've got something. Those of us who have had good work can admit the truth, which is: good work is an accident. That's not being falsely modest, there's a reason that the accidents are going to happen to some of us and will never happen to other people: we've got some sort of knowledge, or instinct, of how to prepare the ground for the accident to happen."

I think this honest statement says a lot about what makes Lumet's films so exciting, jumpy, and inconsistent. In working with each piece as a mosaic tile, Lumet tends to lose sight of a systematic approach to the visual design:

one scene will have breathtakingly composed overhead locations; the next will resort to a TV-movie mash-up of close-ups and counter-reaction shots. Some images will be carefully lit or underlit, as when Andrzej Bartkowiak was Lumet's brilliant DP in *The Verdict*; others will look grainy and slapdash. In the same interview, Lumet surprisingly listed Carl Dreyer as the film-maker he respected most. But it was Dreyer who eloquently lamented the absence of a consistent visual approach in Danish films.

We cannot say that Sidney Lumet rigorously works toward a conscious visual goal. But he does have, I think, an artistic will to complete a picture, whatever compromises that necessitates, and to try to get onscreen some of his own menschy, edgy life force. I watch the backgrounds in his movies with some of the same pleasure that I get from a Renoir or Ophuls film, even if I have to roll my eyes at times at the story in the foreground.

CINEASTE (SPRING 2013)

Chapter Thirty-Four

DAVID LYNCH

Mulholland Drive

Mulholland Drive is a film so compelling, engrossing, well directed, sexy, moving, beautiful to look at, mysterious, and satisfying that it threatens to unnerve the aesthetic prejudices of those, like myself, who are not intrinsic David Lynch fans. For die-hard Lynchians, it will be catnip, but what about the rest of us skeptics? How will we explain to ourselves this sudden embrace of a mannerist who in the past had seemed prone to jejune self-indulgence, capricious phantasmagoria, and vulgarity?

There is the cinema of character (Rohmer) and the cinema of visual dream (Lynch). The first, my preference, is generally what is taught in film schools; the second is often what the young flock to on their own. Of course, one would have to be blind to deny Lynch's brilliance as a filmmaker, his gift for stunning images, passages, and moods that together constitute a private universe. But that was the problem: it was a universe so precious and pleased with itself that it did not seem to need my appreciation. I could simply sidestep Lynch's feast of the uncanny as not my cup of tea. I have no stake in youth culture, no need to appear hip by lauding the overpraised *Eraserhead*, his debut film, with its midnight cult-movie grotesqueries, or the overwrought sci-fi busyness of *Dune*. I was pleasantly surprised by *Elephant Man*'s restraint, but Lynchians dismissed it as a contract-job adaptation, just as they would later mistrust his amiable *The Straight Story*, which also departed from the master's coercive portentousness. *Blue Velvet*, Lynch's signature film, I found ravishing and hypnotic yet periodically silly. I could not take seriously its Boy Scout's allegorical journey into darkness, its fasci-nation with the lurid, its investment in unmasking the American Dream (as if anyone still believed in that), side by side with its quest for innocence. *Wild at Heart* was worse, a half-baked mixture of *Wizard of Oz* faux-naivete and *Touch of Evil* sinister. The television series *Twin Peaks*, intriguing up to a point, became too coy and burdened by surrealist shtick. But I found myself swooning at *Fire Walk with Me*, a *Twin Peaks* theatrical spinoff that worked precisely because it stopped trying to make plot sense and entered a trance space, especially in the nightclub scenes. Given my preference for just those passages in *Blue Velvet* that had been most transfixed, most druggy and slowed-down, I was beginning to think that Lynch succeeded best when he surrendered to a dreamy calm, making time appear to stand still. I was almost willing to declare myself a Lynchian after *Fire Walk with Me*, but I was dis-appointed by the narrative incoherence of his next film, *Lost Highway*, which, despite its alluring visual surface, features so much dissolution of identity that in the end there are no characters to follow. The question of who is in whose dream may make a nice haiku, but it becomes tiresome, I think, as a storytelling premise.[1]

I've dwelled on the pitfalls of Lynch's style to emphasize that *Mulholland Drive* triumphs not from any abandonment of that ominous manner but from its maturation or fulfillment, brought on by small adjustments to the formula. For example, there are still grotesque, surrealist touches, but with-out quite the same preening. Identities are shuffled, as in *Lost Highway*, but not before the characters have been solidly established. A much greater degree of control is in evidence, and there is a new current of adult feeling that even-tually displaces the old, one-note titillation of foreboding or at least coexists with it.

Mulholland Drive begins with a black limousine snaking through the Los Angeles hills, with the lights of the city that W. H. Auden called "the Great Wrong Place" (in tribute to Raymond Chandler's mysteries) shining below. Angelo Badalamenti's score supplies the mood, the ache. A bruised brown and blue palette, tight compositions: a hot, morose brunette in the back seat (Laura Elena Harring) is about to be shot, executed, but is saved by a collision with another car. She stumbles from the wreck in a black cocktail dress and makes her way in high heels down the hill, where she finds an apartment court to hide out in. Suffering from a concussion, she has lost her memory, and her handbag contains no ID, only piles of cash, probably stolen.

We've been here before. Lynch uses film noir as an atmosphere, a gesture, a lost paradise. Until the film takes hold, a sense of belatedness hovers over the enterprise: one thinks not only of older noir (the classically L.A. apartment court of *In a Lonely Place*, the gang's threatened retribution in *The Killers*) but also of the more recent revisionist cycle that plays with the legend of Los Angeles and fiddles with structuralist memory time schemes (*Pulp Fiction*, *Memento*, *The Limey*, *L.A. Confidential*). Then something more gripping starts to happen, partly through the introduction of a counterweight to noir, a perky little blonde named Betty (Naomi Watts), just flown in from Canada, and the resulting chemistry between these two dissimilar women.

Betty is wholesome, optimistic, determined to take the town by storm or to help out a stranger in need because it's the right thing to do. There is something comic in the pairing of the buoyant, new-kid-in-town, Doris Day–ish, resolute Betty and the bewildered, cowering, glamorous, tainted "Rita," still in her cocktail dress. When they first meet, Betty unexpectedly finds this dazed woman is her aunt's shower; the woman volunteers that she has been in an accident but is silent when asked her name. As it happens, a large poster for *Gilda* hangs on the bathroom wall, so when the amnesiac emerges she has an answer for the blonde and an identity: "Rita." Harring recaptures that wounded, duende heritage of Rita Hayworth (herself a changeling, real name Margarita Carmen Cansino), as well as her vagueness, that stunned, incomplete aspect. It's the vacancy that comes with extraordinary beauty and the willingness of those looking at it to project any combination of angel or devil onto her. In this case, she truly doesn't know who she is, so she has to be reactive, agreeable, self-inventing.

What makes most femmes fatales fatal is their unconsciousness; it allows them a dangerous plasticity. All femmes fatales are amnesiac, in that they forget their vows. See Jane Greer in *Out of the Past*, Hayworth in *Gilda*, Yvonne de Carlo in *Criss Cross*, and any number of sweetly accommodating sirens (but never steely, self-aware Barbara Stanwyck) who form the template for Lynch's Rita.

Mulholland Drive not only elicits references to other films; it turns into a movie about moviemaking. This time Lynch's Oz is Tinseltown. Small-town Twin Peaks has been replaced by Hollywood, a milieu that Lynch (whatever his Missoula upbringing) understands by now much more concretely than Middle America and hence is much less apt to patronize. He knows the exercise of arbitrary power by studio heads, easily analogous in film noir terms to mob chieftains. He knows the way pretty young women are passed around

by old men, chewed up and spat out, their spirits broken. He knows the insecure self-absorption of the bit players and can satirize their tenuous hold on
dignity with gentle economy. He knows, too, the way Los Angeles can come
to feel like a company town, provincial in its gossip and interconnections.
When a minor character says his family is "in the business," he apologizes
for the shorthand and explains, "show business." All the apartment court
denizens, including the crazy old psychic, one assumes to have been originally drawn to Los Angeles by the promise of stardom. Thus, the insularity
of the Southern California film community becomes an apt milieu for the
large conspiracy Lynch is always hinting at: everyone is in on it, everyone is
related, and they are all in the same business—of manufacturing dreck.
That's show biz. A part of Lynch loves the dreck or at least its pop vitality
and the labor that goes into achieving that gloss, as he shows in a leisurely
scene of actresses auditioning for a dopey doo-wop number. What he is really
drawn to is the process of performance.

Where identity is not fixed, performance becomes a floating anchor. Betty,
who seems so sunny and perky, practices the lines for her upcoming audition with Rita. The scene they're rehearsing is dreck—something about a
young woman appalled at the behavior of her father's partner—and Betty
plays it with smooth outrage, prompting Rita (who has been woodenly feeding her lines) to marvel: "You're *good*." The next day, at the audition, Betty
finds she has to act the scene with a lecherous has-been, and this time she
does it entirely differently, with equally persuasive lubricity. (It helps that
Naomi Watts is such a phenomenally gifted actress.) With this little turnabout, Lynch demonstrates the playful fluidity that lingers as a promise in
all human character, the reverse side of that anxiety that derives from not
having a stable self.

So when Rita, realizing that she's in danger from the mob, decides to disguise herself, she dons a blonde wig, and the two women compare their
hairdos in the mirror. It could be a moment out of Bergman's *Persona*. Rita's
gratitude toward the more grounded, protective Betty is palpable; no harm,
she seems to believe, can come to blondes. As they track down clues to her
missing identity, the terror recedes, and they turn empowered adventurers
finding connections in a web, like the heroines of Rivette's *Céline and Julie
Go Boating*. We feel the warmth of their becoming pals. Not long after, Betty
tells her new friend she needn't sleep on the couch, they can share the bed,
and Rita goes a good deal further than pals: she strips off her nightgown,
revealing a full figure, leans over the timid Betty, and begins kissing her.

What is remarkable is that we haven't seen it coming yet accept it completely. When Betty tells Rita as they embrace, "I'm in love with you!" it is as if she is understanding for the first time, with surprise, that all her helpfulness and curiosity about the other woman had a point: desire. Who can doubt her? But it took Rita to make the first gesture, the presentation of her voluptuous body to the smaller woman. In this carnal arena, Rita is the skilled performer. When Betty asks, "Have you ever done this before?" (meaning, gone to bed with another woman), Rita, ever the amnesiac, confesses, "I don't know." But the intuitive logic of her generosity seems to flow from the trust and mutual dependency that has been building between them. The two women offer their breasts to each other (and to us). It is a beautiful moment, made all the more effective by its earned tenderness and its utter distance from anything lurid.

We can only speculate why Lynch should have needed the male voyeurism—or sympathetic detachment—of watching two women in bed to permit himself this first convincing portrayal, for him, of an adult love relationship.

Later, Rita wakes up with a premonition and gets Betty to accompany her in the middle of the night to a sort of Magic Theater, à la Hermann Hesse's *Steppenwolf.* In this scene, more than half of the way through, the film seems to ascend or descend to a more unconscious level. Until now, everything that happened, however bizarre, had been causally connected in a linear narrative. Now the two women go home together, carrying a blue box that mysteriously materialized in front of them at the theater, enter their bedroom, a key is inserted in the box, which falls to the floor—and Betty disappears. From this point on, all bets are off. Betty, no longer wholesome-looking, is now living alone in a much rattier apartment court and having a prolonged fever dream. Occasionally Rita visits her and they start to make love, only now Rita seems to be a movie star named Carmela, and all that's left of their relationship is betrayal, humiliation, and abandonment. It's as if Lynch could only sustain the ecstatic rapport, the intimacy of love for a few scenes, before converting it to a nightmare. The threat comes less now from the dark forces of crime (the syndicate hunting Rita having receded) than from the fragility of love. Once Rita plays the sexual card, it would seem, she gains the upper hand and becomes the heartless Carmela, while Betty loses her spunk, turning into the Rejected One.

The events in this last hour, which I'll call part B, may feel fragmented, disconnected, and less compelling than the meticulously ordered part A, but we need part B's disenchantments for emotional balance. The two stories fold into each other, with some details overlapping and others not. What to make of it? Is there a right explanation, which only David Lynch knows or that more clever, diligent film critics than I will have figured out? In any case, several possibilities exist, and being an incurable eighteenth-century rationalist, I feel obliged to enumerate them. 1) It was all a dream—as we used to say at the end of our elementary school compositions. While this may be a consistent explanation, it does not take us very far. It simply reduces the entirety of the film's phenomena to the same flat, random plane. 2) It is a mixture of dream and reality. In this arrangement, some characters from the putative real life would be given other functions in the dream part. The question then remains: which parts represent the reality that the dreaming mind is reprocessing? I have seen it argued convincingly that the second part of the movie should be regarded as reality and the first part as tarnished Betty's wish-fulfillment fantasy of regaining her innocence and true love. 3) The two narrative tracks exist in alternate universes more or less parallel to each other. I can never understand what this increasingly popular explanation means and regard it as the last refuge of postmodernist scoundrels. 4) Since we see Betty masturbating in part B, perhaps all of the narratives could be her masturbation fantasies. If all the events we see are subjective, be it daydream or nightmare, whose subjective consciousness is being tapped? Betty's? Lynch's? Rita's? All of the above? In gestalt therapy, they teach you that you are everyone in your dream. (How could it be otherwise?) Maybe none of this matters. If you surrender to the film sufficiently, it becomes, willy-nilly, your "parallel universe."

Much has been made in the press of the fact that *Mulholland Drive* began as a TV pilot for a series that never got funded. Lynch, deciding to release it as a feature, then went back and shot more footage to flesh it out. Certainly, some of the film's idiosyncrasies might be explained by its television origins: the credits, a fifties-type dance party with special effects that reads like a series title sequence; the episodic nature of the narrative; the many secondary characters who are introduced to us in early sequences but never come back in the story (including name actors such as Dan Hedaya and Robert Forster, who were probably scheduled for later reappearances). The TV-style reliance on close-ups and medium shots is turned into a strength by virtue of painterly lighting and exquisite cinematography. The restriction of visual information reinforces a claustrophobic dreamlike feeling; the self-consciously nocturnal art direction suggests, too, one of those paranoid TV cult shows like *The X-Files* or *Wild Palms*, with Los Angeles contemporary late-modernist villa read as conspiracy décor. The pacing too is like a TV miniseries, with more stress put on atmosphere than on tour-de-force cinematic passages.

I know a number of people who have already seen *Mulholland Drive* several times. When it comes out on DVD, many more will undoubtedly favor it with multiple viewings, partly to try to solve its riddles but also because it has that languid, circular, seductive tempo that invites revisiting, like a favorite tango record. In that sense, it belongs to a newly evolving type of movie (Wong Kar-wai's *In the Mood for Love* is another example) that operates like a fusion between film and pop music: you can enter it at any point; you can leave it on in the background, like a movie screen at a disco; you can be pulled into its unresolved, sensual, less-than-overbearing narrative, with sexy actors contributing to a kind of personal, open-ended fantasy—a machine for yearning. I can certainly see its appeal, but I mistrust this marriage as a wave of cinema's future. As it is, I observe with bemusement the increasing importance of musical soundtracks in providing a subnarrative for movies (such as Sophie Coppola's *Lost in Translation* and *Marie Antoinette* or Wes Anderson's *The Royal Tenenbaums*), tipping off viewers in the know that this particular track by that particular band played over this particular scene creates a special kick. We used to say that slapping a popular rock song on the soundtrack was a form of cheating, a shortcut to provide emotional highs that had not yet been earned by the storytelling. But younger filmmakers and cinephiles have had their brains so wired to pop/rock music that these internalized aural rhythms cannot help but affect their processing and production of screen visuals. This phenomenon of a movie as a sort of mixtape is one mutation I see in current filmmaking. Still, David Lynch has used a talented film composer, Badalamenti, to write a lush, plangent original score for *Mulholland Drive*, and he has made a delicately sensuous and ripe, evocative film, one that deserves to be revisited on its own merits.

FILM COMMENT (SEPTEMBER/OCTOBER 2001)

Chapter Thirty-Five

DUŠAN MAKAVEJEV

The Wolf and the Teddy Bear

The second time I met Dušan Makavejev (the first time was as a journalist interviewing him about *W.R.: The Mysteries of the Organism*) occurred at the Telluride Film Festival, in that old mining and now ski resort/condo mountain area of Colorado. I was there largely as a friend of the festival's co-organizer, Tom Luddy, while Makavejev had come with his new film, *Sweet Movie*. Tom is a human switchboard who connects people he thinks might want to know each other, and in the case of Dušan and me, we hit it off immediately. I like to think it was because we both have a sardonic, impious sense of humor. Someone with a mischievous sensibility can only be reassured by meeting a fellow mocker, willing to look at any subject from an irreverent, contrarian angle. As we came to discover, our sensibilities were fairly different, but there was enough common glue for us to begin a friendship, in the midst of that preening, vainglorious environment which is a film festival.

The three honorees that first year at Telluride, 1974, were Francis Ford Coppola, Gloria Swanson, and Leni Riefenstahl, and the presence of the last provoked controversy. There were even pickets, if I recall. Susan Sontag's great essay written that same year, "Fascinating Fascism," was in part an angry response to her tribute at Telluride: "The purification of Leni Riefenstahl's reputation of its Nazi dross has been gathering momentum for some time, but it has reached some kind of climax this year, with Riefenstahl the guest of honor in a new cinephile-controlled festival held in the summer at Colorado." I remember going up in an elevator with Riefenstahl and Gloria

Swanson, and the two ancient honorees exchanging health secrets (Swanson recommended sunflower seeds). Outrage is my short suit, so I could never muster umbrage at the presence of Riefenstahl. Not that I wanted to cozy up to her, either: her kind had baked my kind. What intrigued me—and Dušan—more was a beautiful print of *The Blue Light*, a silent film that starred the young Leni in her acting days scampering up the mountainside in a short ragged dress. It was the finest example of that German mountaineering genre, pre-Hitler, that celebrated the healthy body in nature. Julie Christie, who was present at Telluride just because she liked seeing interesting movies, had also been taken with *The Blue Light* and, even more fortuitous, had become friendly with both Dušan and me, in the easy, casual way that such an intimate festival made possible.[1]

Probably it was Dušan, with his enthusiasm for improbable schemes, who came up with the idea of shooting a remake of *The Blue Light* then and there, with himself directing, Julie playing the mountain girl, and I writing the script. We even went so far as to hike around the mountains looking for locations. Julie, ever the good sport, posed against various rock formations while Dušan and I snapped photographs. By that time he was an internationally renowned filmmaker and she a major star, but what was I doing there? I had written a book of poetry and begun a memoir about my teaching kids: at this point, I was nowhere in their league. Before I could start to worry myself sick about how I would pull together a script in two days so we could start shooting once the festival had ended, reality intruded: where in the vicinity were we going to get professional camera and sound equipment, much less a budget for even the cheapest production? Had we gone through with the film, it probably would have had a campy, home-movie charm. No great loss. What strikes me today is how unconcerned Dušan was about the source material, with its secondhand Nazi taint. Perhaps he was so secure in his progressive views and had moreover encountered so much bullshit from the Left and the Right in his Eastern European experience, that Riefenstahl was just another piece of twentieth-century history, which fascinated him in toto. If anything, he could always be galvanized by the contradictory pulls of purity and violence, righteous ideology and scandal.

At the time we became friends, I was thirty-one, and Makavejev forty-two—eleven years older. I have the habit of seeking out friendships with older people, who offer a glimpse of the road ahead, and then trying to show them that I can keep up, be as "old," as knowledgeable about their cultural references. Ironically, Makavejev was much more receptive to youth culture than I. Perhaps he mistook me for a young person, instead of the prematurely middle-aged possessor of an "old soul" I thought myself to be.

Makavejev had a way of speaking in short verbal spurts that came out like a dog's bark. He always sounded hoarse. His favorite word was "incredible." He seemed ever on the lookout for the bizarre, and he would get as enthusiastic about the awful as the sublime. In Telluride, his main enthusiasm was for his Yugoslav countryman Nicola Tesla, the inventor of alternating current who had once inhabited these mountains and about whom Makavejev considered doing a movie. He hoped, by remaking *The Blue Light*, somehow to tie in Tesla, who "claimed in the moments of heightened creativity he was radiating a blue light," Makavejev would write in a later essay, "Nicola Tesla Radiated a Blue Light." Wilhelm Reich, too, had a blue-light fixation, he pointed out in that same essay: "Already back in 1934, Reich explained to Erik Erikson that all living creatures radiate a blue light. Erikson did not believe him. Reich invited Erikson—it was in Denmark, during the summer vacation—to observe with him couples making love on the beach, in darkness. He asserted that the blue radiation, which becomes more intense during the sexual act, can be observed by naked eye. Since then, Erikson considered Reich mad."[2]

All these "blue light" convergences were just the sort of thing to get Makavejev's imagination spinning. Did he himself believe (I sure didn't: I was on Erikson's side) that there was any truth to this theory of blue light, creativity, and sex? Hard to say. There was a refreshingly amoral suspension of disbelief to his enthusiasms—at the very least, a reluctance to make the usual condemning judgments. He preferred to exhibit a baffled wonderment: "Incredible!" I realize to some degree his abrupt speech patterns and reliance on certain adjectives may have had to do with English not being his first language: he would skip definite articles, as many foreign speakers do.

Makavejev had a tolerant manner that was (like every enthusiast I've known) inflected by sudden impatience. For instance, if he wanted to talk when you were talking and what you were saying bored him, he would start to close one eye. Then, when you were done, he would take up from where he last left off, maybe grunting "Okay" to signal this continuation. With his bald head, beard, and avid, alert eyes, he kept reminding me of a wolf. There was something lupine, too, about his powerful, hulking build, though he neutralized that physically intimidating quality around women, making himself into more of a huggable teddy bear.

Speaking of wolves, my first encounter with Dušan was, as I mentioned, when my friend Bill Zavatsky and I interviewed him for the *New York Herald* (now defunct).[3] He was explaining to us the principles of montage he used in a sequence of *WR*: "I edited it normally, without Stalin. Then I put Stalin in at the moment when Ilyich is speaking Lenin's words. He hits her. She turns to him, and this is not Lenin anymore, it's Stalin. Pure violence. I cut Stalin in at the place where you expect to see Ilyich. And for me, this is like when children discover that this is not grandma, but the wolf." In the sixties and seventies, Makavejev was an advocate of liberation, especially sexual liberation, but he also warned of the violence that could be unleashed when the self-repressive "character armor" (to use Reich's term) breaks down—or in political terms, when idealism gives way to the urge for domination. It was a salutary warning in the context of that utopian dream of world revolution so many on the Left were indulging: he was looking one step ahead. (Myself, I never took seriously that any sort of liberation was on the horizon. If I found myself marching on the Left, it was because it was the only logical place for a person with my upbringing and moral sensibility).

Dušan placed great emphasis in that interview on the innovative editing techniques he was using for *W.R.* I asked him "When you cut from the phallus to Stalin, it's like a return to the Eisensteinian montage that's gone out of films for a long time," and he bristled, explaining that he too was dissatisfied with Eisenstein's dialectical montage, but he was trying for a more symphonic effect, where a shot might resonate with one that had occurred a half-hour before, rather than always the one just before.

Okay. [With dialectical montage] they never thought about the montage and distance. Because when you pull together something from here and something from there in the same manner, then you have people recalling; you have not only a kind of one plus one equals two, but you have two plus two equals five. If you take very distant things that have something in common, so people can be shocked at it and say, 'Impossible!'—for example, the phallus and Stalin—there is an enormous, tremendous power in Stalin; and this is the same power that is the sexual power of the male member. So there is the same power, and this is just to show them together. And in my opinion, the power of powerful political personalities is the power of symbolic phalluses, or frozen phalluses—not real ones.[4]

Makavejev's placement of Stalin next to the frozen phallus was, when all is said and done, a fairly cheap shot. (Here we see Mak's dichotomy: the intellectually sophisticated cosmopolitan and the somewhat crude, vulgar, provincial operating in the same space.) He then went on to say that each time you view the film again, the connections change: "I developed this idea of shifting gestalts. In one scene, you see one connection; the second time you see the film differently because now you know some other things." At this point I, the sympathetic and for the most part subservient interviewer, asked skeptically: "But how does this 'shifting gestalt' differ from seeing any other film a second time?" He responded with a complicated answer about overlapping shapes, hypnagogic images, borderline experiences between sleeping and waking, and so on. The ex-student of psychology was unloading his whole theory of perception on me.[5] Still, I was not convinced because frankly what had moved me about *W.R.*—and I was very moved, very excited by the film—were not these A+B shock juxtapositions but its romantic, lyrical expressiveness, which emerged in moments like serenading the decapitated beloved with a Mayakovsky poem and in the documentary parts about Wilhelm Reich's son and followers, a poignant tribute to a maligned if deranged psychologist who had tried to synthesize the link between sex and politics, as Makavejev always hoped to do.

It is odd that our first encounter consisted of my asking him questions because subsequently the roles often reversed. In the getting-to-know-each-other phase of our friendship he would ask me questions that came out of the blue, like a European sociologist administering a questionnaire to a typical American: for instance, "What magazines do you read?" At that time I barely read any, except for the *New York Review of Books*, and when I told him that he sounded incredulous, disappointed. "You don't read *Esquire*? *Playboy*? Come on." He thought I was putting on airs, pretending to be a European intellectual, not admitting to my American, animal nature. Similarly, he would try to get me to spill my carnal fantasies, to "talk dirty," man to man. I have noticed with a lot of Eastern European intellectuals, regardless of how brainy, like Žižek, they bond in this stereotypical male way. Dušan liked talking about "fucking" a lot. He was obviously very interested in sex as an indicator of character, and I was as interested in having sex as the next man but did not enjoy talking about it as openly.

Or he would ask me what I thought of some comic strip like Beetle Bailey or *Mad* magazine. I had virtually no interest in pop culture at the time. It sounds odious to put it like that, but one can only be interested in so many things at a time, and my interests, various as they were, did not extend to rock music, comic strips, best-selling novels, and other pop phenomena. The one area in which I tried to keep up with popular tastes was movies since, like most cinephiles, I had a taste for the cheesy, but even then, I never saw any of the Star Wars movies or *E.T.* It wasn't a matter of principle but because I didn't expect to get pleasure from them, pleasure of the heady, complex sort I craved, so why buy a ticket? Of course I saw all of Makavejev's movies, just as I did Bresson's, Fassbinder's, Tarkovsky's, and, later, Hou Hsiao-hsien's and Kiarostami's.

Makavejev rarely brought up other filmmakers in conversation. He was not one of those *Variety* gross-checking, show-biz-obsessed film people. Underneath, he was an intellectual, trained in psychology and cultural criticism. His conversation ranged far and wide, from literature to paintings to science. One time Dušan began telling me about this "incredible" book, *Memories of My Nervous Illness*, by Daniel Paul Schreber, who had suffered at the hands of a brutal father, then grown up to become an upstanding judge, then suffered a psychotic break in which he heard voices and saw himself as a man-woman, and managed to write an account of his schizophrenia that Freud and others cherished. I couldn't quite make out why this book mattered so much to Dušan. Years later I stumbled across Schreber's memoir, read it, and sure enough, it was—incredible! I never knew where Dušan's latest enthusiasm would land next—Reich, Tesla, Schreber, Mickey Mouse—but I kept listening, half-dubious, half-learning.

In a sense Makavejev was a collagist. Like his spiritual godfather, Godard, who put together the day's dialogues at the last moment from snippets on the car radio taking him to the studio or books and magazines he happened to be leafing though, Makavejev laid himself open like a sounding board to vibrations in the air. This meant, on the positive side of opportunism, that he was a skilled *bricoleur*, tuned to the zeitgeist, but on the negative side, that his movies from *W.R.* onward were condemned to unevenness, in which powerful, meaty bits would play side by side with frivolous ones. To take one example at random, the narrative subplot in *Sweet Movie* about a beauty (Carol Laure) married to a Texas billionaire is silly, doesn't contribute anything to the movie. Of course Makavejev meant it to be cartoonish; then he had problems with Laure on the set and in the end couldn't bring himself to jettison it. He was devoted to clashing tonalities, even if it meant using material that was intellectually beneath him.

I am now approaching one of the key problems in our friendship: my judgments about his films, which were not always favorable. As a friend I wanted him to be the best artist he could be, to achieve the greatness that I saw in him. I have made the same mistake with a number of filmmakers who became friends, Rudy Burckhardt, Warren Sonbert, Makavejev, all of whom I kept pushing to do something different when they seemed to be stuck, repeating themselves at a lower level than what I had envisioned for them. A better friend would have embraced whatever it was they had managed to do, knowing how difficult it is to accomplish anything in film. Perhaps I was living too vicariously through them: the filmmaker I'd thought of becoming in college, before giving it up for writing, was competing with them or trying to achieve cinematic expression secondhand. In any case, Makavejev needed his friends to be supporters, not critics.

We had talked from time to time about my writing a screenplay for him. It never came to anything, largely because Dušan was his own screenwriter. He once offered me the chance to hang around the set and contribute ideas that might or might not turn up in the script: he said he had a few such people who were perfectly willing to feed him suggestions, for the greater glory of contributing to a Makavejev film. My ego would not accept this; I had no wish to be part of some other artist's entourage. In retrospect it seems a perfectly generous offer, and I probably would have benefited from the experience—though, knowing me, I might well have ended up the nay-sayer, trying to shoot down his most cockamamie notions, like the dour intellectual cowriter in Fellini's 8½, rather than what he needed, someone who would keep coming up with loony uncensored ideas in a free-associating manner.

Makavejev introduced me to his frequent collaborator, Branko Vučićević, a wise old veteran, cross-eyed and ego-less, as a good co-screenwriter should be. Vučićević, who had worked on *Love Affair*, *Innocence Unprotected*, and *Montenegro*, was not awed by Makavejev, but neither was he critical of him: a fellow Serbian, he was fond of Mak's excesses, he had the proper attitude.

So now we come to the question: What *were* my judgments of his films? I adored the first feature, *Man Is Not a Bird*, and the second, *Love Affair, or the Case of the Missing Switchboard Operator*. They had a rough, passionate, tender humanism, combined with a formalistic playfulness that never strayed too far way from the main characters. They were obviously influenced by Godard but in some ways were a correction of the Swiss master. Precisely because, as I have said, Makavejev was this combination of sophisticated intellectual and slightly crude provincial, he was able in these Yugoslav movies to make a much *warmer*, more heartfelt, careening, passionate, zestful, and erotic film than Godard could. What had unified the bricolage elements in Godard's first, pre-Maoist phase, besides the intelligence of his visual style, was an underlying melancholy—one might even call it a depressive's melancholy. Makavejev's collages were also unified by emotional tone, but it was a more robust sadness. I relished his third film, *Innocence Unprotected*, a mélange of cinephilia, documentary, and narrative. With *W.R.: The Mysteries of the Organism*, he had clearly broken new ground and made his most ambitious work, arguably his masterpiece: on the whole I embraced it, but there were certain parts that seemed to me merely sensationalist or shallow-journalistic—exploitative of the superficial aspects of America, like a pre-*Borat*. I missed the black-and-white, basso profondo, joyous fatalism of his first films.

Part of the problem was that he was now an émigré filmmaker who had lost his grounding, Yugoslavia, and was in the process of becoming homeless. He went from being the greatest filmmaker of a small country to a traveling minstrel of world revolution. The Movement itself was evaporating while his homeland's very name was about to be wiped off the map. Just as Antonioni's *Blow-Up* or *Zabriskie Point* suffered from a thinness of social context when he left Italy's safe confines and began roaming the globe, as did Tarkovsky's last two films made outside of Russia, so did Makavejev's movies begin to exude that deoxygenated atmosphere of the tourist. While it is true that European directors had previously prospered when they came to America, they were then protected by the studio system and the template of Hollywood genre movies. When the studio system collapsed, auteurist émigré directors were expected to come up with something original each movie, and it became harder for them to succeed. In Makavejev's case it was particularly hard because he had grown enamored of the transgressive and was caught between the need to keep transgressing by flaunting taboos and delivering movies commercial enough to stay in business. In his Yugoslavian phase it had been sufficiently subversive to assert the importance of private life and to mock the patriotic group-speak of the state. When he moved to the West, the ante was upped: now he needed to show people literally eating shit, as he did in *Sweet Movie*. I still admired the tragicomic audacity and poetry of that film, but the very notion of the "transgressive" no longer held much appeal for me. It had started to seem mechanical, regardless of who was doing it (even more so when it became academically de rigueur.).

Not surprisingly, Dušan found it difficult to secure funding after the provocations of *Sweet Movie*. One time he called me when he was staying in the Chateau Marmont in Los Angeles, waiting for studio executives and producers, who had previously told him what a genius he was, to return his phone calls. He was in that nowhereland so familiar to those hoping to get a film project green-lighted. Dušan had wanted to make the first "serious film with sex in it." Never mind *Last Tango in Paris*: this one would really do it right. He came up with a screenplay about a white woman and a black man stuck in an elevator for ten hours and their progression from mutual suspicion to hot passion. The actress he had in mind for it was Sarah Miles; the man would be played by the ex-football star Jim Brown. Brown, it turned out, had a scheduling conflict, but the agent offered to replace him with Imam, the beautiful black model who was available and looking to break into movies. On the basis of this whimsical casting switch, the transgressive element would suddenly go from explicit interracial heterosexual to explicit interracial lesbian sex story. Makavejev was still tempted, but the financing fell through.

Splitting his time between Paris and Belgrade, Dušan told me: "When I was making films in Yugoslavia I was toast of Paris, all critics love me, I was everyone's darling. Then I move to Paris, and I become just another French filmmaker scratching for same subsidy money like everyone else. Incredible."

In the meantime he began making a living as a guest professor at Harvard, NYU, and elsewhere. Pedagogy was an interest we both shared. Dušan seemed a natural teacher, given his abundant energy, sympathy for the young, and overflowing ideas.

When my book about teaching creative writing in an inner-city school, *Being with Children*, came out in 1975, Dušan actually read it (unlike most of my other film festival circuit friends). He made a point of telling me more than once that what he liked the most about it were the children's stories and poems in the appendix. The comment wounded me: I liked the children's writing also, had even championed it, but could not help feeling that my 400-page account was not chopped liver either. To me, Dušan's response showed a clichéd counterculture preference for the boldly primitive voices of children over a reasoned and reflective adult voice.

You could also say that as friends we were each trying to reshape the other into our image: just as I wanted Dušan to give up some of what seemed to me his sophomorically orgiastic, "transgressive" shtick, so he wanted to push me out of my measured, rational mode and get me to write from a more elemental place, one that was more in contact with the unconscious.

In 1976 he delivered the aforementioned paper, "Nikola Tesla Radiated a Blue Light," for a conference titled The United States in the World, at the Smithsonian in Washington DC, which was occasioned by America's two hundredth anniversary. It was a brilliantly funny piece of writing, holding in colloidal suspension Makavejev's knowingness and ironic naïveté, his enthusiasm for American freedom and critique of American optimism, from the perspective of one raised half a world away, in a much more limited set of possibilities. Short-paragraphed fragments, like this one, followed each other with surreal deadpan:

I like Instant Coffee and Instant Soup.

When Instant Death was introduced, in 1945, as applied to Hiroshima and Nagasaki, I caught myself, a 13 year old boy, in a dilemma: I liked it very much, although I knew it wasn't nice that I liked it. Then everybody got Instant Excuse: Instant Death has brought Instant End of War.

Instant Beginning and Instant End.

Fast to pick up on the theme of globalization, Makavejev seemed to be "embracing" the United States as his next, inevitable subject matter. To my way of thinking, he did this more successfully on the page than on the big screen: he could control the ironies better. He also started putting together a reel of Coca-Cola ads, to make some McLuhanesque point about consumerism and globalization. These ad clips were also supposed to provide a leitmotif for The Coca-Cola Kid, but when the film came to be shot in Australia, in 1985, the ads fell by the wayside. The Coca-Cola Kid was pleasant, light, and forgettable. The dark side of Makavejev (which had resurfaced in Montenegro) had gone into remission: he had misplaced his energizing Slavic melancholy, either via commercial compromise or the slow accretion of resignation.

In 1988, I was appointed to the New York Film Festival selection committee. There were five of us, Richard Peña, Wendy Keys, David Sterritt, Carrie

Rickey, and I, and we went as a group that May to Cannes to scout films for our own festival. Often we scattered along individual paths to cover more movies, but in the case of an especially promising candidate we would all show up at the same screening. Such was the case with *Manifesto*, directed by Makavejev, a filmmaker we all respected and were fond of. We were each rooting for him to make a comeback, and nothing would have pleased us more than to be able to showcase his newest work in the next NYFF. Unfortunately, none of us liked the film. With *Manifesto*, Makavejev seemed to be trying for a comic romp, a light farce, a fable set in the period of anarchist bombs and *Mitteleuropa* naughtiness, but it came out heavy-handed and forced. Makavejev had sacrificed his natural grit by doing a costume picture, and he did not have the touch of graceful elegance to pull it off. It was just not strong enough, we felt, as we discussed our options over dinner in Cannes that night, to occupy one of the twenty-five slots open at the NYFF: a larger festival could have absorbed it easily.

Who was going to tell him? We all knew Dušan, but rather than pick straws the consensus was that since I was his closest friend in the group, it had to be me. I wish now I had resisted this logic forcefully. If the decision had come from Richard Peña, the festival's director, it might have cushioned the blow with bureaucratic impersonality and seemed less like a friend's betrayal. But a part of me took pride in being the one chosen as the group's messenger, and that part even bought into the proposition that it would be cowardly of me to let anyone else do the notifying. So I left the restaurant to seek out Dušan in the café where I knew he was having dinner and waiting for our decision. I signaled him to come outside—to leave his dinner companions.

We were not going to take his film, I told him right away. Dušan was visibly hurt, stung. If memory serves, he even fell backward a step. Of course every artist worth their salt faces setbacks such as this and must learn to be prepared for them. Dušan took it overall in a subdued, stoic way, but he could not forbear adding that without a New York Film Festival selection, the picture might not even get distributed in the United States or it might have such a tiny distribution as to be invisible (which is in fact what happened). "All right, you didn't like the film, I won't try to argue you out of your opinion," he said. "But when you think a filmmaker is good you should *support* him. You should show his films, even his minor works." (I am paraphrasing from a quarter century ago, but the gist, I know, is correct; the memory is too fresh to doubt). He reiterated the point that the New York Film Festival had supported him in the past; he had counted on us; he had thought we were his friends; and now this rejection.

I could see his argument. I wished I could go along with it. But the only way for me to serve on the New York Film Festival selection committee with integrity was to vote for or against films on the basis of what I actually thought about them; no *politiques des auteurs*, no outside friendships, no previous record should matter. I distinctly recall thinking before I was ever put on the committee that my predecessors must have been idiots to have turned down the latest picture by some distinguished director. Then, sacrilege of sacrileges, once I began serving, I found myself voting on different occasions against a Godard, a Satyajit Ray, a Chantal Akerman, a Zanussi, a Ruiz, a Makavejev, a Fellini—because I couldn't work up enthusiasm for that particular picture of theirs.

None of which changed my awful feeling at that moment that I was hurting Dušan. He was so transparently expressive, his emotions so on the surface, for all his stoicism, that he seemed more vulnerable than wolflike.

Eventually the conversation ended, and I left him at the bistro, walking back to the restaurant where my fellow committee members were having their after-dinner coffee. It remains one of my most painful memories. I still feel ashamed, not that I voted against *Manifesto* but that I allowed myself to be the bearer of bad tidings, the instrument that would wound him in this way.

That Dušan did not hold it entirely against me may be seen by the fact that he called me the next time he was in New York, and we went to the latest David Cronenberg, *Dead Ringers*, which had just opened. He was jet-lagged, tired; I was not, but we both saw eye to eye: a disappointing film, more interesting in concept than in execution. Dušan's taste in movies and mine usually coincided.

Since that time we saw less and less of each other. We would occasionally talk on the phone. Once, I called Tom Luddy in California, and he said, "I have Dušan Makavejev on the other line—do you want to speak to him?" and we had an awkward three-way transcontinental chat. I do think the rejection of *Manifesto* left a scar. But the main reason our friendship dissolved was more mundane: we lived thousands of miles away, and I drifted away from the film festival circuit to concentrate on my writing and teaching, so that we were no longer thrown together by circumstances. It would have taken a continuous effort of will to stay in touch.

The next time I saw him Makavejev had developed scoliosis, and his back curved dramatically. Bent almost double, he seemed to be meeting you more than halfway, stooping courteously like an old nobleman. I asked him why he did not try to make a film about the Serbian-Bosnian War, which was then tearing apart his homeland. He said it was too disheartening; he couldn't find a way to be amused by it, to make it into his kind of cinematic story. That sounded right. In any case, he was more interested now in writing books than making movies. He mentioned having several book projects for which he was researching and gathering materials. Dušan laughed, as if to say: Now we are both in the same arena

Dušan passed away in 2019, at the age of eighty-six, after a long illness. I will always treasure knowing him.

FROM *DUŠAN MAKAVEJEV: EROS IDEOLOGY MONTAGE*
(PRAGUE: LITTERARIA PRAGENSIA, 2018)

Chapter Thirty-Six

KENJI MIZOGUCHI

Ugetsu and *Utamaro and His Five Women*

UGETSU

Often appearing on ten-greatest films in cinema lists, called one of the most beautiful films of all time or the greatest Japanese film ever made, *Ugetsu* comes to us awash in superlatives. No less acclaimed has been its maker, Kenji Mizoguchi: "Like Bach, Titian and Shakespeare, he is the greatest in his art," enthused the French critic Jean Douchet, and not far behind was Jean-Luc Godard, who declared him "the greatest of Japanese filmmakers. Or quite simply one of the greatest of filmmakers" (a photograph exists of Godard reverently visiting Mizoguchi's grave) or the *New York Times* critic Vincent Canby, who extolled him as "one of the great directors of the sound era." In other words, Mizoguchi belongs in the same exalted company as Jean Renoir, Orson Welles, Carl Dreyer, Alfred Hitchcock, Max Ophuls, Sergei Eisenstein, Robert Bresson, and Akira Kurosawa (who looked up to the older man as his master). This near-unanimous reverence for both *Ugetsu* and Mizoguchi among world filmmakers and critics may be puzzling to the movie-going American public. In order to understand what the fuss is about, we need to take a step back from these superlatives or at least put them in context.

Kenji Mizoguchi (1898–1956) began in the silent era and made dozens of fluent, entertaining studio films before arriving at his lyrical, rigorous visual style and patented tragic humanism, around the age of forty. His first masterworks were a pair of bitterly realistic films made in 1936 on the subject of modern women's struggles, *Sisters of the Gion* and *Osaka Elegy*. These break-throughs led to the classic *Story of the Last Chrysanthemums* (1939), set in the Meiji era, about a kabuki actor who stubbornly hones his craft with the aid of his all-too-sacrificing lover. In this film, Mizoguchi perfected his sig-nature, "flowing scroll," "one shot, one scene" style of long duration takes, which generated hypnotic tension and psychological density, keeping the camera well back, avoiding close-ups, and linking the characters to their environments. During the early 1940s the director was hampered by the Japanese studios' propaganda war effort, though he did make a stately, two-part version of *The 47 Ronin*. After the war ended he turned to a series of intense pictures advocating progressive, democratizing ideals, which fell in with the occupation's values, while wobbling aesthetically between subtle refinement and hammy melodrama.

Then, in the 1950s, he regained his touch, and created those sublimely flowing, harrowing masterpieces that represent his pinnacle of directorial achievement: *The Life of Oharu* (1952), *Ugetsu* (1953), *The Crucified Lovers* (1954), *Sansho the Bailiff* (1954), *New Tale of the Heike* (1955), and *Street of Shame* (1956). Except for the last, these pictures were all set in earlier times: Mizoguchi, drawing on Saikaku, Chikamatsu, and other classical writers, had become a specialist in the past, reinterpreting national history as much as, say, John Ford and insisting, like Visconti, on accurate historical detail, borrowing props, kimonos, and suits of armor from museums and private collectors. He attributed his fascination with traditional Japanese culture partly to his own relocation from Tokyo to the Kyoto area.

No doubt, some of Mizoguchi's belated international renown (he won Venice Film Festival prizes three years in a row for *Oharu*, *Ugetsu*, and *Sansho*) had to do with satisfying the West's taste for an exoticized Japan. But he also fit the profile of the brilliant, uncompromising auteur (a perfectionist who would demand hundreds of retakes and move a house several feet to improve the vista). Also, his moving-camera, long-shot approach exempli-fied the Bazinian mise-en-scène aesthetic that the young *Cahiers du Cinema* critics were championing and anticipated the wide-screen filmmaking of Antonioni, Jansco, Nicholas Ray, and others.

Mizoguchi engaged with the past not to recapture nostalgically some lost model of serenity but, if anything, the opposite. In preparing *Ugetsu*, he was drawn to sixteenth-century chronicles about civil wars and their effects on the common people. As a starting point, he and his screenwriter, Yoshikata Yoda, adapted two tales from a nineteenth-century collection of ghost stories,

Akinari Ueda's *Ugetsu Monogatori* (*Tales of Moonlight and Rain*, 1858), retaining the book's images while altering the narrative line. The perennially dissatisfied Mizoguchi stressed in his notes to the long-suffering Yoda: "The feeling of war-time must be apparent in the attitude of every character. The violence of war unleashed by those in power on a pretext of the national good must overwhelm the common people with suffering—moral and physical. Yet the commoners, even under these conditions, must continue to live and eat. This theme is what I especially want to emphasize here. How should I do it?"

Ugetsu ended up concentrating on two couples. The main pair is a poor potter, Genjuro, eager to make war profits by selling his wares to the competing armies, and his devoted wife, Miyagi, who would prefer he stay at home with their little boy and not take chances on the road. (The acting between these two is beyond exquisite: both the brooding Masayuki Mori, who played Genjuro, and the incomparable Kinuyo Tanaka, cast as his wife, were two of Japan's greatest actors, though filmed by Mizoguchi in a determinedly unglamorous, non-movie-star way.). The second couple is a peasant, Tobei, who assists Genjuro in his trade but would rather become a samurai, and his shrewish wife, Ohama, who ridicules her husband's fantasies of military glory. In this "gender tragedy," if you will, the men pursue their aggressive dreams, bringing havoc on themselves and their wives. Still, the point is underlined that the men don't want to escape their wives; they only want to triumph in the larger world so as to return to these wives, made into bigger men by boast-worthy adventures and costly presents.

Are we to take it that the moral of the film is: *Better stay at home, cultivate your garden, nose to the grindstone*? No, Mizoguchi's viewpoint is not cautionary but realistic: This is the way human beings are, never satisfied; everything changes, life is suffering, one cannot avoid one's fate, and if they had stayed home they might have been just as easily killed by pillaging soldiers. The fact that they chose to leave gives us a plot and some ineffably lovely, heartbreaking sequences.

The celebrated Lake Biwa scene, where they come upon a phantom boat in the mists, is surely one of the most lyrical in cinema. Edited to create a stunningly uncanny mood, it also prepares us for the supernatural elements that follow. The dying sailor on the boat is not a ghost, though the travelers at first take him for one; he warns the travelers, particularly the women, to beware of attacking pirates, another ominous foreshadowing.

It is the movie's supreme balancing act to be able to move seamlessly between the realistic and otherworldly. Mizoguchi achieves this feat by varying the direction between a sober, almost documentary, long-distance view of mayhem and several carefully choreographed set pieces, such as the phantom ship. A particularly wrenching set piece involves the potter taking leave of his wife and son: the alternating pattern of cuts between the husband on the boat moving off and the wife running along the shore, waving, comes to concentrate more and more on her stricken, prescient awareness (he, still having no idea what lies ahead, does not deserve our scrutiny). Later, the bestial behavior of the hungry, marauding soldiers coming upon the potter's wife is shot from above, with the detached inevitability of random chaos that makes the savagery more matter-of-fact, the soldiers pathetically staggering about in the background (an effect that must have inspired Godard and Truffaut in their distanced shootouts).

Mizoguchi's artistry reaches its pinnacle in the eerie sequences between Genjuro and Lady Wakasa. *Bolero*-like music underscores the giddy progression by which the humble potter is lured to the noblewoman's house, is seduced by her, and experiences the ecstasy of paradise, only to learn that he has fallen in love with a ghost. Machiko Kyō, one of Japan's screen goddesses, plays Lady Wakasa with white makeup that resembles a Noh mask and slithery movements along the floor like a fox woman. Interestingly, she seduces Genjuro as much by her flattery of his pottery as by her dangerous beauty. Previously, we have seen Genjuro (a surrogate for the director?) obsessed with his pot making, but it is only when Lady Wakasa compliments him on these objects of his which she has been collecting that he appreciates himself in this light, making the telling comment, "I never knew how things could be so enhanced by the proper background." In so doing, he embraces Mizoguchian aesthetics while she raises him from artisan to artist, putting them on a more equal social footing. Their love affair plays out in the rectangular castle of shoji-screened rooms around an open courtyard, an architectural setting more aristocratically formal than the village sequences. There is also a breathtakingly audacious shot which tracks from night to day, starting with the two of them in a bath together then moving across a dissolve and an open field to pick them up picnicking and disporting in the garden.

As Mizoguchi's great cinematographer, Miyazawa, stated in his interview, they used a crane in filming *Ugetsu* 70 percent of the time. The camera, almost constantly moving, not only laterally but vertically, conveys the instability of a world where ghosts come and go, life and death flow simultaneously into each other, and everything is finally transient, subject to betrayal. At her wedding to Genjuro, Lady Wakasa sings, "The finest silk of rarest shade / May fade away, and quickly, too / So may the love I offer you, / If your heart proves false to me." The camera's viewpoint is always emotionally significant: we look down from above at Wakasa seducing Genjuro as she leans over him, as though to convey his fear and desire, while we are practically in the mud with Tobei, crawling along on his belly, before he witnesses his big break: the enemy general's suicidal beheading, for which he will take the credit.

Just as the camera's image field keeps changing without ever losing its elegantly apt compositional sense, so do our sympathies and moral judgments shift from character to character. No doubt Genjuro is right to want to escape the clutches of his ghostly mistress, yet she has given him nothing but happiness and is justified in feeling betrayed by him. Tobei is something of a clown, a buffoon, yet his pain is real enough when, puffed up with samurai vanity, he finds his wife working in a brothel. The complex camera movement that follows Ohama from berating a customer to stumbling upon the open-jawed Tobei and the ensuing passage in which she struggles between anger, shame, and happiness at being reunited with him, demonstrate the way that this director's compassionate if bitter moral vision and his choice of camera angle reinforce each other. Mizoguchi's formalism and humanism are part of a single unified expression.

Perhaps the most striking instance of this transcendent tenderness comes toward the end, when Genjuro returns home from his journey, looking for his wife: the camera inscribes a 360-degree arc around the hut, resting at last on the patient, tranquil Miyagi, whom we had assumed was dead, having seen her speared earlier. We are relieved, as is Genjuro, watching her preparing a homecoming meal for her husband and mending his kimono while he sleeps. On awakening, he discovers his wife is indeed dead; it appears he has again been taken in by a ghost woman. The sole consolation is that we (and presumably Genjuro) continue to hear the ghost of Miyaki's voice on the soundtrack, watching her husband approvingly at his potter's wheel, noting that he has finally become the man of her ideals, though admitting it is a pity they no longer occupy the same world. One might say that Mizoguchi's detached, accepting eye also resembles that of a ghost, looking down on mortal confusions, ambitions, vanities, and regrets. While all appearances are transitory and unstable in his world, there is also a powerfully anchoring stillness at its core, a spiritual strength no less than a virtuoso artistic focus. The periodic chants of the monks, the droning and bells, the Buddhist sutras on Genjuro's back, the landscapes surrounding human need all allude to this unchanging reality, side by side with or beneath the restlessly mutable. Rooted in historical particulars, *Ugetsu* is a timeless masterpiece.

CRITERION COLLECTION, 2005

UTAMARO AND HIS FIVE WOMEN (1946)

"Ukiyo-e" is the Japanese term for "the floating world" of artists, courtesans, wealthy playboys, and fashionable dilettantes who frequented the pleasure quarters of Edo (later Tokyo) in the eighteenth century. The word also designates the popular style of woodcut print championed by Harunobu, Hokusai, and Utamaro, who broke with the aristocratic, Chinese-influenced painters of the generation before them and found a way to capture the earthy, material facts of their mercantile period in a style that remained breathtakingly elegant. This combination of the aesthetic and the populist may have been what attracted Kenji Mizoguchi to the story of Utamaro, since the great filmmaker himself was an exquisite perfectionist who functioned in a popular, collaborative art based on mechanical reproduction. But Mizoguchi first had to convince the U.S. Army's postwar censors, who frowned on period films as possible incitements to Japanese feudal nationalism, that his project would fit into the new democratizing spirit. "So I went to the General Headquarters of the Occupational Authorities and explained to them that Utamaro was a painter for the *people*," the director recalled.

Mizoguchi's identification with Utamaro must have gone further, since the artist was considered unequaled in drawing women and the director had come to specialize in "women's pictures," focusing especially on the suffering and limited options of women in a male-dominated society. While it would be hard to argue that a movie organized around the male gaze and enraptured with female fleshly beauty is feminist, Mizoguchi does show sympathetically how women—oppressed by a social system that makes them the playthings of fathers, husbands, and lovers—fight to emancipate themselves and to express their deepest feelings.

"Man is free," wrote D. H. Lawrence, "only when he is doing what his deepest self likes, and knowing what his deepest self likes, ah! that takes some doing." *Utamaro and His Five Women* is about that process: for Utamaro, it is drawing, and for the women around him, it is loving. Not that they love *him*, by the way. The film's title misleadingly suggests a sultan and his harem, but the protagonist is at most a brotherly protector to the women, a rather asexual portraitist more interested in capturing their lines than in bedding them. He is played by a nebbishy-looking actor (Bandō Minosuke II), raising the question of whether different casting would have produced a more magnetic film or whether someone with more sexual charisma would have ruined the point Mizoguchi was trying to make. The paradox is that Utamaro, in order to achieve that life-giving touch in his art, must detach himself more and more from the hurly-burly. In fact, he recedes to such an extent that he ends up a minor character in his own biopic. A more fitting title might have been, echoing the Ukiyo-e writer Ihara Saikaku, *Five Women Who Loved Love.*

We learn early on that Utamaro has just lost his mistress, the courtesan Okita (played by the magnificent Kinuyo Tanaka, Mizoguchi's favorite leading lady) to the playboy Shozaburo (Shōtarō Nakamura), who is spineless yet has the ability to charm women. Utamaro accepts the loss philosophically; when Shozaburo proves false and jilts Okita, Utamaro advises his ex-lover to "give him up, like a true woman of Edo." You might think that Utamaro is being offered as a model of Buddhist nonattachment, but it is easy for the artist to counsel renunciation in matters of romantic love because that is not where his passion lies. Indeed, when Okita, after stabbing to death her lover and the woman who has taken him away from her, tries to justify her action, she says, "I won't fool myself with lukewarm love. I wanted to be true to myself. Uta, isn't it the same with your drawings?" In this remark she places herself on a par with the artist: they both have been searching for the same authenticity.

In typical Mizoguchi fashion, the movie is filled with incidents of heartless cruelty, rejection, and betrayal. As if in a Japanese version of *La Ronde*, the characters keep changing partners, in search of a fleeting erotic happiness based on novelty and competitive status. Underneath this commotion and turmoil, however, there starts to accumulate a counter-strain of transcendent calm that is largely the fruit of Mizoguchi's visual style. The flowing tracking shots and pans, delicate movements and pauses, patiently held long shots, and elegant compositional reframings engender a sense of poetic sublimity. In a film dedicated to the cult of beauty, the viewer's pleasure overflows in the countryside scenes, where Okita chases her lover down and where the proper Yukie (Eiko Ohara), the artist's daughter, tries to pry her own lover free. Suddenly we are drenched in night scenes, lanterns, rivers, bridges, country inns, and Mizoguchi's visual style at its lushest and most inventive takes over. At the same time, we cannot forget that the most visually sensuous passages are also the most heartbreaking, like the shot of Yukie, devastated by rejection, walking slowly along a country road, sobbing, while Utamaro's servant tries to puzzle out how to console her. There is also a virtuoso sequence near the end in which the camera follows Okita rising to a dreamlike certitude, part madness, part clarity, then pauses on Utamaro while she rushes out of the frame, with the clear implication that she is going to kill herself.

"I don't feel guilty. He told me he was happier with me than with her." So rationalizes a courtesan who has taken away another woman's lover. The man they are fighting over, Seinosuke (Bando Kotaro), is a wannabe artist who had started as a disciple of Kano, a Chinese-style painter, then fallen under the spell of Utamaro. "He draws on women's flesh and mingles with the masses!" says Seinosuke admiringly. But all Seinosuke succeeds in doing is mimicking the easy morality of bohemia, which frees him from any responsibility for hurting others. He never grasps the discipline and commitment that lie at the heart of Utamaro's accomplishment. In the gap between self-indulgence and self-control, passion and renunciation, Mizoguchi opens a generous space for the film's nuanced perspective.

FROM *THE HIDDEN GOD: FILM AND FAITH*
(NEW YORK: MUSEUM OF MODERN ART, 2003)

Chapter Thirty-Seven

MIKIO NARUSE

When a Woman Ascends the Stairs

The posthumous international triumph of Mikio Naruse is one of the most unique corrections in film history. During his lifetime (1905–1969), Naruse toiled away at his craft, largely unsung though respected by his peers, making over eighty pictures. After he died, retrospectives of his work began to tour Europe and America; they excited the enthusiasm of knowledgeable cinephiles and were repeated in periodic cycles. A body of criticism grew around him, and now his films are issued worldwide on DVDs. What is it about Naruse's films that touches this belated responsive chord? They are not flashy, but they ring true. They appeal to our demanding intelligence, our sense of the rigor of daily life, and, seen in bulk, they draw us into an astonishingly consistent, psychologically resonant universe. His work, almost all of which is set in the contemporary era, is about people (very often women) of limited means, trying to keep their heads above water, escape domestic quagmires, and realize their dreams in a world rife with betrayals and self-betrayals. As he famously said about his characters: "If they move even a little they quickly hit the wall." That this rather grim vision should prove delightful in the viewing remains an enigma. Perhaps Naruse's refusal to employ cheap, feel-good shortcuts (or, for that matter, facile apocalyptic bleakness) comes as a relief in contrast to the usual box office fare.

After directing many of his best films during the fifties, including *Late Chrysanthemums, Floating Clouds,* and *Flowing,* Naruse was ready to tackle the newly prosperous, go-getter Japan. Though he had begun making movies from the silent era, Naruse had no trouble adjusting his objective style to a cooler, sixties mode. The crisp black-and-white Cinemascope and xylophone-inflected jazz score and modernist bar interiors give *When a Woman Ascends the Stairs* a glamorous, international style taste that goes down like a dry martini. It seems a departure of sorts from his usually drab, lower-middle-class, scarcity environments, but the preference for enlightened sto-icism over glib redemption is pure Naruse. The film did fairly well in Japan, and when a package of Japanese cinema masters toured the United States in the early sixties, it was this somewhat atypical late work in his corpus that was chosen to represent Naruse and continues to be one of his most frequently seen films there.

At the film's center is Hideko Takamine, one of Naruse's favorite actresses and indeed one of the most striking, gifted, and charismatic stars in Japa-nese cinema. She plays Keiko, a widow who supports herself as a bar madam, the chief attraction in whatever bar she works, by virtue of her beauty and superior refinement. (Hence the honorific "Mama"). In some ways mis-matched for the job, since she does not like liquor, refuses to sleep around, and has a proud, choosy character, she stands out from the stereotypical bar girl, which is why so many of the male characters find her a challenge and want to seduce her. In a sense, she represents a more traditional Japanese set of values, in contrast to the mod, pecuniary libertinism sprouting up around her. The dilemma is that she is approaching an age when her looks might be expected to fade, and so she is encouraged either to start her own bar or get married. Either path seems to involve a sacrifice of independence. To start her own bar, she is advised she will need a patron (i.e., become some busi-nessman's mistress); Keiko tries to circumvent this distasteful compromise by attempting to raise the capital through subscriptions from her wealthiest customers.

The stairs in the title are both literal and symbolic, conveying the idea that Keiko is on a Sisyphean vertical treadmill, trying to get somewhere in this life as a woman on her own. Her voiceovers, on the steps or during documentary-style cutaways of Tokyo, tend to describe in general terms the daily life of the Ginza district and the bar hostess's lot. The film's time struc-ture thus runs on dual tracks: first, the forward linear narrative, packed with incident (suicide, illness, marriage proposals, deceptions, one-night stands, abandonment) and, second, the repeated figure of the stairs, with its philosophic musings, when the film catches its breath and loops back, making you understand that in a sense Keiko is getting nowhere, except in her awareness of what she is up against.

What keeps the film entertaining—even dryly comic—is the tension between the essentially futile struggle of Keiko and the colorful, rapacious types who surround her. Naruse fills the canvas with sharp characterizations: the sexpot Junko, who snatches Keiko's would-be patron for herself; the mother and brother who leech off of her; the long-suffering bartender/manager (played by rising star Tatsuya Nakadai) who unrequitedly loves Keiko but is not above a roll in the hay with Junko; the shrewd, right-to-the-point lady owner of the Carton Bar; the chubby, gentle-mannered suitor Seikine (Daisuke Katō). When Keiko decides to accept Seikine's marriage proposal, we cheer her willingness to compromise by accepting this homely but essentially good-hearted man—only to discover he is not what he appears. The scene where Seikine's real wife tells her that her husband keeps getting into trouble by chasing women and believing his own lies, while his children circle on a beat-up bike trailing a tin can on an empty lot, with power plant stacks in the distance, is classic forlorn Naruse. Another door has closed in Keiko's face.

The film keeps dwelling on that face, Keiko/Takamine's exquisite instrument registering revulsion or censure. Certainly Keiko has more of a conscience than the sleazy businessman Minoru, who wastes no time collecting his debts when his mistress, Yuri, commits suicide, or the opportunistic bar girl who swoops in to resell the suicide's kimonos. But it would be too simple to see Keiko as the saint in a den of sinners. She has her own wayward needs, is in fact in love with a married businessman, Fujisaki (the wonderful actor Masayuki Mori, who played the potter in *Ugetsu* and who subtly communicates here the burden of being "the type women go for"). After the marriage plan with Seikine blows up, she gets drunk and throws herself at Fujisaki. They sleep together, and she awakes, happy and fulfilled, only to learn that he has been transferred to a post in Osaka. When the long-suffering manager discovers she has slept with Fujisaki, he throws the evidence in her face: "I used to respect you," he says. "Sorry, I'm not that good," she mutters. No one is that good—or that evil—in a Naruse movie; he neither ennobles nor demeans but shows realistically that we are all mixed, contradictory creatures.

Though we cannot but sympathize with Keiko, we are also allowed to judge her dispassionately. She comes across at times as self-righteous, at other times, hard. For instance, when she flings the words "I hate you" at her admirer-manager, the balance in sympathy shifts to him for the moment: he has done nothing to deserve such scorn. When her mother begs her for the necessary funds to keep her brother out of jail, Keiko's first response is a haughty refusal; only later does she come around. Asked to help pay for an operation that would correct her nephew's polio, she discards the plea as too expensive, and we never do find out if she springs for the loan. In short, she is a very human mixture of generous and self-protective. She weeps for herself, but do we weep for and with her? We respect her stubbornness and resilience, yes, but what keeps this quintessential woman's picture from descending to weepy melodrama is the objectivity brought to bear. Part of it comes from the detached point of view in Keiko's own voice-overs, part from the careful plotting that makes each successive outcome seem plausible rather than operatic. Most of it ensues from the visual style, which records the drama in even-handed, worldly fashion.

Naruse's visual style, never ostentatious, shows exquisite tact. Like Rossellini, another filmmaker of unfailing intelligence, Naruse directs facts; he constructs the image only enough to get its essential meaning across. There are no bravura 360-degree camera movements, but there are subtle little tracking shots of Keiko walking through Tokyo, with or without company. And when Keiko goes up the stairs to her bar, the camera delicately ascends with her for just two seconds. Kurosawa admiringly singled out Naruse's skill as an editor, and we see plenty of evidence here. In dialogue scenes (such as the one near the beginning, when Keiko enters the party for a bar girl getting married), he employs a highly complex yet for the most part invisible cutting style of close-ups, two-shots and ensembles, with characters shifting from foreground to background. Every cut conveys the partiality of each character's viewpoint, even the most minor: it's everyone for themself. Expressive lighting touches, like the sudden luminosity of Takamine's face in the fortune-telling scene or after she sleeps with Fujisaki are made more effective by their rarity.

Naruse's gift here is being able to keep alive surprise and the fresh possibility of hope, even as you know deep down that he's going to snatch most of that hope away. Endurance is the final antidote to despair, and that he does not extinguish. For a director whose vision is so frequently called pessimistic, what engages and enthralls in *When a Woman Ascends the Stairs* is its lightness of touch, deft and coolly understated, like its cocktail jazz score.

CRITERION COLLECTION, 2007

Chapter Thirty-Eight

YASUJIRŌ OZU

Late Spring

Although the late Yasujirō Ozu never made a bad film, *Late Spring* (*Banshun*, 1949) was the first of two masterpieces (the other being *Tokyo Story* of 1953) that have become cherished classics of world cinema, yielding fresh pleasures after countless viewings. *Late Spring* is perhaps the more delicate and tightly constructed of the two. Indeed, given this Japanese director's penchant for an exhaling, pausing style that favors atmosphere and nuance over plot, it is remarkable how every detail of the film, every dialogue line, seems in retrospect to bear down unremittingly on the central narrative dilemma.

This most implacably fated of stories begins almost nonchalantly, with an easygoing, comic tone. A tea ceremony, a bicycle outing, two scholars bent over their desks and interrupted by the utility company's meter reader—the flotsam and jetsam of daily life sets the stage for the dramatic conflict. A widowed professor, living contentedly with his grown daughter, is brought to understand that he is being selfish in holding on to her and must get her married. The problem is that she does not want to leave, partly because she knows that he will be sad and alone without her, partly because she proudly thinks herself the only one who understands his ways well enough to take care of him, and partly because she is afraid of the unknown responsibilities of husband and children and cannot imagine herself happier than she is with her father. The conflict is not between old and new values but between two traditions: the duty of the parent to see the child safely married, the obligation of the child to care for an aging parent.

Crucial to the film is Setsuko Hara's remarkably shaded performance as the daughter, Noriko: part goody-goody, daddy's girl, part stubbornly defiant rebel, part ingénue in perennial white sweater and skirt, part mature woman, in fact older than her years, with rings under her eyes and an adult sense of self-sacrifice. Her laughter and polite high spirits are so infectious that it comes as a shock when her smile disappears, halfway through the film, as she digs in her heels. But Chishū Ryū is no less extraordinary as the father, Somiya, with his absent-minded-professor grunts; his bemused, baffled smile; and, underneath, his steely resolve. The generational duel of wills is at a stalemate until Somiya pretends that he is remarrying, thereby unleashing Noriko's jealousy, anger, and, eventually, her capacity to embrace a new life. The partnership of Hara and Ryū is one of the great pas de deux in film acting. Although father and daughter can rarely sustain a conversation, much less confront the matter at hand, they read each other's every pause and sigh, and their bent backs mirror each other time and again. (The film is, among other things, a demonstration of elective affinity through genetic posture.) Part of the regret in watching the two separate is the realization that they really do make a great couple, all thoughts of incest aside.

If, as Donald Richie has maintained, "the end effect of an Ozu film . . . is a kind of resigned sadness,"[1] that effect is nowhere more carefully arranged than in *Late Spring*. Many small acts pave the way for our final vision of Somiya, alone and bereft, peeling a pear. Formal rituals of Japanese culture and tradition—a tea ceremony, a visit to a temple, the preparation of a wedding dress—merge casually into the rhythms of everyday life while such ordinary habits as sewing, brushing teeth, or clipping toenails are given an unhurried presentation in real time that elevates them to the status of religious rites. The ocean waves crashing on the shore at the end can be taken as standing for everything that is both changing (the daughter's dread) and unchanging. Or as Audie Bock argues, the director uses such shots not as "symbols in the Western sense, but as vehicles for the transcendent, ineffable quality of life that takes us outside of mere human emotion."

Much has been made of Ozu's master shot, his anchoring of the camera at tatami-mat level, three feet above the ground. The director Paul Schrader in his book *Transcendental Style in Film* is especially eloquent about Ozu's achievement of the statically spiritual through his camera choices and pillow shots. But it also needs to be pointed out that *Late Spring* contains many passages of movement (the bicycle scenes, the tracking shots following the estranged father and daughter on either side of the street), as well as sequences that replace the master shot with close-ups and cross-cutting. Two such sequences stand out: when they attend the Noh drama and, in a wordless montage, we see Noriko jumping to the (false) conclusion that Somiya is about to marry a widow in the audience, and the ensuing dialogue in which she confronts her father and he misleads her into deciding her suspicion is correct. He does this merely by grunting assents to her questions, but the effort of lying makes his upper lip tremble. Ozu films this deception with alternating close-ups, as if to say that his beloved tatami shot is only for showing the truth of everyday life.

So, too, the references to Westernizing influences in postwar Japan (Coca-Cola signs, baseball, classical music, Gary Cooper) demonstrate an Ozu accepting admixtures, He may have been a stylistic purist but he was also a man of his time, and his art was rooted in a particular historical moment. The defeat of Japan in World War II and the adaptations that followed led to an acute generational gap between the prewar elders and the so-called *après-guerre* generation, many of whom had suffered during the war (like the daughter here, whose malnutrition in adolescence has led to a worrisome blood condition, mentioned in passing). Many narratives of postwar Japan show sexually loose young people acting out by drinking, sassing elders, and indulging in other wild Western habits, but Noriko's response to the postwar situation is to burrow deeper into restraint, using ultra-traditional values to protect herself against contamination. This leaves her in a somewhat prudish, judgmentally isolated place (she criticizes the father of a school chum for remarrying, for example) until she reluctantly comes to grasp that embracing life means accepting moral impurities and surrendering to change.

Late Spring kicked off a string of Ozu movies about parents gently pushing their offspring out of the nest even though it meant a future of loneliness for them. The final irony is that Ozu himself remained unmarried, living with his elderly mother. The working-out of the plot of *Late Spring*, in all its ramifications, may have served to purge him of the road not taken.

FROM *THE HIDDEN GOD: FILM AND FAITH*
(NEW YORK: MUSEUM OF MODERN ART, 2003)

Chapter Thirty-Nine

CHRISTIAN PETZOLD

Barbara

The pleasures of this coolly controlled, tensely watchable, subtle psychological thriller are many, starting with the perfect sensibility match between veteran German director Christian Petzold (*Jerichow*) and his perennial leading actress, Nina Hoss. There is no getting around that Hoss is amazing, brilliant, dominant in the title role. As Barbara, a physician exiled to an East German provincial town as punishment for having applied for an exit visa from the GDR (the film is set in 1980, before the fall of the Berlin Wall), Hoss exudes such fierce wariness and disdain for her colleagues, whom she realistically suspects may be spying on her for the Stasi, that the suspense, the ticking bomb becomes less *Will she be able to smuggle herself out of this country she detests?* than *Will she exhibit any humanity, any crack in her icy demeanor?* She does, of course, eventually revealing a warmer, more vulnerable femininity beneath the chiseled façade of disenchantment, but in such precisely calibrated ways that each time it comes as a shock.

For all that the film bills itself as a character study (and a star vehicle), it is at least as much about the dynamics of a whole society under police surveillance. Where everyone is expected to snitch on neighbors, relatives, and colleagues, for the good of utopian if by now worn-out socialist ideals, it becomes harder to despise individual informants. Unlike, say, the heavy-handed way *The Lives of Others* makes villains of its police agents, here we see the characters have little choice but to inform: everyone has his reasons, legitimate reasons, even beyond cowardice, to cooperate with the state.

The adamant Barbara, who will never snitch, is drawn reluctantly to her male colleague at the hospital, Andre, a shaggy, amiable doctor who has secretly been instructed to report on her. As superbly played by Ronald Zehrfeld, Andre's motor seems to be running at half the speed of the tightly wound Barbara's, and that disparity makes for extraordinary partnering. In one of the film's strongest scenes, Andre confesses to Barbara the reason why *he* has been exiled to this backwater. He tells his heartfelt tale, and she receives it in total silence, with pure mistrust, forcing him to comment like an acting student after a failed audition, "What's the matter, did I tell it too smoothly?" You realize suddenly that in this vigilance-driven society, everyone is forced to be an actor, to wear a false mask.

The film zigzags physically between tight, claustrophobic scenes at the hospital and more breathable ones following Barbara on a bicycle into the picturesque countryside, where she tries to find some privacy while pursuing her own double-agent tasks for her West German boyfriend. She is always looking over her shoulder, afraid of being watched, and with good reason, it turns out. Meanwhile, her medical professionalism is aroused by the needs of her patients. Petzold and his cinematographer, Hans Fromm, have framed each shot with consummate intelligence and restraint, capturing both the austerity and the decorousness of this human-scaled environment. We are always made aware, compositionally, of the emotional constraints on the characters, and in the final act, of the temporal limits as well. Time is running out for Barbara. Is the conclusion too neat, too predictable, as a film critic friend of mine complained? Maybe so. On the other hand, there is a thin line between the predictable and the inevitable, and a film that does so many things right is entitled, I believe, to conclude in the manner of its own choosing.

FILM COMMENT (NOVEMBER/DECEMBER 2012)

Chapter Forty

MAURICE PIALAT

Naked Childhood, Van Gogh, and Le Garçu

NAKED CHILDHOOD

In his defiantly maverick directing career, which yielded only ten features in forty years, Maurice Pialat (1925–2003) was a stimulant and irritant, agitating the cozy pool of French cinema. His first effort, the lyrically bitter essay film *Love Exists* (1960), about the suburbs, won a prize at the Venice Film Festival and the admiration of François Truffaut, who offered to help produce his first feature. No doubt Truffaut was also attracted by the subject matter of Pialat's proposed project: a boy abandoned by his mother who is shunted from one foster home to another. But the result was no *Four Hundred Blows* knockoff: if anything, it reversed the experience of that beloved precedent in that Pialat made difficult any sentimental identification with the boy, made it equally hard to indict or applaud the adults, and forced the audience to revise its judgment with each scene.

In retrospect, *Naked Childhood* (*L'Enfance Nue*, 1968) seems one of the most remarkably self-contained and obdurate debuts in cinema history. By his own admission, the director, no youngster but already forty-four, had sought with this first feature to make an "uncomfortable" film for audiences. Although it was hailed by critics, it was not exactly a crowd pleaser, and he vowed to correct his ways and please audiences more in the future. Yet such was his character that he went on to create one gloriously uncomfortable film after another. These included the astringent *The Mouth Agape* (a mother lies dying with cancer while her son seeks erotic release in town); the explosive *À Nos Amours* (a promiscuous teenage girl in a ruptured family); the antiheroic epic *Van Gogh* (the artist seen as a crabby moocher); and his final work, *Le Garçu* (a devastating study of male arrested development). When his eighth feature, an austere drama involving religion, *Under the Sign of Satan* (1987), was announced as the winner of the Palme D'Or at Cannes and drew catcalls from the audience, Pialat showed his contempt for their opinion by making the classic "fuck you" gesture. The confrontational relationship that existed between this famously difficult, temperamental auteur and the French public ought not to be misconstrued as misanthropy. His sympathies for his characters ran so deep that he felt no obligation to sugarcoat their flaws.

In the case of François, the ten-year-old protagonist, we may first want to give him a hug, but before twenty minutes have elapsed he throws a cat over the banister (a deal breaker, understandably, for many viewers), steals a watch and smashes it, and gets in fights with classmates, among other acts of mischief. Our inclination then switches, wanting to see him as a Bad Seed, to wash our hands of him, but he contradicts this picture by certain tender actions, such as caring for the cat he had injured and buying a gift for the foster mother who has just decided she's had enough and he must go. Other factors complicate our judgment: for instance, the young foster mother, pouring out her complaints to the social worker (first he peed in the bed, now he pees around the bed, he doesn't eat, he steals things, etc.) complains that there is something fundamentally nasty about François, the way he stares at their daughter when they give her a bath. The social worker, wearily resigned to having to place the boy in a new home, nevertheless can't resist saying: "You didn't have to bathe her in front of him."

Later, when he is transferred to the home of a kindly elderly couple who are also foster-parenting another boy, the adolescent Raoul, and caring for a bed-ridden grandmother, we see François responding often (if not always) positively to their more benign treatment. He becomes especially fond of the grandmother, who seems able to engage him without cornering him or extracting ritual expressions of affection that are beyond his reserved inclination.

A word should be said about the uncanny performance by Michel Terrazon as the boy. Though Pialat cast nonprofessionals almost entirely for this film, he did not always ask them to play who they were in real life, as he did the elderly couple, the Thierrys: the ten-year-old Terrazon was not abandoned, but a child from a stable family who was called upon to act. His François displays a sly, sneaky manner, a wary half-smile, and a tendency to hide in the background—except when he is openly demanding attention by mischief or destructive tantrums. He is filmed almost always in medium or long shot, in any case, without the soulful close-up treatment Truffaut lavished on Jean-Pierre Léaud. François often remains silent, even when questioned directly by adults. Years later, Terrazon reported that Pialat did not write specific dialogue for the cast but gave them summaries and expected them to come up with their own lines. The young performer's inability to think of what to say perfectly jibed with the character he was playing; such a taciturn boy would likely have had little idea why he was acting out the way he was. Most children cannot give an articulate account of their behavior, and this laconic position would be particularly true for a child whose attachment to his mother was shattered, and with it his sense of personal security. Beyond that, François knows full well that he can be kicked out of a foster home in an instant if he says or does the wrong thing.

The film is thus deeply concerned with psychological behavior, but not with psychological explanation. The audience is called upon to watch this child, whose inner life we can only speculate on and who therefore remains a mystery. That sense of mystery is deepened by Pialat's quirky filmic technique: scenes begin and end abruptly with no preparation or emotional orientation, no music score to tell us how to feel, no cues as to how many hours, days, or months have gone by since the last scene. In short, the viewer in kept off-balance and has to attend to the immediate experience in the moment. Pialat's patient, immersive approach has been legitimately compared to documentaries, and there are many passages in this film that strike a documentary chord: notably, the opening scene of the political demonstration, which would seem to be preparing us for a liberal-left indictment of the French social services. In fact, the purpose of this demo footage is more to give us a social-class context than a political message: to tell us we are about to enter a working-class or lower-middle-class milieu, where economic need may play a role in the decision to foster a child. Even though the first foster mother hotly denies this, saying "I don't need the extra francs you send us every month," the fact remains that these families are not comfortably bourgeois. Pialat clearly sympathized with their straitened economic circumstances, and his attentiveness to the physically worn, dowdy interiors of the two foster homes, with their proud little heirlooms, tells us a great deal about their struggle to hold their head above water. (Later in his career, Pialat, who started out as a painter, would put forth a more polished compositional style, in films such as *À Nos Amours* and *Van Gogh*. But his first film disdained the elegantly pictorial and veered toward a plainer—if equally rigorous— depiction of domestic environments.)

The director explicitly denied that his intent was to make a "social film," and in fact provokingly called himself a man of the Right, thereby distancing himself from politically committed, engagé filmmaking. Yet the extensive preliminary research that Pialat undertook about adopted children and the French social services suggests a more complicated stance. Some of this research made it directly into the film, like the intake scene at the adoption center, where we see the attempt to match orphan with picky prospective parent ("Don't give me a black child." . . ."This boy is a cutie, you'll really like him.") In this intake scene, which straddles the two foster-home narratives, our protagonist François makes no appearance, nor does he in a later scene when his foster-brother Raoul is upbraided for breaking the rules, which suggests that Pialat may have wanted to show us the broader problem of temporary adoptions, above and beyond the plight of this particular boy: that abandoned children brought up in successive foster homes may indeed be prone to aggressive or troubled behavior and that foster parents may approach the task with an unrealistic, consumerist perspective, expecting to find compensation for all their sadness My own suspicion is that Pialat was conflicted: one part of him indeed wanting to address this broad social problem, and another, the proudly artistic side of him, fighting that generalizing, do-gooder impulse with idiosyncratic details that discomfit.

Pialat preferred confessing to a personal, egotistical motive in making the picture: though he was not an orphan himself, having been raised by his biological parents, he nevertheless felt he had been emotionally abandoned by them along the way and that his childhood had been a miserable one. The film's forlorn undertone may well stem from this wound. But just as we think that we are heading into tragedy (the meanness of small-town life bearing down on a troubled child), the film catches its breath with the wedding scene, a working-class documentary passage where everyone rocks back and forth singing "The Blue Java." This is a relaxed tableau, and François is shown enjoying it like everyone else, a minor character responding "normally." At every point, we are presented with conflicting evidence that makes it impossible to decide whether François is essentially a decent kid or a hopeless cause. He does get into fights but is provoked by his classmates. Even in the episode of dropping the cat, he is shown surrounded by other boys, who are no less sadistically curious. And his throwing of railroad ties at passing cars has serious consequences, but again, there are other boys with him doing the same. Should we write off François as pathologically damaged or indulgently argue that "boys will be boys" and consider his only mistake was getting caught? Perhaps neither. All we know is that by the film's end, he is neither redeemed nor irredeemable. Pialat later reproached himself for not having the guts to go all the way and show the boy hanging himself with a dog lead, as one of the boys he had met during his research had done. But that would have been another film—specifically, *Mouchette* (which happened to be made in 1967, the same time Pialat was shooting his first feature)—and suicide for François would have offered a sort of redemption from his troubles, too easy a resolution.

That peculiar obstinate realism of Pialat's, that balance between absence of solace and refusal of pessimistic bleakness, helps explain why he came to be revered by so many younger French filmmakers whom he inspired, such as Catherine Breillat, Olivier Assayas, Erick Zonca, Bruno Dumont, and Gaspar Noe. Kent Jones has clarified "what gives Pialat's best work its existential pull: there is so little evidence of aesthetic attitudinizing or strategizing that we become genuinely attuned to the film as a series of precious moments."[1] In his fascinated attention to the moment, free of narrative agendas, he played a key role in that global shift in cinematic emphasis, which can also be seen in the work of John Cassavetes, Hou Hsaio-hsien, Abbas Kiarostomi, and Jia Zhangke. It is true that Pialat himself never really made it big in the United States, partly because he was part of that underrecognized generation of filmmakers who came just after the New Wave, which included Philippe Garrel, Jacques Doillon, Jean Eustache, and Luc Moullet, and partly because his pictures never offered a scintilla of "feel-good" Gallic charm of the *Amélie* variety.

Maurice Pialat's moral vision was there from the beginning in *L'Enfance Nue*: He could not bring himself to believe in the redemptive promise of enlightened values or love, and he seemed impervious to the delusion of false comfort. Yet the sweetness of the scene where the elderly Memere is sitting on her husband's knee and telling her two foster boys, all ears, about their courtship, leaves an afterglow that cannot be easily forgotten. Stubborn in depicting how precarious and disappointing relationships often are, he was equally insistent on listening to the testimony and experience of those very different from himself who were not as tortured by a fear of abandonment.

VAN GOGH

Hard to single out the most perverse or peculiar film of Maurice Pialat, a maverick master who specialized in the one-off, but *Van Gogh* would be my candidate. Atypical by virtue of being his most ambitious, costly production (backer pressures to recoup expenses forced him to trim it to the still-epic 155 minutes from three hours plus), a costume period drama about the world's pinup darling of beautiful suffering, already a biopic cliché, it yet remains utterly characteristic of this contrarian, personal filmmaker. Pialat must have chosen such a tired subject precisely because it challenged him to liberate Van Gogh from sanctimonious hagiography and to get it right for once. In the process he brought to bear all the earmarks of his provoking, uncompromising, and thoughtful style.

If many viewers find Pialat's films irritating, it may be because he took irritability as his subject matter. It was his bold stroke here to make Van Gogh not a saintly puppy dog who just wants to be loved, as in the Kirk Douglas/ Vincente Minnelli version, but self-absorbed, touchy, shriveled in himself, and incapable of loving anything but his work, about which he also harbors insecurity and distaste. Pialat's Vincent struggles against self-pity and mooching on others, but not hard enough. As the movie progresses, he expresses an instinctive mistrust, bordering on paranoia, toward all those who try to help him, and since, as the saying goes, even paranoids have enemies, he is proven right. But this Vincent is no Christ figure betrayed by his disciples; he is, to put it bluntly, a pain in the ass, badgering his would-be supporters until they turn on him. Vincent even forces the issue by assaulting those he suspects of not loving him enough, to make them acknowledge the antipathy they have for him, as though only hostility was honest.

Key to the success of the film is Jacques Dutronc's lean, crabbed performance, never suing for the audience's sympathy nor attempting charisma. If anything, though in almost every scene, this Van Gogh seems at times a subordinate character, a passive observer to his own life—an effect accentuated by the long-shot cinematography, which frequently marginalizes the protagonist to the frame's edges. The other male leads, Bernard Le Coq's Theo and Gérard Séty's Doctor Gachet, overshadow Vincent at times with their forcefulness and avidity. Pialat's Theo, a hardworking family man and shrewd art dealer, is shown disliking his brother's work and making only ineffectual attempts to sell it while supporting him financially as a family dependent. Dr. Gachet is seen as a Sunday painter who envies the pros and has no real understanding of the artists he patronizes. All six principals in the brilliantly acted ensemble vacillate between considerateness and cruelty, forcing viewers to keep adjusting their judgments. The three female leads, Alexandra London's Marguerite Gachet, the doctor's teenage daughter, who throws herself at Vincent to lose her bourgeois propriety; Jo (Corinne Bourdon), Theo's wife, who alternates between upbraiding her husband for not supporting Vincent enough or helping him too much; and Cathy (Elsa Zylberstein), a prostitute with a soft spot for Vincent though always insisting on payment, embody the film's ambivalence and shifting point of view.

Yet even if they had all been uniformly kind to Vincent, the results would have likely been the same. This film is about (what a strange subject for a super-production!) the will to suicide. In this sense, it is the opposite of *Lust for Life*; it might instead be called *The Death Wish*. We encounter here not the heroic, self-generating, younger Vincent, but a man at the end of his tether, already burnt out, disenchanted, alcoholic, and ultimately turning away from everything that might dissuade him from his suicidal course. Pialat understood that the would-be successful suicide has a mission: to protect, nurture, and hone that impulse into action, regardless of distractions and pleasures along the way. Vincent is seen jumping into the river at a friendly picnic as a provisional suicide attempt. Eventually he succeeds, but the actual shooting takes place off-camera, in keeping with the laconic treatment of the material: all we see is Vincent falling bloodied in a field. There follows a protracted dying in which people take turns sitting by his death-bed while he for the most part shows them and us his back, already a mummy wrapped in sheets. The moment of death itself is handled unsensationally: Theo, leaning over the body of his brother, sees no signs of breathing and says, "It's all over."

Many scenes terminate abruptly, much like in Bresson's *Pickpocket*, in the protagonist refusing community. The editing follows an oddly disjunctive pattern of nonmatching jump cuts within a scene, which reinforces the strategy of keeping the viewer off-balance. On the other hand, there are some beautiful tracking shots, like the one of Vincent and Jo conversing on the riverbank just before he jumps in the water. The extended brothel sequence, with its marching revelers, bawdy songs, and voluptuous surrenders, is like a dreamy interlude allowing the movie to catch its breath before the final plunge. All that erotic release, it turns out, signifies nothing; Vincent goes moody and shoots himself.

There has always been a tension between the libertine and the puritan in Pialat: on the one hand, offering up dollops of sexy detail, exposed bosoms, bottoms, couplings; on the other hand, withdrawing hope that any of this pleasure taking will add up to happiness or even serene resignation. There is something both lush and austere about *Van Gogh*: one has to go back to Visconti's *Senso* to find a similar historical tapestry that so delights in sensual production design and mise-en-scène while enforcing so bleak a feeling of human duplicity and isolation.

How much did Pialat identify with his protagonist? One can certainly see some of Van Gogh's irritability in the filmmaker who told the Cannes award audience to go fuck themselves after their lukewarm response to his winning the Palme D'Or for *Under the Sign of Satan*. And when Van Gogh muses that they keep telling him he's making ugly art, not pretty pictures like Renoir, you can sense some of Pialat's own disgust at the picturesque Gallic charm that represents one pole of French cinema. Pialat championed the other pole, a raw, tough, in-your-face quality, not afraid to risk crudeness. At the same time, the delicacy with which this filmmaker could distance himself from Vincent's morose subjectivity and sympathetically bring to life every other character who interacts with him and embed them all in a visually graceful scheme that honors the ravishments of impressionist painting without slavishly mimicking it demonstrates why Maurice Pialat's passing is, alas, an irreplaceable loss, both for the French and for world cinema.

LE GARÇU

Maurice Pialat's final film, *Le Garçu*, had a great deal to say about father-son relations. Pialat's method, here as in his previous work, was to locate a raw wound and press down hard. His honesty makes you wince; it's not inconsistent with sadism. But in *Le Garçu*, an overwhelming parental tenderness fights cruelty to a standstill. We are presented with a self-absorbed, moody paterfamilias, Gérard (Gérard Depardieu), who is lucky enough to have a beautiful wife (Géraldine Pailhas) and an enchanting boy (Antoine Pialat, the director's own son). Gérard's unsatisfied appetite—Depardieu's bulk registers here—for more of everything leads him to cheat on his wife, walk out on the family, then circle longingly back when they start adjusting to life without him. The scenes with the kid are a triumphant fusion of fiction and documentary since young Pialat does not act so much as be, with the adult actors adjusting around him. Gérard's hunger for a primal closeness with his son is heartbreaking, in view of the child's innate autonomy and sanity. Those with children will especially recognize the fights over childrearing or the wounded feelings when the little boy prefers a male babysitter to his father. Equally moving is the final scene of the estranged couple's uneasy truce. What starts off as a portrait of a narcissist modulates into a broader sadness, in which no one is entirely to blame for the evanescence of romantic love and family happiness.

CRITERION COLLECTION, 2010; *FILM COMMENT* (MAY/JUNE 2004);
FILM COMMENT (NOVEMBER/DECEMBER 1996)

Chapter Forty-One

ALAIN RESNAIS

Middle and Late Resnais

The late styles of elderly auteurs tend toward the sublime or the feeble, though sometimes elements of both recur. How a film critic responds to, say, Ford's *Seven Women*, Fellini's *The Voice of the Moon*, Wilder's *Fedora*, Dreyer's *Gertrud*, Chaplin's *A Countess from Hong Kong*, Oliveira's *Belle Toujours*, or Rohmer's *The Romance of Astrea and Celadon* may hinge in part on one's sentimental need for ancestor worship or, conversely, one's narrow inability to judge any work except by current fashions. I confess wanting to give old masters as much benefit of the doubt as I can.

The late films of Alain Resnais exhibit a freedom and capricious, bittersweet playfulness that may account for their being undervalued. Then again, even when he was younger Resnais always went his own way, ignoring the expectations of others. When he was still the darling of cutting-edge cinephiles, on the basis of his first three fractured, elliptical features, *Hiroshima, Mon Amour, Last Year at Marienbad*, and *Muriel*, he disappointed champions such as Susan Sontag and Annette Michelson by making *La Guerre Est Finie (The War Is Over)*, a powerful, smoothly naturalistic film with an international star, Yves Montand: they saw it as a betrayal, a commercial art house film not that removed from Hollywood storytelling. In retrospect this seems ridiculous. Hadn't Resnais the right to make a realistic film about the aftermath of the Spanish Civil War, especially when it gave him the chance to work from a script by the novelist Jorge Semprún?

One way of looking at Resnais's career is to consider the writers he worked with. Unlike auteurs such as Rohmer or Bergman, who wrote their own screenplays, Resnais happily collaborated with writers as various as Marguerite Duras, Alain Robbe-Grillet, Jean Cayrol, Jorge Semprún, Jules Feiffer, David Mercer, Alan Ayckbourn, Jean Anouilh, Agnès Jaoui, and Jean Gruault and even adapted the plays of deceased writers from the 1920s and '30s, remaining faithful to their scripts. Too, he had his own set of passionate hobbies or interests, in comic books, the theater, music, America, surrealism, which needed expressive outlets. If we can stop thinking of experimental cinema as involving only a small set of modernist-prescribed practices, we can better appreciate that Resnais was always experimenting. A rigorous formalist from the start, he never stopped playing with form from film to film. Some of his middle and late films are extremely tight (like the darkly somber *Love Unto Death*), others shaggy (*I Want to Go Home*), but all issue from the director's warm curiosity, his openness to a combination of artifice and naturalism, and his realistic appreciation of and tolerance of humanity's flaws.

After *La Guerre Est Finie* he made *Stavisky*, a sumptuous period drama about the financier and embezzler Alexandre Stavisky (played by Jean-Paul Belmondo), with a gorgeous musical score by Stephen Sondheim. This *Citizen Kane*–like investigation of an enigmatic character, complete with talking heads speaking to the camera, also signaled Resnais's fascination with the late 1920s and early 1930s. Its self-reflexive perspective was in line with the director's early features, but its nonadherence to a discrete political message displeased many. Resnais, who had begun as a member of the left-wing, committed Left Bank group that included Chris Marker and Agnès Varda, from this point on turned away from politics, toward a more personal and psychological direction. (He complained: I am constantly being scolded by both sides for not being leftist nor rightist enough.) In his next film, *Providence*, his first in English, he collaborated with the English playwright David Mercer and cast John Gielgud as an aging, dying novelist who exerts his imagination to transform his family members into his latest Gothic novel. The alternation between scenes of reality and fantasy suggests a puzzle of figuring out which is which, like the one in *Last Year at Marienbad*, although to my mind the film is far too solemn and portentous. Resnais had conceived of it as a dark comedy, but few audiences would find much to laugh at. In any case, he was trying something new, and not all experiments succeed. The same could be said for *Je T'Aime, Je T'Aime*, a forgettable if marginally enjoyable science fiction film with a premise about going back into the past.

Resnais struck paydirt with *Mélo* (1986), his faithful adaptation of a 1929 play by Henri Bernstein. Working with what would become his regular acting company, Sabine Azéma, Pierre Arditi, André Dussollier, and Fanny Ardant, he drew out all the ecstasy, pain and cruelty in this tragic tale of an adulterous love triangle, at the same time emphasizing its theatrical roots, employing curtains between acts and long dialogue scenes shot in interiors. There is not a hint of camp in the movie: by taking seriously the emotions underlying this forgotten melodrama, this relic of boulevard theater, Resnais achieved a masterpiece. Its shattering effect is particularly significant, given that the director was often falsely accused of making "cold" films.

At a time when most directors his age are shelved, Resnais found a way to keep working by adapting theatrical vehicles and procedures to the screen. From *Mélo* through his other masterpiece of this period, *Same Old Song* (a musical written by Agnès Jaoui and Jean Pierre Bacri) to *Not on the Lips* (a Wildean farce based on a 1931 operetta) to his adaptations of the English playwright Alan Ayckbourn, Resnais perversely swam against the tide of contemporary film idiom by courting a modest, antiquarian, stage-struck manner. How strange for a director once associated with the progressive avant-garde (*Last Year at Marienbad*) to refine a technique—filmed theater—that would strike some as problematically uncinematic. That old stricture that said movies should stay as far away as possible from the theater and strive for "pure cinema" was defied by Resnais, who refused to make a separation between film and theater or to treat them as enemies. And by concentrating on the era of the late 1920s and early '30s, it is almost as if he wanted to explore the neglected possibilities of that transition in French cinema when talkies came in, many plays were adapted to the screen, Marcel Pagnol and Sacha Guitry did their finest work—just before the liquid certainties of Carné's poetic realism and Renoir's *Grand Illusion*.

On the other hand, Resnais might not have been looking backward but forward, to the altered TV image. In interviews, he claimed to be smitten with the inventiveness of camerawork in American television series such as *The X-Files* and *The Sopranos*. The challenges of mounting a fluidly elegant, intimate mise-en-scène in support of the Ayckbourn play *Private Fears in Public Places* (the film's French title is *Coeurs*), whose action takes place almost entirely in a series of interiors (apartments, offices, restaurants), must have appealed to the virtuoso in Resnais—all the more so, knowing that to the degree he succeeded, the results would be unobtrusive. We are only made peripherally aware of the outside environment, the city, the streets, largely through the artificial snow that falls constantly, like a stylized stage effect.

Coeurs needs no special pleading: it is marvelously alert, adult, intelligent, handsome, well acted, and serenely sad—surely one of the most beautiful films ever made by an eighty-four-year-old. Resnais successfully relocated Ayckbourn's ensemble play from London to a wintry Paris, whose denizens are for the most part lonely and lovelorn. To call them "losers" would be too harsh; these are the nonwinners of the urban sweepstakes. As with *Same Old Song*, Resnais uncovers a surprising undertone of desperation and depression beneath the plastic surface of contemporary life. Six lives casually intertwine: a middle-aged real estate agent, played by André Dussollier, and his younger sister (Isabelle Carré) share an apartment; the real estate agent is unrequitedly in love with his pious office assistant (Sabine Azéma), who moonlights as a home-care attendant for the elderly father of a widowed bartender (Pierre Arditi), who works at a club where an unhappy couple (Laura Morante and Lambert Wilson), she a successful businesswoman, he an unemployed, embittered ex-paratrooper, often hang out. The younger sister, who sits in bars night after night hoping to find a man, meets the ex-paratrooper, falls in love, and is stood up by him on their second date. As multiple-protagonist narratives go, think Ophuls's *La Ronde*—a *La Ronde* where the characters don't score, falling back on the resigned dignity of solitude.

Not that all is stoical restraint. Moments of flamboyant carnality erupt: Azéma puts on a sex show, with leather and whips, for her ancient patient, Arditi's father. Carré is repulsed to discover that her older brother watches porn on television, and he is deeply embarrassed. At the film's center is the ever-reliable Dussollier as the mature if frustrated realtor, yearning for his secretary. Resnais has worked with Dussollier so often that it is hard not to think of him as the director's surrogate. Sabine Azéma, Resnais' wife in real life, is an actress whose mannerisms can rub viewers the wrong way, but Resnais brings out her arch, neurotic hysteria and diva-like self-absorption to perfection here. Pierre Arditi is dignified and moving as the widowed bartender; Lambert Wilson departs from his usual elegant leading-man demeanor to achieve a loutish but sympathetic gruffness; Isabelle Carré is luminous in her dewy-eyed ingénue part. The harmony with which wisdom gets distributed, disillusionments are staged, and forbearance achieved gives the whole film the air of a musical. Though not a note is sung, everything is songlike.

In the delightful *Same Old Song*, Resnais assembled an impressive cast of Parisian troupers (Sabine Azéma, André Dussollier, Agnès Jaoui, Lambert Wilson, Jean-Pierre Bacri) crossing one another's paths, grasping for love and meaning in an intricate boulevard-theater plot, stopping only long enough to sing a pop song. These song snatches crystallize yearning or anger, offer platitudes of consolation and self-assertion (Azéma's hilarious "Resist!"), and plenty of rue. *Same Old Song* is that oddity, a musical about Prozac and depression. Its sharply individuated characters race purposively at first toward goals then slow down, suffer panic attacks, face their inner emptiness and lack of control, drifting into benign entropy as if to say: *Relax, this unhappiness is going to last for awhile*. It's a very middle-aged perspective. Resnais's tactful camera revels in the glory of the two-shot, his superb actors feeding off one another. I particularly liked Dussollier, with his toggle coat and oversized sweater, his calm, observant quality a surrogate for Resnais. Certainly the songs are fun, but the main event is watching these passionately intriguing characters and the pain and contact they inflict on one another.

Resnais's last three films—*Wild Grass* (adapted from a novel by Christian Gailly), *You Ain't Seen Nothin' Yet* (a mash-up of Jean Anoulh's *Eurydice* and *Cher Antoine, ou l'Amour Raté*), and *Life of Riley* (another Ayckbourn play)—offer the impression of a graceful leave-taking. In *You Ain't Seen Nothin' Yet*, a troupe of quarreling actors are brought together by the news of their leader's imminent death and must decide whether to put on a final performance. Resnais's lyrical last film, *Life of Riley*, which he completed just before his death, depicts several couples on the brink of dissolution who somehow hold together, either out of middle-aged inertia or a shrewd sense of limitations—recalling the remark of George Harrison's widow, Olivia, that the secret to a long-lasting marriage is not getting divorced. The direction in these three films is functional and minimal, no fancy camerawork, just trusting the actors to deliver the goods.

I invite future film scholars to deconstruct the pleasures and ironies in these late works by Resnais, which have been largely ignored until now. All I can say is that there is much to be discovered.

FILM COMMENT (MARCH/APRIL 2007)

Chapter Forty-Two

DINO RISI

Il Sorpasso

Like the sports car that roars through the streets of Rome in the opening, *Il Sorpasso* charges at a delicious pace from start to finish, each scene uncovering new landscapes, sardonic ironies and oddball secondary characters while adding layers of nuance to its two principals. This miraculously entertaining film has lost not a whit of contemporaneous zing since its 1962 release. If anything, its disappearance from American distribution for many years allows us to appreciate it now with startled gasps of pleasure, as a newly unwrapped, jazz-scored, sleekly propulsive machine from the golden years of the *commedia all'italiana*.

That 1960s–'70s cinematic movement was spear-headed by Mario Monicelli, Alberto Lattuada, Pietro Germi, and Dino Risi, all of whom had roots in *neo-realismo* but felt that its humanistic preoccupation with war and deprivation had played itself out and it was time to tackle the contradictions of Italian society under the boom with more irreverent gusto. Risi, the director of such sharp, mordantly satiric films as *The Sign of Venus*, *A Difficult Life*, *Love and Larceny*, *Scent of a Woman*, and *Il Sorpasso*, was determined to make movies that were both well crafted and commercially popular. He had begun his professional career as a psychiatrist (a fact worth remembering, given his penchant for complex psychological shadings) then had been lured into the motion picture industry, first as a critic and screenwriter then as the director of numerous documentaries.

From 1952 on, he turned out an average of two features a year. It was not until his sixteenth feature, the international hit *Il Sorpasso*, that his unique gifts as a cinematic stylist became more generally apparent—and even now, it must be said, he is underrated, possibly because comedic filmmakers always fight an uphill battle when it comes to being taken seriously. But *Il Sorpasso* is not without its serious side, and its dramatic tensions keep us off-balance and engrossed.

At the film's core is the relationship between two men who meet by happenstance—or, put another way, the extraordinary performances of two magnificent actors who embody these characters: Jean-Louis Trintignant as Roberto, a shy, reserved, well-mannered law student, and Vittorio Gassman as Bruno, a loud, brash, fun-loving Lothario. Roberto is wary of Bruno—understandably so, given the older man's habit of borrowing money and indulging in mischievous pranks. He keeps trying to disentangle himself from the other's commandeering lead. Significantly, we are made privy to the introverted Roberto's thoughts through periodic voiceovers, but never to the extroverted Bruno's. Since Bruno is so quick to act out his impulses and speak his mind with uncensored frankness, we probably don't need to listen in on his mind, but by virtue of having access to Roberto's thoughts, and by that character's relative normalcy, he becomes the audience surrogate, watching and judging the flamboyant Bruno every step of the way, as we are, with fascination, mistrust, amusement, and alarm.

The motor driving the film is Vittorio Gassman's very physical performance as Bruno. Gasssman had the wavy dark hair; lean, muscled physique; and overall good looks of a matinee idol, but he preferred roles that would allow him to mock a character's insecure vanity—the perpetual sneer-smile on his face the quizzical expression of a man trying to put something over on you while fearing being made a patsy himself. It would be tempting to dismiss Gassman's Bruno as merely an opportunistic con man. He is, to be blunt, a jerk, but a strangely sympathetic one. We like him in spite of ourselves. Again and again he slips the noose of our condemnation by acting in a way that shows generosity (for instance, paying back Roberto the money he has borrowed at the first possible opportunity). What he really has going for him is vivacity: he enlivens any scene he enters. In roadside cafes he will suddenly dance over to a waitress to put the moves on her (he hits on every woman in sight). By contrast, Roberto moves in a formal hesitant way that makes his lower body seem frozen, block-like. He also has a slight stammer, which grows fainter the longer he is in Bruno's company. If Bruno is too aware of his charms, Roberto has too little confidence in his attractiveness. The boyish-faced Trintignant aces the role, as he will again a few years later in *My Night at Maud's*, of a repressed, moralistic prude who secretly desires liberation. Roberto clearly wants to learn from Bruno how to be braver, sexier, less inhibited, which is why he keeps hanging out with him against his better judgment. But the uptight law student never gives up trying to rein in his libidinous, rule-bending companion.

In one scene, when they have pursued two pretty foreign tourists to what turns out to be a cemetery, Roberto scolds Bruno, saying that this time he has gone too far, he has crossed the line. But when the men turn around and leave, the women express disappointment that the flirtation has ended. Later on, after Roberto has confided on the road to Bruno his boyhood crush on an aunt, they arrive at his relatives' home. Roberto runs into that same aunt on the stairwell and makes haste to get away from her, as if still smarting from the embarrassment of having confessed his childhood ambition to wed this woman, who is now looking rather plain and middle-aged (and who hopes, perhaps, to rekindle his admiration). Bruno, however, sees that she is still a warm-blooded woman and flirts with her, rearranging her hair and getting her to wear it down. As the two men leave, we see the aunt gazing at herself in an erotic afterglow: she has been brought alive again by Bruno's attentions.

On the other hand, Bruno's ex-wife unceremoniously kicks him off the bed when he tries to seduce her for old times' sake. Sometimes it works, sometimes it doesn't. Bruno goes from cocky bravado to bursts of self-pity, warning Roberto not to end up "a stray dog" like him. Incurious to the point of anti-intellectualism, rejecting out of hand any subject he doesn't already know (Etruscan tombs, medieval architecture), he is by no means stupid; he has an urban peasant's cunning that allows him to see through deceptions. (Note how quickly he uncovers the age-old infidelity of Roberto's sainted great-aunt by observing the gestural similarities between her son and the overseer.) He certainly picks up on Roberto's wary suspicions of him, which wound him. What is clear is that Bruno likes the younger man and he takes seriously his role of tutoring Roberto in life's pleasures, even if it means jettisoning his innocence. Exhibiting a genuine tenderness towards Roberto, Bruno is quick to explain that he's not queer (one of his many semi-disparaging references to homosexuality, a reflexive kind of machismo). But his friendly feeling for the somewhat clueless Roberto is undeniable, and he seems baffled by Roberto's need to keep running away from him.

The film could easily have turned into a schematic melodrama about a worldly, cynical player who destroys a shy, well-brought-up young man, in the manner of Chabrol's *Les Cousins*, but it keeps evading that narrative by instancing Bruno's big-heartedness and Roberto's complicity, until we are obliged to accept that this is the story of a burgeoning friendship. If one of them does not make it out alive, that has less to do with either one destroying the other than with the blood sport of Italian driving. Thus, I think it would be wrong to interpret the film as a morality tale, arguing backward from the ending that it all goes to prove Bruno was a destroyer. Roberto is the one telling Bruno to go faster. He has become a convert to speed. He readily admits that these last few days with Bruno have been the happiest in his life. If anything, what the film demonstrates is the narrow gap between life force and death wish, Eros and Thanatos.

The film's title, *Il Sorpasso*, refers to the Italian custom of overtaking cars on the highway. In its first American release, it carried the English title *The Easy Life*, which now seems a transparent attempt to capitalize on the success of *La Dolce Vita*. The original-language title seems much more fitting, especially as it points to what the movie is really about: the spirit of Italy, for better or worse.

In a humorous essay about Italian driving habits, Jackson Burgess explained: "The paramount feature of Italian highway driving is *il sorpasso*. The word *sorpassare* means 'to pass with an automobile' and 'to surpass or excel.' To *sorpassare* someone is to excel him socially, morally, sexually and politically. By the same token, to be *sorpassato* is to lose status, dignity and reputation. Stopping at a stop sign, for example, is prima facie evidence that the driver, if male, is a cuckold."[1]

This description could account for a good deal of action in the film, and the film's climax thus seen as nothing more nor less than a demonstration of national character. Even in scenes that occur indoors, we are given instances of this Italian tendency to jump the line, to cut corners, to bend the rules—by no means restricted to Bruno. (For instance, the workman who slips ahead of a dignitary waiting in line for a toilet.) But much of *Il Sorpasso* does take place on the road: like all road movies, it adheres to an episodic structure, which puts pressure on the screenplay to come up with surprises, with amusing, revealing, and poignant vignettes. The screenplay, by Risi, Ettore Scola (who would become a fine director himself), and Ruggero Maccari, is a marvel of comic invention, walking the tightrope between satire and sympathy.

The film testifies to the Italian love affair with the car during the boom years as a way to satisfy restless nervous energy and the illusion of getting ahead. Yet it is a truism of enlightened city planning that cars and walking cities are inherently antagonistic. The Italian writer Natalia Ginzburg, speaking to this tension not long after the release of *Il Sorpasso*, commented: "It has become quite difficult both to love Rome and to live in it, since these days it is a jungle of automobiles. If ever there was a city for walking, it's this one; the cars seem to have invaded it by stealth, like an attack of blight. I cannot understand who wanted them, since everyone curses them. They overrun the city like a river at flood tide." Bruno never tires of expressing his preference for the excitements of city life over rural life, yet he loves driving above all else, and his attachment to the car keeps propelling him out of Rome, to crisscross large swatches of the countryside. During this impromptu tour of Italy, we glimpse in the background not only fetching landscapes but dreary, nondescript stretches of suburban sprawl, such as had begun to deface the areas between the historical centers preserved for tourists.

The look of the film owes a great deal to the gifted cinematographer Alfio Contini, who exploited the rich, graphic possibilities of widescreen black-and-white. That format's aesthetic, which reached an apogee in the early 1960s, made the most of swiftly traversed horizontals (such as Bruno's car racing through streets and highways), of architecturally spaced verticals dividing the frame, and of the moody shadows of oncoming night. Risi's training as a documentary filmmaker was displayed in the many cutaways to individual gawkers, faces in the crowd who witness or ignore the protagonists' shenanigans. For all the two-shots of Bruno and Roberto relating to each other in the car, we are never far away from registering the presence of the Italian masses, some bourgeois, others working class. A recurrent motif involves shots of dancers doing the Twist—an American import though with an Italian accent—to a particularly moronic, catchy tune, which conveys the national dedication to having fun. Bruno and Roberto, scoffing at one country dance where a middle-aged farm-hand is grinding away, dub it "the Clodhopper Twist." The point is that whatever their moral or intellectual shortcomings, these ordinary Italians know how to amuse themselves.

There is a memorable moment early on in *Il Sorpasso*, when Bruno says he saw Antonioni's *Eclipse* and it put him to sleep (then he covers himself by declaring that Antonioni is a very fine director). This passage can be read many ways: as a meta-commentary on the film you are watching, its aim to entertain enough to keep you awake; as an assertion by the *commedia all'italiana* school that it is every bit as artistic, in its own way, as its rival, the Italian art cinema; and as a claim staked to portray Italy as it actually was, not as that dour, solemn master of alienation, Michelangelo Antonioni, portrayed it. To take one example: when Antonioni shows a gaggle of young people dancing en masse to pop music in *L'Avventura*, he seems to be deploring it as emblematic of the decline and fall of Western civilization, whereas Risi depicts a similar scene as people just having fun. Risi was a satirist, every bit as aware of the shallowness and soullessness of much contemporary Italian life, but he drew different conclusions from it. He chose to be amused rather than appalled by the petty behavior and boastful vanities he observed. Hence the ambivalent attitude the film takes toward Bruno, who is neither hero nor villain, who is childishly irresponsible one moment and gracious and lovable the next. The fact that his sensible daughter, played by the adorable Catherine Spaak, still is fond of him, despite his many disappearances, counts for a lot. Even his serene ex-wife (Luciana Angiolillo), while not interested in the least in taking him back, continues to have maternal sympathy for this man who reminds her of a lost child. In a sense, that is also Risi's attitude toward Italy: he sees what is foolish, corrupt, profoundly unserious and self-destructive in the country's behavior but cannot help loving it. The result is the bittersweet mash-up of exuberance and regret that is *Il Sorpasso*.

CRITERION COLLECTION, 2014

Chapter Forty-Three

ÉRIC ROHMER

La Collectionneuse, The Marquise of O,
and Le Rayon Vert

LA COLLECTIONNEUSE

La Collectionneuse is a strong, sensuously lush, deceptively slight film, a Riviera fruit with a bitter, uncompromising aftertaste. In retrospect, it is both classically Rohmeresque and atypical, as befits a film in which the director was still finding his way. The first full-length feature in the Moral Tales, the first one in color, the first collaboration between the director and his great cameraman Néstor Almendros, it is also more sexually explicit and linguistically gruff—less chivalric, if you will.

By the time Éric Rohmer began shooting *La Collectionneuse* in 1967, he had already made the first two of his Moral Tales, the short featurettes *La Boulangère de Monceau* and *La Carrière de Suzanne*, and the thematic template of the series had been established: A man, committed to one woman, is tempted by a second but resists having sex with her, in the meantime turning himself inside out with analytical self-scrutiny. He had actually planned to do *La Collectionneuse* as the fourth Moral Tale, after *My Night at Maud's*, but the prospective star of that film, Jean-Louis Trintignant, was tied up with another shooting. And so the director decided to go ahead and direct this feature out of sequence, on a very low budget, with nonprofessionals and limited sets. As James Monaco tells it in his invaluable book, *The New Wave*, "The only expenses that summer were for film stock and rent for the house in Saint-Tropez which was the set and which also housed cast and crew. There was also a small budget line for the salary of the cook who, the stories go, cooked nothing but minestrone during the entire shooting schedule."[1] All this may help explain why *La Collectionneuse* has a somewhat transitional, in-between air: its three main characters, mooching for the summer off their absentee friend Rudolph's beneficence, and Rohmer himself, waiting to start shooting the bigger-budget production that would come to be regarded as his masterpiece, are all marking time.

In this space of freedom, thanks to minimal expectations (he and his producer, Barbet Schroeder, were genuinely surprised when *La Collectionneuse* went on to win the Silver Bear at Berlin and run nine months in a Paris cinema), Rohmer was able to devise several working principles: improvisations with his cast would be codified into a script; extensive rehearsals would be followed by very few takes (a miserly 1.5:1 shooting ratio was achieved); a discreetly spying, unostentatious mise-en-scène was composed, mostly of fluid long shots that would capture the vacationing characters awkwardly sharing the space of someone else's villa, whiling away the summer days and nights in a mixture of lassitude and tension. The sense of contrast between an earthly paradise, in which the loveliest landscapes serve as ironic background for the pettiest exchanges, is heightened by Almendros's extraordinary color photography, with its warm brown tones and deep, rich blues; its preference for natural light over artificial illumination; its use of mirrors to bounce light off, soften and even it out; and its pushing of film stocks to the limit in night scenes and shooting in the shade during the day to avoid the sun's dramatic changes. All these techniques, which would become hallmarks of Almendros's (and Rohmer's) later styles, were worked out for the first time in *La Collectionneuse*, which the cinematographer, not surprisingly, came to regard as his favorite film. He was quick to credit Rohmer's hands-on approach, saying, "Nothing could be done without his knowing about it and agreeing with it. In this he was unlike other directors, who give the cameraman a free hand and don't even want to look through the viewfinder themselves. First and foremost, the people in Rohmer's films are seen realistically. The image is very functional. His criterion is that if the image portrays the characters simply, and as close to real life as possible, they will be interesting." Withal, there was the director's steady emphasis on the slow emergence of character over thespian grandstanding.

Rohmer's use of nonprofessionals is complicated. He had never been as doctrinaire about it as Bresson, but he liked nonprofessionals for the fact that they seemed quieter and less apt to project "Personality," with a capital P.

They were more like empty vessels, ambiguous and harder to read, whom the audience must move halfway to meet. On the other hand, Rohmer often combined vivid professional actors with nonprofessionals, or gave nonprofessionals their first significant roles, which led subsequently to long acting careers. Patrick Bauchau, the star of *La Collectionneuse*, was a fellow traveler of the French New Wave who went on to appear in over a hundred movies; Haydée Politoff, the ingénue here, had a less sparkling career, gracing many Italian horror movies. It is curious that two of the then-nonprofessional leads (Politoff and Daniel Pommereulle) are called by their real first names, Haydée and Daniel, while Patrick Bauchau, the most charismatic, personality-filled, polished of the trio, enacts a character whose name has been changed to Adrien.

La Collectionneuse offers a case study in rationalization. With its unapologetically literary, first-person voice-over narration by Adrien, the film is essentially about the disparity between the main character's subjective interpretations of events and another, wider truth, which may be gleaned by the viewer eavesdropping on the proceedings. Faced with the enticing proximity of Haydée, a bronzed, bikini-clad student, the older man cannot make up his mind whether to hit on and bed her or leave her alone. Here we see one of Rohmer's most original tropes: the tepid attraction. It flies in the face of all cinematic convention, which dictates that the encounter of a good-looking man and good-looking woman must lead to grand narrative passion. But Haydée is not, like Bardot in *And God Created Woman*, an irresistible temptation or force of nature; she is a somewhat scrawnier girl-woman, the cousin of Jean Seberg in Preminger's *Bonjour Tristesse* (another Cote d'Azur movie, made in 1958, which likely influenced Rohmer), who is still trying to figure out the limits of her feminine magnetism. She is certainly not a "slut," a term the two men keep throwing in her face. She is sexually active, not inappropriately for her age, but I choose to believe her when she scoffs at their accusations that she is promiscuous, a "collector" of male lovers. No, she says, she is "searching"; she has as yet had no "lovers" in the affectionate sense of the word.

Why, then, are these men so nasty to her? They are angry because she is a pretty girl who, to their (sexist) minds, imposes on them an obligation to try to seduce her; they are angry that she has attracted them somewhat but not all the way (their own problem, but they interpret it as a kind of tease on her part). They are angry that she represents the utopian sexual liberation of a younger generation, and they are jealous of the cloddish, career-unburdened younger men her own age with whom she sleeps. And finally, they are angry simply because she is a woman, and all women, in their view, threaten to entrap them through the game of love. Haydée is not the most articulate young woman, though she says just enough to cast doubt on the men's interpretations. There will be other Rohmer films that take us deeper into the psyches of women. This one does not, but it gives us a very daring, precise portrait of the misogynistic, entitled, self-loathing psyches of men. And unlike, say, most Woody Allen movies, it does not let the rationalizing male character off the hook. Rohmer has explicitly warned us, in an interview: "You should never think of me as an apologist for my male character, even (or especially) when he is being his own apologist. On the contrary; the men in my films are not meant to be particularly sympathetic characters."

The handsome Adrien acts in a particularly caddish manner: he cynically manipulates his friend Daniel into sleeping with Haydée (and there is the homoerotic suggestion that perhaps he is using her as a substitute for himself); he neglects to defend her when Daniel calls her beastly names; he leaves her with the older American dealer and goes off for two days, as though pimping her; and finally, after eliciting some definitive sign that she really likes him (her stroking his chest repeatedly in the bathroom is one of the sexiest moments of Rohmer's oeuvre), he ditches her on the side of the road. He thinks he is acting out of a need to assert his freedom by abnegating his desires, as though he can only experience freedom through spiting his own interests, but it is no accident that he drives off without her when he sees her talking to two guys her own age. In a sense, he is frightened of her youth, and he also recognizes, however subconsciously, that it would not be right to take advantage of this girl. He does the correct thing, if for the wrong reasons.

In Adrien, Rohmer seems to have presciently diagnosed the emergence of a particular type on the world stage, whom Christopher Lasch would pinpoint a decade later in *The Culture of Narcissism* (1979). According to Lasch, the narcissist could be very charming, with "pseudo self-insight, calculating seductiveness" and "the manipulation of interpersonal relations," though he is haunted by anxiety. His sexual emancipation "brings his no sexual peace. . . . Acquisitive in the sense that his cravings have no limits, he does not accumulate goods and provisions against the future, . . . but lives in a state of restless, perpetually unsatisfied desire."[2] In the movie, Adrien travels light, a middleman for the sale of antiquities, and wants to start his own art gallery. The American collector accuses Adrien in one scene, which gets quite ugly and malicious, of being on "permanent vacation." It is not an entirely inaccurate charge and makes us wonder if the American may be the film's superego—that is, until he slaps Haydée for breaking his Chinese vase and forfeits all our sympathy. Then again, Haydée, in "accidentally" breaking the vase, shows that she is not entirely ready for adult life, either. These people are playing at life, at value and meaning. The tragedy of the narcissist is that nothing matters enough to become tragic. Adrien, alone at the end, tells himself: "I was overwhelmed by a feeling of delightful independence, of total self-determination. But in the emptiness and silence of the house, I was overcome with anguish." Hollowness might be an equally descriptive word.

La Collectionneuse focuses on the colliding needs of two generations, but it is also generationally inflected in another sense: Rohmer was ten years older than his colleagues, Francois Truffaut, Jean-Luc Godard, and Claude Chabrol, and this particular feature film, his second (his first, *Le Signe du Lion*, made in 1959, had been largely ignored) appeared belatedly—eight years after the French New Wave had taken international cinema by storm. If they reinvented film syntax with the brash energy of youth, Rohmer, who was forty-seven when he shot *La Collectionneuse*, would demonstrate what could be done in another, classical vein, with unobtrusive camera movements, invisible editing, suppression of music, and a more detached moral perspective toward its youngish characters. Godard clearly bonded with his childish gangster protagonist in *Breathless*; they are both on the same generational plane. Not so, Rohmer: he interrogates here, in keeping with the overall project of a "moral tale," the drawbacks of neglecting to grow up. He is still young enough to have put in a sex scene (a few seconds of Haydée thrashing in bed with a young man, the first time Adrien glimpses her), which would have been unheard of later in his career, and he incorporates a good deal of the cast's youth slang (much of which he later confessed he didn't understand). But finally, Rohmer views the problems of indolent, potential-laden, prolonged youth in this film from the perspective of the middle-aged artist who knows that the clock is ticking. The "wave" is no longer so "new."

THE MARQUISE OF O

The Marquise of O, which premiered in 1976, has a peculiar, anomalous place in Éric Rohmer's oeuvre. It was shot in West Germany, the only one of his movies not made in French, and it was the first to be based on a literary classic rather than the director's original screenplay and the first to abandon contemporary milieus with naturalistic acting for a historical setting, featuring more formal, stage-inflected performances. In time, he would make four more period pictures: the highly stylized Arthurian romance *Perceval le Gallois* (1978), which followed directly on *The Marquise of O*, then, after a gap of over twenty years, curiously, his last three pictures, *The Lady and the Duke* (2001), which took place during the French Revolution; *Triple Agent* (2004), set between the two world wars; and the lovely medieval pastoral *The Romance of Astrea and Celadon* (2007). We now possess enough examples to contemplate Rohmer's treatment of the past and to consider what themes or procedures might carry over from his contemporary stories: in short, what it might mean to be irreducibly Rohmeresque. But at the time it first came out, following directly on the worldwide successes of *My Night at Maud's*, *Claire's Knee*, and *Chloe in the Afternoon*, *The Marquise of O* seemed a radical departure: many Rohmer fans were puzzled while the majority of the critics, even those who had never taken to this director, hailed it as a masterpiece. It won the Grand Prize of the Jury at Cannes, did excellent business worldwide, and has remained one of his most popular films, a visually gorgeous, morally ambiguous, delicately ironic, and ultimately quite mysterious work that raises intriguing questions about the relationships among painting, theater, and cinema and parental versus romantic love. Beyond that, it asks: how can a film adaptation be utterly faithful and at the same time faithless to its literary source?

We begin with Heinrich von Kleist (1777–1811), the eccentric Romantic genius who wrote major plays (*The Prince of Homburg, Penthiselea*) and some of the most powerful stories in the German language ("Michael Kohlhaas," "The Marquise of O," "The Earthquake in Chile," "The Beggarwoman of Locarno"), before committing suicide in despair. Kleist's forte as a fiction writer was the *tale*, a distillation of fate that pursued the consequences of seemingly forgivable errors or accidents into darker and more inescapable traps. He was not long on psychological analysis: his characters do what they do rashly, almost to their own surprise. On the whole he eschewed scenes for brisk summaries. Characteristically, *The Marquise of O* begins: "In M—, a large town in northern Italy, the widowed Marquise of O—, a lady of unblemished reputation and the mother of several well-bred children, published the following notice in the newspapers: that, without her knowing how, she was in the family way; that she would like the father of the child she was going to bear to report himself; and that her mind was made up, out of consideration for her people, to marry him."

Rohmer opens his film in the same manner, with several men in a tavern reading the notice with wonder, then doggedly follows Kleist's flashback lead. The story reverts to a time when the peaceful Italian noble family is invaded by a Russian army. The beautiful marquise is set upon by ruffians, but rescued by a chivalrous count. As it subsequently emerges, this count, startled by her beauty, takes advantage of her as she slumbers. Months later, he returns, presents himself at their door, and offers his hand in marriage—partly to atone for his crime, though he is not able to bring himself to confess what he had done. The family, pleased in theory with the proposal of this appropriately noble suitor but unwilling to accept his rush to marry without a decent courtship, puts him off. Meanwhile, the marquise begins to experience the first signs of pregnancy, but as she has been completely chaste, she does not understand how this could be. When her pregnancy is medically established beyond all doubt, she must face the mistrust and disapproval of her parents, who cannot believe she has not slept with anyone. The Russian count is frustrated because he is trying to do the right thing but keeps being rebuffed. The audience, which suspects the count is the one who has impregnated the marquise, may find a bit comic the length of time it is taking for the family to figure it out. They cannot imagine that this heroic nobleman, who had appeared like an angel to protect the marquise, can have so diabolically dishonored her.

How can a rescuer also be a violator? Here Kleist and Rohmer are on the same page: the answer is that man is a morally mixed creature. Our appetites and our ethical-religious codes are often at odds. In Rohmer's contemporary narratives, such as *My Night at Maud's* or *Chloe in the Afternoon*, typically the male protagonist is sexually tempted by a beautiful unattached woman but does not act on his desire, either because of moral qualms, cowardice, or both. In *The Marquise of O*, the chivalrous count does violate the sleeping marquise (though we don't actually see it: as usual, Rohmer spares us the sex scene). Perhaps the story's setting in the distant past affords the male protagonist more sway to act on his desire, unencumbered by modern rationalizations and self-analyses.

The Marquise of O in Martin Greenberg's excellent translation, at forty-three pages, is barely long enough to be considered a novella, and it hurtles along in Kleist's condensed, spasmodic prose, not stopping to catch its breath. By contrast, Rohmer's narration moves at a stately pace, making use of every crumb of detail from the original story and staging every hinted-at gesture and action with a real-time fullness that allows us to see each character stand, cross the room, take the other's arm, and so on. Hence, the paradox of its being the most faithful of adaptations while at the same time utterly different in tone. Essentially, the film is an Apollonian, neoclassical contemplation of the Romantic expressive spirit.

Some critics, like Pauline Kael, have complained that Rohmer's version of the Kleist story tamps down the "id" and deprives us of "Kleist's spirit, which made him an avant-gardist and a modern."[3] Jonathan Rosenbaum, while acknowledging Rohmer's "immaculate direction," also opined that the film "subtly betrays the awesome energies of the original." [4] Myself, I think that there are many strands to modernism, and not all spring from the id's energies. Rohmer's quiet modernism resides in its formalism and moral complexity, and his film version of The Marquise of O does not "betray" Kleist any more than Kleist betrayed the old chronicles he used as his source material for the basic plot.

The exquisite visual style of the film reinforces its contemplative, distancing air. The great cinematographer (and frequent Rohmer collaborator) Néstor Almendros bathes his natural-lit compositions in an antique patina that looks simultaneously cool and honeyed. Many shots intentionally echo famous paintings: the marquise's sleeping form recalls Fuseli's The Nightmare, and other compositions featuring the marquise with her curly hairdo seem taken from David's portrait of Mme. Recamier. Some of the interiors suggest Vermeer's Dutch genre paintings or Chardin's still lifes. The net effect of all these pictorial references is to keep us aware that we are watching an artifacted period film, not a documentary. The fighting scenes are staged in tightly framed compositions, almost diorama-like, with a handful of extras, the modest budget reining in any hint of the spectacular—yet still basically realistic, not as self-consciously artificial as Rohmer would later do in Perceval le Gallois.

The film's dialogues are either quoted verbatim from the text or transferred from Kleist's summarizing prose into actual conversation, with minimal changes. Rohmer explained afterward that he stuck so close to Kleist's language because he would have been at a loss to come up with a credible version of how people spoke in that era. That decision also dictated that he choose actors trained in classical theater. He wisely cast Bruno Ganz, a prominent German stage actor, in his first major screen role. Ganz would go on to become an international film star, working frequently with directors such as Wim Wenders, Werner Herzog, and Alain Tanner, and Ganz brings a dark, appropriately stiff impetuosity to his scenes—the willful stubbornness to do the right thing no matter what. He conveys the impression of a man who thinks himself good and cannot quite understand how he was capable of performing such an odious deed. His costar, the dignified Edith Clever, was already a rising figure on the German stage and would subsequently be seen in the films of Hans-Jürgen Syberberg (*Parsifal, Die Nacht*). The marquise's father, played by Peter Luhr, and mother (Edda Seippel), are equally fine in their supporting roles.

The film's measured, gradual pace allows us to savor the irony of this family romance: the parents obviously adore their daughter and vice versa, but outward appearances and social conventions of the day oblige them to act as though their honor has been sullied and to banish her. The innocent young woman impregnated by force and then sent packing was a quintessential narrative of eighteenth- and nineteenth-century melodrama (like *Way Down East*). Rohmer winks at the melodramatic convention while offering a restrained version: the marquise is not kicked out into the cold but takes herself off to a country chateau, still quite comfortable. Thereafter, her mother acts as both tester and go-between, eventually bringing about the reconciliation between the commandant and his daughter. The "proof" that the rapprochement has taken is a scene showing father with grown daughter on his knee, kissing her repeatedly on the mouth. This hint of incestuous eroticism derives directly from Kleist: "Her daughter lay motionless in her father's arms, her head thrown back and her eyes closed, while he sat in the armchair, with tear-choked, glistening eyes, and pressed long, warm and avid kisses on her mouth: just as if he were her lover!"[5] What must have been daring to picture in Kleist's day has become curiously exotic for audiences today, who aren't sure how to take it but who may think: *Hey, maybe that's the way fathers and daughters carried on in the old days.*

Rohmer is able to have it both ways: to mock the rigid intolerance of bygone melodrama by theatrically stylizing the confrontation scenes between parents and child while drawing us into the very real pain of rejection at the heart of this familial disruption. It is only because these three honest, upright family members so obviously feel tenderly toward one another that their baffled estrangement can border on the tragic. The happy ending that caps the prolonged suspense ensures that, in retrospect, all that preceded can now appear in a more comic light.

A comedy of manners with rape in the middle of it? Nothing would seem potentially more offensive, especially when the happy ending of *The Marquise of O* (both story and film) involves the benign marriage of the violated woman with her rapist. But perhaps the issue is fudged somewhat by the convergence of the erotic and the metaphysical: the immanent visit of a god. Kleist, intrigued by the classical narrative of the gods visiting mortals and impregnating them, also wrote the play *Amphitryon*, which is another treatment of the same subject: this time Amphitryon's wife, Alcmene, receives an amorous visit from Jupiter (though she finds it hard to tell the difference between her husband and the god), which results in the birth of Hercules. Undoubtedly, the mystical, Catholic aspect to the Kleist story also attracted Rohmer. The mystery of the virtuous marquise's pregnancy cannot help but recall, as a line in the film reminds us, the only other instance of such innocence: the Virgin Mary. Ultimately, it is up to the eponymous heroine to accept and forgive that the father of her child is both man and beast. As always seems with Rohmer, it is the woman who must employ the principle of grace—who must show more worldly maturity and otherworldly clemency than the callow male.

LE RAYON VERT

For Éric Rohmer, leisure is the supreme spiritual test faced by modern people. As autumn is to Yasujirō Ozu, so summer to Rohmer: the dangerous time for the soul's stock taking. Even the French, for all their *savoir-vivre*, stand revealed by him as being better equipped to work every day in an office than to drift egoless and savor the moment. In film after film (*La Signe du Lion, La Collectionneuse, Claire's Knee, Pauline at the Beach, Le Rayon Vert, A Summer's Tale*), Rohmer used the overly packaged paradise of summer vacation to dramatize the self-deception and inner anguish of people who live in their heads but tell themselves they are up for nothing more than a bit of pleasure and a tan. On vacation, Rohmer makes us see, we are forced back into the recognition of our threadbare resources, emptiness, unanswered desires, inability to rise joyously to the beauty of the natural world, and disappointment with others for not dispensing our loneliness—that loneliness that is hateful but nonetheless prized.

Nowhere has Rohmer more astutely dissected this neurosis called summer vacation than in *Le Rayon Vert* (1986, its title in English variously *The Green Ray* and *Summer*). His method is to zero in on Delphine, one of the most individuated, well-observed characters in his (or indeed anyone's) cinema. Admirably played by the remarkable Marie Rivière, who tries not so much to win the audience's sympathy as to invest it in her contradictions, Delphine is both ordinary and singular, thin-skinned and too hard on herself, attractive and a bit of a pill. We learn in the course of the film that she is a strict vegetarian, disapproves of cut flowers, is made nauseated by swings and sailboats, and does *not, not, not* believe in casual sex. Also, that her fiancé dropped her before the film's narrative begins, and for two years she has been alone, suffering from what our talk show hosts call "self-esteem issues."

Her greatest flaw, though, from the viewpoint of her companion vacationers, is that she is unable to disguise her sadness. Indeed, you would have to go back to Falconetti's 1928 performance as Joan of Arc to find another Frenchwoman who cries as much onscreen. Yet Delphine is hardly being burned at the stake; she is merely flooded with a malaise precipitated by leisure—watching a summer storm, unable to explain why she feels so isolated, or simply frustrated by the difficulty of getting out of Paris.

For Parisians like Delphine, there is a special stigma associated with being forced to spend July and August in town. So she plots to go to Greece with a friend, but the plan falls through; takes up an offer to vacation in Cherbourg, only to feel ill at ease with the strangers she joins there; returns to Paris; rushes off to her ex-boyfriend's ski resort pad while he is away; then can't go through with staying there and returns to Paris, like a colorful beach ball that keeps landing in the same spot; then off to Biarritz for a week or two, again lonely and knowing no one. The boomerang structure of the film is rather comic, like a Jacques Tati acrobatic bit. We almost feel inclined to laugh at Delphine and at the seriousness with which she takes her plight, were it not for the fact that she seems kinder and more aware than many of the people around her. "The discreet cruelty of the bourgeoisie" could be the film's subtitle: one scene in particular, early on, shows a group of friends tearing into her for making too little effort to "meet someone." They offer her advice, astrology, criticism, and smugness—everything, in short, but understanding. In the end it is the spectacle of her hurt that they can't abide and that makes them treat her like a leper. She for her part is still too defensive to admit she *is* miserable, and so she keeps calling up her ex-boyfriend, ostensibly to see if she can borrow his cottage.

Eventually—and there is a sort of progress, in the New Testament sense that if the seed die, it bringeth forth much fruit—Delphine is able to acknowledge aloud that her boyfriend has dumped her. "If I'm dumped, it has to be my fault," she says. "I'm worthless. I have no cards to play." She explains this hesitantly to an easygoing, topless Swedish blonde who tells her the answer is to have fun and not to take men seriously and who then proceeds to pick up two available guys. The chatter between the Swedish blonde and the guys is excruciatingly shallow; we sympathize with silent Delphine for finding it unbearable. As with many dialogues here, Rohmer lets the scene run long, to the point of mortification and beyond.

Although *The Green Ray* is only ninety tightly constructed minutes long, it allows itself many moments of patient respiration and background observation. Scenes often begin in an almost documentary manner, the camera panning over a crowded beach, say, until it picks up Delphine in yet another swimsuit, staring petulantly at the ocean. A perfect beach day is the meditation wall on which she can project her inner demons. But the camera shows its detachment from her morose self-absorption by offering cutaways to another couple, a kid with a sand pail, and glimpses of French families on holiday. The bountiful world is both a reproach to Delphine and a relief to us.

Interestingly, this is not one of those Rohmer films in which every image is exquisitely composed by a master cameraman like Néstor Almendros. This time the director inclined toward a rough-and-ready, pan-and-scan approach and a grainy visual texture, like 16mm blown up to 35. The casual sensuality of a seaside summer, the food and wildflowers and bikinis, are all there but presented in a more throwaway manner. Equally, the delectable physicality of Rivière's Delphine—her long legs continually in view, her expressive, chiseled face, her adorable curly hair—is both impossible to ignore and at the same time an irrelevance since it doesn't bring her any closer to what she wants. All that beauty, offered up to the world and going to waste: ain't it the way? Delphine herself is often observed caressing her legs or adjusting a blouse that keeps slipping off her shoulders, in gestures both autoerotic and conciliatory.

The Green Ray, ultimately, is tender toward the forlorn Delphine. We learn to be with her, in her skin, to feel the sincerity of her pain, and to forgive her silliness, which is mostly youthful shyness. Since Rohmer, like Rossellini in *Voyage to Italy* or *Stromboli*, is a true Catholic filmmaker, he leaves a miracle for the end. First he lets Delphine meet a young man in a train station who does not laugh at her for reading Dostoyevsky's *The Idiot*, and she finds the courage to ask him to accompany her on an outing. Then Rohmer lets her see the green ray, that last blade of light in a sunset which, according to superstition (we've been told earlier), will allow her to know her own heart as well as that of others: in short, to shed her alienation. The gasp of pleasure we hear from her when the sun spurts green is enough to tell us that the crisis of summer is over.

CRITERION COLLECTION, 2006; ARROW FILMS,
ÉRIC ROHMER BOX SET, 2005; FROM *THE HIDDEN GOD:*
FILM AND FAITH (NEW YORK: MUSEUM OF MODERN ART, 2003)

Chapter Forty-Four

RAÚL RUIZ

Time Regained

Time Regained is both an apotheosis and a departure for Raúl Ruiz. This most prolific, self-conscious, and avant-garde filmmaker—who has turned out nearly a hundred movies and videos, many on a shoestring, often casual, parodic, cryptic—suddenly gives us a stately, polished, mimetic, moving, and reasonably faithful adaptation of a literary classic, the last volume of Proust's *In Search of Lost Time*, with a star cast that includes Catherine Deneuve, John Malkovich, Emmanuelle Béart, and Vincent Lopez. Some Ruizians may feel betrayed, to prejudge it as a sort of period costume sellout à la *Brideshead Revisited* or Merchant-Ivory middlebrow production; Proustians, who would find any cinematic version of this most interior of literary masterworks a vulgar reduction, will cringe at this or that casting choice that conflicts with their own mental image of Proust's characters; and the French, jealously guarding their cultural patrimony, are apt to carp that the Chilean exile didn't get certain details or accents right. Meanwhile, the general public—especially if they haven't read Proust—may feel disoriented by this almost three-hour epic, which juggles scores of characters, floats between time frames, and seems to lack a central dramatic focus. If these factors explain why the picture has yet to receive either the cinephiles' enthusiasm or the mainstream approval it deserves, it remains to be said that *Time Regained* is one of the most intelligent and substantial films of our day.

After the title sequence (water running over rocks: time's passing), the movie opens on Proust (Marcello Mazzarella) ill in bed, dictating to his maid

Céleste (Mathilde Seigner). Tiring, he dismisses her and looks through a stack of photographs—presumably friends and family whom he has appropriated for his fiction—with a magnifying glass, which introduces us to both the cast of characters and the theme of distortion. The rest of the film will follow Marcel, Proust's remembered younger self, wandering through other people's lives; trying to make sense of their mores, secrets, and politics; grasping only fragments; getting things wrong; never resolving certain doubts (was Gilberte ever a lesbian?); witnessing their tensions and arguments, denials and evasions; watching them age; wondering what it all meant; and resolving in the end to make a work of literature, which alone might redeem this detritus of unresolved memories, this failed life.

What fascinates me is how much Proust turns out to be ideal material for Ruiz, the confirmation of all his pet theories, while at the same time liberating him from his previous limitations as an overly clever, emotionally distant postmodernist. The Proust project satisfies the following Ruizian conditions, each of which I will try to explain more fully: a) it resists what Ruiz calls "central conflict theory"; b) taps into endless plot possibilities; c) subverts the privileging of the will as the narrative engine; d) explores the subjectivity through which memory and experience are filtered; e) supports narrative simultaneity ("the problem of how more than one fiction can co-exist in the same instant"); and f) asserts that people's identities overlap and that when it comes to character, the one is the many, the many, one.

In his intriguing books of essays, *Poetics of Cinema*, Ruiz argues against central conflict theory, which he sees as the Hollywood paradigm:

To say that a story can only take place if it is connected to a central conflict forces us to eliminate all stories which do not include confrontation and to leave aside all events which require only indifference or detached curiosity, like a landscape, a distant storm, or dinner with friends—unless such scenes punctuate two fights between the bad guys and the good guys. Even more than scenes devoid of action, central conflict theory banishes what are called mixed scenes: an ordinary meal interrupted by an incomprehensible incident with neither rhyme or reason, and no future either, so that it all ends up as an ordinary meal once more. Worse yet, it leaves no room for serial scenes, that is action scenes which follow in sequence without ever knitting into the same flow.[1]

One way to look at *Time Regained*, then, is as a series of "mixed scenes" in which something neutral is followed by something dramatic is followed by something banal or embarrassing etc. I should explain that very few of these scenes occur as scenes in the novel; rather, Ruiz and his co-screenwriter, Gilles Taurand, have lifted lines of a character's dialogue that Proust may have quoted in passing, often in the midst of an interior monologue, and woven them together into dramatic units. There is no attempt to follow the order in which these lines appeared in the novel: some snatches of speech may be combined from hundreds of pages apart, but the dialogue is either taken directly from Proust or paraphrased from the text. In short, in its own way, the film is remarkably faithful to its source material. But it is also faithful to Ruiz's schema that a scene need not revolve around one action or that successive scenes need not connect into one dramatic "flow."

We are constantly stopping and starting, shifting from year to year and character to character, which makes the first half hour perhaps the least engrossing to watch. It is only when we have learned the chronological patterns and sorted out the different characters that we can settle in and observe their separate species of pain. For pain is the spectacle we are offered, basically: Saint-Loup (Pascal Greggory) cheating on his wife Gilberte (Emmanuelle Béart) or Charlus (John Malkovich) complaining of being unsatisfactorily whipped or Oriane de Guermantes (Édith Scob) blurting out her venom and grief.

One of the ways Ruiz had used in the past to get around a central conflict was to employ the paradigm of magic realism, which he defined in terms of the Immortal Story: "all that you see has already happened and will happen many times again." Citing Borges's idea that "destiny adores repetition," he has made many films, such as *The Three Crowns of the Sailor* and *City of Pirates*, that illustrate the Nietzschean principle of eternal recurrence. The upside to this method is that it delivers Scheherezadian storytelling of endlessly playful variation; the downside is that we stop caring since in a world where anything can happen, nothing is ultimately at risk.

In *Time Regained* we have another kind of repetition, but it is more overtly emotional, more character-driven: the pang of rejection in the eyes of Béart's Gilberte, the distressed sneer or nervous giggle emanating from the mouth of Malkovich's Charlus, the rapacious distractedness of Greggory's Saint-Loup. All these figures are condemned to the Proustian law by which experience falls short of one's expectations by some defect in our mental design that deprives us of satisfaction. These are the tics Marcel is condemned to watch. Ruiz has asserted that Hollywood's central conflict theory overemphasizes identifying with the hero's will as an organizing device: "An old

Hollywood saying claims that a film is a success when the viewer identifies with the hero: he accomplishes the action, he must finally win. I think that in any film worth seeing one should identify with the film itself, not with one of its characters." By selecting so observant, so passive, so melancholy, so, in a way, spineless a character as Marcel to be the "glue" of the film, he is certainly diminishing the importance of will and replacing it with sheer consciousness. "What does this Marcel *want*?" the screenplay guru Syd Field or the dramatist David Mamet might ask in frustration. He wants to continue to perceive the film of memory intersecting with the present that is unspooling in his mind and on the screen before us. The action is Marcel's moment-to-moment perception. Ruiz gets to have it both ways: allowing us to identify with Marcel and with the film.

In terms of desire, Marcel, the perennial escort and comfort of old women, the confidant of waiters and widows, seems rather asexual. Had Ruiz adapted an earlier volume of Proust, such as *Albertine Disparue*, the Marcel character might have been more libidinous or obsessively jealous, but the Marcel of *Time Regained* is by now the retrospective analyst rather than the bildungsroman protagonist. If we do not see him in the throes of heterosexual yearning, neither is he presented as gay. He tries to elicit admissions from Saint-Loup about his homosexual inclinations and even stands on a chair to spy on Charlus being flagellated, but the dominant emotion is one of curiosity—that same "detached curiosity" that Ruiz spoke about as an alternative to central conflict theory. And here I cannot overemphasize the admirable, moving performance of the Italian actor Marcello Mazzarella (who remarkably resembles photographs of Proust, with his melancholy eyes and curved mustaches, but who also looks a bit like Raúl Ruiz) in making the most of his part of sympathetically listening to and partnering the other characters' self-absorptions, delusions, and doubts.

There is even an effort to conflate the child Marcel of *Swann's Way* with the older Marcel, sometimes by placing the child actor Georges Du Fresne with Marcello Mazzarella in the same scene. This device also relates to Ruiz's (and Proust's) notions about the instability of identity. Proust, for instance, speaks of a time when "Gilberte, having come across some hidden photographs of Rachel [her husband's mistress], whose name even had been unknown to her, tried to please Robert by imitating certain habits dear to the actress, such as always wearing a red ribbon in her hair and a black velvet ribbon on her arm, and by dyeing her hair in order to look dark." Ruiz conveys this through a scene in which Gilberte makes a theatrical, mocking entrance and the two women's faces dissolve into each other's—much to Robert's annoyance. Proust comments eloquently: "And indeed when we meet again after many years women whom we no longer love, is there not the abyss of death between them and us, quite as much as if they were no longer of this world, since the fact that our love exists no longer makes the people that they were or the person that we were then as good as dead." Ruiz not only puts this sentiment into Marcel's mouth as a line of dialogue but keeps trying to suggest such alterations of identity.

Ruiz has written somewhat mystically about what he calls a "multipersonal world," in which the effort to sustain a single, coherent personality inevitably leads to splitting. For Proust, our multiple selves come from the aging process. The most famous passage of *Time Regained*, which occurs during the big party, has the narrator express his astonishment that these bent, white-haired old farts are in fact the same glamorous people who dominated his younger years. Ruiz has fashioned a tour de force of this concluding party scene (reminiscent of the great ball in Luchino Visconti's *The Leopard*), as Marcel bobs and weaves through the social minefields, politely dealing with importuning wrecks whom he fails to recognize. No attempt is made to age Marcel, as is fitting: we continue to think of ourselves as no older than thirty-five, regardless of what our bones tell us. He comes across a plain, lined, elderly woman, who introduces herself as Gilberte; the rest of their encounter is played by Béart and Mazzarella. An old woman is pointed out to Marcel as Mme. Verdurin, but she is quickly replaced by Marie-France Pisier, the officiously flirtatious Verdurin whom Marcel remembers. In this way, Ruiz shuffles identities and chronologies. I take the Chilean filmmaker at his word when he says that he has been reading and rereading Proust all his life, and preparing for years to make this one film. In a 1986 interview, he said, speaking of his film *In the Mirror*: "It's the first *esquisse*, study, of what I want to make one day, Proust's *Le Temps retrouvé*. A man comes to visit another man who is supposed to be ill and talks with his sitter while he waits. There is a violent struggle, they insult each other, and you never know why. At the end we learn that the text is written by a little boy who is copying what they say, seeing the scene through a mirror, but missing a lot of the words, which is why it's so ambiguous. It's about mishearing and mis-seeing."[2]

In *Time Regained*, Ruiz uses an array of cinematic tricks to suggest this subjective misapprehension: bizarre camera angles and color filters (especially for the distant past) and a host of shadows and mirrors; retarded pacings that suggest a dream in slow motion; characters on moving sidewalks or trains drawn past different landscapes; the youthful Marcel and the adult Marcel in the same frame; powdered manikin-like figures; more peculiarly, in the magnificent concert sequence, rows of listeners swaying in different directions; and during the projection of a World War I newsreel in a crowded café, Marcel, lifted aloft like Peter Pan, floating out of the audience and up to the top of the movie screen. Surprisingly, all these stylized devices fail to ruffle the overall impression of smoothness and restraint. We are never asked to forfeit the illusionism of a costume picture. Much of the credit for this seamlessness must go to the cinematographer, Ricardo Aronovich, and to the opulent, accurate costumes and art direction. "A story is the connection between objects in the set," Ruiz once wrote, sounding like Bresson, and certainly one is made aware of a lot of "stuff": lamps, wallpaper, sculptures that appear insistently in the foreground. These objects help us jump from one discontinuous memory to another.

One of my favorite Ruiz works, an essay film about the French elections called *Of Great Events and Ordinary People*, self-reflects on the ways documentary scenes might be structured to convey the requisite "irregularity" of daily life: you could create categories of actions or ideas, or you could connect scenes by similar camera movements in different locations or even similar shapes or sounds. The resourceful Ruiz does a little of everything in *Time Regained* to provide visual or aural transitions for a nonlinear narrative—moving, say, from a waiter stirring a teaspoon to a railroad worker tapping the wheel of a train with a hammer. What is odd is how respectful he is in making such metaphors, which are never underlined to the point of camp or Brechtian estrangement, as they might be in other Ruiz films, where his mischief must be credited as a joke.

Similarly, the ensemble acting is on a very high level. We are a long way from the cartoonishly crude or intentionally flat performances that Ruiz elicited in so many of his earlier narrative films to build that sense of a "parallel world," one part fairy tale, one part *fotonovela*. I was particularly struck here by a quartet of vivid male performances: Pascal Greggory as Robert Saint-Loup, Vincent Perez as Charlie Morel, Christian Vadim as Bloch, and John Malkovich as Charlus. I have always imagined the baron as much more corpulent than Malkovich. Ordinarily I am not a fan of this actor, finding his self-regarding mannerisms irritating, but here he is a revelation. It is something to see him haughtily "reviewing the troops" in the male brothel sequence or vulnerably begging for a date with Morel or sneering at a journalist's mixed metaphor for Marcel's pleasure. And I can't get out of my mind

Greggory's Saint-Loup tearing into a piece of meat at lunch while discoursing on how nobly the common men die on the battlefields. Or Catherine Deneuve's Odette, directed to a box filled with cash by her ex-lover, coolly masturbating the dying man one last time, out of a mixture of avarice and pity. In that scene, there is the perfect welding of actor, camera movement, and set. There is no leering; it is all done very discreetly. We see what a skillful director Ruiz is, in the classical narrative sense, when he restrains himself.

Heretofore, Proust has been a sort of Bermuda Triangle beckoning the foolhardy and hubristic. We can only imagine what the great Visconti might have done with his projected Proust, before that deal fell apart. Harold Pinter's screenplay tempted Joseph Losey, among others, but was overlong and ended up a paperback. We do have, by way of comparison, Volker Schlöndorff's *Swann in Love*, that solemnly inert curiosity, with a morose Jeremy Irons as Swann drooling over the rounded, soft-core flesh of Ornella Muti's Odette. Now that the bookends of Proust's seven-volume opus have been filmed, what courageous director will take on the middle? Ruiz, I hope. What Proust does for Ruiz is plunge him into the oceanic meditative. In the past, Ruiz has tried to evade the prison of tight narrative construction by producing a plethora of plot, like those Latin American melodramas in which misfortunes rain down on the heads of the characters like unintended miracles. But he has also proposed a "defense of ennui" in the films of Michael Snow, Tarkovsky, Ozu, Warhol, and Straub-Huillet.

It is Proust's observation that the self-destructively restless Saint-Loup practiced "an athletic form of idleness which finds expression not in inertia but in a feverish vivacity that hopes to leave boredom neither time nor space to develop in." It is Ruiz's speculation that our modern melancholy derives largely from a world "emptied by entertainment." Quoting Pascal's statement that all the evil in men comes from their not being able to remain at rest in their room, Ruiz concludes: "So perhaps boredom is a good thing." Substitute "meditation" or "brooding" for "boredom" and you have the Ruizian solution. What need for miracles of plot when there are the mysteries of daily life and irreconcilable memory? With *Time Regained*, Ruiz has taken a significant step in the direction of the quiet, meditative, "boring" masters he so admires and made a beautiful, convincing story-film.

FILM COMMENT (JULY/AUGUST 2000)

Chapter Forty-Five

ALEXANDER SOKUROV

Alexander Sokurov is a devotee of the oneiric, Tarkovsky-wet, *plan-sequence* aesthetic. In 1992, the New York Film Festival showed Sukorov's spectral, nonnarrative meditation on Chekhov, *Stone*. *Whispering Pages* continues in a crepuscular, poetic vein, this time glancing off of Dostoyevsky's *Crime and Punishment*. The best way to take in a film this visually gorgeous is just to watch it, without any narrative expectations. There is no one in cinema today crafting more luminous images. Unlike his mentor, Tarkovsky, who had a futurist bent, Sokurov seems resolutely attracted to the aura of the past: his images here resemble turn-of-the-century gum-bichromate photographs by Stieglitz or Steichen. There are also hauntingly paranoiac scenes of the delirious Raskolnikov figure walking through knots of carousers, which recall the German expressionist street films of the 1920s. Most remarkable are the sequence in which people keep jumping off a balcony to their deaths and another in which the protagonist suckles the lap of a stone lion. The film falters only when it tries to be narrative, vomiting up hammy dialogues between Raskolnikov and Sonya.

What is Sokurov's message? Better not to ask. In interviews he talks all kinds of reactionary Russian-mystic nonsense, but the man makes beautiful movies. Sokurov embodies, even more than did Tarkovsky, the problem of the visionary film artist whose fuzzy, corny content is hard to take seriously, even as his images are so seductive. Does it take having a cockamamie philosophy these days to make rigorous, visionary films?

Alexander Sokurov proves himself to be the cinema's supreme landscape artist in *Mother and Son*. Wind moving through branches, a storm building, the drama of light and clouds, horizon and atmosphere, all are rendered in strangely marvelous, lens-distorted images, like old-fashioned stereopticons. Dominated by Nature, the two protagonists execute gestural pas-de-deux with the slowness of Robert Wilson's theatrical performers in *Einstein on the Beach*. Torture to watch at times, both because we are seeing unalloyed suffering, aestheticized, and because its deliberateness requires a patience bordering on prayer. The film is an inside-out version of Sokurov's *The Second Circle*. Together, they constitute a filial diptych: where the earlier movie focused on a son's preparation of his father's dead body for burial, roaming around a bare-bulb apartment, this one dwells on a son's caring for his dying mother in a lush if lonely country setting. "Let's go for a walk," he says, and proceeds to carry his mother on his back, staggering like Frankenstein's monster through the Gothic landscape. The spare dialogue provides hints of their relationship: she was a schoolteacher who her son feels never gave him the assurance that he was more than "Satisfactory"; she regards him as a man of the head rather than the heart. They have brief philosophical discussions about the meaning of life and the purpose of death. She, petting his hair, worries about his grieving too much after her death and tells him, "Be patient. Wait for me." It should be very moving, and it almost is. But the austerity of this arty visual experiment mutes the human drama. After watching them for seventy-three minutes, I wanted to know a little more about these two so that their anguish could move from generic to specific. Sokurov has been called, perhaps unfairly, Tarkovsky's disciple: the difference is that Tarkovsky kept trying to inject larger ideas and conflicts into his stories as they went along, whereas Sokurov builds each of his films around one idea, one note. My eyes tell me it's great filmmaking; my mind continues to doubt.

FILM COMMENT (NOVEMBER/DECEMBER 1994; NOVEMBER/DECEMBER 1997)

Chapter Forty-Six

PAOLO SORRENTINO

The Great Beauty

It begins with a quote from Céline, that sardonically comic writer whose humanity was as laudable as his politics were dubious, advocating travel as a spur to the imagination: "All the rest, he writes, "is delusion and pain." Fair warning: we are about to watch the doings of a deluded upper-class circle that never leaves Rome. The film opens with placid, picturesque shots of the city waking up and going about its routines: a tourist's Eternal City. Later someone remarks that tourists are the best people in Rome (they travel, after all). In this first sequence a Japanese tourist happily raises his camera—and promptly drops dead. Soon enough, we are plunged into a disco bacchanal, each of the dancers revolving in a cone of grotesque self-absorbed autoeroticism, enacting with various degrees of success and ridiculousness their notion of sexy-cool. A call goes up for *la colita*, a group line dance, in which the participants keep moving and returning to the same place: emblematic, we will discover, of this privileged crowd's existence. From the mass scene we pick out a grinning, exuberant, well-tailored man who, we are told, is having his sixty-fifth birthday. "Jep! Jep!" women salute him, sidling up from all sides. He seems essential to their fun, their ringleader, though it is not long before we see him retreating in a more melancholy, contemplative mood to his own backstage, a bachelor apartment with a terrace to die for, overlooking the Colosseum.

Sumptuously sensual, crammed with gusto, vitality, spectacle, and invention, *The Great Beauty* is also a cautionary tale about the heedless pursuit of pleasure. Director Paolo Sorrentino pulls out all the stops visually, layering one stunning, eye-opening image onto another. For all this, the film is also, paradoxically, austere. How it manages this feat seems partly the result of its director's split personality: part showman, entranced with the sheer audacity of flimflam, Sorrentino is also drawn to characters who are highly disciplined, even monklike in their isolation (*The Consequences of Love, Il Divo*). With his seven features, he has amassed a body of stylish, flashy work that has made him a leading Italian auteur at international film festivals. *The Great Beauty* is his best film so far, a culmination of his inquiries into the clash between the human as social animal and introvert.

Sorrentino was born in Naples in 1970. In addition to filmmaking, he is also the author of a novel, *Hanno tutti ragione*, translated as *Everyone's Right*, though a better title might be "Everyone has his reasons," a line famously associated with *The Rules of the Game*. Like the maker of that film, Jean Renoir, Sorrentino takes an overall impartial, nonjudgmental, if slightly satirical attitude toward the aristocrats and high-lifes he depicts, generating suspense as to what price may eventually have to be paid for all this sybaritic activity. No one is accidentally shot in the final reel, though a few deaths occur along the way. A more important consequence is the emptiness that accumulates around all this busy diversion, a hollow pang at the core that is entirely intentional on Sorrentino's and his co-screenwriter, Umberto Contarello's, part.

With its marathon parties, fleshy displays, bizarre extremes (one dwarf, one giraffe), and its journalist hero whose episodic adventures wandering around an ancient/modern Rome modulate seamlessly from the absurdly humorous to the forlorn, the film has inevitably been compared to *La Dolce Vita*. Since Sorrentino himself clearly had this precedent in mind, it may be instructive to ask in what ways *The Great Beauty* differs from as well as resembles or extends that earlier film. Fellini's protagonist, Marcello, looked to be about forty. He was on a quest, whether to find the purpose of his life or to bed more beauties, and he was also still capable of being shocked by an act of senseless violence, such as the intellectual Steiner killing his children and himself. Fellini, a child of neorealism for all his via Veneto flashiness, conveyed a fresh, wide-eyed shock at the way the fun-loving Romans in 1961 seemed to be losing their moral bearings in selfish pursuit of pleasure. *The Great Beauty* gives us a Rome fifty years later, having undergone decades more of political disillusionment, corruption, incompetence, and triviality and hence, shock-proof. Jep Gambadella, the aging protagonist, is a detached, intellectual bon vivant, aware of his limits (he has a bad knee and wears a truss for his back) and no longer particularly looking for answers; rather, he is playing out the string. With lust no longer a factor, he will obligingly have sex if the woman expects it, in the manner of a *cavaliere servante*. When his friend Romano envies him the attentions of the beautiful, rich Orietta, he says, "At my age, a beauty isn't enough." Though he resents feeling old, it also gives him the courage to think "At my age I can't waste my time doing things I don't want to do," and, as if to demonstrate, he creeps out of Orietta's bedroom before she can show him on her laptop the nude photos she took of herself.

One of the film's triumphs is the complexity of its main character, brought to stunning life by the magnificently flexible, ironic, soulful performance of Sorrentino's favorite actor, Toni Servillo. Jep may live a frivolous existence as a night owl and parasitic chronicler of high society, but he reveals in voice-overs a deeper awareness of his own flaws and those of his set. Surrounded by self-deceiving acquaintances, like the failed actress who says she is considering either writing a Proustian novel or directing a film or Viola, the anguished mother of a seriously disturbed son who insists he is much better now, Jep alone refuses to fool himself. While others treat him as a still-practicing literary author because of a novel he wrote forty years ago, *The Human Apparatus*, he knows that he is not working on a second book and suspects he has nothing more to say. He has made himself useful to high society as the likable "extra" single man at dinner parties, his witty, gossipy aphorisms according a dignity to their time-wasting activities.

Lest we see him too hastily as a kind of secular saint, everyone's friend and confidant, there is a stunningly powerful scene in the middle of the film in which, goaded by Stefana, an attractive Marxist novelist, to defend his lack of service to society, he mutters that she is hiding "a series of untruths." She demands that he explain what he means by her "lies," and, dropping his customary diplomatic mask, he calmly takes apart this woman's claims to distinction in front of her friends. He enumerates her seamy past, her opportunistic politics, her lame abilities as a writer, her failure as a wife and mother. Jep's nastiness is a revelation, suggesting the harsh judgments he may be harboring toward all his companions. Yet this unmasking can also be seen as containing a grain of compassion and even affection for his tribe. "You're fifty-three, with a life in tatters, like the rest of us," he ends his diatribe, on a note of fellow feeling. It would seem to Jep that the problem is not with having erred: the only unpardonable sin is not to gain wisdom from one's shallowness, one's mistakes, and Jep is pushing her to open her eyes. An hour later in the film, when he finds himself dancing with this same Stefana, he tells her it seems like an oversight that they have never slept together. The fact that she takes this statement with tolerant amusement and good grace shows either that Jep's earlier character assassination has been forgiven or that nothing is important enough in this tribal existence to leave a permanent mark.

The name "Silvio Berlusconi" is never uttered throughout the length of the film, yet the picture we get of Italian society seems a mirror image reflecting Berlusconi's tarnishing impact. The filmmaker, whose earlier *Il Divo* focused on another Italian kingmaker, Giulio Andreotti, and was all about the inside game of Italian politics, has said in interviews that he did not want *The Great Beauty* to be a commentary on this specific historic moment. Rather, he wanted to show how Rome was both a marvelous playground and a trap, promoting inanition. The Eternal City is eternal not just because it has been around for so long but because nothing is allowed to change (at least if you belong to the upper classes), and those who surrender to its magnetic pull can spend the rest of their lives in gilded entropy. This point is made graphically via a few scenes in which the art crowd politely applauds avant-garde acts: first we see a woman performance artist strip naked and butt her head bloody against an aqueduct column, then later we watch a child throw herself and buckets of paint against a canvas, creating in this way the latest "art" sensation. The Eternal City can absorb any experimental provocation without turning a hair, without ceding its indifference.

Boasting that their party's train dances are the best in Rome, Jep explains: "They're the best because they go nowhere." In the face of this inertia, only death has a chance of breaking out of the conga circle. The suicide by Viola's spoiled, resentful son, who drives his car with eyes closed, occasions a lecture by Jep about the proper etiquette at funerals: one is never supposed to cry, it will upstage the family's grief. He delivers this mock-pedantic lecture to Ramona, a voluptuous-figured, sad-eyed stripper whom he has been befriending. At the funeral itself, though he had shown little feeling for the young man earlier, he weeps as he carries the suicide's coffin out of the church—thereby breaking his own rule. He may be weeping at the thought of his own approaching mortality or at the very pointlessness of their lives: either way, it is a rare departure from his usual stoical front. With these people, the line between stoicism and indifference remains blurry.

Earlier, he learns that a woman who'd been his first love has just died. The woman's husband tells him that Jep was the only one she ever loved. The two men make a good-faith effort to bond over their shared grief, and Jep has several flashback moments recalling this pretty teenager on the beach (rather like the angelic Claudia Cardinale character in *8½* whom the hero keeps glimpsing and idealizing). But though the film seems to want to assign this first love a key, a Rosebud, to Jep's story, what is striking is how little her passing matters to him, finally. Jep sinks into his usual nocturnal patterns. His narcissistic self having eroded over time, it has given way to an almost purely watchful, *flâneur's* role. He wonders, like a good Catholic, if religious faith might have answers for him, but the cardinal whom he accosts for spiritual advice runs off for a skunk hunt. This hilarious cardinal wants to talk only about cooking. Meanwhile, like a good Roman, Jep visits exquisite old houses with artistic treasures—Roman statues and painting collections—presided over by wizened, card-playing princesses. The nobility is on its last legs, and the impecunious ones even hire themselves out for parties.

One justification for the length of the film, two and a half hours, is that it wears down expectations of tidy narrative and coaxes the viewer into a free-fall space of borderline-surreal antinarrative, where a magician makes a giraffe disappear, a mystic quack dispenses healing for a price, and a 104-year old saint (a dead ringer for Mother Teresa) arrives and summons migrating flamingoes. She alone manifests discipline, crawling up a set of stairs on her hands and knees. In the end none of it really matters to Jep, beyond the bittersweet awareness that he just has to keep on living until the end destined for him. Sorrentino specializes in figures trapped in a system of corruption who nevertheless want to retain a sense of honor or loyalty to an old, half-forgotten code. Perhaps art will do for a code, considers Jep. If, as the magician says, making a giraffe disappear is just a trick, then perhaps he can now resume writing, with the awareness that art itself (and perhaps this very film) is just a trick. "Our journey is entirely imaginary, which is its strength," Céline's initial quote tells us.

From time to time, Jep is asked or asks himself why he never wrote another novel, and he comes up with various lines like, "Rome makes you waste a lot of time," or, "I went out too much at night," or, "I was lazy," or, "This is my life, and it's nothing. Flaubert wanted to write a book about nothing, and *he* couldn't do it." When Jep is asked by Sister Maria, the 104-year-old saint, why he never wrote a second novel, this time he answers wistfully, "I was looking for the great beauty."

Is "the great beauty" of the title quite simply Rome, that courtesan that saps the energy of ambitious provincials with its thousand and one diversions? Or is it some hoped-for aesthetic pattern, some Platonic form underlying our seemingly pointless, soul-wasteful experiences, which will finally reveal the transcendental grandeur of life on earth? All along, Jep, when not exasperated by his friends and acquaintances, has been a connoisseur savoring simple moments, usually involving the ongoing life of the city. In the movie's exquisite, concluding title sequence, we are in a boat rolling down the Tiber, and we pass various tourist sites of Rome. No longer seeing Jep or any of the film's characters, the viewer has become just another spectator, another tourist, like those in the opening scene. The invitation seems to be to forget plot, just keep looking—and there is much to look at in life, especially if you have a pair of sensitive eyes to guide you, like Sorrentino's. So Fellini yields to Antonioni-esque shots where the actors have left the frame and the camera keeps on unblinkingly, severely, rapturously recording.

It is odd that Sorrentino, who is so accomplished a storyteller, who has such a propulsive, heart-pounding way with montage; with rhythmic combinations of tracks, zooms, pans, close-ups, and crane shots; with the whole bag of cinematic tricks, should also be drawn to the calm emptying out of narrative. But so it is, and *The Great Beauty* succeeds in continually diverting us while questioning the very need for diversion and bringing us to a rather contemplative place, a serene site where the eternal has acquired, by the end, more positive connotations.

CRITERION COLLECTION, 2014

Chapter Forty-Seven

JEAN-MARIE STRAUB

Not Reconciled

One German generation explaining to the other the losses it suffered and mistakes it committed in a seventy-year span, going right through the Nazi era and beyond, may be one way of stating the subject of this unique film experience. But an experimental work as seminal as *Not Reconciled* sends reverberations in too many directions to be easily summarized. First, how was the director, Jean-Marie Straub, able to take Nobel Prize–winner Heinrich Böll's effective if somewhat conventional novel, *Billiards at Half-Past Nine*, a family saga with a large cast of characters spanning three generations, and condense it into a severe film of only fifty-one minutes? Straub's solution was daring and original: not by trying to cram as much dramatic incident into it as possible, like most movie adaptations, but by concentrating on just those undramatic, static, mundane moments that crisscross decades. The traumas take place off-screen. What we see are an old woman quietly pouring tea and recounting stories to a bellhop, a middle-aged architect treasuring a cigarette at the top of a staircase—those privileged moments of in-gathering before going down to face the compromises of survival. A grandfather tells how every morning for thirty years he had sat in the same café taking his breakfast coffee and paprika cheese.

Straub shows a fascination for the cleanliness, regularity, and *gemütlicht* attractiveness of the German bourgeois household, which is both its genius and its undoing. The sunlight on a tea service, the customary billiard game, all rendered in orderly, Vermeer-like black-and-white images: these constants almost level historical upheavals to a murmured interruption at the door of peaceful family life. Yet the turmoils that are never shown onscreen are always spoken of and explained, compulsively, until you are made to understand the permanent uneasiness that Junkerism and Nazism have left on this fragmented family. "I have lived through two world wars and I have never seen men as bad as these are now," says the grandmother about the new type of businessmen who've inherited the so-called miracle of West Germany. *Not Reconciled* is a film whose political outrage, from the understated title outward, is understood without having to be shouted. It is a master class in duration and an aesthetic experience of the highest order—one that makes no compromises with the audience's expectations for easy pleasure.

To quote the film critic Richard Roud: "I found the resulting mosaic all the more satisfying in that I, as spectator, had been obliged to help put those pieces together. Viewing such a film is not a passive activity; it is a highly stimulating form of controlled participation."[1]

Straub, along with his wife and codirector, Daniele Huillet, continued for more than four decades to make a stream of features and shorts that were challenging, difficult, intransigent, experimental. They reinterpreted the past, adapting parts of the Western canon they admired from a radically leftist perspective, infused with rigorous Brechtian-inflected aesthetics. Their films included *The Chronicle of Anna Magdalena Bach*, Arnold Schonberg's opera *Moses and Aaron*, *Class Relations* (based on Kafka's *Amerika*), *Sicilia!* (from an Elio Vittorini novel), a meditation on a set of Pavese's texts (*From the Clouds to the Resistance*), and ruminations springboarding from Montaigne, Corneille, Engels, and so on. Not all their experiments succeeded: some were off-puttingly dry or impenetrable. But they occupied a defiant pole of what an intellectual, essayistic cinema, freed from commercial considerations, might look like, as well as one that was oppositional in its politics, refusing ever to be *reconciled* to social injustice.

NEW YORKER FILMS CATALOGUE (1976–77)

Chapter Forty-Eight

ANDREI TARKOVSKY

Solaris

Andrei Tarkovsky belongs to that handful of filmmakers (Carl Dreyer, Robert Bresson, Jean Vigo, Jacques Tati) who, with a small, concentrated body of work, created their own universe. Though he made only seven features, thwarted by Soviet censors and then by cancer, each honored his ambition to crash through the surface of ordinary life and find a larger spiritual meaning: to heal modern art's secular fragmentation by infusing it with a metaphysical dimension. To that end he rejected Eisenstein montage and developed a long-take aesthetic, which he thought better able to reveal the deeper truths underlying the ephemeral moment.

Since Tarkovsky is often portrayed as a lonely, martyred genius, we'd do well to place him in a wider context, as the most renowned of an astonishing generation—Larisa Shepitko, Aleksei German, Andrei Konchalovsky, Sergei Parajanov, Otar Iosseliani—that effected a dazzling, short-lived renaissance of Soviet cinema. All had censorship problems. In the early 1970s, Tarkovsky, unable to get approval for a script that was considered too personal-obscurantist (*Mirror*), proposed a film adaptation of Stanislaw Lem's novella *Solaris*, thinking it stood a better chance of being green-lighted by the commissars as science fiction seemed more "objective" and accessible to the masses. His hunch paid off: *Solaris* took the Grand Jury Prize at Cannes. Tarkovsky had arrived on the world stage with his most accessible work. While hardly a conventional film, *Solaris* is relatively straightforward and stands as a fulcrum in Tarkovsky's career: behind him was his impressive debut,

Ivan's Childhood, and his first epic masterpiece, *Andrei Rublev*; ahead of him lay *Mirror* (brilliantly experimental and, yes, personal-obscurantist), *Stalker* (a great, somber, difficult work), and finally, two lyrical, meditative pictures he made in exile, *Nostalghia* and *The Sacrifice*. He died shortly after completing this last film, in 1988, at age fifty-four.

We know that Tarkovsky had seen Kubrick's *2001* and disliked the picture, finding it cold and sterile. The media played up the Cold War angle of the Soviet director's determination to make an "anti-*2001*," and certainly Tarkovsky developed more intensely individual, humanized characters than Kubrick had and put a more passionate human drama at the center. Still, hindsight allows us to observe that the two masterworks are more cousins than opposites. Both set up their narratives in a leisurely, languid manner, spending considerable time tracking around the space set; both employed a wide-screen, mise-en-scène approach that drew on superior art direction; and both generated an air of mystery that invited countless explanations.

Unlike *2001*, however, *Solaris* is saturated by grief, which grips the film even before it leaves earth. In this moody prelude, we see the protagonist, a space psychologist named Kris Kelvin, staring at underwater reeds as though they were a drowned woman's tresses. Played by the stolid Donatas Banionis, a Russian Glenn Ford with five o'clock shadow and a shock of prematurely white hair, Kris looks forever traumatized, slowed by some unspeakable sorrow. His father and aunt worry about his torpor and chide him for his plodding, bookkeeper-like manner. He is about to take off the next day for a mission to the space station *Solaris*, a once-thriving project that has gone amiss: it will be his job to determine whether to close down the research station. In preparation, he watches a video from a scientific conference (allowing Tarkovsky to satirize bureaucratic stodginess) about the troubles on *Solaris*.

On Earth, the humans seem in thrall to machinery and TV images, cut off from the natural life surrounding them (underwater reeds, a thoroughbred horse, a farm dog). In his haunting shots of Moscow freeways, Tarkovsky disdains showing any but contemporary cars, just as Godard did with the buildings in *Alphaville*: Why bother clothing the present world in sci-fi garb, when the estranging future has already arrived?

At the planet Solaris, Kris finds a shabby space station, deserted except for two preoccupied if not deranged scientists, Snouth and Sartorius. A colleague whom Kris had expected to meet has already committed suicide, leaving him a taped message warning of hallucinated Guests who have "something to do with conscience." Sure enough, Kris's dead wife Hari materializes at his side, offering the devoted tenderness for which he is starved. Kris, panicking, shoves her into a space capsule and fires it off; but Hari No. 2 is not slow in arriving. As played by the lovely Natalya Bondarchuk, this "eternal feminine" is the opposite of a femme fatale: all clinging fidelity and frightened vulnerability. We learn that the real Hari had committed suicide with a poison Kris had unthinkingly left behind when he quit her. The hallucinated Hari No. 2, fearing Kris does not love her, takes liquid nitrogen and kills herself as well. By the time Hari No. 3 appears, Kris will do anything to redeem himself.

Solaris helped initiate a genre that has become an art house staple: the drama of grief and partial recovery. Watching this 167-minute work is like catching a fever, with night sweats and eventual cooled brow. Tarkovsky's experiments with pacing, to "find Time within Time," as he put it, has his camera track up to the sleeping Kris, dilating the moment, so that we enter his dream. As in Siegel's *Invasion of the Body Snatchers*, to fall asleep is to risk a succubus's visit. However, this time the danger comes not from any harm she may do the hero: true horror is in having to watch someone you love destroy themselves. The film that *Solaris* most resembles thematically is not *2001*, but Hitchcock's *Vertigo*: the inability of the male to protect the female, the multiple disguises or "resurrections" of the loved one, the inevitability of repeating past mistakes.

The film's power derives ultimately from Kris's reawakened, anguished love for Hari—his willingness to do anything to hold onto her, even knowing she isn't real. (Like Mizoguchi's *Ugetsu*, this is a story about falling in love with ghosts). The alternations between color and black and white convey something of this ontological instability, and the jittery camera explorations over shelves and walls suggest a seizure. Hari wonders aloud if she has epilepsy, and later we see her body horrifically jerking at the threshold between being and nonbeing. A gorgeous, serene floating sequence, when Kris and Hari lose gravity, offers another stylized representation of this borderline at transcendence.

Meanwhile, Tarkovsky peppers the dialogue with arguments about reality, identity, humanity, and sympathy, buttressed by references to Western civilization's linchpins—Bach, Tolstoy, Dostoyevsky, Goethe, Brueghel, Luther, and Cervantes. The Soviet censors, who demanded that the filmmaker "remove the concept of God," may have been mollified by the absence of the G-word, but Tarkovsky took the standard science-fiction theme of spacemen establishing "contact" with other forms of intelligence and elevated it implicitly to contact with divinity (as symbolized by the planet's oceans, which have been granted sentient powers.)

Lem and Tarkovsky, both Eastern Europeans, were critical of what they saw as Anglo-American science fiction's shallowness and wanted to invest the form with intellectual and emotional depth. Tarkovsky took a good deal directly from Lem's book, but he also expanded, reordered, and beclouded it with characteristic pseudophilosophizing. (If there is a dubious side to Tarkovsky's achievement, it is that his spiritual messages can come across as pompously simplistic, not always matching the level of his visionary visuals.)

As it happened, Lem did not much care for Tarkovsky's elliptical reworking of his material and was looking forward before he died to the remake by Steven Soderbergh. The Soderbergh version, starring George Clooney in the leading role, proved to be an intelligently restrained, uncluttered, if almost too quiet version of the Lem novel. Soderbergh had promised a cross between *2001* and *Last Tango in Paris*, but the resulting film was measured, not nearly as sensationalistic as threatened. Just as Tarkovsky had sought to reverse Kubrick and ended up extending him, so Soderbergh's version could not help but honor his majestic predecessor. Such was a fittingly filial, Freudian coda to Tarkovsky's *Solaris*, which concludes with the space station's claustrophobic concavities yielding to the rain-sodden beauty of this island earth and the returning Kris embracing his father's knees.

CRITERION COLLECTION, 2002

Chapter Forty-Nine

FRANÇOIS TRUFFAUT

One good thing about biting your nails, François Truffaut once told a friend, is that there would always be women who tried to break you out of the habit. The filmmaker deployed his shyness cannily, both as a seductive tool and a way to keep more self-assured people who threatened him off-balance. Yet in spite of his calculation, Truffaut remains for us a charming and sympathetic figure. Perhaps we forgive him his act because it grew out of modest self-assessment. As he told a fellow film critic: "I'm just lucky to have some understanding of cinema, to like it, and to work like a dog."

The life of François Truffaut is so compelling that parts of it arrest us like a fairy tale. An unwanted illegitimate child, raised initially by his grandmother then taken in by his mother and the man she married, to whom she is routinely unfaithful, he enters adolescence rebellious, love-starved, and movie-mad, steals lobby cards and typewriters to support his movie habit, is sent to juvenile detention center. The great critic André Bazin, impressed by his precocity, takes him under his wing, but he frequents prostitutes and contracts syphilis, enlists in the army, deserts, is jailed, tries to kill himself, and gets rescued by a claque of intellectuals, including Sartre. Delivered to freedom, he becomes a slash-and-burn film critic, attacking (unfairly) the allegedly bad old fogies of French cinema for their polished adaptations of literary classics, defending the good fathers (Renoir, Guitry, Ophuls, Cocteau); abandons rhetorical violence to turn into the apostle of cinematic tenderness as a key member of the French New Wave; becomes an international celebrity; has affairs with countless beautiful actresses; learns who his real father is (a Jewish dentist in Belfort); moves politically from right to left but quarrels with the ultra-left Godard, who accuses him of being a middlebrow sellout; has depressions; persists; makes good movies and bad; and dies abruptly of a brain tumor at age fifty-two.

Such a life! The filmmaker himself dipped into it at will for his many movies. Now the story is retooled in a sympathetic biography by two *Cahiers du Cinema* editors, Antoine de Baecque and Serge Toubiana. De Baecque is currently writing a history of the French New Wave, and the chapters devoted to this gang of enthusiasts-turned-auteurs are particularly rich. "It was like an underground group preparing a revolution," recalls the actor Jean-Claude Brialy. No matter how many times one hears about it, there is something improbable and thrilling about the Nouvelle Vague, particularly for the French, who see it as both a nationalist triumph and a spiritual renewal (with André Bazin as John the Baptist). "The most important postwar critic passed away as the New Wave was being born, just as Truffaut was filming the first scenes of *The Four Hundred Blows*," intone de Baecque and Toubiana.[1]

All that talent, audacity, lightness, raw insouciance: the problem for the New Wave, Truffaut not least, was, having put their youth on-screen, how to maintain that freshness while still growing older, changing and maturing— that is, without falling into a mannered arrested development. Truffaut heroically sought to change and did change, in some respects, while dragging his feet in others. The teenaged fanatic ("Lets admit it. François' aggressiveness, his state of perpetual agitation, like a crazed mosquito, got on our nerves," remembers the screenwriter Jean Gruault) became the measured presence in tailored dark suits and narrow ties. The Robespierre who attacked older directors for using screenwriters and making adaptations—i.e., for not being true auteurs of personal films—would evolve into the studio head keeping groups of screenwriters busy at the same time on several literary properties. And why not? He did not want to waste his backers' money; hence, even when his gorgeous, cherished by him *Two English Girls* was dying at the box office, he cut twenty minutes of it so that the distributors could squeeze in an extra show. Godard accused him of being a businessman in the morning and a poet in the afternoon: not a bad combination for a filmmaker, come to think about it. One could say the same about Lubitsch, Preminger, Hitchcock. Godard, the greater artist of the two, comes off as the bigger jerk. Truffaut, for all his faults, seems more decent—true to the "humanist" label Spielberg gave him. He may have stopped writing criticism because "criticizing a film comes down to criticizing a man, and this I no longer want to do," but his unforgettable letter chastising Godard for opportunism and antisemitism shows that some of the youthful fury persisted in Truffaut, albeit tempered by a fine outrage.

The drama of Truffaut's life is a duel between self-loathing (he once called himself a "self-hating autodidact") and smugness, a longing for maturity and a neurotic refusal to change what basically worked, however unhappy it made him. Having identified so totally with the struggles of adolescence, he had a hard time imagining adulthood. Antoine Doinel could not be permitted the career commitment his creator enjoyed, and so he grew ever more tiresome in his efforts to stay free to follow his instincts. A friend of Truffaut, Georges Kiejman, seeing the filmmaker in the spring of 1968 bolting over cars to "reach the front ranks and join those who were about to get beat up by the police," remembers thinking, "No matter what age he lived to, he would remain an eternal adolescent."

Truffaut's strenuous efforts at artistic self-renewal disguised from himself what was an alternation between two static modes: modest brashness and aristocratic restraint. Each effort to fling off the present and start in a new direction—for instance, by breaking up with the current woman in his life— only masked the old patterns of romantic enthrallment and flight, just as each new film project tried to regain a youthful, New Wave freshness or perfect a classical smoothness, as though for the first time.

His whole romantic conduct can be seen as a continuously repeating pattern of approach-avoidance. The biographers are assiduous in recording Truffaut's pursuit and conquest of his leading ladies (Jeanne Moreau, Françoise Dorléac, Catherine Deneuve, Julie Christie, Jacqueline Bisset, Isabelle Adjani, Marie-France Pisier, Alexandra Stewart, Claude Jade, Fanny Ardant) but have little to say about how and why these affairs with these dream girls terminated. The closest we get to the nitty-gritty is Alexandra Stewart's testimony: "Women, for him, were always part icon, part woman. That's why he loved his actresses: It made his life easier—loving cinema more than anything else. Above all, it was a way of perpetuating childhood: woman as mother, woman as doll, woman as fiancée." That Truffaut himself had precious little self-awareness or insight into his skirt chasing may be seen by the disturbingly vacant, self-approving film he made on the subject, *The Man Who Loved Women*. (Though his earlier film, the wonderfully self-contained, perfectly executed *La Peau Douce* [*The Soft Skin*], showed more insight into the perils of womanizing.)

Dave Kehr, in a perceptive article assessing Truffaut's achievement, divided the filmmaker's work into "dark" and "light," arguing that his darker works—*The Soft Skin, Mississippi Mermaid, Two English Girls, The Story of Adele H., The Green Room, The Woman Next Door*—are his most enduring.[2] I would, on the whole agree, although I will always be faithful to the inventiveness and tenderness of his first features, *The Four Hundred Blows, Shoot the Piano Player,* and *Jules and Jim.* What I can't abide are the coyly charm-mongering complacency of comedies like *Bed and Board, Love on the Run, Small Change,* and so on. I have mixed feelings about *The Last Metro* and *Day for Night,* attracted as I am to their Renoireque celebration of group performance but wincing at their Panglossian resolutions. If there is a tragedy in Truffaut's career, it is that when he tried to make personal films of serious complexity, like *Two English Girls* or *The Green Room,* he was shot down by the public, and when he gave in to shallow glibness, he was wildly rewarded.

FILM COMMENT (JULY/AUGUST 1999)

INTERMISSION
Documentaries and Essay Films

Chapter Fifty

FREDERICK WISEMAN

Composing an American Epic

Who is the greatest American filmmaker of the last thirty years? Martin Scorsese, Steven Spielberg, Francis Ford Coppola, Stanley Kubrick, Woody Allen, and Robert Altman all have their partisans. But if the criteria includes the most number of masterpieces, maybe we should be talking about Frederick Wiseman.

Since 1967, when *Titicut Follies*, his scathing portrait of a state prison for the criminally insane, made its debut, he has directed a total of thirty complex, disturbing, illuminating documentaries, on the average of one a year. If this towering achievement has been underrecognized, it may be because documentaries get little respect; because Wiseman's have mostly been shown on television, rather than in theatrical release; and because his style is demanding, presenting often painful realities in a nonunderlined way that makes the viewer work.

If Walt Whitman's grandiosely democratic aim was to capture "the poem of these United States," then Frederick Wiseman, in a more diffident vein, is his one true grandson. "My goal is to make as many films as possible about different aspects of American life," Wiseman has said. So far, he has tackled education, welfare, medicine, religion, the military, the police, the workplace, leisure, retail, food, housing, the arts, and community. Like Whitman, who wrote a single ever-thickening book, Wiseman regards his collected work as "all one long movie."

"Wiseman is one of my heroes," said Errol Morris, himself a superb documentary filmmaker. "One hallmark of a great filmmaker—Renoir, Hitchcock, Bresson, Wiseman—is to have created a body of work that is a cosmos. Give up that old distinction between documentary and feature film. Call it what it is: a vision, a simulacrum of the world. No one has exceeded in scope and intensity the simulacrum that Wiseman has given us."[1]

The Cambridge, Massachusetts, filmmaker, now in his mideighties, grew up in an atmosphere of social concern. His mother was the administrator of a children's psychiatric ward, and his father, a lawyer, served on hospital boards and charitable organizations. Wiseman attended law school at Yale and passed the bar but did not practice, though he taught academic law and married a law professor, naming his production company, "Zipporah," after her. His first film, *Titicut Follies*, financed on credit, confirmed his hunch that contemporary life might be explored by focusing on institutions. It also got him into trouble (the film was censored for twenty-five years, as the State of Massachusetts did not take kindly to this exposure of Bridgewater Prison's cruelly inadequate facilities). Undaunted, he went on to reel off an unprecedented string of brilliant films.

From the start, Wiseman appropriated the techniques of cinema vérité—synch-sound, lightweight portable equipment—plunging the viewer into the moment without explanatory voiceovers, mood music, interviews, reenactments, flashbacks, or titles identifying time and place. These austerities encourage the impression that one is watching life as it happens, and they force the viewer to make sense of scenes and relationships glimpsed in medias res. Of course the "truth" in cinema vérité is still a highly artificial, selective fiction. What counts is that Wiseman has taken the journalistic technique of cinema vérité and elevated it to a form of personal expression.

Part of what makes Wiseman unique is that he follows location, not character. He roots in one place for days, weeks, months, obeying the philosophy that reality is not in some glamorous "elsewhere" but wherever you happen to be. Wiseman insists that, Heisenberg's principle aside, his filmmaking presence does not alter the subjects' behavior. The minimal crew consists of Wiseman himself, taking sound, and a cameraman whom the director instructs via ear mike. A great deal must still be left to the cameraman's discretion, and Wiseman has long had the benefit of two superlative cameramen, William Byrne and John Davy. Copious footage is shot. A four-hour event might be edited down to ten minutes yet give the impression of occurring in real time.

An acknowledged master editor, Wiseman is above all a storyteller who can keep his finger on the pulse of a scene while letting it remain open. As he once said: "To take a simple example, you could just cut to the one-liner that's really good. But I think the one-liner that is really good is much better if it is submerged in a context, so the viewer has to grope for it a little bit by participating in the scene."

His early films, like *Titicut Follies, High School, Law and Order, Hospital,* and *Welfare,* were initially received as muckraking social criticism, in line with sixties protest culture. But if Wiseman had a reformist axe to grind in the first two (which he now concedes were "too didactic"), he soon began to baffle his anti-establishment fans by his even-handed treatment of the police in *Law and Order* (1969) and by the portrait of the army's professionalism in *Basic Training* (1971). Increasingly, his sympathies were not only for the schoolchildren, patients, and criminals processed by the state but for the harried caregivers, officials, and peacekeepers trying to do their best.

Thirty years later, these films look a little different. We can appreciate more that they are about the fragility, suffering, and resilience of the human condition. The jailers and the jailed in *Titicut Follies* are both locked in together. Many of the lessons the high school teachers are trying to instill in their charges actually make sense. The telephone confrontation in *Hospital* between the bald male doctor and the unseen Miss Hightower, who refuses to put the doctor's ailing transvestite patient on welfare, captures the intractable flavor of the Age of Bureaucracy.

Bureaucracy is one of Wiseman's key subjects. His treatment of it reached an apotheosis is *Welfare* (1975), perhaps his greatest film. The amount of thorny, complex reality it offered, without rushing to resolution, was unique for television; the nearly three-hour length (it was the first of Wiseman's films to move beyond the tight ninety-minute structure) gave it an epic dimension. Also, the piece had an over-the-top, operatic quality, with duets and arias, including the amazing soliloquy of the last client, who is both paranoid and eloquently sane in his rambling prayer. (Not surprisingly, *Welfare* was turned into an opera years later.) One saw that underneath the social critic was the philosopher: all these people in waiting rooms, who stand for us, are petitioning a silent god of justice, as in Kafka's parable "Before the Law."

What to do about the welfare system? Wiseman refused to "pontificate" and offer policy solutions. "I am incapable of pronouncing general truths," he insisted, aligning himself instead with "the complexity and ambiguity of human behavior." Whatever institutional reforms might ensue, we would still be suffering, craving an explanation and waiting to die.

Nowhere is that point made clearer than in the six-hour *Near Death* (1989), which takes place in the terminal ward of a hospital. This fascinating if excruciating film has several long discussions between the medical staff and a patient's dazed family, who are told the pessimistic circumstances of their loved one and, indirectly, encouraged to pull the plug. It is as much a study of language and colloquy as it is about medical technology and the final moments of life.

My film critic's tendency is to want to divide Wiseman's "one long movie" into triumphs, near misses, and duds. Certainly it is easy to isolate such masterworks as *Welfare, Hospital, Titicut Follies, Law and Order, Juvenile Court, Near Death*, and *Public Housing*, where the drama of suffering is most intense or comically appalling, the confrontations between servers and clients at their starkest, and to find blander his studies of fashion models, Aspen skiers, Central Park volunteers, or the actors in the Comédie-Française. But even those less intense works inform us of a world, and he can be acutely observant with less overtly dramatic subject matter. *Essene* sustains the tension of a crackling intellectual argument, as notions of participatory democracy and group therapy are shakily introduced to a religious order. *Meat* (1976), though the cows and lambs who are the victims can't argue back, is an oddly touching, gruesome western.

"Most documentaries date, the further they get from their historic context," observed Richard Pena, the director of the Film Society of Lincoln Center, which is sponsoring a Wiseman retrospective. "With Wiseman it's the opposite: the issues are still relevant, but now we can see their formal artistry and their poetic, abstract quality."[2] In their elegantly composed cutaway shots and ten-second vignettes, Wiseman's documentaries display a surprising affinity with the work of experimental filmmakers such as Ernie Gehr and Rudy Burckhardt.

Wiseman has always been a passionate devotee of the theater, and there is a theatrical underside to his work. From the revue staged in *Titicut Follies* to the client at the end of *Welfare* who even cites *Waiting for Godot*, there is a focus on performance (how well or badly the bureaucrat disappears into his role or the healer into hers). Wiseman's institutions are not just sociological constructs but stage settings inviting a theater of the absurd. Often some grim humor breaks through the surface. Whether it's the hippie on a bad drug trip, terrified of dying and vomiting for ten minutes in *Hospital*, or the technicians in *Primate* masturbating the chimpanzee or the sour-faced Brother Wilfred whisking a flyswatter in disdain at the Abbott's New Age innovations in *Essene* or the lower-class, Black inhabitants of the projects in *Public Housing* listening in silent disbelief to the Black middle-class, former basketball player entrepreneur who tells them they should start an elevator-repair business, there is a surreal gap between problems and solutions.

Pauline Kael said about his unflinching camera: "You look misery in the eye and you realize there's nothing to be afraid of."[3] But not only misery. In *Canal Zone* (1977), the Panamanian patients in a mental health clinic sit stolidly in the waiting room watching television, an Abbott and Costello film dubbed into Spanish. With puckish calm, Wiseman gives us more than a minute of this film clip, minus English subtitles, followed by a Kentucky Fried Chicken commercial. We are welcome to interpret the scene as a commentary on cultural imperialism,but it is also a statement of our hopelessness before the entropic absurdity of life.

Several Wiseman works, such as *Canal Zone* and *Meat*, end with a curious diminuendo. "He addresses our greatest fear, stasis," notes Errol Morris, "everything grinding down slower and slower to some kind of sad halt."[4]

There is also a meditative, almost pastoral side to Wiseman: the pleasure of looking at the world around us in all its contradictions, with a calm, hypnotic, Zen stoicism. This contemplative manner is manifest in *Belfast, Maine*, which can be seen as a summation of everything Wiseman has done. It captures the rhythms of a community, with scenes of lobstering, factories, moviegoing, emergency clinics, outreach programs for sheltered elderly people, hunting, amateur theatricals, high school (a teacher gives an impassioned defense of *Moby-Dick*), and the after-effects of domestic abuse. Fastening with close-ups on everyday implements, the aging Wiseman, holding on, shows himself less to be an angry prophet than a grateful mystic of the materialist realm.

So many American movies are about desire, forbidden or otherwise. Wiseman's films are more about the reality principle: work, survival, illness, death. Yet underneath his stern drive to make us experience greater doses of life as it is lies a wonderment at reality's strange, oneiric forms. The fog-bound final images of *Belfast, Maine* suggest that life is also a dream.

NEW YORK TIMES, JANUARY 23, 2000

Chapter Fifty-One

ALAIN RESNAIS

Night and Fog

François Truffaut once called *Night and Fog* "the greatest film ever made." If you don't believe me, here's the exact quote: "The effective war film is often the one in which the action begins *after* the war, when there is nothing but ruins and desolation everywhere: Rossellini's *Germany Year Zero* (1947) and above all, Alain Resnais' *Nuit et Bruillard*, the greatest film ever made."[1] Certainly it is one of the two or three most powerful and intelligent nonfiction films ever made (I hesitate to call it a documentary, for reasons that will follow), and it is also, among those many movies that have taken on the loaded subject matter of the Holocaust, perhaps the most sophisticated and ethically irreproachable.

The rap against Holocaust films is that they exploit the audience's feelings of outrage and sorrow for commercial ends, and by pretending to put us vicariously through such a staggeringly incomprehensible experience, they trivialize, reducing it to sentimental melodrama. Resnais has done nothing of the kind. Making this film in 1955, only ten years after the liberation of the concentration camps, with the wounds so fresh, he did not presume, first of all, to speak for the victims and survivors of the camps: he chose as his screenwriter the novelist Jean Cayrol, a man who had actually been imprisoned in one. Second, neither he nor Cayrol presumed to offer a comprehensive guide to the concentration camp universe. Quite the contrary: the voiceover is filled with skepticism and doubt and a sympathetic awareness of the viewer's resistance, conscious or unconscious, to grasping the unthinkable. "Useless to describe what went on in these cells," and "Words are insufficient," we are told again and again in the voiceover narration. "No description, no picture can reveal their true dimension." And: "It is in vain that we try to remember." Meanwhile, the viewer is calmly given information about the Nazis' extermination procedures. Thus the dialectic is set up between the necessity of remembering and the impossibility of doing so.

Night and Fog is, in effect, an antidocumentary: we cannot "document" this particular reality; it is too heinous. We would be defeated in advance. What can we do then? Resnais's and Cayrol's answer is: we can reflect, ask questions, examine the record, and interrogate our own responses. In short, offer up an essay. Moreover, by choosing to compress such enormous subject matter into only a half hour (think, by contrast, of Claude Lanzmann's great, monumental, nine-hour *Shoah*), the filmmakers force themselves into the epigrammatic concision and synthesis of essayistic reflection.

This effort at analysis and reflection is one of the ways the filmmakers work to evade pious sentimentality: indeed, the narration (spoken by Michel Bouquet) is delivered in a harsh, dry, astringent voice, filled with ironic shadings (though, according to Resnais himself, he asked Bouquet to deliver his lines in a "neutral tone.") The magnificent score by Hans Eisler is also employed ironically: the lovely, lyrical flute passages collide with the harrowing images; the Schoenbergian pizzicato strings signal the revving up on the Nazi machine. Just as Cayrol's text is unusually elegant, dense, and poetic for a film voiceover, so the Eisler is not your typical movie background score but an independent piece of modern music that has since been performed in concert halls.

The visuals mix color photography, for the present, and black-and-white for the past. While some of the black-and-white stills and film footage are absolutely horrific (the shoveled corpses, the piles of women's hair), there is no attempt to recapture the horror in the present-day footage of the camps. Resnais, by his own admission, strove there for "the most realistic color, the most faithful reproduction of the actual place." The color photography employs a tentative, probing tracking shot and panning approach. "We go slowly along, looking for—what?" the narrator asks dubiously. In brooding about the connection between location and history, architecture and death, the film makes the ironic point that the buildings of each concentration camp went up matter-of-factly, by ordinary construction methods ("contractors, estimates, competitive bids, and no doubt a bribe or two"), that the watchtowers had different design motifs ("Swiss style, garage style, Japanese style"), that they could even be picture-postcard pretty, that "nothing distinguished the gas chamber from an ordinary blockhouse." Past and present finally converge in a chilling pan shot of a ceiling, over which the narrative voice tells us: "The only sign—but you have to know—is this ceiling, dug into by fingernails. Even the concrete was torn." This "but you have to know" (*mais il faut savoir*, in the original French) has a double meaning: you wouldn't see it unless tipped off to what it meant and you must take this in now, you can no longer escape knowing it.

The black-and-white archival footage and the color photography are conjoined entirely by straight cuts, no process shots, and the whole is a triumph of editing. We remember that Resnais began in movies as an editor, and his first filmic efforts, shorts that also included *Van Gogh, Guernica, Statues Also Die*, and *All the Memory in the World*, were all impressive assemblages, which accentuated by montage the disjunctions and continuities between past and present. *Night and Fog* looked forward, in Resnais's career, to other films that would obsess over memory and forgetfulness, such as *Hiroshima Mon Amour* (1959), *Last Year at Marienbad* (1961), *Muriel* (1963), and *Providence* (1977).

The film also helped promote a fascinating genre, the essay film, championed especially by Chris Marker (who collaborated with Resnais on this picture and *Statues Also Die*) and practiced as well by such diverse figures as Agnès Varda, Michael Moore, Jean-Luc Godard, Ross McElwee, Alan Berliner, Harun Farocki, and Yvonne Rainer. All these filmmakers rejected the objective neutrality presumptions of traditional documentaries, and tried to turn film into a medium expressive of personal, idiosyncratic thought.

Finally, it may be well to take up the suggestion by Truffaut, quoted earlier, that *Night and Fog* has special significance as a film against war, against violence itself. Movies that purport to dramatize "war is hell" almost invariably make the experience of battle adventurous and exciting. Only by looking back reflectively and trying to understand the suffering and disasters of history—"when there is nothing but ruins and desolation"—can we begin to commit ourselves to prevent further atrocities, a point made loud and clear in the final voiceover, which for once abandons the tone of modest scrutiny and allows itself a moment of well-earned, didactic passion.

CRITERION COLLECTION, 2003

Chapter Fifty-Two

JEAN ROUCH AND EDGAR MORIN

Chronicle of a Summer

In 1959, Edgar Morin, a prominent sociologist and cinephile who had written several books about the movies, approached Jean Rouch, the pioneering ethnographic filmmaker. Rouch had already distinguished himself with a series of celebrated semidocumentaries (*Jaguar, Moi, un Noir, La Pyramide Humaine*) shot in Africa, which had invited the subjects he filmed to have a hand in shaping, fictionalizing, and reacting on camera for these films—a practice he called "shared ethnography." Morin invited or challenged Rouch to collaborate with him on a movie shot closer to home, in Paris, 1960—to relinquish the exotic cover of Africa for the more mundane lives of bourgeois and working-class Parisians. The result, *Chronique d'un Été* (*Chronicle of a Summer*), one of the supreme masterworks of nonfiction cinema, which I would rank just below Chris Marker's *Sans Soleil*, has nevertheless been rather difficult to see in this country for some time.

When I saw it in the early sixties on its initial release, I was blown away by its freshness, audacity, and emotional power. It seemed to open a continent of possibilities. Now it has been reissued on DVD, thanks to a restoration by the Cineteca di Bologna. I was both eager and afraid to watch it again, lest it prove disappointing, but it turns out to be just as surprising, just as remarkable. How to account for that uniqueness?

Let me attempt a rough description. The film begins with Rouch and Morin explaining to their assistant Marceline Loridan that they are going to embark on an experiment. (The word "experiment" is key, as it places the enterprise in the vicinity of the essay film, keeping it open, flexible, and play-fully receptive to contradiction and imperfection.) She is instructed to go into the street with a colleague and stop passersby and ask if they are happy. These scenes, which yield the expected evasions and terse admissions, give way to longer, more piercingly in-depth interviews with a dozen or so sub-jects who are asked to explain how they live, what they live for, how they feel about their working lives and their chances for personal happiness. The film's allure hinges in large part on the subjects selected, who are generally articu-late, young, attractive, intelligent, and afflicted with a kind of self-aware paralysis.

Morin, besides being a sociology professor, was a left-wing activist involved at the time in protesting the Algerian War, and he drew many of the inter-viewees from his political circle, especially the faction calling itself Social-ism or Barbarism. There were several group meals staged, political discus-sions among young radicals (including the then-boyishly charismatic Régis Debray), workers obliged to confront students, whites and Africans made to talk about their feelings toward each other. Inclined toward psychoanalysis and Marxism, Morin seemed to be pressing the point of how alienated peo-ple were in their jobs, how discontented they were as individuals, whereas the less ideological Rouch tried to lighten the mood with scenes of people having fun—even moving the action to St. Tropez for some beach action.

Burning holes in the center of the film are two riveting dramatic monologues—arias, if you will—by a pair of women. Marceline Loridan-Ivens unforgettably walks through the streets of Paris remembering her incarceration in Auschwitz and Bergen-Belsen and her family's destruction in these concentration camps. Rouch and Morin had been experimenting with lightweight synch-sound equipment, and the force of this sequence derives as much from the airy freedom of a long continuous hand-held shot as it does from its contrastingly dark content. The second sequence, equally dramatic but claustrophobically constrained within a room's interior, involves Mary Lou, a beautiful, unhappy Italian secretary who pours out her feelings of being miserable and lost as an émigré in France, drinking and sleeping around, to the sympathetic Morin. In a later sequence we see Mary Lou sud-denly radiant, her mood improved by a new lover. (Cineastes, take note: her secretarial job happened to be at *Cahiers du Cinema*, and her fugitively glimpsed lover, none other than the director Jacques Rivette.)

It seemed to be a naïve hope on the filmmakers' part that they could knock down walls between people in different socioeconomic strata and effectuate a sense of community by getting them to see how similar their problems were. (They seem to pounce embarrassingly, for instance, on an awkward moment when a worker, Angelo, tells an African student, Landry, he likes him, as though this were a major breakthrough in human affairs instead of a polite remark, which is how Landry takes it.) The kicker comes when they bring the interviewees together for a screening of the film's rough cut. The cast turns on the filmmakers for exploiting them and invading their privacy and questions the sincerity of the two most dramatic participants, Marceline and Mary Lou, as divas performing for the camera. So some essential questions of documentary filmmaking come to the fore: What is truth? Is it possible for people to act naturally when a camera is on? How can documentarians avoid manipulation, or is it even worth trying? Beyond cinematic considerations, there are larger political doubts raised about the chances of transforming human nature to bring about a more mutually cooperative society. In a last, postmortem sequence, our two disillusioned filmmakers, like Bouvard and Pécuchet, are shown walking haltingly down the Musée de l'Homme hallway, trying to make sense of their "failed" experiment. Regardless of their not having achieved all their quixotic goals, this self-reflexive ending is an artistic triumph, deliciously comic and pleasing for skeptics like me.

The Criterion Collection has done an indispensable service by not only releasing the restored version in a clean transfer but also supplying meaty supplements that place it in historical and aesthetic context. There is an amazing seventy-five-minute documentary entitled *Un Été + 50*, directed by Florence Dauman, which contains outtakes of the original film and interviews with Morin and several of the participants, including an ironic Debray looking back on his radical youth. Here we get to see extended political discussions about the Algerian War and the Congo, which the state censorship at the time would not have permitted, as well as hammy personal encounters that fortunately did not make it into the final cut. We see the thirty-five-year-old Marceline Loridan, unhappily in love with Jean-Pierre, a twenty-year-old skirt-chaser, rehearsing their breakup scene over and over. (Loridan would later become the wife, working partner, and widow of the great documentarian Joris Ivens). These sequences, intriguing as they are, would have bloated the final film and destroyed its delicate arc. They confirm by their absence what a miraculously artful construction is the seemingly casual *Chronicle of a Summer.*

Appearing at the peak of the French New Wave, the film could not help but be subsumed in its wet embrace. There was considerable overlap in the visuals (black-and-white cutaways of everyday Paris, gritty locations, shot in part by the New Wave's favorite cameraman, Raoul Coutard, though it was Michel Brault, imported from the direct-cinema movement of Canada, who best fielded the mobile equipment, employing the first handheld, sync sound 16mm camera ever used in France), in the preference for natural light, voice-over, and self-reflexivity. But Rouch, we see in an interview supplement, was touchy about being associated with the New Wave, as well he might be, since the influence really flowed from the older man to the younger filmmakers. Godard had already declared Rouch's *Moi un Noir* "the greatest French film since the Liberation" and praised "its wonderful verve and spontaneity." An accompanying essay by Sam di Torio helpfully pinpoints all the cross-currents between *Chronicle* and subsequent film culture, as well as the politics of the time. (It is not a stretch to see *Chronicle* as a harbinger of the events of '68.) Finally, there is an illuminating interview with the scholar Faye Ginsburg about the tensions between Rouch and Morin on the set. Auteurists might be inclined to give the lion's share of the credit to Rouch, simply because of his splendid oeuvre, but it may make more sense to argue that the achievement of this particular film, its interplay of gravity and sprightliness, is precisely the result of these two very different sensibilities working together. Rouch may have made more radical films on his own, but he needed Morin to make one as deeply satisfying, as resonant and as touching as *Chronicle of a Summer.*

CINEASTE (SUMMER 2013)

Chapter Fifty-Three

ALAN BERLINER

In this age of memoir, when, thanks to simplified technologies, everybody's life becomes potential movie material, documentary filmmakers all over America have taken to mining the stories of their immediate families. But a gulf separates these family chronicles, many of them myopic, sentimentalized, or resentful, from a handful of truly well-made documentaries.

No one has been more dogged or more successful with this difficult form than Alan Berliner, whose trilogy of feature documentaries is being shown at Lincoln Center's Walter Reade Theater.

Berliner's first feature, *The Family Album*, made in 1986, consists of found home movies and audio tapes that are edited together to tell the story of American family life. While the images celebrate, as home movies tend to, the optimism of social rituals, holidays, and horsing around, the voices on the soundtrack often tell a more troubled story.

In his second feature, *Intimate Stranger*, Berliner focused on his maternal grandfather, Joseph Cassuto, an Egyptian Jewish cotton merchant who ended up working for a Japanese firm and living away from his family eleven months out of the year. Cassuto comes across as a hero to his Japanese colleagues (to whom he sent food and medical supplies after the war), a goodwill ambassador to the world, but a stranger in his own household. "I never met anyone who didn't like him—outside of his immediate family," says one son. Yet Cassuto's daughter Regina, the filmmaker's mother, continues to idealize her father. We are left with a complex portrait of a man who had a talent for friendship but was weak in the domestic area. The filmmaker presents conflicting judgments of his grandfather, who died when Berliner was a teenager, but abstains from passing judgment himself.

In his next, most powerful film, *Nobody's Business*, Berliner, who was forty during the shooting, did not have the option of detachment because this time he made a film about his own father. He tries to draw out his reclusive, stoical, bitter, taciturn father, a retired sportswear manufacturer who has entered a brokenhearted old age. The first efforts are comic, like trying to get a stone to speak. His father, Oscar, refuses to see why his story would interest anyone else. "My life is nothing. You have one bad habit," Oscar admonishes his son. "You think if something's important to you, it has to be important to everyone else."

Undaunted, the filmmaker confronts his father with a variety of strategies (research into family roots, tough probes about his parents' divorce) to get him to open up. The purpose is both aesthetic and personal: to find the meaning of this man's life, for the sake of the documentary, by transmuting it into artistically tellable form and to have a long-deferred talk with his father.

Recurring clips of prizefighting wryly comment on this duel between clamlike father and stubborn, prying son, who does not seem to want to knock out his father as much as to get him off the mat to go a few more rounds. Oscar Berliner comes across as a typical postwar dad, a hard-working, honorable guy who fitted in best with his army buddies during World War II. Then he married the glamorous, exotic aspiring actress Regina, with whom he was classically mismatched. "We crossed paths in a head-on collision," Regina comments in the film. "He was ready to get married, and I was ready to leave my father's house." The filmmaker's sister, Lynn, who provides a balanced, sympathetic voice, says: "He married the wrong woman. End of story."

Yet Oscar Berliner, now in his late seventies, keeps surprising viewers with his combativeness and the integrity of his indifference. When the filmmaker tries to interest him in research about their rabbinical ancestors, Oscar dismisses it as phony nostalgia.

"There was one tombstone standing all alone, and that one I chose to see as your grandfather's," Alan Berliner tells his father.

"Hooray for you," comes the sarcastic reply.

It's a measure of the filmmaker's generosity that he lets his father win his share of the arguments. What initially seems like a one-sided fight generates immense, perverse sympathy for this difficult old man. Though Alan's sister insists her father's capacity to love has dried up, Oscar catches us off guard at the end when he dotes on his new grandchild.

"There's a general sense that Alan Berliner has figured out the family documentary form," says Jack Salzman, media director at the Jewish Museum. "He really does explore family relations in an energetic, vital way. Alan manages to impose his presence and voice on the film, without getting narcissistic."[1]

How do Berliner's explorations manage to evade the pitfalls of the family film? For starters, they are dramatically tight (each no more than an hour long); they are full of juicy conflict and contradiction, innovative in their cinematic technique, unpredictable in their structures. And they spring from a high degree of preliminary analysis. This is cooked, not raw material.

"Alan Berliner represents to me the most exciting breakthrough out of the impasse of the family film," says Richard Pena, program director of the Film Society of Lincoln Center. "Most documentaries end up planting the camera and waiting for something to happen. With Berliner, one sees a much more playful, essayistic thought process at work."[2] Pena compares *Intimate Stranger*, with its multiple, contradictory narrators, to *Citizen Kane*. Berliner agrees that *Citizen Kane* was an influence. The point is that Berliner's storytelling may have more in common with the subjective psychology of characters in fiction films than with the traditional documentary's display of fact as objective truth.

Commenting on Joseph Cassuto's seemingly nutty habit of wiring Presidents Kennedy and Nixon with offers to advise them on matters of state, one relative says: "Look, Alan, you live in your head; he lived in his head. In his head your grandfather saw himself as a statesman." The wounded patriarchs of these two last films are, in different ways, solitary *Luftmenschen*.

Berliner himself is a thin, bearded, gentle-voiced, slightly formal man whose nervous laugh disguises a fierce will underneath. In his TriBeCa loft, his extensive collections of photographs, family films, and notes are archived with a neatnik's color-coded obsessiveness. Berliner, who was raised in Far Rockaway, Queens, trained as an experimental film maker at the State University of New York at Binghamton. His early shorts were all geometric and structuralist. "The idea that I would someday make a film outside a minimalist, abstract vocabulary was implausible," he says. Then humanism struck. He found himself doing highly accessible, emotionally gripping, narrative work. I know no one working in personal films today who brings so dramatically alive the intense and ambivalent love within families. His technical mastery of the relation between sound and image is consistently employed in the service of psychological truths.

Yet there are still traces of the experimental filmmaker in Berliner's style, like the device of using images and sounds of a manual typewriter to help structure *Intimate Stranger* or the boxing ring that becomes a leitmotif for *Nobody's Business*. The experimental training also surfaces in the abundant techniques used in the soundtrack, which avoids a literal connection with the visuals. For instance, while his estranged parents are each telling about their marriage breaking up, we see not their faces but footage of a hurricane-swept house falling into the river below.

Berliner compares hovering over a Steenbeck editing table to sitting at the Steinway. Having made his living for years as a sound editor, he continues to be a film artist for whom editing is central. "Editing is constructing and articulating a flow of thought," he says, and "flow of thought" is one way to define Berliner's essay films.[3]

The Family Trilogy follows a trajectory of increasing vulnerability, from the relatively impersonal *Family Album*, in which the voices of Berliner's family (among others) are heard but never seen, to *Intimate Stranger*, which has some embarrassing revelations about his grandfather, and finally, to *Nobody's Business*, with its no-holds-barred encounters. What next? Will he make a film about himself? Berliner is unsure what his next project will be, but feels he is still too young for an autobiography.

What of the emotional pitfalls of working with one's family as primary material? Hurting the feelings of loved ones? When Berliner's mother asked him why it was necessary to include unflattering aspects in his portrait of his grandfather, he told her he was trying to get a fuller understanding of who this person was. In his journal, however, he recorded his own doubt: "Who am I as his grandson to burst into these sacred places and start rushing about making trouble, causing tears, opening wounds, exposing scar tissue and raising the dead? My uncle Al said he had a love-hate relationship to this project. That's the appropriate tension for all of us."

Regina Berliner, the filmmaker's mother, revealed another sentiment. "The films were very touching," she said. "I was in tears in some parts. Perhaps I would have liked to see the films first and edited a few things out. I asked Alan, 'Why must every part of my life be exposed to the public?'"

"To make a good movie,' he said.

"I accepted it. I wasn't very pleased, but I accepted it."

NEW YORK TIMES, JANUARY 12, 1997

POSTSCRIPT: *WIDE AWAKE*

As was perhaps inevitable, Alan Berliner, after making a brilliant pair of family portraits, *Intimate Stranger* (about his grandfather) and *Nobody's Business* (about his father), would run out of patriarchs and have to turn the camera on himself. In *Wide Awake*, he examines that self through his lifelong insomnia. The filmmaker, it seems, has always been a bad sleeper and feels as though in a constantly woozy state of jet lag. Now, having become a father for the first time, he must figure out what to do to be there for his son. So he consults a slew of doctors, interrogates his past, confronts his mother and sister about the possible childhood roots of this problem, and digresses in a dozen different directions about the science and folklore of sleep.

Berliner is an inventive formal stylist, and part of the pleasure in watching this movie is to see him come up with new visual and aural strategies to hold our attention. He is a master at intercutting found footage from old films and home movies with shots of the contemporary urban landscape. Seeking to rationalize and shift the blame for his insomnia to his mother, modernity, cities, sensory overload, and anything else he can think of, he recognizes finally that the culprit is himself: he has come to love the early hours of the night and to identify his filmmaking creativity with that cocooning solitude. How now to reconcile the old habits of an artist loner with the new demands and rewards of family life? Somehow, if he wants to share the same planet and time zone with his newborn son, Eli, he must learn to make an adjustment. The film leaves us in an unresolved quandary. If we are sometimes at the brink of losing patience with this self-conscious, self-absorbed filmmaker-protagonist, we must admit that he has done a thoroughly honest job of uncovering the all-too-human strategies of neurotic self-protection.

Chapter Fifty-Four

ROBERT GARDNER

Dead Birds

In 1964, Lyndon B. Johnson had just assumed the presidency after Kennedy's assassination. We were in the thick of the Cold War. Patrice Lumumba had been unseated by a CIA coup and killed in the Congo. The Cuban Missile Crisis was so recent as still to raise a shiver of apocalyptic foretaste. The first American troops had been sent as "advisors" to Vietnam. And I turned twenty-one and graduated from college. It was a nervous yet idealistic time, when helping to make a better world, either through joining the Mississippi Freedom Summer or signing up for the Peace Corps or waging revolutionary armed struggle with Che Guevara or doing socially engaged art all seemed valid possibilities. In that precarious mood, Robert Gardner released his documentary feature *Dead Birds*, which reflected both the violence and hopes of the time, and it has remained imprinted since, however subliminally, on our culture's mind-screen.

In retrospect, *Dead Birds* can be seen as a threshold, dividing all that had preceded and followed it in ethnographic cinema. Certainly, there had been popular, colorful, anthropologically naïve documentaries about people of the wild, such as *Nanook of the North* and *Grass*. And there had been ethnographically scrupulous documentary shorts made in the field by such distinguished anthropologists as Margaret Mead and Gregory Bateson, destined as audio-visual classroom aids. John Marshall had shot thousands of feet on Bushmen of the Kalahari Desert, and the results were edited by Gardner and him into *The Hunters* (1958), an informative, genially episodic film.

Dead Birds was something else: a powerful story of chilling relevance about the Dani, a Neolithic farmer-warrior group in New Guinea that practiced a kind of tit-for-tat killing game with a nearby rival Indigenous group. The film showed how these likable, friendly (to the film crew, anyway) people nevertheless believed that the universe was out of balance unless they could go one-up homicidally on the other group. And since the other group believed the same, individual losses on each side kept being avenged with reciprocal murders, either by doing battle openly or by sneaking up on an unsuspecting enemy (a child, a woman, an old man, didn't matter) who had wandered into no-man's-land.

The narrative was organized around a few key protagonists, including the warrior Weyak, who mounted watchtowers to keep an eye on the enemy, and the young boy Pua, who herded pigs when not distracted by daydreams and envy of others' activities. Some of the most memorable images involved the battle scenes, where lines of warriors taunted each other, and the funerals, where the dead person would be tied to a chair near the pyre, and for which pigs had to be slaughtered with bow and arrow at close range to make the feast. If all this blood-letting seemed, on one level, senseless, it was perhaps no more so than the periodic massacres occurring in civilized society. *Dead Birds* implicitly asked us to ponder the nature and function of human aggression by watching it operate in these highly controlled, ritualized, and, in a way, humanely limited circumstances (a single death usually being sufficient to stop the killing for awhile).

In documentary filmmaking, the period of fundraising and preparation work usually far exceeds the shooting time, and the correspondence, diaries, and documents the filmmaker kept from that period (published both in Robert Gardner's *The Impulse to Preserve* and *Making "Dead Birds"*), give us inside glimpses of the patience and persistence necessary to drill through layers of governmental and eleemosynary bureaucracy in order to get the project off the ground. Gardner, trained as both an anthropologist and a filmmaker, took great pains to ensure that both the scientific and artistic parts of the venture would be respected. Inclined from the start toward a humanities-oriented, one might almost say belletristic anthropology that valued subjective perceptions and personal accounts, in contrast to the more quantifiable structural anthropology then in vogue, Gardner tried to learn as much of the language and circumstances of the Dani as he could before setting off. He was determined to spend enough time with them so that the results would not be a hit-and-run documentary, and he surrounded himself with professionals whose perspectives could check his own. The team included the still photographer Eliot Elisofon, the senior anthropologist Jan Broekhuijse, the writer Peter Matthiessen, the botanist Chris Versteegh, the young anthropologist Karl Heider, who would be left behind to do fieldwork after the shooting finished, and the sound engineer Michael Rockefeller.

From the start, Gardner pondered a way of organizing the overflow of impressions and data about the Dani into a single cohesive story. In this, his first major project, as he would with his later films, such as *Rivers of Sand*, *Forest of Bliss*, and *Ika Hands*, he sought a ruling metaphor to convey his core understanding of the people under scrutiny. Before he left New Guinea, he knew he would use the fact that the Dani identify with birds and refer to their victims' captured weapons, ornaments, and corpses by the term "dead birds" as the symbol he needed. At the same time the filmmaker consciously decided to exclude various subplots, agricultural or otherwise, that would not fit into this theme of mortality and revenge killing.

In many respects, the Dani do not come across in the film as bloodthirsty people. Quite the contrary: they seem charming, reasonable, self-contained, yet spontaneous. All the more appalling that their very identity (especially that of the men) seems to hinge on spilling blood. Gardner took the non-judgmental point of view that this was the reality of the situation. Was this amoral spectatorship or scientific detachment?

The filmmaker's attitude toward the Dani's ritual warfare seems, in retrospect, rather complicated. He became understandably indignant when false rumors circulated that he and his crew were instigating the fighting, and he went to great lengths to rebut these allegations. He knew that he was merely documenting a way of life that had gone on for centuries: in no way was he the cause of them. Still, since this ritualized vendetta had been chosen as the main subject, he clearly had a stake in the continuation of the fighting. No warfare, no film. When Margaret Mead counseled him against making a film about tribal warfare, he chose to interpret her advice as a statement for the public record rather than a true reflection of her beliefs. When attacks and war parties experienced a lull, he expressed disappointment at the prospect that the fighting might cease altogether. He got annoyed at local missionaries and officials who seemed set on putting an end to the fighting, and he hoped to keep the police and army out of the area during the filming, as these law enforcers might have a restraining effect on normal tribal behavior. From the missionaries' perspective, if these filmmakers were not actively trying to stop the killing, they were implicitly condoning and promoting it.

Gardner grasped that the Dani men derived their sense of manhood from these war exercises. As he put it in a 1961 journal entry: "That there is ritual war in the Baliem Valley is something all people who have lived in that valley know for a certainty; but what no one has bothered to find out is what warfare means to those who make it or what it could mean to deprive them of it."[1] As a filmmaker, he was attracted to the "extraordinary theatricality and raw energy" of this spectacle of "300–500 decorated and armed warriors dancing against 8000-foot peaks."[2] He was also, he confesses now, "in the grip of almost obsessive thinking, in which naïveté combined with ambitious goals had me supposing that a film concerned with hand-to-hand violence with ritual purpose could speak in a general way to the understanding of human aggression."[3]

Yet his nonintrusive stance could be inconsistent, as when he intervened to save the life of a runaway Wittaia woman whom the Dani were planning to lure into killing. "But I could not be witness to such an event, despite what some might think its cinematic value," he wrote, explaining his intervention.[4] Nowhere does his ambivalence emerge so starkly as in the question of whether to document the amputation of young girls' finger joints, a part of the grieving ritual. Clearly sickened and appalled by this practice, he nevertheless wondered in a diary entry, with a note of self-irony: "Has anyone filmed such an event and, if not, has it some irresistible cinematographic allure?"[5] Deciding he did not have the heart to, he forfeited the chance, though he was later tempted to get footage of the amputations when the producer Joseph E. Levine showed interest in acquiring *Dead Birds* for large-scale distribution. Levine, a vulgarian who had made a pile with some cheap Hercules movies shot in Italy, was branching out into classy projects such as Godard's *Contempt*, as well as sensationalistic, pseudo-anthropological exploitation pictures such as *The Sky Above, the Mud Below*. Gardner could hardly be blamed for thinking that his film, to which he had given his lifeblood, had a chance for much wider circulation with super salesman Levine and wrote Heider, still in the field, to ask if it might be possible to film a joint-amputation ritual. When Levine demanded a total remake of the film, Gardner wrote Heider to forget it, reasoning that in any case it was more effective to show mutilated hands without the actual grisly ceremony on-screen.

Far from trying to hide these ethical dilemmas, Gardner has always been quick to raise the issue of documentary filmmaking's moral quandaries and honest about the degree to which he may have overstepped the line. By temperament a worrier, eaten by a Yankee puritanical conscience, what seems to intrigue him most is the problematic, impure, and unresolved nature of the experience: the impossibility of avoiding what Sartre called "dirty hands." Blessed with lank, movie-star good looks (he started out as an actor), a privileged background (related to art collector Isabella Gardner, who bequeathed her museum to Boston), and the inherited social ease that allowed him to correspond with foundation heads and public officials on an equal footing, he also betrayed at times a fragile, self-doubting emotional structure. Of course, no one who has managed to finish a series of noncommercial movies while administering the Harvard Center for the Visual Arts and the Film Study Center could be said to lack self-confidence, yet he gives the impression in person of being a painfully modest man. There is, withal, a streak of solemn sadness in him, which he readily acknowledges. When asked why he has always felt like a "refugee" and identified with marginalized cultures, he said: "I think I was born a melancholy person, and it was not difficult for me to see that film was a melancholy way of looking at the world. If I stayed at home, I might not find enough melancholy or be able to express the kinds of melancholy I thought I could in an environment or culture I was less familiar with." Asked why he thought film was intrinsically melancholic, he said: "I view the world in terms of 'then' and 'now.' The 'now' is sliding into 'then' at which point the 'now' is forever lost. I think that is melancholic. Film incarnates death for me because when I see a film, particularly actuality film, or when I look at the wonderful renderings of humanity by the great photographers of the world, it seems to me that in those images is the story we can tell without knowing what the whole story is, but that it will surely end in death."[6]

Gardner has written that he used anthropology as an instrument of self-discovery and self-comprehension. Interestingly, for all his confessional honesty, he has never specified which personal threads of suppressed aggression or internal anger or moody impulse might have attracted him to this bloodthirsty material. Perhaps a temperamental pessimism drew him to the subject of ritual war. My instinct tells me that the film has less to do in the end with killing than with mourning.

Certainly, death plays a key role in *Dead Birds*. Above and beyond bloodshed, the philosophical question is posed on the voice-over: What effect does a person's knowing they are mortal have on the conduct of their life? The shadow that one particular death cast on the film has been lasting and profound. In a startling diary admission on location, Gardner recorded he had had to hush up the fact that Michael Rockefeller was grazed by an arrow in battle, to keep the authorities from stopping the film. Perhaps some grain of remorse for exposing his companions to danger lodged retrospectively in his heart when Rockefeller disappeared later off the coast of New Guinea. Though the young, talented, idealistic sound engineer/photographer did not die on the set but shortly afterward, on a separate trip he made looking for indigenous art, the simultaneity of that loss with the final stage of editing the film haunts all of Gardner's recollections about the making of *Dead Birds*. The idea that these two scions of America's ruling class should have joined forces to document one of the world's poorest groups is in itself remarkable. The filmmaker accompanied Michael's father, Governor Nelson Rockefeller, to New Guinea in a fruitless attempt to get to the bottom of the tragedy.

In the forty-some odd years since it was first shown, *Dead Birds* has been screened at conferences and film festivals, shown regularly in the classroom and on television, rereleased on DVD, and acknowledged as a classic of ethnographic cinema.

It happens that ethnographic cinema is a highly problematic field—and the more interesting for being so. There is inevitably some guilt surrounding the potential for colonialist intrusion and exploitation of indigenous people. There is the risk of not being able to satisfy the sometimes contradictory demands of anthropology and film, the danger of sentimentalizing or patronizing the group being studied by overstressing exotic folkloric elements and of insufficiently registering cultural change for the sake of presenting a romantically static, cordoned-off picture of the "primitive." There is the temptation to distort reality by staging reenactments or instigating events or scrambling chronologies, continuities, and spatial contexts through editing, the hazard of altering the group's behavior merely by the camera's presence and awakening needs and appetites that may destabilize a whole culture and economy through the inadvertent introduction of novel objects from the developed world (watches, cell phones, etc.).[7] And finally, there is the possibility of intervening inappropriately in rituals and of not intervening enough when to do nothing would border on immoral.

Guilt comes with the territory of documentary filmmaking and specifically ethnographic cinema. Ever since Buñuel's dispassionate filming of the donkey's demise in *Land Without Bread*, the ethics of documentary filmmakers have been interrogated: should they not intervene to prevent cruel acts? Critics often make the point that almost all antiwar movies have an ultimately prowar effect by glorifying its excitement. Seen in that light, *Dead Birds* is also not entirely pacifist: it exalts the skill of hand-to-hand combat and the cunning necessary to take another person's life. Shuddering at "the sudden and pointless bloodiness of the affair," after witnessing a battle, Gardner nevertheless forced himself to ask in a journal entry, "I even wonder, if it may not be true, that to take a life is the most intense, possibly ultimate, human experience there is."[8]

Since *Dead Birds* was first shown, the field of ethnographic cinema has developed stricter guidelines, as Karl Heider (who had been part of the original expedition) articulates in his standard text on visual anthropology, *Ethnographic Cinema* (1976). For instance, it is considered desirable that whole acts and entire bodies be presented whenever possible and close-ups avoided; that the ethnographer's presence be self-reflexively acknowledged, rather than pretending to be a fly on the wall; and that ideally the ethnographic film should be backed up by written material, which further explains and analyzes the visual record. Heider, noting that in many ways *Dead Birds* instinctively satisfied the criteria of ethnographic truth, from its coherent spatial presentation of the hilly terrain to its feelings for the Dani as complex individuals, nevertheless pointed out that "the battle sequence in *Dead Birds* combined footage shot at different battles" and "even though Robert Gardner filmed most of the battle scenes in *Dead Birds* with normal focal-length lenses, they had the effect of foreshortening the scene, and so the front lines appear to be much closer to each other than they actually were."[9] Another distortion of the record was the use of "wild sound," recorded separately by Michael Rockefeller and then added to the images because cheap, lightweight synchronous sound equipment was not yet available.

Unlike today's digital video filmmakers, Gardner's task was made more arduous and chancy because he could not see the rushes. Much of his anxiety came from shooting "blind" and never knowing if there was a crack on the camera lens or if the f-stops were correct or if the nearest developing labs he was obliged to trust would scratch the negative. Other hardships he and his crew faced: a brutal sun, almost impassable swamps, copious flies, drenching rain, dysentery, sand fly fever, crocodiles, canoes capsizing with all the equipment, humidity so intense it caused the film stock to swell and the camera to jam, hostile officials, stray arrows, native children who kicked the tripod, not to mention loneliness, boredom, fear of failure. But as Werner Herzog has said, "Humiliation and strain are essential parts of filmmaking," and Gardner would appear to share with Herzog the premise of moviemaking as a self-imposed ordeal. There were also missed opportunities, as happens to any documentary filmmaker, such as his having to change film magazines while the dead boy's body was carried to the fire. By the same token, there were hunches that paid off and sudden improbable pieces of luck, like finding the very cowrie shells he would need with which to buy the goodwill of the natives in the nearby home of a Massachusetts collector.

Gardner has had half a lifetime to play back in his mind the moves, the miracles, the triumphs and regrets of that first adventure that launched him on his filmmaking journey. One qualm or bit of second-guessing on the filmmaker's part should be addressed: his worry about placing "the burden of language" on *Dead Birds* through its voiceover narration. He has stated that he considered going back to "rewrite the narration, which I have often thought too heavy and occasionally arch."[10] His self-doubts on that score may have been triggered by the criticism of colleagues, who regarded as presumptuous the soundtrack's imputing of thoughts and feelings to the Dani.

The field of ethnographic cinema seems to have developed a general prejudice against the alleged intrusiveness of voiceover: Karl Heider argued, for instance, that narration in ethnographic cinema is a "cinematically weak" distraction that draws our attention away from the immediacy of the images. Because I think spoken words belong in motion pictures as much as images and welcome articulate voiceover narration, I disagree with this position.

Gardner's retrospective hesitations about the narration may also reflect his own evolution as a documentary filmmaker toward a preference for wordless images without voiceover commentary or dialogue, a feat he achieved most spectacularly in his other masterpiece, *Forest of Bliss*. That movie, however, shows Hindus preparing corpses in Benares, a procedure that would be readily understandable by most Western viewers, whereas very few of us could have known what was going on with the indigenous people in New Guinea unless we were given some rudimentary information.

The splendid voiceover narration in *Dead Birds* gives much more than contextual information: it supplies a personal and poetic dimension and a quintessentially mournful tone, superbly delivered in Gardner's grave, somber voice, which crystallizes and unites the images. There is generosity in the filmmaker's attempt to put into his own eloquent words the significance of the events we have been allowed to witness. In this respect, *Dead Birds* is not only a classic of ethnographic cinema but also a bridge to the essay film, that tricky subgenre in which the filmmaker tells us what he or she is thinking. We do learn considerable amounts about the Dani from the narration, but we also learn about Gardner's perspective toward them and understand better why he has maintained that anthropology can be a voyage to the self.

Ethnographic filmmakers, it seems to me, are caught in a bind: on the one hand, they are asked not to interpret the events on-screen with voiceover narration, under the apparent assumption that to let the images speak for themselves would be more "factual," more "objective"; on the other hand, they are expected to signal the viewer "self-reflexively" that they are on the premises, making a movie, so that the subjective, fabricating factor of filmmaking can be taken into account. In a sense, the ethnographic profession is in the same dilemma as journalism schools, which have had increasingly to acknowledge that there may be no such thing as objective reporting while clinging obstinately to that ideal. We do not have to reprise the familiar arguments here about the distorting nature of photography. Moreover, most audiences of even moderate sophistication are aware when they are watching a movie that they are not seeing unmediated reality and that decisions have been made behind the camera and in the editing room. Additionally, most moderately sophisticated viewers would know how to adjust to the convention employed by Gardner when he relates in voiceover, say, the purpose that a particular Dani has in mind in setting off to perform some action. The filmmaker is not "presuming" to channel the Dani's thoughts so much as he is synthesizing what he knows to be true and summarizing it in a concise manner, without an awkward aural trail of footnotes to explain how he came by that knowledge.

To the degree that the ethnographic filmmaker is an artist, it is inevitable that a strong shaping impulse will streamline and omit much daily social reality of the group under investigation. The better the storyteller, the more the omissions. As Alfred Hitchcock famously said, "Movies are life with the boring bits left out." Does that mean that the ethnographic film that entertains us, with a dramatic arc similar to a commercial feature, necessarily falsifies too much? I think not. Even if we were to consider *Dead Birds* or indeed any ethnographic film a fiction, we would need to recall the ways that fiction can capture its own set of truths.

FOREWORD TO ROBERT GARDNER, *MAKING "DEAD BIRDS":*
CHRONICLE OF A FILM (CAMBRIDGE, MA: PEABODY MUSEUM PRESS, 2007)

Chapter Fifty-Five

SAM GREEN AND BILL SPIEGEL

The Weather Underground

The Weather Underground provides a rousing introduction to those revolutionary celebrities, those daring young outlaws of the recent past; offers audiences on the Left an excuse to cheer favorites and boo establishment war criminals as they flash on the screen; and is a serviceable *aide-memoire* to veterans of the sixties who may be on the brink of memory loss. Beyond that, it is not a very good documentary. I did not expect it to be very good, but I was still intrigued to see whether the ways in which it failed might be instructive and curious how the evasions, truths, political rhetoric, and rationalizations would play out. More than that, I suppose, I wanted to catch a glimpse of some people I knew, however slightly, talking about a period of my life and a struggle I had witnessed and participated in, however tangentially.

To come clean: I had been somewhat friendly with Mark Rudd during the 1968 Columbia University protest, as one of the "radical alumni" lending support. The last time I saw Mark was at the 1969 Counter-Inaugural demonstrations against Richard Nixon, when I became disenchanted, or rather, horrified at SDS and the Yippies using young high schoolers as cannon fodder in skirmishes with the DC police, though they seemed to see it as seasoning or toughening the kids into "street-fighting men." My own efforts against the Vietnam War were certainly a lot tamer than the Weathermen, whom I viewed then (and still view) as largely self-deluded and dangerous poseurs. That said, I could never dislike them as individuals: years later, I became the genial ex-Weatherman Bill Ayers's writing teacher, helped him complete a memoir, and got to know his wife, Bernardine Dohrn, and their three terrific sons. Not only that, but I also came to know and like Todd Gitlin, who is used in the film as the mouthpiece of the "responsible Left," attacking the hooliganism of the Weather Underground.

All these slivers of acquaintance with the principals may have contaminated any chance for me to have an objective critical take on the film. But I doubt it. For sure, I could not come to it with a neophyte's gratitude at the information it was recapitulating for the zillionth time, that progression of images that inevitably summarize the sixties and seventies in this kind of documentary (the Vietnam War clips, Jimi Hendrix, Bob Dylan, be-ins, Nixon with Billy Graham, and on and on). A young person, seeing all this history play itself out for the first time, might understandably be fascinated and might rate the film more highly than I could. Myself, I was looking for some reflective intelligence, some analytical perspective on this historical material, and what I kept hearing were crude voiceover generalities like: "As the seventies drew to a close, America seemed to be falling apart." Well, yes and no. "America was increasingly polarized and, for a while, the Weather Underground seemed to have its hand on the pulse of culture." Really?

I can't quite figure out what exactly is the point of view of the filmmakers, codirectors Sam Green and Bill Spiegel, toward their subject. They seem to regard the Weather Underground as a neat avant-garde manifestation of youth culture and political commitment and are clearly in sympathy with its progressive, anti-imperialist, antiracist positions. I suspect they disapprove of tactics like bombing the Capitol and the Pentagon and may have been looking for a certain amount of mea culpa self-scrutiny, which is pretty scarce. That they let the two most rueful, agonized voices, Brian Flanagan and Mark Rudd, have the final word, suggests some agreement with them.

Toward the very end, they ask Mark Rudd why it is so hard to talk personally, and Mark, white-bearded and looking very uncomfortable, blurts out like a cri de coeur: "My mixed feelings . . . my feelings of guilt and shame . . . how hard it is to tease out what was right from what was wrong." Well, *that* would have been an interesting movie, but it isn't the one we get. Instead, the veterans of the Weather Underground lead the filmmakers on a merry chase down the highways and byways of their old idealistic political rationales, which are repeated with very little self-examination.

Again and again, we are told: "America was murdering innocent Vietnamese and oppressing Blacks in the ghetto, so we had to do something." So they set off bombs. They planned to bomb a dance at Fort Dix, which would have killed dozens of innocent people, but the bomb exploded their own townhouse, and several Weathermen were killed. After the Greenwich Village townhouse explosion, the Weathermen decided to go underground. They also realized that they'd made an error in having almost unleashed indiscriminate violence on ordinary people. (Interesting that it was only when they suffered casualties of their own that they realized unleashing indiscriminate violence was a mistake, but nobody comments on that.) Still, the bombing continued: prison offices, government buildings, monuments. Bill Ayers says on camera: "But we never did hurt anybody. We placed bombs but didn't hurt people." He neglects to mention the security guard and state troopers who were shot to death after the botched Brinks job. The narrator informs us that that job was committed by a radical splinter group, yet David Harris, who participated in that robbery, is one of the regular talking heads chosen by the filmmakers to represent the Weather Underground. Selective honesty. It is hard to know whether the shortcomings of the filmmakers as probers or the wiliness of their interviewees is to blame for the lack of candor. Possibly both. But the result is a feast of disingenuous half-truths left unchallenged.

For instance, Naomi Jaffe, ex-Weatherperson, glibly insists that, "Doing nothing is also a form of violence." But is it, strictly speaking? At least Jaffe is honest in saying she wanted to "be part of" the big parade of world revolution. After all, it wasn't just disinterested idealism that drove the student radicals: they loved to party, and occupying campus buildings or smashing cars in the Days of Rage was another form of partying. They loved the romance of Che Guevara and being outlaws. But they don't ever say in this film, "We got swept up in the bravado of it all." No, they say that the murder of Fred Hampton raised the stakes for the Weathermen. They say that they wanted to organize white revolutionary youth to fight alongside Black and Brown insurgent groups. (Not that the favor was always appreciated: a Black leader is shown sneering at the Weather Underground for its "Custeristic" ways of leading people who are ill-prepared to fight into a "massacre.") So much of the group's hunger for revolutionary legitimacy merges with envy of people of color and their oppressed authenticity: this, too, goes unexamined.

Another rationale that comes into play here is the insanity plea. As articulated by Brian Flanagan, it goes like this: "The Vietnam War had made us crazy, so we did horrific things." Mark Rudd says: "I was overwhelmed by hate. Demented." I have no doubt that the enormous wrong of the war, combined with the Weathermen's own tendency to exacerbate the sensation of crisis by acting as if a gun were constantly being held to their heads, did make them feel, at moments, crazed or demented. Still, the members of the Weather Underground were, by and large, not psychopathic types but rather grounded, intelligent, playful, privileged, well-bred, *polite* kids (when not engaged in civil disobedience) who got caught up in a role. Their lurid accentuation now of the "madness of the times" serves to distract us from how much they seem to have been actually quite levelheaded, most of the time, but engaged in dangerous acts, partly for excitement, partly as a "gut check" (to use a phrase that props up in the film) and a way to keep from looking cowardly in front of one's pals.

What comes across clearly in the movie is how charming the Weather Underground leaders were and remain. Each has retained the political organizer's ability to come across as vulnerably engaging: full of charismatic bravura in addressing crowds, seductively gentle in looking back. No one seems sweeter than David Harris, who has been serving a life sentence for his accomplice role in the Brinks armed robbery and homicides. He looks so wistful and diffidently handsome, you want to give him a hug or some chicken soup. The young, foxy Bernadine Dohrn is shown flirting with reporters and TV media in front of the SDS convention. Brian Flanagan, now a bartender, is masculine Irish charm itself as he stares the camera in the eye and says: "There were armed robberies. I'm not going to tell you which ones I did or who did what." And why should he? But by the same token, you're not going to get much genuine, groping insight out of these folks; they're cagey, and, like all professional charmers, know how to get by on a wink and a smile. Significant gaps in recollection occur or are left to stand. (One fascinating subject that gets barely thirty seconds is how most of them managed to avoid doing jail time.) You wonder if these memory gaps are caused by the passage of years or by the need to protect themselves and others.

Part of their discomfort with self-analysis has to do with the New Left's mistrust of psychological motivation and of individuality itself as bourgeois constructs. So all personal actions tend to be justified and explained in retrospect by a political line consensually arrived at long ago, however farfetched then or tenuous now.

The Weather Underground's continued bombings and other acts of sabotage strike me as having become increasingly symbolic, irrelevant, theatrically forced expressions of solidarity: because of such and such outrage done by the American government or bad deed committed against the environment by a corporation, we are retaliating by . . . bombing a statue of a policeman (or something equally random and adventurist, like springing Timothy Leary from jail so he can fly to Algeria to sport a Black Panther beret and mouth revolutionary sayings alongside Eldridge Cleaver).

No one bothers to take up the question: Did the Weather Underground's actions in fact hasten the end of the Vietnam War? Was any of this effective? All we get is the repeated formulation: because the bad guys did X, we were forced to do Y. You keep waiting for the logic between the two halves of the sentence to close up, but it never does: somewhere in that comma, in the crease between clauses, the distance in between cause and effect keeps widening. The filmmakers try to shorten that distance by montages that give us something to look at while sopping up the audio of rationale and recollection. But an odd thing happens: the authenticity of past and present are both undercut and the passage of time denied by shuttling the two eras indiscriminately. For example, some "Days of Rage" news footage is set up by ominous strains of the film's Philip Glass–like music score, with a voiceover of the "square" newscaster of the day, then a graybeard activist reminiscing. The multiplicity of narrators dilutes the intensity and reliability of each—which may explain why we never come near gaining the visceral sense of what it was like to live underground that we do in a memoir, such as Ayers's *Fugitive Days*.

When the filmmakers are not stitching together old news clips, they are padding the visual record with "filler" shots of walking down corridors or moody cityscapes. The most dubious instance of this filler footage is a staging of headless bodies engaged in a silly, stilted sexual orgy, while a voiceover explains that it was the Weather Underground's policy to "smash monogamy." (Some honestly recollected anecdotes about how badly that policy played out would have been refreshing here, but of course, there are strict limits in place as to how much "the personal is political," lest prurient interest distract from the dignity of the political struggle.) With all this busy compilation of images, it's surprising that only a few seconds of a decent older film about the Weather Underground, by Emile de Antonio and Haskell Wexler, get used: perhaps the rights were too hard to obtain, or perhaps Green and Spiegel did not want to be upstaged by their elders.

Some attempt is made to counter-balance the Weather Underground's rationales by roping in a disbelieving Todd Gitlin from time to time. Still smarting decades later from their takeover of SDS ("organizational piracy!"), he says bitterly: "They had the Bonnie and Clyde factor working for them. They wanted action, they wanted to kick ass." Or: "They brought themselves to the point where they were willing to be mass murderers. They had a grand project for purification of the world, and in the face of that project, ordinary life was dispensable." This has an element of truth but overstates the case the other way since the Weathermen mostly got around to no more than property damage. It is a measure of the filmmakers' haphazard approach to putting forth their own viewpoint that they simply throw in all these shrill, ten-second voices and hope for the best. The fact that this has become standard operating procedure for many documentaries about controversial issues does not in any way dispel the moral and political confusion underlying the film.

Yet given our present dismay at the Bush administration's military interventions or tax ripoffs for the rich and our feeling of political paralysis in the face of these misguided policies, there is something very timely about a documentary that excavates the rebellious example of the Weather Underground. That service alone may be seen by some to outweigh its cinematic deficiencies. Though the film probably has nothing practical to teach us about where we go from here, I am left to ponder the disturbing consolations of Mark Rudd's summary: "We finally realized the violence didn't work. But I still think we were right about America's place and role in the world."

CINEASTE 28, NO. 4 (FALL 2003)

Chapter Fifty-Six

JAFAR PANAHI

This Is Not a Film

That one of the most consistently amusing and enlivening movies to emerge from this year's crop of festival films should have been made by an Iranian filmmaker under house arrest, his hands pretty much tied, his budget and equipment nil, just goes to prove that you can't keep a good filmmaker down. I stress the playful charm of *This Is Not a Film* by Jafar Panahi and Mojtaba Mirtahmasb because the circumstances surrounding this singular work (and most attempts to describe it) inevitably portend something grimmer. For allegedly promoting antiregime activities, Panahi was banned from making films for twenty years and sentenced to six years in prison. Idled while appealing his sentence, bored and jittery, he decides to circumvent the ban through a technicality. He will read his last screenplay, which the authorities had refused permission to film: he explains slyly that he was forbidden to direct, write, or give interviews, but not to read aloud on camera. So he invites a friend, the documentarian Mirtahmasb, over to his apartment to record him reading the script.

Part of the jest is that Panahi is such a commanding personality, he cannot stop playing at being a director. He tells his colleague "Cut," but is reminded that giving such an order constitutes directing. An auteur with a string of international successes (*The White Balloon, The Circle, Crimson Gold, Offside*), Panahi comes across as an immensely vibrant, moody artist at the top of his form. In his black T-shirt, jeans, sandals, and tinted glasses, he is like a caged animal prowling his opulent apartment filled with the latest appliances and electronic gadgets, talking on speaker phone to his lawyer (she pessimistically prepares him for doing some jail time), switching on the (censored) cable news to see footage of the typhoon in Japan, and watching snippets from his movies, as though to reassure himself of his identity. His true costar is the family pet iguana, Igi, another caged animal, who keeps upstaging him by exploring the apartment and distracting the great man, digging into him with sharp nails as Panahi plays with his laptop. There is also a neighbor woman who keeps trying to get someone to watch her dog, Mickey, while she goes off to the fireworks. Mickey barks ferociously when he sees Igi, the offer is rescinded, and life goes on.

The premise is that we are watching an artless home movie documenting a day in the life of Panahi as he awaits the court's final decision. In fact the film was shot in one week—some parts written, some sketched out, and others serendipitous—with a combination of HD camera and low-definition camera phone, and despite the graininess of the latter, most of it looks pretty smooth.

The film draws further attention to its artifice by Panahi's questioning whether all this pretense of straight documentation is phony. Iranian cinema has often traded in such self-reflexive moves, letting meta- collide with neo-realism. Panahi conducts a little seminar on using nonprofessional actors in his films, approving the way they often come up with surprising bits that he could have never thought of or they refuse the "lie" of acting. In doing so, they direct him. But this time, he is the actor, directing himself, and he does a good job of animating what might have been an inert situation.

Similarly, despite his periodic protestations that nothing is happening except two men reduced to filming each other, the actual seventy-five minutes are packed with incident: Panahi maps off his rug to enact parts from his screenplay, lying down and hammily playing his suicidal heroine with tears in his eyes; listens on the phone to his wife issuing instructions about feeding the iguana; impatiently watches the construction cranes from his balcony; answers the doorbell for food delivery; basks in favorite scenes from his movies and—and this becomes the climax of the film—engages with a young, exuberantly polite art student who is picking up the building's trash for his brother-in-law custodian.

In the elevator, the student starts to tell Panahi his account of witnessing the police coming to arrest the filmmaker but keeps being interrupted by the need to collect trash on every floor, until Panahi, exasperated, gives up on hearing this vignette in which he clearly hoped to be the star and asks the young man what he plans to do when he graduates with a master's degree. Self-absorbed vanity yields to genuine curiosity about other people. This is another familiar trope of Iranian cinema: in films as diverse as *The Apple*, *The White Balloon*, and *Through the Olive Trees*, any pretence of plot grinds to a halt as we watch some ordinary shopkeeper or farmer whose craggy individuality is suddenly not to be denied.

For all its everyday brio, we are reminded in the last scene that serious courage has been involved here. "Be careful, Mr. Panahi, they'll see your movie camera," warns the student as they leave the building proper. The filmmaker records, just beyond his apartment building's gates, some conflagrations in the street that seem to have been part of a prodemocracy demonstration. There are no direct discussions about political injustices; the sense you get is it's too obvious for cultivated Iranians to need to reiterate this— and too sensitive. Panahi's codirector, Mirtahmasb, is currently in jail, and Panahi is still waiting to find out about his final sentence. The edited film was smuggled out of Iran (in a cake, according to one report) and shown first at the Berlin Film Festival and subsequently at the New York Film Festival and elsewhere. The final credits thank a series of unnamed, asterisked benefactors. As for the movie's title, it can be seen as both a bit of faux humility and a cheeky, preemptive plea of innocence: if this is not a film, by all means let us have many more such "not films."

FILM COMMENT (MARCH/APRIL 2012)

Chapter Fifty-Seven

DOCUMENTARY SPLENDORS AND ERRORS

I often hear, from my friends who are movie buffs, that they find documentaries more interesting these days than features. This snobbish, debatable assertion, which pits itself against popular taste and commercial reality—those few documentaries that do manage to open usually disappear within a week of their release—still has a certain validity. You are more likely to encounter complex characters and plausible, unresolved dilemmas in documentaries than in scripted dramas. Feature film screenwriters tend to jam all the loose behavioral threads of human nature into a hard-driving plot, hoping that audiences will be carried past the gaps by attractive actors and a transition-friendly music score to the climax. Of course we go to narratives not only for verisimilitude—sometimes, indeed for wild, exaggerated behavior—yet we still may feel a longing for psychological truth in the depiction of character.

I had the good fortune to attend the 2013 New York Film Festival and Telluride Film Festival, and what lingered in my mind after were the documentaries. Some were brilliantly controlled by masters of the form who knew how to put across all the meanings and subtexts the audience might receive. Others were a fascinating mix of the purposeful and the inadvertent: because of documentaries' propensity to let more truth seep in around the edges than the filmmakers might have intended, shards of raw oppositional reality clashed with the picture's message. When a melodrama ceases to convince, it leaves a deadness behind, and a desire to forget the whole implausible mess. When a documentary fails to win its point, it leaves unsettled, frustrating, yet exciting traces of counterintuitive arguments and half-buried paths.

The best film I saw was Rithy Panh's *The Missing Picture*, which was less a standard documentary than a personal essay film, one exploring memory. Panh, a Cambodian filmmaker who had previously made powerful films such as *S21: The Khmer Rouge Killing Machine* and *Duch, Master of the Forges of Hell* about the perpetrators of genocide under Pol Pot, this time told his own story. Via a chillingly calm, eloquently step-by-step voiceover narration, we learn about his family's removal to a collective farm and their destruction through execution and starvation (only Panh seems to have survived). Because the Khmer Rouge, unlike other totalitarian regimes, did not go in much for filmed propaganda, there was almost no documentary footage of the years in question—hence the title *The Missing Picture*. Panh had to supply images by reconstructing these childhood experiences from memory, using clay, plasticene, fabric, and other materials. Reenactments in documentaries are usually a mistake (think of those true-crime television shows that clumsily employ the device). However, because these scenes were reenacted here not by human actors, which would have vulgarized and cheapened the atrocities, but by clay figurines, the models have a dignity and haunting presence that, paradoxically, ensures their authenticity.

To jump to a different genocide, Claude Lanzmann's *The Last of the Unjust*, is a compelling, near-four-hour follow-up to his monumental masterpiece, *Shoah*. The heart of the film is a lengthy interview with Benjamin Murmelstein, the last surviving elder of Theresiendstadt, which the Nazis put forth as a "model" concentration camp. We are inclined to regard those Jewish leaders who were appointed by the Nazis as deeply compromised, tragically deluded figures. Murmelstein, fully aware of the contempt in which he is held, proves to be an intelligent, amusing, clear-eyed, wryly self-aware witness as he reports on his scary encounters with Adolf Eichmann and other Nazi bigwigs, and he attempts to contextualize if not exonerate his actions as a go-between with the Devil. Lanzmann, who shot the Murmelstein interview at the same time he was compiling materials for his great 1985 film, left it out of the earlier work because, by his own admission, its sometimes humorous tone would have clashed with the overall sobriety of *Shoah*. The interview has been surrounded, perhaps unnecessarily, with shots of Lanzmann, now in his eighties, revisiting Holocaust sites and commenting in his boastful, vain manner about the subject he has made his own and seems to feel he

owns. The real value of this documentary lies in the tense footage of Lanzmann interviewing Murmelstein. Some critics feel that Lanzmann let his
interviewee off the hook too easily and doubt that Murmelstein was telling
the whole truth. I found him to be a reliable witness (but what do I know?),
and I give the usually gruff Lanzmann credit for softening to the other man's
charm. A good documentarian is able to be open even to those subjects initially counted as the enemy.

Would that Errol Morris had been equally receptive to the complex intelligence of his subject, Donald Rumsfeld, in his newest documentary, *The
Unknown Known*, shown at Telluride. Morris, the director of such brilliant
films as *Gates of Heaven*, *Vernon, Florida*, *The Thin Blue Line*, and *The Fog
of War*, seems out to "nab" a war criminal, one he clearly assumes to be the
Prince of Darkness, and tangle him in his own contradictions through skeptical interrogation. It was an approach that worked beautifully in *The Fog of
War*, his masterful examination of Robert MacNamara. The difference is that
MacNamara was genuinely self-divided, so there was more room to expose
guilt and regret, whereas Rumsfeld presents a unified front and is never in
doubt. That he occasionally made contradictory statements should not be
surprising, given a public career that spanned a half century, and they roll
off his back. Moreover, Rumsfeld is no dummy. He comes across in the interview as something of a thinker (indeed, his famous statement about the
known knowns, the unknown knowns and the unknown unknowns seems
to me elegant, not stupid at all) while Morris, like many on the Left, consistently underestimates the smarts of the Right; he tries to mock Rumsfeld's
need to define his terms as the sign of a pathological control freak. Even if
you find Rumsfeld's role in promoting the Iraq and Afghanistan Wars a
ghastly crime against humanity (as I do, being 100 percent opposed to both
wars), you may concede that, given his initial premises about America's role
in the world and the dangers it faces, his conclusions follow logically. Morris's own position, that history is madness, governed by greed and the demonic
will to power, comes across as faddish and glib in the face of Rumsfeld's
demurral that, no, history is often the rational contestation between various
ideologies, each of which proceeds from a more or less sane if self-serving
agenda, and the trick is to negotiate those contesting claims when possible,
and if not, you may have to go to war.

The more the filmmaker tried to catch Rumsfeld in a lie, the more I began
to sympathize with the heretofore hateful former secretary of defense: it was
rather like that moment in *Bowling for Columbine* when you suddenly feel

sorry for Charlton Heston, whose home has been invaded by the anti-gun-crusading Michael Moore.

Over the years, Morris has developed an elaborate, baroquely self-conscious documentary style, which includes chapter titles, graphics that creep around the talking heads, reenactments expressionistically lit, pounding Philip Glass scores, shots of oceans, airplane noses, you name it. This time he has overloaded the gimmicks, perhaps in response to his own frustration at being unable to crack Rumsfeld's blandly cheerful midwestern demeanor. If *The Unknown Known* is, all things considered, an absorbing documentary, it is partly because Morris, that immensely gifted filmmaker, provides us with enough material to allow us to draw our own conclusions, even those that may disagree with his.

I should mention that Errol Morris is actually an acquaintance/friend of mine, and when I bumped into him at a reception after the screening of the film and he asked me what I thought, I said that Rumfeld came across as something of an intellectual. Errol scratched his head and said, "If he's an intellectual, what are we?" I had no reply on hand. What I should have said was that, in our polarized politics, it seems harder to grasp that those in the opposite camp may have a consistently reasoned, if loathsome to us, position.

Documentaries rarely treat with any nuance the give-and-take of primary education. In *To Be and to Have*, we are not only brought closely into that process but treated to an encounter with a whole human being whose melancholy serenity has a heaing effect on the world around him. The verteran French documentarist Nicolas Philibert brings a restrained, patient style to his portrait of a teacher, Georges Lopez, and his pupils in a one-room schoolhouse during the course of a year. Everything about Lopez, his quiet voice, the way he cocks his ear while listening to his charges or mediates their fights, his openness to their childhood sorrows, alongside his refusal to let them stray from the task of learning, is impressively of a piece. Anyone who has worked with children will be fascinated by the impromptu choices this teacher makes in responding to his charges (and, concurrently, the tactful decisions the director makes to stay with a scene or cut away). Educational reformers may be dismayed to see that Lopez is a traditionalist when it comes to curriculum or classroom layout. What is radical is his manner, allowing him to approach each child as a thoughtful, reasoning human being.

Chapter Fifty-Eight

ROSS MCELWEE

Bright Leaves

For over twenty years, Ross McElwee has been performing with rare success a cinematic high-wire act of daring and complexity: the personal essay film. From his poignant 1984 *Backyard*, which examined the immediate circumstances of his southern upbringing, to the hilarious *Sherman's March* (1986), about his romantic misadventures, to the delicate *Time Indefinite*, wherein our hero settles down and confronts the trade-offs of middle age, to *Six O'Clock News* (1996), which takes in the larger world's sorrows, and now *Bright Leaves*, McElwee has generously unwrapped for us his mental and physical landscapes. These autobiographical meditations are all the more unusual in that McElwee seems so obviously a modest, self-effacing person, not given to showing off in the brazen manner of Michael Moore. His decision to keep returning to his unsensational life and plumbing its meaning suggests a faith in the mystery of the everyday—adjusting to family life, making a living, falling in and out of love, puzzling over one's responsibility to strangers and neighbors, and meeting sickness and death, when they come, with dignity.

How to take these quiet, plain materials and give them entertainment value without over-dramatizing one's persona? McElwee, like all good essayists, has become a master of tweaking his language with a humorous spin here, an irony there, and digressing in such a way that will expand and deepen the picture.

His latest work, *Bright Leaves*, is a triumphant braiding of the small and the large, the personal and the general. He returns to North Carolina to consider his familial connection to the tobacco industry, for better or worse. In a sense McElwee has always been a regional (or should I say, bi-regional) filmmaker, an émigré from the South to New England who keeps ruefully reflecting on the abandonment of his home ground.

A veteran personal essayist is faced with the double challenge of finding new autobiographical material, having cannibalized much of his life already, and at the same time using his I-character to retrieve chunks of the world at large so as to avoid a claustrophobically narrow self-absorption. This time he reaches back to his great-grandfather, John Harvey McElwee, a nineteenth-century tobacco grower who originated the popular Durham Bull brand and then lost his business to the more competitively ruthless James Duke. McElwee, the most filial of filmmakers (a tender regard for his surgeon father animates almost all his work), takes up the chivalric cudgels here for his great-grandfather. But he does so with tongue planted firmly in cheek, letting us know *he* knows every family has its neglected genius ancestor whose invention has been stolen by another. So it is with self-mocking chagrin that he declares, gazing at the Duke mansion: "If things had gone slightly differently, this would have been all mine. I'd be sitting on a considerable fortune."

On discovering an old Warner Brothers costume picture, *Bright Leaf*, directed by Michael Curtiz, he becomes convinced that the Carolina tobacco grower played by Gary Cooper must have been based on his great-grandfather, which occasions even more grandiose musings: suddenly he is the fourth-generation love child of Gary Cooper and Patricia Neal (since they did have an affair on the set).

McElwee balances this comically resentful family pride with a guilty awareness that the cigarette habit has killed millions. He takes us into the hospital wards, following his doctor brother (the third generation of McElwee physicians) on his grim rounds. But solemnity is never allowed the final word: the filmmaker's voice-over slyly comments that even if his tobacco-growing great-grandfather did not deed them a fortune, "he did leave behind a sort of agricultural/pathological trust fund" in the form of lung cancer patients. That "sort of" syntactical hiccup typifies McElwee's hesitantly comic delivery, as well as his refusal of dogmatic certainty.

"Mixed feelings" is the answer an interviewee gives on camera about the tobacco industry: bad for your health, good for North Carolina's economy. And indeed, everything McElwee touches in this film becomes imbued with a warm ambivalence, signaled often by the split between image and sound. The visuals of green tobacco fields are both lush and sinister, like mutant cabbages. Some of McElwee's most beautiful shots have a melancholy tranquility that simultaneously declares, "You can't go home again," and, "You can't *not* go home again." The filmmaker's friends Brian and Emily, an extremely likable couple who keep popping up in the movie, trying to kick the nicotine habit and failing, embody this conflicted irresolution. (They do, however, finally get married, even if they can't give up smoking.)

In the midst of it all, McElwee cunningly inserts a stick of dynamite: Vlada Petric, his film theorist friend, bursts in with acerbic Eastern European energy, demanding to know what the point of all this dithering is. Petric insists that everything in a film be harmoniously integrated into a single "cinematic vision"; by his purist standards, even Michael Curtiz is a sloppy hack. What, then, about Ross McElwee and the gently meandering film we are watching? McElwee confronts this auto-critique audaciously and even surmounts it by shifting the focus slightly from tobacco to filmmaking itself.

In the last third, the picture becomes more self-reflexive, inviting speculations about the purpose of filming anything. In a lovely, candidly antinarrative moment, he admits, "Sometimes I feel it's such a pleasure to film, especially down South, that it almost doesn't matter what I'm filming." The pertinent and the accidental (a dog running into the shot and "spoiling" it) have, existentially speaking, equal weight. He compares filming to smoking a cigarette, a narcotic habit that makes time seem to stand still. The urge to "preserve a moment" is thus allied with the hope of staving off loss and arresting death. Yet he acknowledges that when he watches footage of his deceased father, the man is beginning to seem less real to him, almost a fictional character. He admits that he filmed his son Adrian incessantly when he was a tot, in part to keep him from growing up so fast—to no avail: you can't arrest the onrush of time by "capturing" it on celluloid.

McElwee arrives at the same bracing awareness that was Montaigne's: namely, everything is connected to everything else, if in no other way, then via the mind of the essayist. The true subject of any essay is ultimately the author's flow of consciousness. McElwee's drive, to uncover the underlying meaning of his native land's tobacco fix by investigating his roots, gives way eventually to a calmer acceptance of entropic helplessness and curiosity for its own sake. The South's unimposing yet enticing nature has liberated the filmmaker to surrender to that curiosity, and *Bright Leaves* is, in the last analysis, the artistic expression of a free soul.

POV (PBS WEBSITE)

Chapter Fifty-Nine

MARK RAPPAPORT'S ESSAY FILMS

The essay film, that protean and ever-emerging subgenre of the documentary, full of promise yet deucedly hard to pull off, has shown a particular affinity for ruminations on place and spectacle. Not surprisingly, meditations on the cinema are a favorite subject since the essay filmmaker is first of all a filmmaker and knows quite a lot about, or is often obsessed with, its craft and traditions. Welles's *Filming Othello*, Pasolini's *Notes Towards an African Orestes*, Godard's *Histoire(s) du Cinéma*, Varda's *Varda by Agnès* are all examples of auteurs taking us behind the scenes. As well, countless supplements to DVDs and streaming services (such as David Bordwell's excellent commentaries) are in effect essay films that explore and deconstruct the medium.

No one has done more or better work in this regard than Mark Rappaport. Having begun his career with a series of dramatic arthouse features (such as *The Scenic Route* and *Impostors*), he has since devoted himself exclusively to making essay films. The first two feature-length ones, *Rock Hudson's Home Movies* (1992) and *From the Journals of Jean Seberg* (1995) received extensive coverage and exposure.

In the late 1980s, for a period of two and a half years, Rappaport was quite sick with a mysterious illness, which turned out to be chronic fatigue syndrome. Bedridden, he found himself unable to do much of anything except watch favorite movies or tape TV shows on his VCR. He conceived the idea of taking bits and pieces of the movies he was watching and making a "collage film." As he recounted: "I thought, at that time, that there was a strong possibility that I might never be physically capable of working again the way I had in earlier years, that I might never have the strength to do another feature. I thought that this kind of compilation was something that could be done as a mildly low-level work involvement . . . just me sitting in front of an editing machine, with very few other people involved in the making of the project, and relatively little money to spend on the whole work."

Rappaport had supported himself for years as a film editor, so this was something he felt quite able to do. He was also inspired, he says, by Godard's *Histoire(s) du Cinéma*, which he saw at the Berlin Film Festival "in 1990 or so. I was bathed in a cold sweat by the end of the screening. It was an existential experience. I made *Rock Hudson's Home Movies* shortly after that." It needs to be said that Rappaport's warmly skeptical, immensely lucid voice-over narrations could not be farther from Godard's gnomic pronouncements, but his borrowings from Godard were more in the visual realm: superimposing images from two films on the same clip or using shock juxtapositions.

In any case, Rappaport's decision to focus on Rock Hudson grew directly out of his preoccupation as a gay man with the AIDS plague and with society's twisted representations of masculinity. He employed two rather daring devices for the film. The first was to stage it as a fictional autobiography, pretending that Rock was narrating his recollections from beyond the grave, the actual text being written by Rappaport : he even had an actor, Eric Farr, play Rock and address the camera, though Farr is a slighter man and only vaguely resembles the screen idol (which was probably the point). The film's basic premise was that Rock had been trying to display his secret homosexuality all along on-screen if you knew how to look. And here Rappaport employed his second inventive device, the notion you could narrate a screen performer's life by looking no further than the footage from his or her filmography. It has long been grasped that a star like John Wayne or James Stewart built up a complex persona additively, cumulatively from film to film, over the years, but Rappaport went further, illustrating the actual facts of an actor's life by referencing only the on-screen performances. Sometimes these clips would show the uncanny concordance between the two, and sometimes just the opposite—the gap between an actor's off-screen and on-screen selves. Rappaport did research the biographical details of his subjects, but the result was something very different from the standard celebrity biography we see on television, which dredges up candid footage of the subject relaxing on holiday and includes talking-head interviews with friends, colleagues, family members, and critics.

Rappaport has stated he wanted to use Hollywood clips to explore "ideological attitudes that commercial films subliminally offer above and beyond the story, the stars, the scenery, and the price of admission—messages and value assumptions that linger on long after the plot is forgotten." In saying that, he openly acknowledged his debt to feminist and queer theory. Yet his reliance on video rather than film also supported his undogmatic essayist's style: "I realized that video is a much more gracious and relaxed format than film for something as personal and cranky as an essay." Also cheaper. His preference for film clips stemmed from the fact that no matter how he might try to describe some on-screen bit on the page, his words could never match the simple concrete reality of the footage; it was physical evidence, not to be denied, despite the footage having been taken from a staged, fictional tale. Rappaport was in a sense building on Godard's remark that every dramatic film is also a documentary of the actors performing.

In his next film, *From the Journals of Jean Seberg*, he again channeled his subject's voice from beyond the grave, this time using a fine actress, Mary Beth Hurt, to impersonate the star, largely by standing in front of a screen on which Seberg's dazzling image had been projected and speaking her lines in a dry, ironic voice. (The fact that Hurt looks nothing like Seberg enforced a necessary distance.) The filmmaker's feminist sympathies were fully engaged in this narrative about a beautiful woman who had been victimized, first by being miscast by Otto Preminger in *Saint Joan*; later by being called on to enact misogynistic fantasies by her director husband, Romain Gary; and finally by the FBI, who tarnished her with false rumors that she had been impregnated by a Black Panther and drove her to suicide. Perhaps he lets Seberg off the hook too easily, minimizing her self-destructive complicity with her downfall in this tale of female victimhood. In the midst of this sad story, the filmmaker inserted the idea that Seberg, by violating the cardinal rule and gazing steadfastly into the camera with a face expressing nothing, introduced a new kind of screen acting and became the first modern movie star. Backing up this claim are digressions on the Kuleshev experiment and her costar Clint Eastwood's expressionless face. Rappaport was evolving an unmethodical method that he would employ consistently in the short essay films that followed, of digressing whenever it pleased him. There are fascinating insights about the auteurs (Otto Preminger, Jean-Luc Godard, Robert Rossen) who used her, about Seberg's blank stare as a trend-setting harbinger, about her role as a social activist compared to Vanessa Redgrave and Jane Fonda, about her growth as an actress (*Lilith* is given its proper due), about the degrading performances that her husband, Romain Gary, put her through in his movies, about the role of gossip in film history, and a dozen other subjects. The iron law of an effective digression in narrative is that it must seem to deepen or complicate the initial subject upon its return—and even if it doesn't, it can still work as long as it entertains us sufficiently for us not to notice its random nature. Rappaport invariably satisfies the second condition and usually the first as well.

Much less well known than these two features are the dozen shorts he followed them up with, ranging from ten to thirty-six minutes. It is these shorts that I would most like to explore. The short films range from examining an actor's career to studying a particular film technique or directorial trope. More than half are minibiographies of performers: John Garfield, Conrad Veidt, Paul Henreid, Anita Ekberg, Debra Paget, Marcel Dalio, Will Geer, and the child actor Christopher Olsen, an ordinary boy whose one talent was that he could cry on cue. In some cases, Rappaport continues to employ the conceit of a confessional autobiography, employing actors with the proper accents to deliver the voice-over lines. In others, he elects a third-person narrative voice. Occasionally, as in *Debra Paget, for Example*, he mixes both first- and third-person. Consistently, there is some exploration of the hidden or not entirely explicit facet of the actor's real life and the gap between actual and screen self. The title he gave to one of these essay films, *The Double Life of Paul Henreid*, emphasizes the sort of split that occurs in almost all the biographical shorts.

Rappaport, being Jewish and gay and a left-wing expatriate who lives in Paris, is very apt to ferret out connections to Judaism and homosexuality and, to a lesser extent, European cinema and progressive politics. In *John Garfield*, we learn that the actor, né Julius Garfinkel, was never cast explicitly as a Jew until he made *Gentleman's Agreement* toward the end of his career, when he was hounded by the House of Un-American Activities Committee for his involvement in left-wing causes.

The ironic situation of German refugee actors fleeing Hitler, limited by their accents, forced to play Nazis, was explored in his short on Conrad Veidt. The star of German expressionist cinema, from *The Cabinet of Dr. Caligari* onward, Veidt was not Jewish but married a Jewish woman and impishly signed a document saying he was a Jew just to annoy Goebbels. He also played the lead in the English film *Jew Süss*, saying, "Maybe it takes an honorary

Jew to play a Jew." He then went to Hollywood, where he acted as a succession of Nazi villains and con men. "I profited from the war as long as I could play Nazis," Rappaport has Veidt say ruefully. In one film, Veidt played twins, one good, one evil, which enabled Rappaport to make a droll digression on that plot premise literalizing the divided self.

Paul Henreid, by contrast, was allowed to play the Good European, the Resistance fighter in *Casablanca* and Bette Davis's cigarette-sharing dreamboat in *Now, Voyager.* Why wasn't he cast as a Nazi? Perhaps his sensitive, cultivated features and his plummy voice saved him from that fate. The filmmaker has Henreid say: "As a performing artist, you can never project the trajectory of your career, and you never know where your life will take you."

In *I, Dalio*, Rappaport, fascinated with the fate of those capable actors who never make it to the top rung of stardom, asserts: "No one starts out as a character actor." Dalio is shown playing a succession of cowards, betrayers, informers, and blackmailers in French films of the thirties—with the implication, though it is never said, that he is acting this way because he is a quintessential Jew. He also plays shady Arabs. Only in the two Renoir masterpieces, *Grand Illusion* and *Rules of the Game*, is the Dalio character explicitly outed as a Jew, albeit in a sympathetic manner. Then he moves to Hollywood in the forties, where he is cast as the archetypal Frenchman, "Frenchie," often a waiter in a fancy establishment pouring wine for the Americans or a groveling cameo in *Casablanca*, before returning to France for a succession of roles as a pimp, a conniver, and again, a Jew. "I always come to a bad end."

Will Geer played aging roles from the start. "Maybe some people are just born to be old, and I was one of them." His double life consisted not only of pretending to be older than he was, but of being gay and a communist to boot. Though blacklisted, he restarted his career as "the sidekick who is the amiable eunuch" and finally as "America's grandpa" in *The Waltons.* Having attained genuine seniority, his being gay became a nonproblem: "No one mentioned our secret. We were too old to scold."

The ways that beautiful women have suffered shortened careers are explored in the essay films devoted to Anita Ekberg and Debra Paget. The well-endowed Ekberg was made into a joke in Frank Tashlin's *Hollywood or Bust* then exploited in a series of other pictures, usually filmed lying down making love to the camera, before finding her immortality in Fellini's *La Dolce Vita.* But sex goddesses age, and we are gallantly given only an instant to contemplate a shot of the obese Ekberg in her retirement.

Debra Paget is presented as an exemplary studio contract player in the forties and fifties, inserted whenever needed as the damsel in distress, sacrificed to the gods, often cast as the exotic Other, Indigenous American or Polynesian, Princess of the Nile, though she was just a brunette from Denver, we are told. Cast as a dancing girl in *The Ten Commandments*, she ended up working in Fritz Lang's last-gasp, cockeyed diptych, *The Tiger of Bengal* and *The Indian Tomb*, before retiring at twenty-nine. Rappaport has great fun summarizing the absurd plots of her movies, with wry asides like, "For a little local color in the harem, they have hired Peruvian singer Yma Sumac." But he also wonders "why a certain kind of kitsch has a hold on us greater than art." In some cases, it is simply that these were the movies he saw as a boy, that stayed anchored in his consciousness, and that he now wishes to revisit.

An avid cinephile, his overall taste is for high art, with a dedication to the auteur pantheon, as evidenced in his essay shorts about film technique. *Tati vs. Bresson: The Gag* demonstrates how both employ a similar gag, underlining that the two directors "regard sound not as a handmaiden to the image, but as an equal partner." To reinforce the point, he digresses to *Strangers on a Train, M*, and *The Big Combo. The Circle Closes* investigates the use of recurring objects in Hitchcock, Buñuel, Ophüls, and Anthony Mann. *The Vanity Tables of Douglas Sirk* is a reflection on the ways that director shows women entrapped in their houses and their social roles. "When men use mirrors, they are only mirrors," though there is an eloquent aside on Alain Delon overseeing his dandy outfit and getting ready to commit mayhem in *Le Samouraï*.

Sergei/Sir Gay has Eisenstein explaining how he smuggled his homosexuality into his films by camera placements ("men are way too close to each other in the close-ups"), by shots of men bound up and contorted like St. Sebastian ("Maybe I like to see men humiliated. It has happened to me so often"), and by emphasizing boots ("So I was a fetishist. So what?). Insisting that none of this should detract from the value of his art, he wishes he could have made movies featuring a boyfriend, the way Visconti, Cocteau, and Fassbinder did.

In his haunting essay film *The Empty Screen, or the Metaphysics of the Movies*, Rappaport assembles a series of clips about characters trying to interact with the screen, including Buster Keaton's *Sherlock, Junior*, Hitchcock's *Saboteur*, Woody Allen's *The Purple Rose of Cairo*, and several Godard films (*Les Carabiniers, Masculin Féminin, Vivre Sa Vie*, and *Contempt*), to reinforce the melancholy realization that while we may love the figures on-screen, "they can never love us back."

Perhaps the most tender movie love evinced in these short essay films is *Max and James and Danielle*, which focuses on the great Max Ophüls and two of his favorite actors, James Mason and Danielle Darrieux. Rappaport is clearly taken with *The Earrings of Madame de . . .* , and why not? He tells us that Ophüls wanted to make a movie pairing Garbo and Mason, but "the vagaries of filmmaking" prevented it. He managed to cast Mason in two of his Hollywood pictures, *Caught* and *The Reckless Moment*, and might have been tempted to use him in *Madame de . . .* as well. Rappaport Photoshops Mason's face over Vittorio DeSica's in the waltz scene to see how that might have worked out. He digresses to point out that Mason and Darrieux did act together once, in Mankiewicz's *Five Fingers*. More digressions and parentheses follow, only to keep returning to the waltz ("Dancing together is their purest expression of love.") It is as if he were reprising the triangle in *Mme. De . . .* among Darrieux, De Sica, and Boyer, this time via the director and his two actors. The speculative, what-might-have-been if only circumstances had played out differently occurs as a continuing tug of regret under these otherwise sprightly investigations. A line from *Rock Hudson's Home Movies*— "Finally it's about death and the fragility of beauty"—might characterize the whole project.

So often, essay films skimp on the language part of the equation, with tentatively written narrations. In the case of Mark Rappaport, a talented writer, his well-chosen words and fluent, apt images combine to exhibit a playfulness, aphoristic wit, worldly perspective, and stylistic brio that one associates with the best of literary essays. What is equally remarkable is the freedom with which he pursues his subjects, purely for his own amusement, it would seem. He keeps making these little, gemlike essay films on cinema history, which are funded not by grants or commissions but out of his own pocket. Some end up as supplements on DVDs, some are shown at film festivals, and some are only circulated among his friends. Regardless, they constitute one of the most unique, expressively willful and satisfying bodies of essay films extant.

CINEASTE (SPRING 2020)

Chapter Sixty

MARCEL OPHULS

Marcel Ophuls is a Socratic philosopher with a camera, a gadfly who prods the world with embarrassing questions. The gist of his philosophy can be absorbed in his noble, engrossing, and marvelously entertaining historical inquiries. Argument and counterargument, apology and misgiving follow each other, until the viewer is left with a broader if more perplexed wisdom about how complicated the past is.

History records other father-son fimmakers (the Oswalds, the Tourneurs) but none so major as Max Ophüls and Marcel Ophuls. The father cornered the market on bittersweet French and Viennese eroticism, graceful camera movements, and female sensibility in films such as *Letter from an Unknown Woman* (1948), *La Ronde* (1952), *The Earrings of Madame de . . .* (1953), and *Lola Montès* (1955). The son began by wanting to make musical comedies but, as it turned out, staked out other territory: violence, guilt, memory, the nature of evil. ("Did it bother me that my films were not as beautiful as my father's? Not at all—because no one else made films as beautiful, either," Marcel said. "What bothered me was that he got to sleep with Danielle Darrieux.")

His first masterpiece, *The Sorrow and the Pity*, showed daily life in a historical furnace—Nazi-occupied France—and how choices made under those circumstances continued to haunt the people involved, decades later. *A Sense of Loss* explored the tragic collision course of competing moral claims in the Irish conflict. *The Memory of Justice* wove together the Nuremberg trials,

Algeria, and Vietnam to ask in what ways war crimes can be punished. *Hotel Terminus* started with the crimes of the Nazi official Klaus Barbie and uncovered an amazing web of old-boy networks and spheres of mutual protection for Nazis all over the globe.

Ophuls is curious about the way things connect through the chains of casual events. Skeptical, restless, ironic, humorous when the situation allows, he lets civility take him as far as it can, after which he is up against the cliff side of the incomprehensible. Indeed, all his work revolves around the limits of tolerance and liberal-democratic values in a ferocious time. He is a collector, a loving archivist of the detritus of civilization in upheaval. He is an explorer: the émigré who can fit in everywhere yet seems not quite at home anywhere. More and more, Ophuls appears as a character in his own films: mocking the illusion of objectivity, he adjusts his persona from that of the quintessentially decent, cultured European to the angry prosecutor or impish provocateur. (See his mischievous baiting of the spymaster Markus Wolf in his *November Days*.)

There are two facets to the documentarist's art: first, fetching the materials through research and filming and, second, assembling and editing. Much as Ophuls has excelled at the former, he has transformed the latter with symphonic, monumental constructions. Questions of length and scale are pushed to the limit. For how do you know, in dealing with complex historical materials, when you have come to the final truth? There is always someone else the events affected: a neighbor who saw the convoy take off, the chauffeur of a bigwig. Tenderly, patiently, he gets them talking.

Ophuls is preoccupied with the dynamics of rationalization. Self-excuse is classically a comic theme; but Ophuls's camera uncovers the darker, more regrettable consequence of lying to oneself. Beyond the unmasking of his interviewees, he challenges the audience to consider what we might have done in the same circumstances. He seems to want us to grasp that we are all, finally, residents of the Hotel Terminus.

FROM *MARCEL OPHULS: A COURSE IN RESISTANCE*,
WALKER ART CENTER, NOVEMBER 4–27, 1992

Chapter Sixty-One

CITY ESSAY FILMS

Cities and movies have long flirted with each other and hinted at marriage. The two fields have so much in common that it is tempting, if tricky, to fold one into the other as a single entity: cinemaurbanism. For essay filmmakers, particularly, who must get tired of cannibalizing their past lives and their relatives, the temptation to work with place as subject matter is ever present, waiting to be photographed. Since most essay filmmakers live in cities, it's only natural that they would meditate about the urban environment. There is the historical genesis of filmmaking in cities like New York and Paris, the density of information in streetscapes, Georg Simmel's point in his famous essay, "The Metropolis and Mental Life," that the modern metropolis privileges the eye above all other senses, and so on.

I propose to discuss the following films: *À Valparaíso, Love Exists, London, Of Time and the City, My Winnipeg, Tokyo-Ga, Los Angeles Plays Itself,* and *Helsinki, Forever.* A scream will be heard in certain quarters at omissions such as *Berlin: Symphony of a Metropolis, Rien Que les Heures, À Propos de Nice, Menschen am Sonntag,* or *The Man with the Movie Camera*—all marvelous documentaries and cine-poems, but they don't seem to me true essay films. In a previous article, "In Search of the Centaur: The Essay-Film," I argued that, first, an essay film must have words, in the form of a text, either spoken, subtitled, or intertitled. Say what you like about visualization being at the core of thinking, I cannot accept an utterly silent flow of images as constituting essayistic discourse. Second, the text must represent a single voice, a strong, personal point of view. It must attempt to reflect on or work out some problem or problems. Finally, the language in the text should be eloquent, expressive, well written, not merely drily informational.

The city essay film as a subgenre of the essay film can be divided between those works focusing on the filmmaker's own city, native or adopted, and those in which the filmmaker is a visitor or a tourist. *À Valparaíso* (1963) belongs to the second category. A dazzling, gorgeously packed half-hour short, it would be interesting if for no other reason than as a singular collaboration between two titans of nonfiction cinema: the Dutch documentarist Joris Ivens, who directed it, and the French auteur Chris Marker, who wrote the narration. Marker had not yet become the grand master of the essay film (*Sans Soleil*, *Le Joli Mai*), but his commentary, spoken in voice-over by an actor, already displayed that crisply sardonic, aphoristically bemused manner that would soon be recognized as his signature.

The film's analysis of the Chilean port is organized along two axes: the first, topographical, makes much of the fact that the city is built pressed against a steep hill, with the poorer inhabitants occupying the higher zone. The rituals of ascent and descent are caught in numerous shots of cable cars transporting those who can afford the few cents' fare while the others are obliged to climb on foot. "One descends laughing. One ascends panting." Meanwhile we see a wealthy woman decadently walking a penguin in the lower zone. The second organizing principle is by the elements, enumerated as Sun, Sea, Air and Blood. Marker comments about the city: "Her lie is the sun; her truth, the sea." We learn that Valparaiso was a fabulously successful port until the Panama Canal came along and cut into its business; now it struggles to stay busy, though even the poor have enough fish to eat. The section on Blood offers a collage of violence: pirates, earthquakes, slavery, and colonial oppression.

A curious tension develops between the different manners of the two auteurs: Marker's narration is relentlessly ironic, but Ivens's images are Popular Front upbeat. The People, yes! We see celebrations of the working class: part Family of Man, part house style of the New Deal–spawned U.S. Film Service (for whom Ivens made *Power and the Land* earlier) and part Soviet documentaries (Ivens, a devoted communist, made several films in the USSR). So Marker will say: "Men don't know, men don't want to know. When worry touches them with its cold nose, instinct brings them toward the warmth and light," and we see picturesque shots of taverns and folk dancing. The images here (by Georges Strouve) are luminous and strikingly well composed, with sharp sun-drencehd contrasts. They are, dare I say, more visually accomplished than Marker's own visuals would later prove. On the other hand, it is Marker's dubious, melancholy voice-over narration that dominates our take on this particular city. The two manners support each other admirably until the end, when the black-and-white switches to color and we get a kitschy sequence of kite flying, weddings, and the promise of social justice, as Marker's bemused skepticism gives way to Ivens' revolutionary positivism.

Á Valparaíso distances itself from nostalgia, asserting that the new adventure will bring improvements to the life of the people. But virtually all subsequent city essay films express a melancholy sense of loss regarding the altered urban environment. One reason for this disillusionment is that these filmmakers all witnessed the destruction of traditional neighborhoods, through the global set of misguided policies known as urban renewal, and the concomitant privileging of suburbs and highway transportation.

The growth of the suburbs was the subject of Maurice Pialat's acerbic, lyrical short, *L'Amour Existe* (*Love Exists*). Pialat, who would go on to direct such disturbing, powerful features as *Naked Childhood* and *À Nos Amours*, was thirty-five when he made this, his first professional movie, in 1960, and it won him the Prix Lumière and a prize at Venice. Essay films, more than documentaries, test the toleration of audiences for complex spoken language—none more so than *L'Amour Existe*. Its harshly poetic voiceover is dense and defiantly literary. The film begins with shots of crowds cramming into trains and cars, leaving the city in droves for the suburbs. A voice is heard on the soundtrack, striking a personal note: "I lived in the suburbs a long time. My first memory is of the suburbs." A section of childhood recollections begins: escape through movies, an innocent gaze bestowing beauty on slag heaps, quiet streets, biking, first flirtations, everything frozen in place. "Boredom is the principal erosive agent in these impoverished landscapes." But gradually things start to change, and for the worse: "Where are the open-air cafes, the stands selling fried foods? Paris no longer dances to the accordion tune." The tipping point is the destruction of the Méliès film studio in Montreuil, "delight and wonder disappearing without a sound." Soon the suburbs begin to spread, "to splinter into individual plots. The detached home reigns supreme in the farthest suburb and 'little' is all the rage." Pialat presciently saw that suburban sprawl would mean an end to the countryside that used to surround Paris: "Greater Paris has less green space than any other city in the world, yet the systematic massacre of ancient parks continues, fed by the hunger for 'faux luxe' houses." The other housing vogue that provokes his ire is the apartment block. "The age of barracks for civilians has arrived. Concentration camp living in easy installments, urban planning a maze of roads, shoddy materials that fall apart before construction's even finished." The filmmaker has no qualms expressing his opinions: hearing them so eloquently put is exhilarating, counterbalanced only by their unremitting gloom.

Pialat's take on the new consumer society adds up to "a lifetime spent buying everything retail while selling oneself wholesale. . . . No promotion, no retirement plan, no amount of money can seal the wound." Meanwhile, just two miles from the Champs-Élysées, immigrants lie in makeshift, kerosene-lit, flammable shacks, some of which we see burning down. This unsparing jeremiad is accompanied by visuals consoling by their Atget-like elegance: nighttime shots of streets and riverfronts, fluid car and motorcycle pursuits. The visual treatment is superb, except for a clumsily reenacted sequence meant to show teenagers fighting. (Curiously, there is a similarly awkward staging of a fight in À Valparaíso. These essay filmmakers should stay away from staged action.) "Love exists"—surely the title is ironic, unless it is meant to imply that love had better exist, because everything else is so helpless and fallen.

A similar pessimism hovers over *London*, the first in a trilogy of essay films by Patrick Keiller (to be followed by *Robinson In Space*, 1997, and *Robinson in Ruins*, 2010). All three films employ the conceit that the filmmaker is reporting the thoughts of his friend and ex-lover Robinson—a device clearly modeled on Chris Marker's masterpiece, *Sans Soleil*, where a mythical Sandor Krasna stands in for the filmmaker. It is also an archaizing device since classical essayists such as Addison and Steele, Charles Lamb and Washington Irving invented personae as a playful way to have their cake and eat it too, enunciating impish attitudes that they could then distance themselves from by fobbing them off on their surrogate selves if need be. "Robinson" also pays tribute to the minor character of the same name who keeps popping up in Céline's novel *Journey to the End of the Night* (and indeed, the first words we hear on the soundtrack, in the drily sonorous voice of the narrator Paul Scofied, are, "It is a journey to the end of the world.") The narrator says he has been absent from London for many years as a sailor and photographer traveling the globe: this entitles him to take the estranged viewpoint of the returning prodigal son who finds his native city much changed—one of the many alienation devices that gives the film the feel of a science fiction meditation on a lunar landscape.

The main source of estrangement, it soon becomes clear, is political. Keiller and his putative friend Robinson are appalled at the Thatcherite policies of the Tory-led British government, which have weakened the social-democratic achievements of the postwar Labour government and exposed everyone not rich to the unsparing forces of a neoliberal market economy. At the film's midpoint, there is a sequence showing the election of the Tory candidate, John Major, as prime minister, which elicits the comment, "It is difficult to recall the shock with which we realized our alienation from the events that were taking place before us. . . . It seemed there was no longer anything a Conservative government could do to cause it to be voted out of office. We were living in a one-party state." Of course, the filmmaker could not have anticipated the Tony Blair years, though it is doubtful they would have made him much happier nor changed his mind about the city's condition. "London, he said, is a city under siege from a suburban government, which uses homelessness, pollution, crime, and the most expensive and rundown system of public transportation of any metropolitan city in Europe as weapons against Londoners' lingering desire for the freedom of city life."

Cities have long been associated, at least since the Middle Ages, with individual freedom, including freedom from sexual repression and forms of puritanism. "Robinson is not a conservationist, but he misses the smell if cigarette ash and urine that used to linger in the neo-Georgian phone boxes." The situation of Robinson as an aging gay man who lectures at the university and is constantly afraid of losing his job under the new Tory austerity gives him an outsider's jaundiced perspective on the new metropolis. Today's London is not only complacent, he finds, but also virulently anti-intellectual, which drives Robinson into a series of expeditions to recover traces of an earlier, culturally richer time. These ventures into the sources of English Romanticism, as well as the living quarters of foreign visiting writers such as Verlaine, Rimbaud, Apollinaire, and Herzen, provide a structure of sorts for the film and a pretext for the filmmaker to roam on foot as a flâneur. There is a fascination with the city's bohemian past, and the very act of walking is asserted as both subversive and quaintly antiquarian.

What is noteworthy about Keiller's enterprise is the combination of progressive left-wing radicalism and a clinging to dusty remnants of old. The film keeps stopping and starting: pausing to take in shots of monuments, old bridges, crosswalks, flowers, waterways, which follow each other statically, while the commentary is bracketed on both ends by silence. Some of the comments are witty, like one about a disappointing visit to Ikea, "tainted by the ill-humor that so often accompanies questions of interior design." Others offer merely dry tidbits of information. There are also references dropped to what might be called Urbanism's Greatest Hits: Poe's "The Man of the Crowd," Walter Benjamin, Baudelaire, the Situationists' "drift." The movie begins to resemble more a syllabus than a worked-though analysis. The coy, teasing manner of the Robinson trilogy helps explain how these films can be so playful and cultivated, on the one hand, and so elusive and frustrating, on the other.

By comparison, Terence Davies's *Of Time and the City* wears its heart on its sleeve and is personal to the point of confession. The city of the title is Liverpool, where Davies grew up, and much of the film is an autobiographical evocation of the lost world of his boyhood. (Or "girlhood," as he puts it at one point, alluding to the conflict between his strict Catholic upbringing and the guilt that arose when he discovered he was gay.) Again, having a gay observer allows for an outsider perspective on the normative city, but in Davies's case there is more of an ache to identify with or situate himself within the cocooned security of the traditional family: parents, grandparents, siblings, infants. Davies revisits the material of his two rapturous earlier memoir-films, *Distant Voices, Still Lives*, and *The Long Day Closes*, in both of which the parameters of his working-class childhood (street games, love of the sacrificial mother and fear of the father, holidays at home, escape to Hollywood movies) were raised to an operatic level. In those two memoir-films, he achieved his sacral elevation of the commonplace, partly through burnished, exquisitely staged tableaus, partly though soaring musical quotation. In *Of Time and the City*, he is obliged to surrender some visual quality since he is working for the most part with newsreels and other found materials, but the same ache is realized through the historical poignancy of archival footage, which shows the ordinary dignity of working-class people going about their business against a backdrop of brick tenements and narrow alleys, listening to the radio, children going off to school—and through a much more outspoken, poetic text than heretofore. Davies mixes the recitation of poetic fragments about time from writers such as Eliot, Shelley, Engels, and Joyce with his own general and specific ruminations.

"We leave the place we hate, then spend a lifetime trying to regain it," he says ruefully. Though there is much to dislike in the conventional Liverpool of his youth, such as the sexual repression of the church, he is disdainful of the present consumerist license. "In deconsecrated Catholic churches, now made into restaurants as chic as anything abroad, the congregation can eat and drink in the sight of God, who will no doubt disapprove of cocktails in the building." In his commentary he comes across as a left Conservative: politically progressive, aesthetically attached to the restrained England of old. He compliments the football players of his youth, who moved with grace and "knew never to punch the air in victory." He is proudly out of step with contemporary mores, disliking not only the exhibitionism but also the pious rigidity of political correctness. As the screen shows pretty women on parade in the fifties, we hear his comment: "Bathing beauty competitions, in their day harmless, now as quaint as the bustle, now as unacceptable as Chinese foot-binding." The main villain is time's arrow: all traditional civilization has been swept away. "These golden moments pass and leave no trace," he quotes Chekhov.

A further lyricism of loss is achieved through the film's musical commentary, which blends classical music (Liszt) with pop songs of a certain era ("The Folks on the Hill," "Dirty Old Town"). In one of his most audacious asides, Davies trashes Liverpool's greatest icons, the Beatles: "John, Paul, George, and Ringo—not so much a musical phenomenon, more like a firm of musical solicitors. And the witty lyric and the well-crafted love song seemed as antiquated as antimacassars or curling tongs." Some viewers will doubtless find Davies's contrarianism sour and distasteful, but I found it honest. From his idiosyncratic perspective, rock music was a falling-off from the mellifluous perfection of Peggy Lee. "After the rise of rock and roll, my interest in popular music waned, and as it declined, my love of classical music increased." He names Sibelius, Bruckner, and especially Mahler, relishing "every overwrought note." You can see how Davies's need for emotional catharsis led him from *Singing in the Rain* and Doris Day musicals to Mahler, bypassing the cheery repetitiveness of "She loves you / yeah yeah yeah" (which he sarcastically quotes).

Davies is equally hard on the monarchy, "the Betty Windsor Show," deploring the wastefully expensive coronation taking place in London while "the rest of the nation survived on rationing in some of the worst slums in Europe." Liverpool was and is a major industrial port, but not the capital city, and its destiny has been to remain provincial, both cozy and defensively so, as Davies demonstrates. During the Victorian era, at the height of the British empire, Liverpool, along with Manchester, Birmingham, and other English cities, received a monumental buildup in the public realm such as had previously occurred only in London. Several times, Davies's camera tracks around the classical colonnades and elaborate ornamentation in Liverpool Philharmonic Hall and other splendid public buildings and equestrian statues. Is he mocking the world-city pretensions of overreaching Liverpool or lamenting what might have been? He is much more explicit in his response to the razing of old neighborhoods and their replacement by shabby housing projects. "We had hoped for paradise. We got the anus mundi." A montage of demolition, graffiti, boarded-up shops, and dismal apartment blocks follows, supporting that claim. Even the new downtown of glass skyscrapers and parking garages testifies to "the British genius for creating the dismal." Davies has been effectively ejected from the Eden of his childhood, with no possibility of going back.

"But where are you, the Liverpool I knew and loved, where have you gone without me? And now I'm an alien in my own land," he concludes.

If Davies cannot seem to reenter his native city, the narrator in Guy Maddins's *My Winnipeg* cannot get away from his. Every time he tries to separate himself and make a run for it, some lethargy takes over. We see the actor playing Maddin slumped in a train hurtling through snowy streets while the voice-over intones, "My home for my entire life. My entire life! I must leave it. But how to wake myself enough for the frightening task? How to find one's way out?" He is like the protagonist in Scorsese's *After Hours*, who finds himself unable to flee New York's Soho district. Of course, this being a Guy Maddin film, there is much that is preposterous, comic, and erotically taboo, all filmed in quasi-silent-movie style. The line between dreams and waking is purposely smudged by double exposures, negative black-and-white, flashing titles, a perpetually snowy surround that erases horizon lines (thanks to Jody Shapiro's cunningly oneiric cinematography), and the narrator's incantatory voice-over. The musical score conjures a film noir nightmare, which association is reinforced by casting Ann Savage (the original actress in Edgar G. Ulmer's classic *Detour*) as Maddin's mother. One of *My Winnipeg*'s imaginative tropes is that the filmmaker protagonist, like a hapless noir narrator, schemes to "film my way out of here" if only he can "properly recreate the archetypal episodes of my family history. Only then can I isolate the essence of what in this dynamic is keeping me here in Winnipeg, and perhaps once this isolation through filmed reenactment is complete, I can free myself from the heinous power of family and city, and escape once and for all." Maddin has great fun playing with the oedipal metaphors, such as that one's native city in the primal one out of which one crawls (not very far, in his case) and that sends endless mixed signals to the child about masculinity and femininity.

Yet behind the zany panic and shameless Freudian send-up, one senses a deeply felt essay, working out the love-hate relationship this regional artist has with his provincial city. The complacent local pride of the Winnipeggers is both mocked and celebrated. "We're the coldest city in the world. What enchantment must the coldness offer up for people with the right attitude," says the narrator, and we see archival footage of ice skaters with goofy contented smiles. Maddin keeps trying to decode "this city of palimpsests." He gives us a geography lesson about the significant meeting of two rivers and multiple railroad lines in a city built at the "center of the continent." He recounts episodes of local history involving labor strife, nightmare debauches, paranormal activities, sports heroes, a devious mixture of fact and mythology that gives way to a long sequence about the demolition of a beloved hockey rink and its replacement by a soulless stadium, sitting there "like a zombie in a cheap new suit." This act of urbicide is conflated with the death of his father, prompting Maddin to soliloquize, Hamlet-like: "Why was this allowed to happen? My father. The arena. The paternal amphitheater of our games, murdered, all because he lacked luxury boxes! Here we pride ourselves on the tradition of labor, and we allow our shrine to be outraged for lack of luxury boxes. I'm ashamed to be a Winnipegger." Again, the mischievous emoting does not negate Maddin's sincere outrage at such a treachery foisted on "this sleepy working-class town."

All the filmmakers in question here seem to share the values enunciated by Jane Jacobs in *The Death and Life of Great American Cities*: preserving old neighborhoods for mixed uses, appreciating the "sidewalk ballet" of pedestrians, opposing master planning, especially of the highway/tower-in-the-park variety. But they were filmmakers before they were urbanists, so their interest in the city fabric keeps being encroached upon or inflected by a deeper attachment to cinematic history. Three cases in point illustrate the diversity of this intersection: *Tokyo-Ga, Los Angeles Plays Itself,* and *Helsinki, Forever.*

In *Tokyo-Ga* (1985), Wim Wenders went searching for traces of his beloved master—the Japanese director Yasujirō Ozu, who had died twenty years before—in contemporary Tokyo. The result was one of Wenders's subtlest and most intelligent movies. The text is eloquently written and keeps reaching for larger questions about the way we live in this globalized, postmodern era. What does it mean any more to be local, to live in a specific city such as Tokyo, when, Wenders asserts, "the TV set is now the center of the world"? While we glimpse shots of TV programs, a vulgar mélange of underwear ads, samurai flicks, game shows in a moving taxi, we hear Wenders's voice-over: "The more the reality of Tokyo struck me as a torrent of impersonal, unkind, threatening, yes, even inhuman images, the greater and more powerful became in my mind the images of the loving and ordered world of the mythical city of Tokyo that I knew from the films of Yasujirō Ozu. Perhaps that world no longer existed: the view which still could achieve order in a world of disorder, the view which could still render the world transparent. Perhaps such a view is no longer possible today, not even for Ozu, were he still alive. Perhaps the frantically cloying inflation of images has already destroyed too much."

In this disenchanted perspective, we are not far from Susan Sontag calling for an "ecology of images" or from Roland Barthes's bemused take on the mysteries of Japanese culture in *Empire of Signs*, or indeed from the images of that self-same eighties Tokyo in Chris Marker's *Sans Soleil*. Marker, by coincidence, was shooting that film at the same time Wenders was shooting his, and Wenders incorporates a sequence paying tribute to the camera-shy French director, who allows one eye to be photographed from behind a newspaper held before his face in a Shinjuku bar.

Wenders went to Tokyo as a cine-tourist and shot more or less everything he came across—pachinko parlors, golf practice, parks, and streets. Like most tourists, he was basically restricted to public spaces, recreation and retail establishments, the work world and the domestic world being off-limits. (Actually, it was Ed Lachman, his gifted cameraman, who took most of the footage, though Wenders never mentions that assistant, saying instead: "I set up my camera as usual . . ." The poignant aloneness of the foreign traveler would ostensibly be compromised or diluted by mentioning he had companionship.)

Every time the cacophony of contemporary Tokyo starts getting to him, Wenders runs for cover to Ozu-world, either through quotes from Ozu's films or visits to Ozu's grave or interviews with his favorite collaborators, the actor Chishū Ryū and the cameraman Yūharu Atsuta. These emotional interviewees stress that they were obedient servants of their master, trying only to carry out the filmmaker's instructions. "He was more than a director. He was like a king," says Atsuta. How interesting that the hip, progressive German Wenders seems so drawn to the *Ordnung* in Ozu's world—and to the patriarchal system of father/king/director.

Also happening to be in town was Wenders's friend and fellow filmmaker Werner Herzog, interviewed atop a skyscraper, shown gazing down disapprovingly at Tokyo below. Herzog, looking natty in a jacket and tie, pontificates about how hard it is to locate "true images, everything is so built-up," and vows to climb mountains or endure any hardship (see his *Aguirre* and *Fitzcarraldo*) to "find images that are pure and clear and transparent." To a city lover like me, this is nonsense: there are plenty of stunning images of city life available, as *Tokyo-Ga* shows. Wenders himself acknowledges: "No matter how much I understood Werner's quest for pure and transparent images, the images I was searching for were only to be found down below, in the chaos of the city. In spite of everything, I couldn't help being impressed by Tokyo."

Note the reluctance with which Wenders enunciates his admiration for contemporary Tokyo. It bears remarking, too, that use of his word "chaos." If there is anything to be learned from Jane Jacobs, it is that the modern city is not chaotic: it functions every day, if on a level that may appear scattered or serendipitous. Wenders's ambivalence expresses his loss of the seemingly ordered, historical 1930s–1950s city as it appeared in Ozu's highly selective lens (though it seemed to many observers at the time equally disordered: see Lewis Mumford's cautionary writings about cities getting too big or Ralph Steiner's anti-anthill polemical film, *The City*). The age-old, Jeffersonian antipathy to city life as innately sinful and disordered must be taken into account here. It is a tribute to the complexity of Wenders's essay film that we are allowed to experience this ambivalence—his love of city life's proliferation and his mistrust of it—without false resolution.

If images of Tokyo from classic cinema redeem the modern city in Wenders's eyes, the opposite is true for Thom Andersen in *Los Angeles Plays Itself*. As he says flat-out in his narration: "People blame all sorts of things on the movies. For me it's the betrayal of their native city." The narrated text establishes the speaker as a local curmudgeon ("Why should I be generous. . . . If you're like me and identify more with the city of Los Angeles than the movie industry, it's hard not to resent Hollywood") who is both begrudging of motion pictures' self-aggrandizement and quick to mock himself or express an essayist's self-skepticism. "Maybe this effort to see how movies depict Los Angeles may seem more than wrongheaded or meanspirited," he offers. This essay film attempts to read backward, from the distortion and misrepresentation of the most photographed city in the world to the real Los Angeles, in what he calls "a city symphony in reverse."

The nearly three-hour *Los Angeles Plays Itself* is certainly ambitious, richly complex, and interesting: admittedly overlong, its leisurely pace pursues concentric subtopics in the free manner of literary essayists at their most unbuttoned. Within a chapter structure (City as Background, City as Subject, and so on), there is ample opportunity for Andersen to discourse on such matters as how difficult it is to get Los Angeles right (putting a largely horizontal city in a vertical frame or filming a smoggy atmosphere "where everything dissolves into the distance" or "because traditional public space has been largely occupied by the quasi-private space of moving vehicles"); how the initialism L.A. seems like "a slightly derisive diminutive"; how the city became perceived as "the capital of adultery and murder"; how the LAPD controlled the city; how Hollywood loved to destroy the place in apocalyptic disaster movies; how and why nostalgia played such a big role in period films in a city supposedly without history; how its glorious modernist domestic architecture was used to signify "epicene villainy"; how certain sites, like the Bradbury Building or Frank Lloyd Wright's Ennis House, were shot differently in a multitude of genre movies; how there is a difference between high-tourist and low-tourist directors; how *The Long Goodbye* is Robert Altman's best movie but Altman little understood the suburbanites he condescended to in *Short Cuts*. . . . Perhaps the collector-like breadth of topics has something to do with the film's being assembled almost entirely from film clips and not requiring much of a shooting budget or with Andersen's not being a feature director taking a holiday with a nonfiction work (like Wenders or Davies) but an essay filmmaker primarily. This is his life's work—certainly an advance over his previous essay film, *Red Hollywood*—and so he could afford to be more personal and more encyclopedic.

One of Andersen's strengths here is his research into the actual history of Los Angeles; one of his weaknesses, preaching about it to raise our political consciousness. In discussing at length *Chinatown* and *L.A. Confidential*, two excellent period movies that purported to disclose the city's "secret history," Andersen astutely maintains that there was no conspiracy or cover-up but rather, something sadder: the public's open rejection of progressive policies. A proposal for public housing was discussed for months on the front pages, and its defeat was "a tragedy from which Los Angeles has yet to recover." Andersen is at pains to correct the political apathy that cynicism promotes. "Cynicism tells us we are ignorant and powerless," he says. In other words, organize. Fight the power.

Racism and social inequality (illustrated here by the Zoot Suit Riots, the Watts riots, incidents of police brutality) are the true dirty secret about Los Angeles, the film argues, that rarely gets into Hollywood movies. In his search for authentic, nondistorting models, Andersen alights on Kent MacKenzie's *The Exiles*, a semidocumentary/semifiction independent film made in the early 1960s about Indigenous Americans living in the Bunker Hill district. "Better than any other movie, it proves that there once was a city here, before they tore it down and built a simulacrum." The old working-class district of Bunker Hill was eradicated through slum clearance and replaced by high-rise buildings. Andersen approvingly categorizes *The Exiles* as "a type of American neorealism," and indeed it is a miraculous, one-of-a-kind film, but there is something too convenient about using MacKenzie and several African American filmmakers who worked in Los Angeles, Haile Gerima, Charles Burnett, and Billy Woodberry, as a club with which to clobber Hollywood feature films. By romanticizing the poor or less fortunate as the People, Andersen in effect dismisses all other social class's claims to authenticity. Beyond that lies another paradox: the rough, grainy, but "truthful" footage so positively cited from the films of MacKenzie, Burnett, Gerima, et al. cannot hope to measure up to the glossy, tacky, melodramatic Hollywood film clips that Andersen had earlier so lovingly assembled but now is reluctant to acknowledge his love for. Perhaps all anti-Hollywood essay films must inadvertently, in the end, glorify Hollywood, like it or not.

Peter von Bagh's *Helsinki, Forever* ruminates tenderly on the city's history during the twentieth century, largely through film clips and newsreels. Von Bagh, long active in Finland's scene as the Midnight Sun Festival's director, was the ideal person to assemble the choicest footage from the national film archives. Part of the film's charm is the offering of treasured nuggets from this distinguished but largely unknown (to us) film heritage: beautifully composed shots of black-and-white movies from the 1930s through 1950s succeed one another, their order in the film determined largely by district. The same main boulevards, the same public squares, are shown in different eras, looking alike but different, as Finland's "megastars" (so we are told) dash through these streets in various decades of their careers, looking harried, happy, or lonely as each scenario dictates.

The seamless way that feature film sequences are folded into historical newsreels makes the opposite point from *Los Angeles Plays Itself*: here, everything is to be trusted, every image is pertinent, contributing to our understanding of a changing Helsinki. The same market square is shown in color and black-and-white, one time harboring ordinary happiness, the next, class warfare. Historical tragedies are not minimized, but a sort of benign impersonal sorrow presides over the narration. We see baffled newcomers from the countryside trying to survive crossing a street for the first time in the Big City or bloodied criminals stumbling through the railway station or divorcees window-shopping elegant apparel now beyond their means. Helsinki is "forever"—except that it too is seen to have suffered the scars of urban renewal. "The 1960s was more fatal to buildings than the war," remarks the narrator, adding that in 1965 a beloved movie palace "was torn down so fast, there was no time for conservation acts." So it would seem that the inhabitants of cities, be they Helsinki, Paris, London, Tokyo, or Valparaiso, have more in common with one another than they do with their rural countrymen.

In *London*, there is a passage on the soundtrack that the narrator attributes to Robinson: "He argued that the failure of London was rooted in the English fear of cities, a Protestant fear of popery and socialism, the fear of Europe that had disenfranchised Londoners and undermined their society. . . . At the historical center there is nothing but a civic void that fills and empties daily. . . . The true identity of London is in its absence. As a city it no longer exists. In this alone it is truly modern. London was the first metropolis to disappear." Since the evidence on-screen and off- shows that London is still going strong, we have to assume that this is merely fashionable palaver of a paradox-promoting kind. However, before we dismiss it completely we must acknowledge that it does point to a concern expressed by many of the filmmakers discussed in this very preliminary survey: that while pointing the camera at the city, the city eluded them. There was another city, a shadow city, standing in its place, mocking the attempt.

We need to deal here with a confession of failure. But is it the city that has failed, by becoming a Baudrillardian simulacrum, or the filmmakers, by being unable to capture these human hives or come to terms with their multiplicity? Neither, I would argue. Cities continue to stagger along, if not thrive, just as they continue to elude our hunger for neat solutions or apocalyptic denouements. By thinking hard as essayists about their chosen metropolises, these filmmakers have given us useful insights into the way we who are city dwellers live now and the self-conscious ways we regard the urban experience. Whether the city in question has been approached from the angle of a travelogue, a jeremiad, an elegy, a site of memory, a parody or surreal farce, a cinephile's rhapsody or image critique, the result has yielded in each case a vivid map of the filmmaker's consciousness. In doing so, these films have approached as closely as any to the ideal enunciated by Alexandre Astruc: the *camera-stylo*, following one's thoughts with the camera as a flexible writing implement.

THE NORMAL SCHOOL (FALL 2012)

FILM CRITICS

Chapter Sixty-Two

THE MAKING OF MANNY FARBER

When it comes to major American film critics I am a polytheist; each has their sublimities, there is no need to assign rank. That said, the one who fills me most with awe is Manny Farber. There is something so stimulating, so eternally fresh about his dense, back-tracking writing style, which piles doubt upon doubt and never allows you to rest for long in the conviction that you know what's coming next. It puts me in mind of Montaigne's late, free-fall essays, of Jackson Pollock's (and of course Farber's own) all-over paintings, of a sheer vertical rock face whose purchase is always precarious and dangerous. But so compelling! Where did that "cubist" prose style come from—or that mind that saw things in so many dimension at once? Knowing the pieces in his sole collection, *Negative Space*, constituted only a small part of his film reviewing, I often wondered about the pieces he didn't put in and why he chose to leave them out. How could *anything* Manny Farber wrote, I thought, be less than fascinating?

Now, thanks to Robert Polito, who has tracked down and edited the complete film writings by Farber, newly published by the Library of America, we have the opportunity to read these missing pieces. And you know what? I can see why Farber omitted them. Especially the early ones, from 1942 to 1947, They're not bad; in fact, they're superior film criticism for that period. But they're not yet Farberesque. Reading them is a bit like looking at the photographs Diane Arbus took before she patented that enigmatically perverse style of hers—quite adequate, even good, but not yet what we think of as Arbus.

When Farber began writing film criticism in 1942, he was, it seems to me, very much under the influence of the great Otis Ferguson, who died on active duty when his ship was bombed in 1943. Farber was quite open in later years about his admiration for Ferguson. He followed the house style of Ferguson and the *New Republic* in stitching together short reviews of three movies a week for a single column, and he followed Ferguson's populist (as opposed to aesthete-longhair) approach to movies, which included the employment of jazzed-up prose and slang words like "hokum." Ferguson was also never less than clear and straightforward, and so was Farber, at the beginning. Now, clarity would seem to be an asset for any reviewer—except Farber, perhaps, because we don't necessarily go to Farber for clarity; we go to him for stimulating confusion and his ability to keep us off balance. But it would seem that he needed to develop his aesthetic first by working out ideas in a transparently lucid style before he could trust a more clotted, textured one.

Another influence on him in these early stages was his friend James Agee, who preceded him at *The Nation*. Farber was ambivalent about his friend's criticism, as we see in that famous essay, "Nearer My Agee to Thee." But what surprises me about Farber's earliest pieces, 1942–1947, is how often he falls into an Agee-esque moralism and political preaching, deploring the shortcomings of Hollywood. His writing style may have been more Ferguson-like at this point, but in his readiness to scold Hollywood and in his hunger for the real, for ordinary people on-screen, he was actually closer to Agee than to Ferguson.

In these early reviews, Farber kept hammering away at certain principles that, to me anyway, seem simplistic—especially compared to his later positions. One was that the Hays Office censorship was mostly responsible for the immaturity of American films. Another was that films must not be "theatrical" or "literary"; they must "show, not tell"; they must avoid talk and voice-over narration and make their points mainly through "the camera eye." All this was a pretty standard aesthetic line for film buffs from the 1920s onward. Farber would build on this sensitivity to the visual and would come to excel at descriptions of nonverbal behaviors and lines of force on-screen while moving away from the rigid position that films must achieve their destiny only cinematically and strive to keep a distance from other media. But in the beginning he was a pitchman for "pure cinema."

It is a treat to see the judgments he made about films of the World War II and postwar period, how often he got things right (that is to say, jibed with our current opinion) and how often not. I don't fault him in the least for his lack of enthusiasm about movies we now hold in the highest esteem, such as *The Magnificent Ambersons*, *Casablanca*, *Laura*, *Picnic on the Grass*, or *Open City*: he was responding with maverick honesty to these new releases in their time, without our perspective of period nostalgia and auteurist reverence. Still, it does seem odd that he and Agee should have seen the forties as such a sterile desert, movie-wise.

Later on, he would learn how to capture the unevenness of a movie as something engrossing, fascinating, rather than sourly disappointing. That is, he would develop a viewpoint that was multidimensional, no longer shrilly moralistic. And from about 1948 on, he would devise that baroque prose style to insinuate and embed the maximum complexity tolerable in a sentence. How did that radical change come about? I don't know, but I suspect it had something to do with his revelation that the language of film criticism, the arena of the page itself, could be worked on as a medium in much the same ways he was exploring space in his paintings. As Robert Polito puts it in his superb introduction, "Farber advanced a topographical prose that aspired termite fashion through fragmentation, parody, allusions, multiple focus, and clashing dictions to engage the formal spaces of the new films and paintings he admired." But it didn't happen immediately, and the unveiling of that slow process by which he acquired mastery is an inspiration to us journeymen critics, and one of the many gifts of this truly invaluable volume.

MUBI NOTEBOOK (BLOG), NOVEMBER 19, 2009

Chapter Sixty-Three

ROGER EBERT

Life Itself

Film critics as a rule are prickly, truculent, not exactly huggable, but Roger Ebert (1942–2013) came as close as any to being universally well loved. He had a huge, dedicated fan base in print, on TV, and on the web. Even art-film snobs, inclined to sneer at his thumbs up/thumbs down judgments, had to admit that beneath that bluff, huggy-bear exterior resided a truly knowledgeable cinephile. On top of that, he was a thoroughly nice guy. In my own encounters with Roger, at the Telluride or Cannes Film Festivals, I found him to be unfailingly gracious, approachable, and, well, *nice*. All of which led me to approach this documentary celebration of Ebert with curiosity: How to sustain interest and tension in a film about a really decent guy, the people's favorite, and keep it from turning hagiographic and sentimental?

Life Itself, by the skilled, veteran documentarian Steve James (*Hoop Dreams*), does not evade those traps: there are plenty of gooey, fawning moments in the film, and a full enjoyment of this rich, seven-layer-cake offering may depend on embracing sentimentality for once, for a good cause.

James also balances the goo by bringing out some dark complexities and contradictions in Ebert's character. Using the film critic's own memoir, *Life Itself,* as a springboard, he has gone back and interviewed old newspaper cronies, *Siskel and Ebert* television producers, rival film critics. The picture that emerges is of someone who grew up in a working-class environment;

found writing easy from the start; wanted to go to Harvard but, lacking family funds, ended up in a local Illinois school; edited the college newspaper; went to work for the *Chicago Sun-Times*; bought hook line and sinker the romance of the hard-drinking reporter; and almost by a fluke fell into the movie reviewer job when the previous one retired, thereby becoming the youngest daily film critic in America. Early on, he seems to have been a show-off, a bar-room monologuist, a compulsive eater and alcoholic. Some nights he would stagger home from the tavern and wish he was dead. The hangovers finally got to him: In August 1979, he took his last drink and joined AA. It was at an AA meeting, at the ripe age of fifty, that he met an African American woman named Chaz, the mother of several kids, and fell in love. Their marriage had a stabilizing effect on Ebert and brought him happiness. Also maturity: the film thus traces an arc, showing his progression from being a self-destructive jerk to a *mensch*, largely thanks to the influence of Chaz and her family, who welcome him as step-grandfather and benevolent paterfamilias. The scenes with Chaz helping Ebert through his last illness and the interview with her after his death are some of the most moving. Bearing out Ebert's description of her as "a strong woman," she also comes across as singularly eloquent, caring, and honest.

The film ping-pongs between Ebert during the last four months of his life, in the hospital, and a more or less linear biography via interviews. James was invited by the Eberts to record candidly the film critic's battle with cancer, and some of these scenes are graphic and powerful, if hard to take: much of his jaw had been eaten away; he was fed by a G-tube that needed to be suctioned periodically; and he could speak only with a voice synthesizer. What's so impressive is that he continued to write, keep a blog, and answer emails almost to the very end while maintaining serene composure and humor. I kept thinking of another documentary, *Lightning Over Water* and how Wenders's shoot seemed more cluelessly invasive of Nick Ray's privacy in his last hours than James's of Ebert's. Still, it is not always clear how the illness narrative in *Life Itself* and the other parts cohere. Sometimes the film seems to be pulling in too many different directions and repeating its points. At 118 minutes, it is also twenty minutes too long.

As in other James films, the politics are implicitly progressive, starting with Ebert's avowal that he learned to vote Democratic and be prolabor from his electrician father and moving on to his early editorial outrage at the Birmingham church bombing. The film is very Chicago-centric, one might almost say Chicago-proud, with the suggestion that there is something more blue collar, earthy, or "real" about that metropolis than New York or Los Angeles. Ebert is cast as a true Chicago type and lauded for continuing to write loyally for the *Chicago Sun-Times* (a paper whose readership is said to tilt more working-class and Black than the establishment-oriented *Chicago Tribune*) even after he won a Pulitzer Prize and was courted by the *Washington Post*. We are also told that Ebert was a "populist film critic," though what this might mean other than that he shied away from academic lingo is uncertain: one would need to deconstruct the word "populist" a little more than this film is willing to do.

Notwithstanding the many compliments heaped on Ebert for his importance to the field, there is a frustrating inability to get at what exactly his writing was like, what made it so special, and how it fit into the larger historical context of American film criticism. We get some footage of Pauline Kael and a still of Andrew Sarris and supportive testimony from fellow critics Richard Corliss and A. O. Scott. Jonathan Rosenbaum is brought on to represent the view that Ebert was the epitome of mainstream film criticism, whose overall effect is to marginalize and ignore eccentric low-budget films. This critique is redressed by the testimony of several deeply grateful, bordering on sycophantic, independent filmmakers who were promoted by Ebert. James himself was one such filmmaker: Ebert championed *Hoop Dreams*, and so this documentary is, by his own admission, a way of paying back the debt. Which is fine, but it makes for a cozy, festschrift atmosphere that at times leaves the viewer feeling left out.

Thank goodness for Gene Siskel, who brings a salutary tension to the proceedings. One of the film's most satisfying strands covers Ebert's ambivalent relationship with his fellow critic and cohost. Siskel's widow, Marlene Iglitzen, shrewdly analyzes the sibling rivalry between them. We get to see some priceless outtake footage in which they keep one-upping each other while trying to share the show's opening introduction, along with some of their on-screen jousting. I had always regarded Siskel as a cinematic middlebrow compared to Ebert, but he holds his own well in the sequences here, and his opinions seem reasonable, less kneejerk-auteurist than his partner's. It becomes clear that Siskel, though the younger of the two, regarded Ebert as an overgrown kid, a fanboy still living in a garage apartment. When Ebert announced he was getting married, Siskel rejoiced at the thought that now he would have to get a mortgage and buy furniture, like the rest of humanity.

The love they came to feel for each other is touching if at times unrequited. "He's an asshole, but he's my asshole," Siskel told Marlene. *Life Itself* performs an essential service in offering up both sides of Roger Ebert: saintly lover of life and (surprise!) petulant asshole.

CINEASTE 28, NO. 4 (FALL 2003)

Chapter Sixty-Four

STANLEY KAUFFMANN

Stanley Kauffmann is no longer with us. He'd seemed one of our constants, having begun a weekly film review column for the *New Republic* in 1958 and continued it for over fifty years, the longest tenure of any American film critic. His unruffled, civilized tone was an anomaly; his measured sobriety, a rebuke to every partisan punster, fanboy, and hipster. He was the critic for all the professors who listened to NPR in the hinterlands. He cared not a whit about the cutting edge.

From the start he seemed to be looking at film with middle-aged human-ist values, impervious to the speeded-up demands of youth culture, its jump-cut sassiness or provocative languidness. Refusing to place bets on up-and-coming auteurs, he approached each film with an open if skeptical perspective. The most excitement he permitted was for directors like Anto-nioni and Bergman, whom he thought were making large social statements about the way we live now. He always evinced more interest in "problem" films from Eastern Europe or England than the latest formalist hotshot.

When I first began reading film reviews as a teenager, I found him stuffy and old-fashioned. I was a fanatic, for whom movie love was a sort of hero worship. Later, having done plenty of film reviewing myself (and grown middle-aged), I came to respect immensely his craftsmanship, that ability to cobble week after week a shapely piece that took readers through care-fully staged doubts, praising what could be praised, demurring when neces-sary, rendering justice. In selecting for my anthology, *American Movie*

Critics, I read hundreds of his reviews and never came across a badly written one. Reviewing *Bonnie and Clyde*, he threaded the needle between Pauline Kael's crush and Bosley Crowther's denunciation, pointing out patiently the film's strengths and weaknesses.

Several times we did panel discussions together at the Skidmore summer writer conferences. Stanley would be invited to pick a film, and it was usually something serious and dour, like *The Spy Who Came in from the Cold*. With the best will in the world, the cinephile in me could not work up much enthusiasm for Martin Ritt's overly controlled spy film, though I could see why Kauffmann thought it admirably grown-up and courageous in addressing Cold War politics. Kauffmann returned the favor when he consented to appear on a panel honoring the publication of *American Movie Critics*: the movie I chose to show that night at Lincoln Center was one of my favorites, Godard's *Contempt*, and when it was Stanley's turn to speak, he grumbled that he still couldn't see it as anything but a muddled mess. For narcissistic reasons alone, practically all cinephiles love *Contempt*, just as we love the voyeuristic *Vertigo*. Stanley was not a cinephile. He wrote a million words about film but didn't have a passion for it. He did for the theater, and his sense of plot construction and consistent psychology derived from that training ground. He wrote plays, novels, even a western (*Shootout Canyon*) under a pseudonym for money, dubbed pictures in Rome, produced a radio show, hosted a PBS program, worked in publishing for decades, was the *Times*' drama critic for eight months, and taught in universities. He zestfully covered all these occupations in his 2007 memoir, *Albums of a Life*, yet curiously, said little about film reviewing, the one he did longest. Worldly, he brought to the job those wider life experiences, as well as resistance to the narrow glamour and buzz that dominates film culture.

He never served on the New York Film Festival selection committee. Why? Was his taste deemed too middlebrow? I asked Richard Pena why he'd never invited Stanley to be on the committee during his twenty-five years of chairing it. "Stanley was always friendly when he saw me, very complimentary. Then he would write extremely harsh, hostile things about the festival, saying it was elitist and obscure. I also sensed he wouldn't have functioned well in a committee. He always seemed a loner, above the fray." We need such above-the-fray voices in our hothouse film-buff climate. It is good to have some critics who *don't* fall in love. More than perhaps we ever realized, we needed and still need Stanley Kauffmann.

Chapter Sixty-Five

PAULINE KAEL
A Biography

The time is ripe for a life of Pauline Kael. Ten years after her passing, her insistent, astute voice continues to resonate in the culture. The Library of America has just published a hefty selection of her best pieces, which makes the case definitively for her mastery as a prose writer—probably superior in that regard to any other film critic. What follows, naturally, is curiosity about the woman herself, such as only a biography can supply. Brian Kellow, a seasoned biographer of Ethel Merman and the Bennett sisters, editor at *Opera News*, film buff, and Kael admirer, would seem right for the job, and he has written a decent, balanced, revealing and informative book. He has done his research and interviewed everyone who knew her (including me). If there is finally something muffled about the result, it may have less to do with the biographer's shortcomings than with the difficulties posed by this particular subject.

For starters, Kael was extremely guarded about her private life and changed her versions of the past frequently. The freshest material here, for those who know her public persona well, are the first chapters, when Kellow takes us through her childhood in Petaluma, California, in a community of Yiddish-speaking émigré farmers; her chilly, discontented mother and expansive, adulterous father; her dropping out of college in senior year; her first unhappy sojourn in New York City (which crystallized a lifelong dislike of the place); her failure at playwriting; her love affairs with several gay or bisexual men. One such liaison, with the experimental filmmaker James Broughton, produced a child, Gina, whom she raised by herself, Mildred Pierce–like, and heroically supported both of them with a number of odd jobs, including running a laundry. Gina's heart condition needed to be corrected by expensive surgery, and Kael ended up enticing Edward Landberg, the owner of a local art house, Berkeley Cinema Guild into marriage. It proved a fiasco, but Landberg agreed to pay for Gina's operation, which Kellow suspects had been Kael's motive all along.

By this point she had begun writing program notes for their art house and for Pacifica radio, then reviews for little magazines, then *New Republic*, *McCall's*, and eventually the *New Yorker*, where she joined the staff in 1967 at age forty-eight and reigned for the next thirty-plus years. Her first book, *I Lost It at the Movies*, sold around 150,000 copies, an unimaginable success for a collection of film criticism. From here on in, Kellow takes us through all the familiar highpoints and flashpoints: *Bonnie and Clyde*; *Funny Girl*; her chummy relations with directors Altman, De Palma, Peckinpah; her falling-out with Woody Allen and Paul Schrader; the *Shoah* review; the Hollywood gig debacle; her changing cast of Paulettes; and so on.

The problem for the biographer is that, after a certain point, Kael seemed to have no private life: by the time she was forty she had given up on men, and even her friendships seemed limited to one topic. "Her existence revolved around going to movies, talking about movies, lecturing on movies, being interviewed about movies." Anyone who has hung around film critic circles will know that narrowing thinness and provincialism that can set in when there is no other focus but movie talk. Kellow, with no access to her inner life beyond her reviews, is reduced to slogging through the major releases year by year, offering plot summaries and reporting what Pauline said and how other critics differed. The biographer himself refrains from offering his opinion, which is a pity; it reduces him to a maitre d' seating quotes. Occasionally he allows himself to demur, as when he chides Kael for presuming to know Ellen Burstyn's motives ("quite out of critical bounds") or for saying that Claude Lanzmann "'could probably find anti-Semitism anywhere.' It was a stunning lapse of judgment, considering that Lanzmann was looking for anti-Semitism in the most obvious of places—the death camps."

Kael's fans tend to be idolaters: for them she is not merely a good film critic but the only film critic, an attitude she encouraged by her frequent disparagement of her colleagues as idiots, schmucks, cowards, and sexless drones. There could be only one valid judgment, especially since she refused to see a film twice; changing one's mind seemed to her a sign of weakness. Kellow, smitten by her reviews from adolescence, situates himself well within the Kael party line. For instance: "Pauline's review of *Last Tango* did more than anything else to date to boost her reputation as the era's wisest and most searching film critic." Really? I thought it quite uneven, especially in the Leaud secondary plot. Okay, fine: one would not expect a biographer to be at odds with his subject. But for those skeptical that hers is the only true opinion, it makes for claustrophobic predictability.

The biographer shows more independence in assessing Kael's treatment of her daughter, Gina, whose ambitions to become a dancer or a painter she did little to encourage, preferring to keep her on "a silver cord . . . as secretary, driver, reader, sounding board." Gina, for her part, was mistrustful of the dynamic she witnessed between Kael and her acolytes. "As Gina often pointed out, Pauline liked to be surrounded by people whose feelings about the arts and politics were close to her own. She often told friends that she found it difficult to form a close bond with someone who disagreed with her about more than three movies."

I think Kael had as high a critical batting average as any critic of her time. I would not dream of castigating her because she got this or that film "wrong": it's the fate of film critics to make many assessments that look questionable in light of later opinion. Still, it's instructive to look at her likes and dislikes for patterns. She was an advocate of the American studio film and increasingly incurious about world cinema. Kellow notes: "She was particularly piqued that she had not been able to have an effect on the tastes of most of the senior writers and editors at *The New Yorker*, who dutifully continued to attend art films by Fassbinder and Bresson that they thought were good for them, and looked askance at her praise for *Carrie*, *The Fury*, and *The Warriors*." She preferred De Palma to Hitchcock, detested *Last Year at Marienbad*, found *Badlands* "over-intellectualized" and *Au Hazard Balthazar* "grim." Kellow concludes that formidable intellect aside, her life as a critic was "a triumph of instinct over intellect. Her highly emotional responses to art were what enabled her to make so indelible a mark as a critic."

The paradox was that someone who had such quick access to her emotional responses could be so clueless about her effect on others. Kellow registers bemusement at her naïve surprise when her savage criticisms wounded the recipients. He also shakes his head at her naïve expectation that she could go out to Hollywood and single-handedly make it a more creative place. Gina's trenchant remarks at her mother's memorial tribute are quoted near the end. After noting Kael's inflexibility and insensitivity to others, she said:

"Pauline's greatest weakness, her failure as a person, became her great strength, her liberation as a writer and critic. She truly believed that what she did was for everyone else's good, and that because she meant well, she had no negative effects. She refused any consideration of that possibility and she denied any motivations or personal needs. . . . This lack of introspection, self-awareness, restraint, or hesitation gave Pauline supreme freedom to speak up, to speak her mind, to find her honest voice. She turned her lack of self-awareness into a triumph."

Kellow has left it to Gina to connect the dots, which he has been too polite or discreet to do. His subtitle, *A Life in the Dark*, may allude to the pathos underneath the triumph. Or it may reference the *Kane*-like testimony of ex-Paulette Owen Gleiberman, quoted here: "She was a great, fascinating woman who had her dark side."

FILM COMMENT (NOVEMBER/DECEMBER 2011)

Chapter Sixty-Six

STANLEY CAVELL

In the big parade of American writing about film, Stanley Cavell occupies a strange, outsider position. A Harvard professor of philosophy, he is not, by his own admission, either a film critic or a film scholar, yet he has written with persistent trenchancy and brilliance about movies. First, in *The World Viewed*, he cobbled together a stimulating theory of film as a medium, without recourse to the usual academic jargon; then, in *Pursuits of Happiness*, his best-known book, he mapped felicitously a genre that he called the comedy of remarriage; lastly, in *Contesting Tears*, he analyzed "the melodrama of the unknown woman" (formerly, "the woman's film") in surprising ways. He brought down to earth the discussion of philosophy through concrete examples provided in movies and imparted a seriousness and depth to the criticism of film narrative by calling upon philosophy to illuminate its underlying moral choices.

Now Cavell, in his late seventies, has given us a volume that synthesizes his life's work in philosophy and film while adding a third leg to the triangle: teaching. *Cities of Words: Pedagogical Letters on a Register of the Moral Life* is based on a celebrated course of lectures he gave several times before he retired from the classroom, which alternated discussions of philosophical or literary texts and films. Thus, Emerson is paired with *The Philadelphia Story*, Locke with *Adam's Rib*, Nietzsche with *Now, Voyager*, John Stuart Mill with *Gaslight*, and so on. Sometimes the pairings seem arbitrary: I am still trying to figure out what Kant has to do with *It Happened One Night*.

But there are some terrifically apt combinations, such as Henry James's story "The Beast in the Jungle" with Ophüls's *Letter from an Unknown Woman* (in each case, a woman tries to convey to a man the meaning of his life by getting him—albeit too late—to recognize her), or Shakespeare's *A Winter's Tale* and Rohmer's astute reworking of the same material in the *A Tale of Winter*. And even when the dazzling ideas from either world merely glance off each other, there is pleasure and edification enough in following, sentence by sentence, Cavell's enormously original, mature, well-stocked mind.

Do not be put off by the fact that these pages began as lectures. Here is an author who has the guts to admit, "I love the sound of interesting, which means interested, academic lecturing," and goes on to show in what that art consists: first, demonstrating a generosity and enthusiasm for the subject at hand (you feel Cavell trying to cram everything he knows into these 450 pages); second, performing in front of students, or readers, the actual process of thinking, through a doggedly honest, skeptical self-scrutiny. The prose here often wades into a new, untried thought through hesitant speculations, digressions, and questioning of prior assertions.

Neither should you jump to the conclusion that this volume is merely a "greatest hits" rehash of Cavell's past books because it again takes up, say, *The Lady Eve* or *Stella Dallas*. The author has been mulling over some of these movies for a lifetime, and he revisits them in the same way that Northrop Frye (an acknowledged influence) might return to Shakespeare's late comedies again, as inexhaustible texts. He is well aware that many will think him foolish to take so seriously what is after all, "only a movie." He writes:

In a film, unlike a painting or sculpture or piece of theater, we are given (captivated by) a forever fixed, captured, image of a human being in this precise environment, in these precise attitudes and relations, remaining silent or saying precisely these words precisely this way. (In film, contrary to theater, the actor takes precedence over the character.) The events are made to be examined and reexamined, to make one voluble, to be read for their possibilities, like a field of battle or a crime scene. It is a mystery why the convention developed, still in the process of being broken, of viewing a movie only once and, moreover, of accepting as criticism of a film the brief results of impressions upon seeing it once.

While I myself am perfectly willing to grant him the freedom to uncover every possible meaning or nuance in movies I accept as classics, such as *The Awful Truth* or *His Girl Friday*, I initially balked at the same respectful treatment accorded such dustier (to my mind) films as *Mr. Deeds Goes to Town* or *Now, Voyager.* As it turned out, these chapters were some of the freshest in the book, forcing me to reconsider my prejudices.

I have sometimes found myself thinking that Cavell's method of dissecting the ethical and psychological dilemmas in a film plot, analyzing its narratological branchings and roads not taken, unduly favors the script over cinematic form or individual acting style. But in fact he often has good things to say about these aspects as well, as when he comments sharply on Ophüls's camera position changes in *Letter from an Unknown Woman,* or speaks about "Bette Davis's powers as a screen presence, having to do with her virtuosic ability to project moods edged with hysteria, a power that enables her notable capacity for enacting extremes of self-revelation and self-concealment."

When he invokes the doctrine of "moral perfectionism," as exemplified by Emerson, I can see that it fits in with his generally ameliorist viewpoint, allowing for growth, self-improvement, and even happiness. There is, in Cavell, an unfashionably optimistic strain that refuses to see the world as a demonic hell ruled by Satan. His faith that such a thing as a "good marriage" is even attainable stems from his conviction in the possibility of a conversation between men and women as friends, just as his love of Emerson, Thoreau, and Wittgenstein, dead authors fully alive to him, drives his cautious belief in the ongoing possibility of democracy. Ultimately, whether it is a matter of marriage, world politics, or the classroom, he believes in keeping the conversation open and "voluble" as long as possible.

In Cavell's first book about movies, *The World Viewed,* he wrote: "It is generally true of the writing about film which has meant something to me that it has the power of the missing companion. Agee and Robert Warshow and Andre Bazin manage that mode of conversation all the time; and I have found it in, among others, Manny Farber, Pauline Kael, Parker Tyler, Andrew Sarris." Alongside these names so companionable to film buffs, I would happily add another: Stanley Cavell.

FILM COMMENT (JULY/AUGUST 2004)

Chapter Sixty-Seven

JAMES HARVEY

Though his actual first name was Howard and he signed his books "James Harvey," in the twenty-plus years of our friendship I always knew him as Jim. In our household, my wife, daughter, and I also had a nickname for him, "the Owl," because of the night hours he kept. I am a morning person, and sometimes the difference created tension between us, if, say, we were having dinner after a film and it was going on ten-thirty and I could barely keep my eyes open, I would stand up to signal I was done and ready to leave while he was still nursing his espresso, just getting started, and he would get a wounded look in his eyes and let me know he thought I was being rude. It's true, I can be abrupt, and he was the opposite, apt to make a more gradual, mannerly leave-taking.

We were both great walkers, he even more than I, but being such a passionate lover of animals he would stop to pet every dog whose path we crossed and chat with the owner, which irritated me. Each of us had little habits or eccentricities we had to forgive in the other, like an old married couple. Such is the nature of enduring friendship.

I found him an open, generous conversationalist, always asking after one's mental state and family members, willing to entertain any topic, not shying away from giving or receiving personal disclosures, but of course we would always get around to what movies or other cultural forms we had seen recently. He had a broader range than I and was a regular opera-, theater-, and ballet-goer, whereas I would only dip into those other art forms occasionally, being film-monogamous. We would talk on the phone and discuss the various movie possibilities in town (sometimes mighty slim) and meet up at the theater, I always getting there early, he sometimes arriving maddeningly close to show-time.

Our opinions about a movie were generally in sync; I would say 80 percent of the time we agreed. He had higher standards and a tendency to be picky and critical. If I mostly liked a film or thought it had good elements, I would wax enthusiastic, and he might sigh and say it was "okay." Having come to cinephilia in the sixties through André Bazin, Andrew Sarris, and auteurism, I was more of a formalist in my takes and would expatiate about the compositional or cutting style. He noticed those things too, but they mattered less to him than the overall moral and psychological stance of a film. Was it unnecessarily mean to one of its characters or dismissively caricaturing?

We both disliked nasty movies, by which I mean those that achieved effects through sensationalist appeal, sadism, or cruelty. In short, we were no longer thrill-seeking adolescents and were looking for wisdom and worldly perspective, perhaps even some kindness or tenderness. I am no spring chicken myself, but Jim was a good thirteen years older. He had a different historical frame of reference and experience of life, which was partly why I cherished his company and looked up to him for guidance.

With the passing of that whole generation of older film critics—Pauline Kael, Andrew Sarris, Manny Farber, Richard Schickel, Stanley Cavell, and now Jim Harvey—we have lost an incalculably valuable grasp of cinematic tradition. I mean something like when Kael pointed out in her barbed critique of *The Graduate* that there is nothing new about the sexual *mésalliance* of a younger man and an older woman, it goes back to the silent era. I remember as a young man in my twenties, hero-worshipping Godard, when I read with incredulous shock Manny Farber discussing the (to him, younger) Jean-Luc as though he were still a work in progress and needed to mature. I now think he was right. In Jim's case, it meant discussing in his first, now classic book, *Romantic Comedy in Hollywood: From Lubitsch to Sturges*, the plots of the Jeannette MacDonald/Maurice Chevalier Lubitsch musicals not condescendingly as campy shenanigans but as serious moral dilemmas. Or his drawing a sharp distinction between the personae of Mae West and Jean Harlow in favor of the latter. In his second book, *Movie Love in the Fifties*, he was able to penetrate deeply into the melodramas of Douglas Sirk, whom he actually knew and had interviewed. His analysis of Sirk's *Imitation of Life* uncovers all its heartbreaking paradoxes and contradictions, the nobility of Juanita Moore against the stagy falseness of Lana Turner, and the tragic Susan Kohner caught in between.

It was Harvey's critical technique, a risky one, to work patiently through a movie scene by scene, interpreting the choices and subtexts along the way, rather than glibly summarizing with a few witty ripostes. In his third book, the brilliant *Watching Them Be*, his sympathetic but clear-eyed study of star presence from Garbo to Balthazar (the donkey), he was able to get to the heart of Ingrid Bergman's different acting under David O. Selznick and Roberto Rossellini, John Wayne's partnership with John Ford, Godard's close-ups in *Masculin Féminin*, Bette Davis as directed by William Wyler. He was by no means stuck in Hollywood's Golden Age and could discourse as happily on Tarantino's singular achievement in *Jackie Brown* as on Garbo, but when he approached the icons of the past he did so with the understanding of a contemporary who had seen their movies when they first opened.

We often showed each other drafts of what we were writing. Jim responded invariably with praise. His critical suggestions for improvement were never over matters of style but rather morality, such as if he thought I was being unfair toward someone I wrote about. His own manuscripts, quirky-syntactical and densely thoughtful, were typed old style with erasures and penciling, which made me gasp when I first saw them. Wanting to spare him the dismissals of editors, I offered to retype them for neatness's sake into my laptop, but he would have none of it. In his last years, approaching ninety, it became harder and harder for him to finish a piece to his satisfaction. He regarded my productivity with bafflement if not mild disapproval. Yet he was the quintessential loyal friend and would always attend my public events and read my pieces when they appeared in print.

Jim had been raised Roman Catholic and turned more and more to the church in his later years. He even tithed, which I warned him to stop doing when he worried about financial matters, but he did not take my suggestion seriously. Since I was a secular, skeptical Jew and he a practicing Catholic, it was one more matter for us to view with different lenses. I ecstatically embraced Noah Baumbach's *The Meyerowitz Stories*—it was mother's milk to me—but he was put off by something: perhaps it was too sardonic, too familial-quarrelsomely Jewish. On the other hand, when we saw Martin Scorsese's *Silence* together, he left the theater deeply moved; I found it leaden, solemn, over-cooked. (I was turned off by the endless close-ups of teary-eyed Andrew Garfield, out of his thespian depth). We agreed to disagree about some of Terence Malick's recent movies, like *To the Wonder*. He thought them bravely spiritual, and to me they seemed self-indulgent. Increasingly, he was sensitive to the spiritual dimension of movies and wanted to write a final fourth book about the movies and religion. It never got past the book proposal.

Jim lived alone. He told me it was by choice. A bachelor his entire adult life, whose signal desire when younger was to get away from his conventional parents, he could not see sharing his living space with any other creature besides a cat or a dog. His refrigerator was bare. He did not cook except to heat up the occasional frozen meal, and he took most of his meals in restaurants, as often as possible in the company of a friend. He had many, many friends, in fact a genius for friendship; it was his preferred mode. Politically on the left, a self-described "democratic socialist," he kept MSNBC on all day when he was not writing or watching a movie; he was both dreading and looking forward to the 2020 presidential election. But in the last year of his life he developed a blood disease and had to go into the hospital regularly for infusions. He started falling, the hazard of the elderly, and since he would not give up his marathon strolls (sometimes leaving me in Manhattan to take the subway home while he walked home across the Brooklyn Bridge), these tripping incidents occurred in the street more and more often. The last time it happened, he was walking his dog and the leash entangled his leg when the animal bolted. He went into the hospital to have a leg operation, and two months later he passed away.

Ordinarily I would have visited his hospital bedside, but he had the bad luck to fall ill at the onset of the COVID pandemic, when visitors were not permitted. He dearly wished he could be released and allowed to convalesce at home. Since he lived in a third floor walkup and couldn't rise out of bed by himself, it was clearly never going to happen. A friend, Dan Kleinman, gave him a laptop and loaded it with ballets, which he watched with satisfaction. I am told that toward the end he accepted with resignation the fact that he was dying. He died in mid-April, 2020, at ninety years of age. Characteristically, he died alone.

INDIEWIRE, MAY 29, 2020

Chapter Sixty-Eight

JONATHAN ROSENBAUM

If pressed to name the best regular film critic in America today, I'd have to say Jonathan Rosenbaum. His weekly articles in the *Chicago Reader* are so thoughtful, so informed and informative, so well written that they function more as reflective essays than hasty reviews. He also takes a stance that is utterly independent of pressures to placate the industry or write down to his readers, as his top-ten list of 1994 (headed by *Sátántangó, The Second Heimat,* and *That's Entertainment III*) can attest. Rosenbaum pays his readers the compliment of assuming they are as intellectually curious as he is while deftly sketching in the career backgrounds of filmmakers such as Joris Ivens or Béla Tarr. The fact that he operates out of Chicago rather than New York may give him greater freedom to play the teacher and the lone voice in the wilderness. But Rosenbaum's new collection, *Placing Movies,* which includes generous selections from earlier reviewing in *Sight and Sound, Film Comment,* and the *Soho News,* as well as more recent *Chicago Reader* pieces, shows that he was always one to go his own perceptive, eccentric way.

Rosenbaum's specialty is the "difficult" film, which he patiently disentangles through description, analysis, and research. Take his masterly dissection of Carl Theodor Dreyer's *Gertrud*; it is inestimably aided by his going back and reading the original Söderberg play in a French translation, as well as a French biography of Dreyer, to get at the filmmaker's psychological intentions. From there, he unravels the cinematic allure of the nonnarrative in this narrative film. The *Gertrud* piece is one of three invaluable probings of difficult modernist films with roots in seemingly dated texts (Resnais's *Mélo* and Oliveira's *Doomed Love* being the other two). Equally impressive is his analysis of Chantal Akerman's *Jeanne Dielman*, which interweaves frank comments about his bafflement and irritation with a steadily growing understanding of what the film might be about.

Rosenbaum uses candor to cut through otherwise obscure matters in discussing the avant-garde. For instance, he admits that avant-garde insiders tend to accept uncritically the works of their heroes while most reviewers dismiss the products thoughtlessly—which is why he strives for a mixture of intellectual preparation and a subjectively honest, nonacademic approach. The book's ostensible larger theme is, as its subtitle puts it, "the practice of film criticism," and each of its sections is preceded by an introduction that shows the down-to-earth aspects of a film critic's life: how this editor fired him or that publicist snubbed him or how disappointed he was with the reception of his last book. While these passages have a somewhat embarrassing revenge-of-the-nerds quality, I have to take my hat off to Rosenbaum for developing a literary persona that is singular and courageously self-exposed. Two of the best pieces—on mentor-critic Manny Farber and Jacques Tati, who hired Rosenbaum as a scriptwriter—are fully accomplished personal essays that bring alive their subjects via their interactions with the author, who portrays his clumsiness with humor.

He writes with equal passion about old and new films. With his keen sense of the past, he celebrates the fifties chemistry of Marilyn Monroe and Jane Russell in Howard Hawks's *Gentlemen Prefer Blondes*. He sorts out the historical strengths and weaknesses in Clint Eastwood's *Bird* or the Coen Brothers' *Barton Fink*. Or he enthusiastically reapproaches a classic like Jean Vigo's *L'Atalante*: "Michel Simon, as Père Jules, offers what is just about the most wondrous character acting I know of in movies; but even this performance would be substantially less than it is if it weren't for Vigo's superb sense of how to integrate him with everything else in the picture. At once the film's only pure infant and its only pure adult, he embodies a kind of polymorphous-perverse behavior that perfectly exemplifies the film's capacity to integrate fantasy and reality."

Intelligent, industrious, learned, frank, adept at conveying both the formalist joys of mise-en-scène and the thorny content of politics and morality, both the virtues of commercial movies and those of avant-garde cinema—are there any weaknesses in this exemplary critic? Unfortunately, yes. It is not enough that Rosenbaum is so often right: he has to tell you he is and insult those colleagues he deems wrong. There is a petulant, quarrelsome tone that creeps into his prose from time to time, especially toward other critics that enjoy a higher profile, like Andrew Sarris, Pauline Kael, and Vincent Canby. He seems not to appreciate the difference between honesty and incivility. To mock one's fellow critics and get away with it, one needs the malicious wit of a Hazlitt or Mencken. Rosenbaum too often attacks "ignorance" with the solemn, self-righteous superiority complex of a teenager with an authority problem. Adolescent, too, is his overly romantic defense of filmmaker martyrs (Welles, Cassavetes) "killed" by evil critics. Rosenbaum's castigation of distributors for not booking Rivette's nine-hour *Out 1: Spectre* or Michael Snow's experimental films into theaters immediately or for closing the latest Kiarostami feature after two weeks, before the hungry masses could get a chance to see it, also seems a trifle naïve. He should realize there are certain joys, as Stendhal says, for the happy few and leave it at that.

Placing Movies shows there are two sides to this critic: the wise Dr. Rosenbaum, who champions the mature, complex, compassionate, postcolonialist, feminist in cinema; and Kid Jonathan, the aggressive radical macho who puts in a good word for "hatred and anger, emotions that are undervalued in more cowardly periods like the present." That hatred and anger can be defended on political or aesthetic grounds I have no doubt, but I see them as less useful in the writing of sound film criticism. Fortunately, it is Dr. Rosenbaum who predominates in this brilliant, essential collection.

FILM COMMENT (JULY/AUGUST 1995)

Chapter Sixty-Nine

JONATHAN BAUMBACH

With this welcome collection, Jonathan Baumbach, known for his wry, take-no-prisoners experimental fiction, is revealed in retrospect to have been a brilliant film critic. In an era bristling with formidable commentators on the movies (Andrew Sarris, Pauline Kael, Manny Farber, Parker Tyler, John Simon, Dwight Macdonald, Molly Haskell, Vincent Canby, Stanley Kauffmann, and William S. Pechter, just to name a few), Baumbach, we see now, was one of the sharpest. Writing for quarterlies such as *Film Culture* and *Partisan Review*, he could absent himself from the hype-manufacturing competition of daily/weekly reviewers and weigh in with thoughtful, elegant prose, astute judgment, and a dose of skepticism after the initial hoopla had died down. If that old, questionable distinction between movie reviewing and film criticism makes any sense, then we must place him in the latter category, where he would place himself.

In his initial analyses of liberal "message" pictures such as *Edge of the City*, *Twelve Angry Men*, and *State of Siege*, we see him patiently sifting cinematic aesthetics from thematic assumptions. Already there is a preference for formalist rigor over the pieties of content. Baumbach was a sophisticated, auteur-oriented cinephile from the first, drawn to the complexities of international art cinema over mediocre commercial product, which he called "debased populism." Robert Bresson, that austere master of mise-en-scène, was his artistic gold standard; the inventive Godard, his main man; Antonioni and Chabrol stood high in his regard; and when it came to American film, he favored independent stylists such as Sam Peckinpah, Terence Malick, or the Roman Polanski of *Chinatown*. He was not swept away by the New Hollywood's "super-kitsch of Altman and Coppola" and could separate what was exciting in a film like *Nashville* from Altman's "crassness." In this, he was the opposite of Pauline Kael, whose hyperbolic enthusiasms he analyzed with acuity in his shrewd critique:

On the evidence, Kael prefers the hot to the cool, gut experience to intellectual, subject matter to form; she is a moralist, has a liberal journalist's respect for important social content (is a sucker for good causes like *Serpico* and *Conrack* and *Sounder* and *State of Siege*), is wary of easy sentiment, is moved by the star turns of charismatic performers, gives more weight to the sound of a film (clever dialogue gets high marks) than its look, distrusts visual elegance (and beauty, one might add) almost as if it were a species of fraud, as if there were something decadent or anti-human in esthetic suasion.

Reverse almost all the statements in the above paragraph and you arrive at a quick summary of Baumbach's own film aesthetic. His taste was that of a certain educated class of cinephile who frequented New York Film Festival, hoping for surprises. I used to see him at NYFF press screenings, and we struck up a friendly acquaintance. Though Jonathan was ten years older than I am, we shared many of the same experiences in the dark. Perhaps for that reason, I usually agreed with his judgments. Even when I disagree today (like rating Sidney Lumet higher than he does), at the time I usually leaned his way. For instance, we sixties and seventies cognoscenti were snobbish about Ingmar Bergman as the darling of the middle-class suburbanites, and hence his dismissal of the over-determined *Cries and Whispers* would have garnered my strenuous assent. Decades later, as so many more trendy directors have disappointed, the Ingmar Bergman of *Fanny and Alexander* and *Scenes from a Marriage* looks more and more titanic. (In fact, Baumbach does give a positive review to *Scenes from a Marriage*). In any case, we should judge a film critic fifty years later not so much by a scorecard of how many he got "right" or "wrong" by contemporary standards but by the spirit and intelligence of his writing, the humanity of his wisdom. By these standards, Baumbach shines.

Still, I would like to tease out certain paradoxes in his criticism, not to find fault but to pinpoint the complexity of that balancing act. He comes down on the side of pleasure, saying that "suffering in a movie theater is not always redemptive" and "the pains of viewing *Cries and Whispers* . . . outweigh the pleasure." But he gives high marks to Godard's *Every Man for Himself* for frustrating the audience: "There is in Godard's work a temperamental resistance to giving the audience what it perceives itself to want." He tries to reconcile the anti-satisfaction side of Godard by stressing his craft: "Godard's pleasure in filmmaking . . . is at odds with the moral statement his films want to make. Impulse triumphs over puritanical vision." He sticks loyally with Godard long after some of us have gotten off the boat. He mocks Kael as a "moralist" yet dismisses Pasolini's intriguing *Salò* on similar moral grounds: "In its assaults on its audience, *Salò* becomes in effect the Fascist ethic it instructs us to despise. There is considerable audacity, of course, in making a film as brutal and dehumanizing as this—mutilation and scatology its main pleasures—but no reason but self-contempt for an audience to suffer it."

Like any good writer or critic, Baumbach does have a moral vision, but he is so mistrustful of self-satisfied moralism that he cannot always own up to it. Some of this reluctance may also have to do with his commitment as a fiction writer to experimental narrative, which brings with it a certain disdain for conventional realism.

Just as we are wondering what connection there is between the perspicacious film critic and the risky experimental fiction writer, Baumbach clarifies all that with a beautifully candid personal essay, "Seeing Myself in Movies." In it he tells us how he fell in love with movies as a child, drawn to their dreamlike invocation of fantasy, mystery, and desire and their relaxation of the strictures of everyday reality. Movies were "an outlaw pleasure." When he grew up and became an accomplished writer, he tried to incorporate that same oneiric sense of freedom and narrative possibility into his fictions. In one of his novels, *Chez Charlotte and Emily*, "daydreams [are] made manifest," and he hopes it will demonstrate "how one escapes the banality of everyday life—how one renews life for oneself—through the generative power of the imagination." A discontent with the banality of daily life seems to be one of his constants. Putting in a good word for the murderous, eponymous heroine of Chabrol's *Violette*, he writes: "Her rebellion is . . . an acting out of the unexpressed rages of stultifying respectability."

From this we may posit three entities: Baumbach the movie lover, Baumbach the film critic ,and Baumbach the experimental fiction writer. There are traces of the boy entranced with movies' dream structures in the film critic's infatuation with the Arabian Nights endless plots of Jacques Rivette's

Out 1: Spectre and *Céline and Julie Go Boating.* The film critic is inclined to indulge the far-fetched elements in Brian De Palma's *Dressed to Kill* because it accesses our desires for violence, sex, and mayhem. De Palma is also excused his baroque excesses because his movies are self-referential, making us conscious of borrowings from other movies (here, Baumbach is being less the awestruck boy than the sophisticated postmodernist theorist).

At one point, the judicious film critic even delivers a passionate defense of experimentalism—coming to the aid of his alter ego, the fiction writer, as it were: "There is much insistence these days in places like *The New York Times*, that 'experimental' art (also called postmodern) is a thing of the past. For some time, the word 'experimental' in the context of the arts has been loaded against itself, has been a code word for pretension and obscurity. Radical art is the sworn enemy of the prevalent populist aesthetic: if it doesn't make any money, if it doesn't persuade a large audience, it has no right to exist. Establishment culture has, of course, a large stake in opposing art that doesn't pay its way. The attack on experimentation is, in disguise, an attack against all art, against the uncompromised nature of art."

This passage, which can be read as an *apologia pro vita sua*, seems to equate unremunerative experimentalism with art itself. In his recurrent use of terms such as "radical," "anti-psychology" and "serious," one hears echoes of Susan Sontag, though perhaps it is only that they both operated under the intellectual canopy of the same zeitgeist. The curious thing is that Baumbach the film critic often chastised a movie's characters for their inconsistency or lack of psychological depth. In the case of his beloved *Breathless*, he also noted, in spite of applauding Godard's "anti-psychology," that the courtship scenes charm by their behavioral realism. It is also noteworthy that Baumbach chose to write his fine, clear, nuanced critical essays in a manner that is not in the least experimental. I would further add that for all their surreal plot turns, much of the pleasure I have gotten from reading his novels and short stories has come from his accurate observations of male egotism, his aphoristic insights about rationalization, and his worldly, sardonic narrative voice (not that far removed from his film-critical voice). Stoical resignation in the face of life's limitations and the desire to upset the apple cart are forever alternating in Baumbach's novels. But this is not the occasion for analyzing his fiction. I only bring it up to point to the stimulating tensions between the realistic, psychologically astute side of Baumbach and the defiantly outlaw, immature à la Gombrowicz, avant-garde provocateur.

A fourth entity might be perceived in the shadows: Baumbach the putative filmmaker. That was the road not taken. "Do I write novels that are related to films because I am unable (for financial reasons, for reasons of personality) to make a film? It's possible—indeed, not unlikely." It is common for film critics to harbor fantasies of making their own movies: Sarris and Agee wrote screenplays (a few, in Agee's case, actually got made); Kael spent an uncomfortable season in Hollywood trying to sway productions. In a final essay, Baumbach acknowledges the fact that the closest he came was to father a celebrated filmmaker, Noah, in whose pictures he is occasionally given a cameo part. (Another son, Nico, is a film scholar and Columbia University professor of film.) Baumbach sounds graciously resigned to playing a morally ambivalent role in his filmmaker son's "dreamlike romantic comedy about transcending the terrors that keep one from becoming fully alive." Whatever those personal terrors might be, in his case, his film criticism brings us into the healing presence of a fully evolved, lively intelligence. We are grateful to have this scintillating and engaging and long-overdue collection of his film criticism.

FROM *SHOTS IN THE DARK: WRITINGS ON FILM*, BY JONATHAN BAUMBACH
(BARCELONA: CAT THREAD BOOKS, 2019)

EXIT MUSIC

A Few Last Thoughts

Chapter Seventy

REPERTORY MOVIE THEATERS,
RAVISHING REVIVALS

I have spent large chunks of my life in repertory movie theaters. Coming to cinephilia at the height of auteurism, and being both an auteurist and a completist, eager to see all of my favorite directors' works, I would track down obscure titles, like *The Model and the Marriage Broker* during my George Cukor phase or *Two Men in Manhattan*, by Jean-Pierre Melville. Often these minor films were not that great, but they taught me something about a master's artistic range and development. (And sometimes they *were* great, like Mizoguchi's *Miss Oyu*). Since I knew that these rarities typically had short runs, perhaps only a day, I would scan the listings of the repertory movies theaters for revivals and prepare to pounce. In this way, I haunted the Thalia, the New Yorker, the Charles, Theatre 80 St. Marks, the Regency, the Elgin, the Bleecker Street Cinema, Film Forum, and many another venue that revived older films. Of course, I still kept up with the new releases, but I was eager to fill in the historical gaps.

A new study by Ben Davis, *Repertory Movie Theaters of New York City: Havens for Revivals, Indies, and the Avant-Garde, 1960–1994*, with copious photographs, has just been published. I confess I approached it with trepidation, fearing it would get wrong the passion to which I had devoted so much time and energy, rather like going to a political demonstration and coming home to see it distorted in the nightly news. I also worried that this subject that was so meaningful to me would not matter much to the reading public and in seeing it thus diminished, I would realize that I had wasted my life.

Not that I would take back any of the sublime movie-going moments that I had experienced from youth to middle age; just that I would be embarrassed to find myself grouped with a pack of obsessive, nerdy aesthetes who in their prolonged-adolescent fandom had overvalued their idols and mistaken the shadow for the act.

As it turns out, Davis has done a superb job of capturing the phenomenon of New York repertory movie theaters and placing it in historical context. His prose is clear, intelligent, engaging; his anecdotal examples colorful and often humorous; his research impeccably extensive; and his facts for the most part accurate. He has interviewed everyone on the scene who is still alive—including me. The book is divided into a first wave, taking us through the sixties, with chapters on Dan Talbot's New Yorker, Lionel Rogosin's Bleecker Street Cinema, Walter Langsford and Edwin Stein Jr.'s Charles, and Martin and Ursula Lewis's Thalia, followed by a second wave, from the seventies on, focusing on Chuck Zlatkin and Steve Gould's Elgin, Howard Otway's Theatre 80 St. Marks, Frank Rowley's Regency, the Thalia reborn under Richard Schwarz, and Sid Geffen and Jackie Raynal's Carnegie Hall Cinema.

The peculiarities of each of these owners and their venues are duly noted: Rowley's meticulous presentation of MGM classics, including stationing underlings to clap at the end of big musical numbers; Schwarz's temper tantrums and love of B movies; the Thalia's impossibly parabolic slope and permeable acoustics; the Bleecker Street's tendency to run behind schedule so that its small lobby was often packed with disgruntled queues; Theatre 80's odd, fuzzy rear-view projection; Sid Geffen's imperial schemes in complete disregard of his lack of capital. . . . Overall, these pioneers come across as a bunch of wildly idealistic missionaries, lovers of film much more interested in spreading the gospel of cinema than in making money. They took chances, played hunches, went against the grain of commercial conformity, artfully constructed balanced double bills, connived to get their hands on the best possible prints, and eventually, most of them went under.

Davis explains: "It was not the VCR revolution that did the theater in, but the real estate revolution. Much like the closing of the Elgin, the Bleecker's closing pitted a real estate developer who saw the property as a profitable investment against a theater owner who treasured it as a cultural resource. It was a doomed struggle."

Since the book is structured along a rise-and-fall arc, it concludes with a brief chapter that finds faint signs of revival in the "microcinemas"—casual venues such as Rooftop Films, Light Industry, and Union Docs—which have sprung up recently. Myself, I do not think we need to lament so lachrymosely the decline of the repertory houses since new ones in New York such as the Metrograph and the renovated Quad keep appearing, the venerable Film Forum keeps chugging along, and the nonprofit institutions, such as MOMA, the Film Society of Lincoln Center, the Museum of the Moving Image, Japan Society, BAM, and the Asia Society do a bang-up job of presenting new and old global cinema. Probably every intriguing new film will pass through New York at one point or another, and the city continues to rank with Paris as the premier place for watching movies. Added to these showcases, the televised distributers, like Criterion and Turner Classic Movies, have done a remarkable job of rescuing worthy old films.

What has changed, then, is not so much the opportunity to see good films but the way they are packaged. In brief, we have gone from a time in the fifties and sixties when the emphasis was placed on making an accepted canon available to the novice film buff (*Battleship Potemkin*, *Passion of Joan of Arc*, *Sunrise*), though that historical narrative was simplistic in its ignoring of much world cinema, to a smorgasbord of "edgy" hors d'oeuvres and a neglect of meat-and-potatoes classics. This trend began with the rediscovery of film noir and pre-Code Hollywood, then extended to "bad movies" featuring the likes of Ed Wood, to J-horror, giallo, softcore porn, sexual-preference or ethnic-identity niche packages, and so forth. All of these fringe subgenres have a value in filling out the capacious rewards of cinema, but the end result is that it is now easier to see a sadistic gore-fest like Takashi Miike's *Ichi the Killer* than the transcendently compassionate works of Murnau and Borzage, or a Dario Argento horror film (visually elegant as those are) than the masterworks of John Ford. Many of the old Thalia/New Yorker staples rarely get projected: Hollywood seventies movies seem to have replaced the second-tier classics by G. W. Pabst, Marcel Carné, V. I. Pudovkin, Rouben Mamoulian, René Clair, Robert Flaherty, Jacques Feyder, Julien Duvivier, etc., etc.

Paradoxically, it was the inventive enterprise of the repertory movie theaters in rescuing neglected or forgotten films that helped undermine the old narrative about the development of film art, from Griffith to German expressionism to the Soviet montage directors to the French poetic cinema. But not to worry: it is still possible to track down anything and everything, provided one has sufficient patience. Meanwhile, Ben Davis has performed an extremely useful service in recapturing this piece of the endangered past and arguing for its importance as an archive that preserved the history of movies as an art form.

For me, also, the book has been a poignant and at times painful walk down Memory Lane. It made me recall showing Jonas Mekas in the Charles lobby the schedule for the film program I had organized as an undergraduate at Columbia and his sniffing at my inclusion of Henry King's *The Gunfighter* (a pretty good film by an old veteran), saying I would have done better to exhibit Edgar G. Ulmer's *The Naked Dawn* (a much hipper auteur). I remember taking a date to Theatre 80 St. Mark's for its ritual New Year's Eve champagne show, Preston Sturges's *Unfaithfully Yours*, and the movie if not the champagne was completely satisfying. I remember writing articles for *The Thousand Eyes*, the Carnegie Hall Cinema's ambitious rag, and someone sending in an angry letter attacking me for clinging to narrative film. I remember my itch to work at a repertory theater, which led me to apply for a job with Ursula Lewis, the owner of the Thalia, who was looking for a programmer for her uptown theater, the Heights: needless to say, I didn't impress her with my unprofitable schemes for showing obscure back titles of minor would-be auteurs like Paul Wendkos and Gerd Oswald. (I too was into the forgotten film). Finally, I remember the late Dan Talbot, a friend, dissuading me from my dream of working under him at the New Yorker: "Phillip, there's no glamour being an assistant manager of a movie house. You end up having to roust overdosed junkies in the toilet and mopping up their vomit." That image has stayed with me.

Though I consider myself fairly levelheaded, not given to mysticism, I've had certain movie experiences that I would say approached the sublime. Often they involved revivals of previously unavailable films I was dying to see. As most of this hunting took place in the days before VCRs and DVDs, I had to keep an eye out for rare titles popping up at a revival house, film festival, or museum. Was my ecstatic response determined by the picture's quality or my pride in catching up with it? Both. I've been particularly drawn to earlier works by great filmmakers on their way to creating their ripe masterpieces. There is something delicious about retroactively discovering the promise of a mature manner before it has been totally perfected, like Bertolucci's first film, *The Grim Reaper*.

For instance, when Antonioni's *L'Avventura* and *La Notte* were the rage, it became imperative to see the maestro's apprentice films. I heard that a bootleg print of *Le Amiche* had been smuggled into the United States and was to be projected one night at the Charles, a revival house on the Lower East Side. The film had no subtitles, so a bilingual speaker, stationed to the side with a microphone, translated the dialogue into English seconds after it was uttered in Italian, in a flat, bored monotone intriguingly at odds with the intense drama of alienation, suicide, and careless love being enacted onscreen.

The New York Film Festival was a reliable source for filling in the gaps in great auteurs' oeuvres. In this manner I caught up not only with Antonioni's bracingly bitter *The Lady Without Camelias* but also several of Max Ophüls's stunningly lovely, worldly-wise, 1930s works, such as the romantic, snow-kissed *Liebelei* (with Magda Schneider, Romy's mother), the backstage drama *Divine*, and the starlet tragedy *La Signora di Tutti*, with its exquisite lakeside-sequence tracking shot that rivaled a similar one in Mizoguchi's *Ugetsu*.

Speaking of Mizoguchi, when my first wife, Carol, and I were living in Madrid in 1965 and were poor as church mice, we were determined to see *Princess Yang Kwei Fei* when it showed at the Cinemateca. We had saved our pesetas only to discover at the box office that the screening had sold out. We lingered at the entrance, crestfallen, until an usher took pity on us and let us in a side door for free. The titles were just going up as we found places on the carpet steps, and we watched, in thrall to this ravishing color film, not really sure what was going on, trying to keep up with the fast Spanish subtitles.

My most exalted movie experience occurred not in a movie theater at all. I was visiting the Bay Area and dropped in on my friend Tom Luddy, at that time director of the Pacific Film Archives, later the cofounder of the Telluride Film festival. Tom sometimes let me go through the film cans that happened to be on hand in the PFA archives and pick out something I wanted to see. He would then have the staff projectionist screen it for me, and I would watch it alone in the auditorium, blissfully spoiled. One afternoon I arrived late, and Tom mentioned they had just got in a 16mm subtitled print of Visconti's *Ossessione*. Previously unseen in the United States because of a contract dispute (Visconti had never paid for rights to the James M. Cain novel *The Postman Always Rings Twice*, which he'd freely adapted), *Ossessione* ranked highest on my wish list. The problem was that the PFA was about to shut down for the night and I was flying back to New York the next day. To my amazement, Tom kindly let me borrow the print and a 16mm projector. I took them back to the house of my friend, the educator Herbert Kohl, where I was staying. I lost no time borrowing a sheet from Herb and tacking it against the wall. Threading the projector, my hands trembled, fearful of harming the only print of *Ossessione* in America. Herb liked movies well enough but was stunned to see the reverence and tremulous ardor with which I blocked out the light and set up the proper throw. I invited him to watch it, but he left soon after the first few minutes, pulled away by the swirling life of his children. Those familiar with the film and its aching, fatalistic rural atmosphere of longing and eroticism, can picture the dusky black-and-white cinematography as it was projected on a wrinkled white sheet. The neorealist acting by Clara Calamai and Massimo Girotti seemed much more modestly believable and naturalistic than the glamorous stylings of Lana Turner and John Garfield in the Hollywood version of the Cain novel. As I lay on my borrowed single bed, the images transporting me, I was happy beyond belief. Years later, I saw *Ossessione* again at the New York Film Festival. It was still noble, tragic, and poetic, but I regard the time I saw it on a hanging sheet in Berkeley as the perfect incarnation of that movie.

One last memory: it was snowing heavily in New York, and the public school where I taught was closed for the day. I enticed my friend Peter Minnichiello away from his serious, responsible desk job so that we could catch *The Bad and the Beautiful*, which was showing that afternoon as part of a Vincente Minnelli retrospective at the Carnegie Hall Cinema. Midtown had slowed down, there were barely any cars, and people were walking down the middle of the street without fear of being run over; some were even skiing along Seventh Avenue. Nothing could have suited the free holiday spirit more than this half-comic, half-melodramatic confection about moviemaking, with Kirk Douglas playing a rat producer and Lana Turner displaying her charms. We surrendered to it; we were in bliss. My friend Peter is no more (as is true, alas, of my late friend Tom Luddy)—they are both maybe watching films together in heaven—but I still think back to those screenings as instances of pure grace. Magic, if you will.

METROGRAPH JOURNAL (SUMMER 2016)

CONCLUSION

The Faith of a Cineaste

The other day a friend of mine who teaches a film course told me he was afraid to show Minnelli's *The Bad and the Beautiful* to his undergraduate class because he was sure they'd find it slow and confusing. "They just don't know how to look at classic movies like that. They're used to a faster pace." I commiserated with him, remembering how I had once screened Max Ophüls's tender, romantic *Letter from an Unknown Woman* for a roomful of seemingly sophisticated Princeton students, only to be told by one young man that he found it "cheesy." (I guess it was the constructed sets of Old Vienna that put him off.) Still, I resist the notion that the glories of past cinema will be forever lost to future generations of sensation-hungry mutants because I keep meeting young people who have an insatiable curiosity and appetite for good movies, past and present.

Moreover, the "slow cinema" movement that has percolated worldwide in the past decades (Chantal Akerman, Pedro Costa, Albert Serra, Lav Diaz) demonstrates that a short attention span and a rapid cutting technique will not necessarily have the final word. We are invited to drink in the image, to meditate on its moment by moment welling up, long past the time the scenic information it initially seemed intended to deliver.

Similarly, I have no use for the "Death of Cinema" diagnosis that Susan Sontag, Paul Schrader, and Jean-Luc Godard were peddling awhile back, and which seems to me no more true than the Death of the Novel, the Death of New York, and the Death of Liberalism, all of which I have lived through and beyond. Maybe there are fewer towering cinematic masterpieces than in the past, but that leaves all the more room for surprises: pleasurable films that have striking performances, intriguing plots, fetching camerawork, or simply moments of sharp truth.

Let us admit that movies may never regain the currency or centrality in the culture that they held in previous generations. During the 1930s and 1940s, it seemed that everyone, male and female, went once or twice a week to the cinema, regardless of whether the film was a gem or a dud. In the late fifties and early sixties, movies began to be talked about as an essential art form, with each new masterpiece eagerly awaited. Fellini's *La Dolce Vita* or Visconti's *Rocco and His Brothers* opened in Broadway playhouses, where it was necessary to buy tickets in advance. The entertainment pages of newspapers were filled with think-pieces about the latest Godard or Bergman. Not only is that sort of coverage rare today, but newspapers themselves have been disappearing at an alarming rate. Still, movies persist, the industry buoyed by the latest superhero or Disney hit while we are getting used to thinking of serious art films as a niche, semi-underground endeavor.

My sense is also that the level of acting is as high in movies today as it's ever been. We may not have the kind of larger-than-life luminaries such as Bette Davis or Barbara Stanwyck, but when I watch those films with Davis or Stanwyck on TCM, they are often surrounded by dreadful sticks, empty suits, mustachioed placeholders, or vacant bimbos. Now we are getting a whole new crop of talented, versatile performers, and the challenge will be to find them enough scripts that will show just how far they can reach.

Part of these scripts may turn up on television. I remember well when film programmers started saying the more interesting work these days was being done on TV rather than the movies, and the conversation turned to asking which series I was watching. This was not the old water-cooler chatter about last night's popular game show: larger claims were being made that we were living in a golden age of television. And indeed, there did seem to be a plethora of unusual, engrossing series from all over the globe, suddenly available to American home viewers. Being a diehard cineaste, I did not agree that cinema had lost its edge to the younger medium. A dozen or two striking, challenging, handsome films were still showing up each year, and from what I could tell, they were far more visually complex than TV series, which tended to rely on close-ups and reaction shots because of the medium's shallower depth of field and smaller screen. I still prefer projected images in theaters to televised ones at home, but the whole idea of comparing the two media as though one had to choose is foolish. If television did momentarily have the upper hand, it was in the enrichment of character. The average movie protagonist has at most two personality traits (usually contradictory for the sake of tension), and supporting characters have only one. But because of the protracted time frame of TV series, you can watch the same characters over a period of years getting into scrapes, undermining their best intentions, demonstrating their precise limitations, as well as their potential for growth. (Think of the mother and daughter in *The Gilmore Girls* or Tony in *The Sopranos*.) We get to see them more slowly and realistically moving toward their fate.

Certainly, the technological changes in accessing moving images, as well as the shift from celluloid to digital format, have had and will continue to have a deep effect on film culture. With so many ways to watch, from iPads to Netflix streaming to cell phones, it may become necessary to entice people back to theaters by making each screening feel more like a special event: a newly struck print, an expert or cast member introducing the show. Recently I watched Douglas Fairbanks Sr. leaping acrobatically about in a new print of *The Mark of Zorro*, and the audience, myself included, took in that silent film with a joy that made me understand the excitement at its original reception. But repertory cinemas face a scarcity of prints; digital transfers of old movies are becoming increasingly expensive; many of the art film distributors have gone out of business; and the old financing model for independent filmmaking has collapsed and needs to be reinvented.

Through it all, strange, exhilarating, tormenting films continue to be made, enough to supply annual film festivals and hungry, demanding movie buffs for the foreseeable future. Meanwhile, the riches of the cinematic past mount up: a priceless record of intelligence, beauty, behavioral complexity, anguish, and desire. The point is that there is no shortage of artful movies old and new to encounter, not to mention stimulating television; so please enjoy them all while you can. As for me, I will continue to be in thrall to the moving image until they pry the remote from my cold, dead hand.

NOTES

4. CHANTAL AKERMAN: *NO HOME MOVIE*

1. Chantal Akerman, *My Mother Laughs* (New York: Song Cave, 2013), 138.

5. ANTONIONI'S *LE AMICHE*: ANOTHER LOOK

1. Tony Pipolo, "Friends—Italian Style," *Le Amiche*, Criterion Collection booklet, 2016.
2. Pauline Kael, *I Lost It at the Movies* (Boston: Little, Brown, 1965), 179–96.

8. ROBERT BRESSON: *MOUCHETTE*

1. George Bernanos, *Mouchette* (New York: New York Review Books, 2006), 87–88.

21. JEAN-LUC GODARD: *BREATHLESS* AND *BAND OF OUTSIDERS*

1. David Sterritt, *The Films of Jean-Luc Godard* (Cambridge: Cambridge University Press, 1999), 49–50.

31. HAROLD LLOYD: *SPEEDY*

1. Harold Lloyd, *An American Comedy* (1928; New York: Dover, 1971), 3–4.
2. James Agee, "Comedy's Greatest Era," *Life*, September 5, 1949, 79.

34. DAVID LYNCH: *MULHOLLAND DRIVE*

1. *Inland Empire*, the film with which Lynch followed *Mulholland Drive*, proved to be a reversion to this mode: an episodic attenuation of cryptic funhouse illusion-and-reality enigmas.

35. DUŠAN MAKAVEJEV: THE WOLF AND THE TEDDY BEAR

1. I later came to appreciate that Telluride was not quite as democratic as I'd imagined; the simple truth was that I was in the in-group, for a change, as a friend of Luddy and so got to hang out with the celebrities while the hoi polloi looked on, with no hope of making the acquaintance of Ms. Christie, Francis Ford Coppola, et al.
2. Dušan Makavejev, "Nicola Tesla Radiated A Blue Light," Fall 1980 paper in Studies of Visual Communication, University of Pennsylvania.
3. Makavejev must have liked the interview because it was reprinted as the introduction to the paperback of his *W.R.* screenplay.
4. Dušan Makavejev, *WR: Mysteries of the Organism: A Cinematic Testament to the Life and Teachings of Wilhelm Reich* (New York: Bard/Avon Books, 1972), 17–18.
5. He went so far as to identify himself in the Tesla paper "Writer, Filmmaker, Psychologist."

38. YASUJIRŌ OZU: *LATE SPRING*

1. Joseph L. Anderson and Donald Richie, *The Japanese Film* (Princeton, NJ: Princeton University Press, 1982), 359.

40. MAURICE PIALAT: *NAKED CHILDHOOD, VAN GOGH,* AND *LE GARÇU*

1. Kent Jones, "Pialat's Naked Childhood," audio commentary, Criterion Collection, 2010,

42. DINO RISI: *IL SORPASSO*

1. Jackson Burgess, "Sex and the Italian Driver," *Holiday*, January 1, 1970.

43. ÉRIC ROHMER: *LA COLLECTIONNEUSE, THE MARQUISE OF O,* AND *LE RAYON VERT*

1. James Monaco, *The New Wave* (New York: Oxford University Press, 1976), 288.
2. Christopher Lasch, *The Culture of Narcissism: American Life in an Age of Diminishing Expectations* (New York: Norton, 1979).
3. Pauline Kael, "No Id," *New Yorker*, October 25, 1976, 67.

4. Jonathan Rosenbaum, *Monthly Film Bulletin* 43, no. 515 (December 1976).
5. Heinrich von Kleist, *The Marquise of O— and Other Stories* (New York: Frederick Ungar, 1973), 79.

44. RAÚL RUIZ: *TIME REGAINED*

1. Raúl Ruiz, *The Poetics of Cinema* (Paris: Editions Dis Voir), 11.
2. Raúl Ruiz, "In the Mirror" (Interview, YouTube).

47. JEAN-MARIE STRAUB *NOT RECONCILED*

1. Richard Roud, in *New Yorker Films Catalogue* 1 (1976–77): 71.

49. FRANÇOIS TRUFFAUT

1. Antoine De Baeque and Serge Toubiana, *Truffaut: A Biography* (New York: Knopf, 2000).
2. Dave Kehr, "Film: A Poet of Darkness Who Longs for the Light," *New York Times*, May 16, 1999.

50. FREDERICK WISEMAN: COMPOSING AN AMERICAN EPIC

1. Errol Morris, in conversation with the author.
2. Richard Pena, in conversation with the author.
3. Pauline Kael, *For Keeps: 30 Years at the Movies* (New York: Dutton, 1994), 339–43.
4. Errol Morris, in conversation with the author.

51. ALAIN RESNAIS: *NIGHT AND FOG*

1. Truffaut, quoted in "*Alain Resnais'* Night and Fog," Criterion Collection booklet, 2003.

53. ALAN BERLINER

1. Jack Salzman, in conversation with the author.
2. Richard Pena, in conversation with the author.
3. Alan Berliner, reading from his diaries to the author.

54. ROBERT GARDNER: *DEAD BIRDS*

1. Robert Gardner, *The Impulse to Preserve: Reflections of a Filmmaker* (New York: Other Press, 2006), 46.
2. Gardner, *The Impulse to Preserve*, 16.

3. "Meet the Maker with Robert Gardner and Phillip Lopate," conversation and interview, Donnell Media Center, New York Public Library, October 5, 2006.
4. Gardner, *The Impulse to Preserve*, 68.
5. Gardner, *The Impulse to Preserve*, 62.
6. Gardner and Lopate, "Meet the Maker."
7. Decades later, when Gardner returned to the area, he found the surviving tribe members who had participated in the filmmaking conducting *Dead Bird* tours! Modernity had caught up with the Dani.
8. Gardner, *The Impulse to Preserve*, 34.
9. Karl Heider, *Ethnographic Film* (Austin: University of Texas Press, 1976), 117.
10. Robert Gardner in conversation with the author.